STUDIES IN INTERNATIONAL POLITICAL ECONOMY
Stephen D. Krasner, General Editor
Ernst B. Haas, Consulting Editor

Unequal Alliance

UNEQUAL ALLIANCE

The World Bank, the International
Monetary Fund, and the Philippines

ROBIN BROAD

UNIVERSITY OF CALIFORNIA PRESS
Berkeley · Los Angeles · London

University of California Press
Berkeley and Los Angeles, California

University of California Press, Ltd.
London, England

© 1988 by
The Regents of the University of California

Library of Congress Cataloging-in-Publication Data

Broad, Robin.
  Unequal alliance.

  (Studies in international political economy)
  Bibliography: p.
  Includes index.
  1. World Bank—Philippines. 2. International
Monetary Fund—Philippines. 3. Philippines—
Economic policy.   I. Title.   II. Series.
HG3881.5.W57B76   1988   332.1'52   87–10745
  ISBN 0–520–05905–0

This book is distributed in the Philippines and Asia
by the Ateneo de Manila University Press (P.O. Box
154, Manila) and in the rest of the world by the
University of California Press.

Printed in the United States of America
1   2   3   4   5   6   7   8   9

To three Filipino nationalists whose lives serve
as beacons of a more promising future:

Senator Jose "Pepe" Diokno, lawyer, political
detainee, and human rights advocate,
1922–1987

Ceferino "Jun" Flores, Jr., hotel worker and
union leader, missing since January 28, 1983

and

Alberto Gonzales, industrial engineer and
youth organizer, killed when military forces
violently dispersed a strike at the Bataan
Export Processing Zone, January 31, 1987

CONTENTS

LIST OF TABLES

LIST OF FIGURES

LIST OF ABBREVIATIONS

ADFU	Apex Development Finance Unit
AID	Agency for International Development
CBP	Central Bank of the Philippines
CDCP	Construction and Development Corporation of the Philippines
DBP	Development Bank of the Philippines
ECB	Expanded commercial bank
EDI	Economic Development Institute
EFF	Extended fund facility
EPZ	Export processing zone
FTZ	Free trade zone
GATT	General Agreement on Tariffs and Trade
IBRD	International Bank for Reconstruction and Development
IMF	International Monetary Fund
LDC	Less developed country
NDC	National Development Corporation
NEDA	National Economic and Development Authority
NEPA	National Economic Protectionism Association
NIC	Newly industrializing country
OECD	Organization of Economic Cooperation and Development
PDCP	Private Development Corporation of the Philippines
PISO	Philippine Investments Systems Organization
PNB	Philippine National Bank
SAL	Structural adjustment loan
SDR	Special drawing right

SGV   SyCip, Gorres, and Velayo
TNB   Transnational bank
TNC   Transnational corporation
UNCTAD   United Nations Conference on Trade and Development
UNIDO   United Nations Industrial Development Organization

PREFACE

Look—your Bank, I don't like it so much. It scratches
where it doesn't itch.

*Guatemalan Indian (referring to
multilateral development bank)*

The term at the tip of everyone's tongue in establishment development
circles is *structural adjustment*. It is the be-all and end-all phrase of the moment—the answer to the Third World's ills.

The world economy, most recognize, is harsh and competitive. In order
to compete, Third World countries must adjust their economic structures.
For the second half of the 1980s, according to the World Bank, the International Monetary Fund (IMF), and most within the U.S. government,
what is required of developing countries when they adjust is adherence to
one basic tenet: submit your economies to international market forces.
And that means privatize, open up, liberalize, offer more incentives to private foreign investment—in short: inject Reaganomics into the Third
World.

As a result, structural adjustment policies are permeating the African,
Asian, and Latin American continents. As former IMF managing director
Jacques de Larosière announced triumphantly in 1984, "Adjustment is
now virtually universal. . . . Never before has there been such an extensive
yet convergent adjustment effort."[1]

Not only is structural adjustment viewed as the key to growth and development; it has also been transformed into the easy answer to the most
pressing global problem of the day: the international debt crisis. The
World Bank, the main source of external development funds for about one
hundred countries, has been thrown centerstage in the debt drama. At this

writing, it is negotiating or has recently granted broad structural adjustment or sector loans to thirteen of the fifteen countries for whom the gap
between debt service owed and ability to pay is greatest.[2] This, we are assured, will solve the crisis.

The tragedy is that this particular brand of structural adjustment works
to the benefit of the few. Recent history demonstrates that it has helped
some transnational banks and corporations and a very thin stratum of
transnational elites in developing countries. Structural adjustment has also
been, over the past half-decade of general stagnation in world trade, a disaster for the majority of the Third World, that is, for most workers, peasants, and small entrepreneurs producing for the domestic market. Structural adjustment has retarded development in the broader, participatory
and sustaining sense of the term.

This is the conclusion that emerges from detailed study of the World
Bank's test case for structural adjustment lending, the Philippines, during
1979–1982. That failure is the subject of this book.

Behind the closed doors of high-level policy-making in Manila in the
early 1980s, a major transformation of the Philippine political economy
was being planned and implemented. For an outside researcher, what
leaked through seemed initially little more than a trickle of unrelated facts
and actors: new policy initiatives consolidating light-manufactured exports
as the wave of the future; World Bank missions constantly shuttling in and
out of certain offices to lay the groundwork for one of the Bank's first structural adjustment loans; the IMF representative maintaining his organization's decade-long watch at the Central Bank; presidential strongman
Ferdinand Marcos's ace team of young, Westernized technocrats tightening
their grip on the various government ministries.

After some months, these and other clues began to fit together to form
an often remarkable, at times shocking, tale of how policy is formulated in
a developing country being pushed, pulled, and, on occasion, forced into
structural adjustment.

Piecing together the details of the Philippine structural adjustment experiment in the early 1980s was aided by an important sociological factor.
Top Philippine government officials directly involved in the negotiations
were, it turns out, more often than not delighted to tell their stories to an
American researcher connected to a prestigious U.S. university.[3] And talk
they did—almost nonstop for eight months. To some extent, this book

tries simply to reconstruct events, to let the reader hear the discussions, the debates, and the strategizing that occur behind closed doors—to recreate the actual process of the transformation.

Those concerned with development, be it in Africa, Asia, or Latin America, would do well to study the Philippine experiment and experience carefully. Through 1985, the World Bank had lent the Philippines $4.5 billion in 101 project and program loans.[4] In the twenty-three-year span from 1962 to 1985, the IMF had overseen seventeen standby arrangements and one extended fund facility, a rate of one arrangement every 1.3 years.[5] It was the Philippines, with its eager corps of technocrats in command, that was chosen as the guinea pig for structural adjustment lending in the late 1970s. Five years later, when the results were in, the Bank and the Fund refused to take any blame for the Philippine economic failure—its negative economic growth rates, its foundering light-manufactured-export earnings, and its soaring, unpayable debt service. Instead, the Bank and the Fund, the international purveyors of structural adjustment, blame the failure of their Philippine experiment on the political turmoil that engulfed the country following the assassination of opposition politician Benigno Aquino in mid-1983.

To suggest so is to deceive. It is a deception because the Bank itself considered the Philippines a success story by mid-1982: a success in eliminating many "inefficient firms," a success in rooting out economic nationalists from the government, a success in depressing wages to "competitive" levels, a success in expanding private foreign economic interests in the Philippine domestic economy.

In earlier years, policies that bore some resemblance to those wrought by structural adjustment in the Philippines promoted growth (though not necessarily development) in other countries, such as Brazil, South Korea, and Singapore. They failed to do so in the Philippines in the 1980s in part because world trade stopped growing in precisely those light-manufacturing markets (apparel and semiconductors, in particular) where the Philippine economy had been steered. As world trade growth halted, developed countries barricaded themselves behind rising protectionist barriers. Competition among developing countries that were encouraged to try the same development tactics as the Philippines became fierce.

Regardless of success or failure in the growth arena, however, structural adjustment has been a disaster in terms of development that might benefit the poorer majority. This is no accident. Structural adjustment is not meant for these social strata.

These conclusions are likely to fall on deaf ears at the U.S. Treasury Department (which controls U.S. participation in the international financial and development institutions), the World Bank, and the IMF. In late 1985, these quarters reacted to the growing instability and misery of a Third World staggering under enormous external debts by launching the so-called Baker Plan. The plan represented a shift of sorts in debt management. It exhorted the fifteen most troubled debtor nations to make Reaganomic-type adjustments. In return, the Baker Plan promised a continuation of private transnational bank lending—a promise that the banks, already in search of more profitable investments outside the shaky Third World, have attempted to ignore. And, most important, it promised a large increase in World Bank structural adjustment and sector lending to shift countries toward what Baker and the Bank billed as "adjustment with growth."

In part, this plan represented a passing of the mantle of chief debt negotiator from the IMF, which had filled this role since 1982, to its sister institution, the World Bank. The Fund was battered by both the bread riots and the bad press that inexorably followed its austerity programs and by a shortage of funds in the wake of three years of large-scale lending.

The shift was also, in many ways, the culmination of a change in World Bank emphasis that began with the Philippine experiment of 1979–1982. It was a change from narrower project lending (for dams, infrastructure, agricultural projects, and so on) toward broader sectoral or multisectoral, economy-wide, nonproject lending accompanied by macroeconomic conditions. In the words of former senior World Bank official Stanley Please, up to the 1980s the Bank had been a "hobbled giant," constrained by its emphasis on individual project lending from mobilizing its enormous resources and expertise for broad-based economic adjustment.[6] The advent of structural adjustment lending and the Baker Plan ensured that the Bank would hobble no more.

The World Bank's preeminent role in debt-related adjustment also made sense because the troubled countries were predominantly the "newly industrializing countries" (NICs) of the 1960s and 1970s (e.g., Brazil, Mexico, South Korea) as well as the twenty to thirty countries that the World Bank had been helping shift toward export-oriented light manufacturing in the late 1970s and early 1980s. Those countries were the very ones that had already been targeted for (if not already endowed with) structural adjustment loans.

Among the fifteen nations that Treasury Secretary James Baker (in consultation with Federal Reserve Board Chairman Paul Volcker and Secretary of State George Shultz) selected as most in need of this help in late 1985 was the Philippines. The Philippines of 1979–1982, with its ascendent technocratic corps in key ministries, would arguably have been an ideal candidate for a "Baker loan"—indeed, it had, in essence, received a precursor to the Baker loans. Much, however, had transpired since 1982. The economy had collapsed. Social unrest had escalated in the wake of the 1983 assassination of Benigno Aquino. Many of Marcos's cronies, who controlled large portions of the economy, had been bailed out of business dealings based more on palace connections than business acumen; their assets had been taken over (some partially, others in full) by the government. And, finally, in a four-day "snap revolution" that was broadcast to living rooms around the world, Aquino's widow Corazon assumed the presidency in February 1986.

Ironically, at this writing (April 1987), the Philippines, even with all these changes, remains a prime candidate for Baker/World Bank–style restructuring. Crucial to such restructuring is the continued receptivity of technocrats occupying the top posts in two ministries: the Ministry of Finance and the Central Bank. The World Bank and the IMF could not have been more delighted with Aquino's selections: Jaime Ongpin (brother of Marcos's industry minister, Roberto Ongpin), the powerful Harvard M.B.A. who had headed the Philippines' largest mining company, as finance minister; and Marcos's own Central Bank governor, Jose Fernandez, remaining in his post. Not that there were not new obstacles—primarily the nationalists who had been placed in some of the other ministries. An internal World Bank memorandum noted in May 1986: "Cabinet members have not yet adopted the discipline of an agreed policy line. . . . Perhaps none of this is surprising in the circumstances, but for us it means that the Minister of Finance and the Governor of the Central Bank do not have an easy time when they present 'technocratic arguments' and proposals to the Cabinet, and this is bound to complicate our work."[7]

Already in March 1986, within a month of Aquino's ascension to power, the World Bank held lengthy individual meetings in Manila with

Jaime Ongpin, "Jobo" Fernandez, Minister of Trade and Industry Jose Concepcion, and other ministers. The first three indicated their willingness to work closely with the Bank and the Fund, Ongpin asked that the Bank set up a Manila office to facilitate this, and Fernandez pursued the issue of the Baker Plan's application to the Philippines.[8]

By October 1986, the IMF had approved a financial package of $510 million for the Philippines. As part of the package, the World Bank dusted off a $300 million sectoral adjustment loan (which it had prepared but not finalized under Marcos's rule) to restructure government-owned financial institutions—all in exchange for trade liberalization and the other usual adjustment measures.[9] Simultaneously, a wave of World Bank missions began that would, by the end of 1986, complete the Bank's first major industrial-sector report on the Philippines since its work in 1979 prompted by the structural adjustment loan. In other words, all indications were that four short years after the disastrous Philippine structural adjustment experiment, the World Bank and the IMF had every intention of trying exactly the same experiment once again.

Our plea, to both the Philippine government and the governments of other nations being sold the rhetoric of structural adjustment, is this: Do not enter these negotiations with your eyes closed. World trade continues to stagnate. Markets are glutted; protectionism, of the vicious beggar-thy-neighbor variety, is growing everywhere. And capital from transnational banks and corporations, which the Bank and the Fund always promise will flow following adjustment agreements, is no longer moving to the Third World. That capital has instead already turned toward new arenas for short-term rewards at home—consumer credit, corporate mergers, and the get-rich-quick gimmicks of financial speculation.[10] The beneficiaries of the Bank/Fund version of structural adjustment are few. Those who will suffer are many.

There is a desperate need for fundamental rethinking of development strategies in a world economy of vastly reduced growth. That rethinking is unlikely to occur in the confines of the World Bank and the IMF; they have too much vested in the status quo. But the Bank and the Fund need not have a monopoly on what constitutes acceptable adjustment and acceptable development models. Rethinking is already beginning in the universities, research institutions, and opposition parties of several Third World countries. It deserves to be heard—and to be broadened and shared. In this debate lie the seeds of a more just and humane version of adjustment and development.

Robin Broad
John Cavanagh

ACKNOWLEDGMENTS

When a book's research and writing span three continents and half a dozen years, numerous people are owed not only thanks but also "debts of gratitude," *utang na loob,* as they say in the Philippines. Remarkable people dragged typewriters miles for me, set up interviews with friends-of-friends-of-friends, and spent hours lingering over coffee, discussing and debating what my research had to say.

Financial backing from the Woodrow Wilson School of Public and International Affairs at Princeton University made my 1980–1981 research trip to the Philippines possible. In the Philippines, the College of Public Administration of the University of the Philippines provided institutional support during my tenure as Visiting Research Associate. The Asian Institute of Management, the Ibon Databank, and the Third World Studies Center of the University of the Philippines allowed me extended use of libraries and other facilities. In Switzerland, the United Nations libraries at the Palais des Nations and the World Health Organization supplied me with space to continue my research and begin writing.

My research in the Philippines took place during Ferdinand Marcos's rule and I, understandably, expected to refrain from mentioning most Filipino friends and self-proclaimed research assistants by name. Not having had the chance to ask each if this silence should still hold, I feel it best to continue to leave them unnamed—but not unthanked. Without their trust and indefatigable efforts to make my stay a productive one, this book would not have been possible. I am similarly grateful to the many Filipino friends throughout the country who persisted in pressing me on the relevance of my work to their struggles. A few who deserve special thanks can be mentioned: the Diokno family allowed me access to the treasures of their library and the warmth of their family; Hilarion Henares and Alejandro

Lichauco carefully schooled me in the beliefs of Filipino nationalists; and members of the staff at Ibon Databank in Manila were always there with answers to tough questions.

The heart of this book grows out of the willingness of more than one hundred very busy people to take hours (and sometimes full work days) from their hectic schedules to sit and talk with me. Most did so patiently and honestly, for which I thank them. Some of my Filipino sources will undoubtedly either not find my work as flattering as they had hoped or be dismayed with the composite picture. To them, I can only reiterate that I have tried my best to be faithful to their every word. If the whole is distressing, then I can hope only that it makes certain persons in the Philippines ponder their roles in it. One high government official I interviewed told me that he had read a book about "neocolonialism" and found it astonishingly accurate. But, he quickly added, he vowed never again to read another book on the subject, for it had the power to shatter everything he had believed until then. The advent of the Cory Aquino government, with many fresh faces and many old ones (including, it appears, a majority of my interviewees), provides a perfect opportunity for such shattering. I am appreciative of the few at the World Bank and the IMF who agreed to talk "on the record." I am sorry more of their colleagues would not do so, even anonymously. That, in itself, is a sad commentary on those institutions.

Outside the Philippines, Richard Falk, whose feedback over the years has sharpened my critical understanding, provided welcome encouragement at important moments in my research and writing. I thank Walden Bello, Henry Bienen, Edward Broad, Richard Feinberg, Gary Hawes, Teresa Hayter, David Hsieh, Ben Kerkvliet, Cheryl Payer, Joel Rocamora, Robert Stauffer, Lynn White, and John Willoughby for somehow finding the time to read various versions of my manuscript carefully and critically. In my three years in Washington (two at the U.S. Treasury Department and one in the U.S. Congress), I gained insights into international economics and the process of development from many people, but especially from Thomas Burke at the Treasury, Alexey de Synegub at the Inter-American Development Bank, Congressman Charles Schumer, former congressional staff director Jan Shinpoch, and Barbara Upton and Kathryn Boyd at the Agency for International Development.

Frederick and Gertrude Clairmonte, George Davol, John Kelly, Lee Kolman, Jorge Sol, my family, the Cavanagh family, and many individuals at the Institute for Policy Studies and the Amsterdam-based Transnational Institute offered both inspiration and support throughout this effort. Dr. James E. Cavanagh deserves separate mention, for he provided a serene spot in upstate New York for finishing this project. Special gratitude goes to Elizabeth Cavanagh and Eliana Loveluck for helping with the messier side of putting a book together, while somehow maintaining their interest in what those pages said. At the University of California Press, editors Naomi Schneider, Mary Renaud, and Marilyn Schwartz and copyeditor Jane-Ellen Long provided skilled and expeditious editorial assistance.

My coauthor of the preface and conclusion, John Cavanagh, actually deserves credit for much more. It was his unwavering conviction that this project not only was worthwhile but had to be done that sustained it from start to finish.

These, as I have said, are merely the words of thanks. The *utang na loob* will, I hope, be repaid in better ways.

1

Introduction

The Philippine Setting

Manila, 1981. A chauffeur-driven white Mercedes weaves in and out of the traffic backed up along what could well be a street in downtown Manhattan. This is Makati, its modern skyscrapers housing the business and financial elite of the Philippines. In the back seat sits a well-dressed Filipino businessman whose fortune has been amassed over the decades through production of goods for the domestic market. This man has earned the epithet of economic "nationalist" by keeping his hands fairly clean of involvement with foreign corporations and foreign markets. But times are changing. "Export or perish," he repeats several times. First stop: the investment house of the Philippines' largest commercial bank, to converse with influential friends in the hope of obtaining a sizable loan to convert his production processes to suit the export market. Second stop: a government office to register for tax exemptions bestowed upon exporters. "A tragedy," he explains on his way back to the limousine. "The Philippines is importing a perfect substitute for what I will be producing. . . . But

1

with all the loans and tax exemptions reserved solely for exporters, how can I afford not to export, instead of producing for the local market?"

Manila, 1981. Marikina, Manila's shoe district. On the door of an old, nondescript building that had housed his small footwear factory, a man, less well dressed than the exporter above, nails a hastily painted sign: "Out of business." A group of uniformed, giggling schoolgirls skip by. He stares at their shiny yellow, blue, and pink plastic shoes, the kind from Japan, South Korea, or Taiwan that have been flooding the domestic market this year, ever since the drastic reduction in shoe import tariffs. Then he looks at his own leather shoes, the type his small business had produced until its bankruptcy a day or so before. He continues hammering.

Manila, 1981. Magallanes Village, one of the favorite and poshest residential areas for foreign business executives, as well as for the lucky Filipinos who are allotted high positions in foreign corporations. Inside one of the securely fenced houses (a modern rendition of an old Spanish villa), a smartly dressed Filipina, whose husband is involved in various joint ventures with American and Japanese corporations, sends her maid for an assortment of snacks. Swiss chocolates: "So much nicer than our own candies," the wife gushes to her guests. Sausages from the United States: "We really don't have anything that can compare with these," she continues. Apples from Taiwan: "As cheap as our own mangoes . . . they're all so reasonably priced now"—now that taxes on imported goods have been slashed and bans on the import of certain luxury goods have been lifted.

Manila, 1981. North Forbes Park. Crème de la crème of Manila's residential subdivisions. Exquisitely sculptured gardens. Tightly guarded mansions hidden behind forbidding walls topped with a layer of jagged glass. Diosdado Macapagal, Philippine president from 1962 to 1965, stands in his extravagant stone entryway, surrounded by priceless wood carvings depicting his administration's greatest moments. Waving a copy of a recent statement he wrote as a spokesperson for today's elite urban opposition, Macapagal remains a politician to the core. The loser in the 1965 election that ushered in Ferdinand Marcos's extended reign, he finds few kind words for the role played of late by the World Bank and the International Monetary Fund, or their corporate allies. "A pack of wolves has jumped on the carcass of the Philippine economy," he says. There is bitterness in his voice.

Manila's disenfranchised national entrepreneurs did not start lobbing bombs in 1972 when two-time presidential winner Marcos declared martial law and sealed his rule for another decade and a half. They waited until nearly eight years later, when President Ferdinand Marcos and his elite corps of technocratic aides had implemented policy changes transforming the economy into an export enclave for garments, electronic components, and other light-manufactured goods destined for developed-country markets. And then—for a few months—some heaved bombs in earnest.

Elsewhere in the Philippine capital city, there was further evidence of change, further portents that the early 1980s marked a turning point for the Philippine political economy. Boards, sometimes lettered, sometimes not, sealed the doorways and windows of small businesses—shoe, dressmaking, and tailoring shops—that had produced for the domestic market. Nailed there to proclaim a phenomenon that was becoming ever more common—closed; bankrupt; out of business; cannot compete.

Across the bay from Manila, in Bataan near the famous Second World War battle site, the unbroken din of sewing machines could be heard from newly built factories; other buildings in the Bataan industrial export complex were quieter, filled with rows of microscopes and chemical baths for electronics assembly—modern factories, busy or not so busy, depending on the vicissitudes of the world market, to which all production was geared. The underpaid labor force, predominantly under twenty and female, hurried to piece together their quota of shirts, brassieres, microelectronic circuitry, and the like.

Hurried as ordered, until June 1982, when ten thousand of these workers did exactly what their government had promised transnational corporations they would never do. They walked off their jobs—not simply in a single strike action (which itself was illegal, but not unknown), but in a mass walkout, a general strike.[1]

The disintegration of the social fabric visible in these actions by businessmen and workers alike was not only the result of internal squabbling among Philippine classes. It was also the outcome of a development path chosen and molded by Philippine technocrats together with officials from the World Bank and the International Monetary Fund (IMF). That export-oriented industrialization path, conceived and implemented over the course of the 1970s and early 1980s, carried with it the seeds of this disintegration. For although it benefited some (most notably the transnational corporations and banks with alliances to a small class of Filipinos dominating the industrial and financial sectors), it hurt many. For workers and peasants, this economic model proved a convincing recruiter for a rapidly growing insurgency. For much of the middle class and portions of the upper classes, it was an important factor in their decision to participate in the overthrow of Marcos.

As the restructuring of the economy took root, a series of events and developments shook the Philippines. In the boardrooms of Makati. In the small industries of Marikina. In luxury villages like Magallanes. In the streets among the occasional overflowing of demonstrators. In the fetid slums that surround Philippine cities. Events that, in one way or another, hark back to the economic restructuring; events that broke open wide chasms in Philippine society.

The Newest International Division of Labor

The international division of labor is in a state of rapid flux. A once simple division of labor between industrialized, developed countries and raw-materials-exporting, developing countries emerged in the middle of the last century and lasted through the middle of this century. Such a basic international division of labor—between former colonizers and colonies, North and South, industrialized and nonindustrialized—has been replaced. In the place of the former colonies stands a highly differentiated developing world order that defies easy categorization.

Two identifiable groups of less developed countries (LDCs) began to shatter the primary-commodities-exporting mold in the 1960s and early 1970s. During the 1960s, seven LDCs began to penetrate the world market as exporters of manufactures. These were the so-called newly industrializing countries—the NICs of Taiwan, South Korea, Hong Kong, Singapore, Brazil, India, and Mexico[2]—and the disruptions they wrought on the older world order were enough to spawn an entire literature on the "new international division of labor." These seven were followed by a second stratification in 1973–1974, when the thirteen nations of the Organization of Petroleum Exporting Countries (OPEC) harnessed their power over oil and attempted to translate their financial success into development grounded in construction and heavy industries.

Beginning in earnest in the late 1970s, another grouping attempted to break out of dependence on primary commodity exports, a set of countries that has sometimes mistakenly been analyzed as a new generation of NICs. Indeed, as this third group of twenty to thirty LDCs began to complement their raw material exports with labor-intensive manufacturing, they often took up the rhetoric of successful NIC industrialization and declared themselves future NICs.

But there were important distinctions that relegated the "would-be NICs" to a different plateau of development from the original NICs. Primary among these distinctions was the historical moment: the decade-plus that separated the NICs' debut from that of the would-be NICs witnessed technological advances in several industrial sectors that changed the industrial offerings for Third World countries looking to world markets. By the late 1970s, technological changes (including a communications revolution) made the fragmentation of production across several countries or even continents profitable and desirable. Whereas the NICs had received complete industrial processes, such as shipbuilding and machinery, the would-be NICs received fairly marginal segments of worldwide assembly lines for semiconductors, consumer electronics, textiles, and apparel.

By the mid-1980s, the developing world could be categorized into these three divisions plus two others:

- Thirteen OPEC countries, each with rapidly constructed industrial shells that are suffering from the post-1983 oil glut
- Seven NICs, several now foundering under the weight of immense debt burdens
- Twenty to thirty would-be NICs
- Sixty-odd LDCs whose economies are still predominantly grounded in the export of raw materials and minerals, although some of these sixty have set up small assembly-type industries
- The final thirty to thirty-five so-called least developed countries, with only meager natural resource bases and little export capability.

Each of these five divisions begs individual analysis. But it is the most dynamic of the divisions today, the would-be NICs, that is the least understood and the most rapidly changing.

General Analytical Framework

As the international division of labor is far from an immobile configuration, so too it is hardly a natural setup. The simple colonial division of labor of the nineteenth century was imposed by direct force as well as by subtler means such as taxation. Part of the purpose of this book is to delineate the forces, both domestic and international, that explain the appearance of the would-be NICs. From Asia to Africa, Latin America to the Middle East, would-be NICs span the globe. One of these countries is the Philippines, moving out of its agricultural-export mold to be pulled into the light-manufactures pattern as rapidly as any other of the twenty to thirty would-be NICs.

Since the bulk of the developing world won political independence, several sets of international institutions have played major roles in molding and shifting these countries' domestic economic policies. Very little has been written on the process of policy formulation in LDCs, however, and even less on the interplay of national and international forces that affect the process. This book examines the influence of one set—multilateral institutions—on macroeconomic policy-making in LDCs, with special emphasis on the Philippines as an example of a would-be NIC. Among multilateral institutions, the dominant two, the World Bank and the International Monetary Fund, stand as the central concern of this work.[3]

In general terms, three sets of international institutions influencing LDC macroeconomic policy-making can be differentiated:

1. Private institutions, consisting primarily of transnational corporations (TNCs) and transnational banks (TNBs).

2. "Core" states (to use Immanuel Wallerstein's terminology), which comprise principally the former colonial powers and which exert influence through their departments of treasury, state, and overseas aid.[4]

3. Multilateral institutions, which, in addition to the IMF and the World Bank, include the General Agreement on Tariffs and Trade (GATT), regional development banks, and United Nations agencies.

The dynamics of interaction between these three sets of international actors and LDC states in policy-making are schematized in Figure 1. In influencing economic policy-making in LDCs (an effect denoted in solid rays), each of the three sets interacts with and nurtures a corps of technocratic bureaucrats who share a conviction of the importance of maximizing economic linkages with the world economy. Opposing these technocrats stands a group of LDC bureaucrats committed to developing the national market first. In the simplified schematization of Figure 1, the LDC state is therefore split into two factions: a transnationalist component, and an economic nationalist one.

The other major set of national institutions influencing policy formulation—domestic private corporations, financial institutions, and capitalists—can also be divided into two factions. Each tends to reflect a mindset grounded in economic interests. The overwhelming majority of entrepreneurs in any developing country are engaged in economic activities that serve national markets. Most of these entrepreneurs are small businesses; a few grow to be giant conglomerates. But whether big or small, their own interests and preservation tend to lead them to favor economic policies that protect themselves and their country's resources from the whims of the world market. Thus, they can be called economic nationalists.

Since the Second World War, a numerically small but, in some cases, economically powerful group of businessmen and -women have linked up with transnational banks and corporations in joint ventures, licensing agreements, marketing arrangements, and connections that tend to wed them ideologically to policies furthering free international flows of goods and capital. This faction can be called transnationalists.

Quite often, representatives from each of these private-sector factions are shuffled in and out of government positions. Hence the existence of nationalist and transnationalist factions within the state is often grounded in part in the economic interests of the bureaucrats. Indeed, in a Philippine government advertisement placed in an international business magazine to attract foreign investment, the transnationalist technocrats were billed as "transplanted businessmen" with an "international outlook."[5]

None of this is static. The absolute and relative size of each faction in both the private sector and the state sector varies widely from LDC to LDC and across time. The broad masses, who influence certain policies in more democratic LDCs, are excluded from any appreciable impact on macroeconomic policy-making in the bulk of LDCs. Formal and informal collaboration, based on shared interests, exists among a number of the major sets of actors, however, and is denoted by connecting lines of squares in Figure 1. Just as the three international sets of institutions and the local elites

Figure 1. External Influences on LDC Policy Formulation

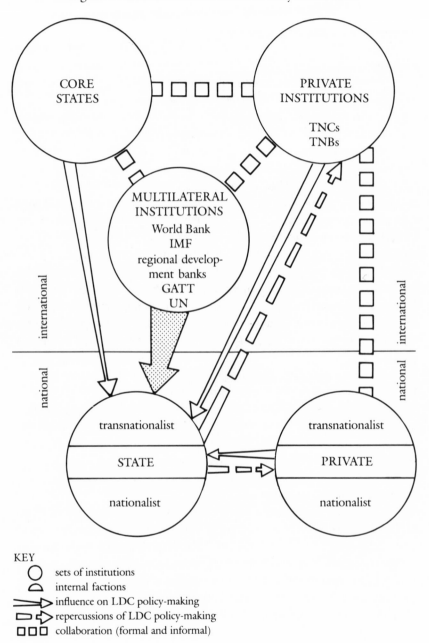

KEY

○ sets of institutions
◠ internal factions
⟹ influence on LDC policy-making
□ □ ⟹ repercussions of LDC policy-making
□□□ collaboration (formal and informal)

influence LDC policy-making, economic policy decisions of LDC states have repercussions on each set of institutions and on factions thereof (indicated by the broken rays in Figure 1).

In this mix of influence and control, it is the multilateral institutions' influence on LDC policy-making—the shaded ray at the center of Figure 1—that constitutes the major force in the emergence of the would-be NICs. It is here that answers lie to how the World Bank and the IMF contribute to shifts in an LDC's dominant paradigm of development: in particular, why would-be NICs were emerging; why it was that a country like the Philippines was shifting its overall economic direction from primary-commodity-export–led growth to export-oriented industrialization in the late 1970s and early 1980s; and how it was that, by this period, the Bank's and the Fund's positions in Philippine policy-making were sufficiently well entrenched to enable them to play a major role in the transformation of industry and finance in that country.

Whereas development literature has heavily critiqued development paradigms and policies, scant attention has been devoted to the mechanisms of interaction between international and national actors in policy formulation. Consequently, there is only shallow understanding of the crucial arena of how and why such shifts in an LDC's overall development path occur. This book attempts to help fill this void.

The Philippine Transformation

How can one step behind the closed doors and into the largely "confidential" process by which World Bank and IMF prescriptions are translated into policies that touch the lives of millions? That process and the interaction among Bank, Fund, and LDC state officials it entails are closed to the public. Moreover, each of the relevant actors has a vested interest in keeping it so.

In the case of the Philippines, a two-pronged approach succeeded in lifting the veil. First, a series of high-level leaks of Bank and Fund documents during the late 1970s and early 1980s provided access to thousands of pages intended for insiders' eyes only.[6] Encompassing practically all categories of confidential and restricted documents,[7] this continuous flow provided invaluable insights. Yet, rich as the documents were, they were only one part of the story; much of Bank and Fund influence is channeled through "policy dialogues" with LDC government officials, dialogues that are translated into the printed word only in generalizations, if at all.

Thus, a second tack involving interviews with key actors was taken. These were the very people who normally would not be expected to talk freely and certainly not about policy-making, an acutely sensitive arena in a country like the Philippines during a period when democratic processes were noticeable only by their absence. Yet over a hundred interviews— many with policymakers, some with Bank and Fund officials—were conducted in the Philippines from November 1980 to June 1981 and from July to August 1982.[8]

Surprisingly, there was little reticence. One- or two-hour slots stretched into long sessions (at times, a full working day) and several extended to more than one encounter per interviewee. People talked who had never talked publicly before. Partly they did so because of the greater ease a Western academician has with LDC bureaucrats. But some also spoke because the far-reaching policies of export-oriented industrialization were pitting nationalist bureaucrats against transnationalist colleagues in what seemed to many to be the final offensive. Divisions and loyalties could no longer be obscured. Nor could the identity of short-term winners. While some were eager to brag of successes, others felt the need to share their despair.

Most of the story can be understood through events surrounding two World Bank loans—a "structural adjustment loan" for the industrial sector, and an "apex loan" for the financial sector—which together were resounding successes in stimulating policy change in the early 1980s. Yet, just prior to these Bank loans, from 1976 to 1978, the IMF had tried to no avail to initiate a series of similar policy shifts. What changed? Why did the Bank succeed when the IMF had not? And how did that success affect different groups?

The gist of the story, culled from months of interviews, can be outlined in brief. The September 1980 signing of a $200 million structural adjustment loan for the Philippine industrial sector, after two years of intense dialogue between the World Bank and government officials, represented an excellent example of learning from history. The IMF had failed in its attempt to sell a similar package, attached to a loan of approximately $250 million, in part because it could not shake its image as purveyor of austerity and social upheaval. Beyond that, the Fund failed to neutralize nationalist factions in the government, especially in the Central Bank. Determined not to suffer the same fate, the World Bank shifted roles and steered policies skillfully around the Central Bank. It was aided by its more benevolent image as a lender of funds for long-term development projects. Clothed in this benevolence, the Bank was able to carry out the short-term stabilization role of the IMF. It put together a $200 million structural adjustment loan package (the Bank's fourth, the Philippines' first) as broad balance-of-payments support, attached not to a specific project but to a set of policy stipulations consolidating an export-oriented course for the Philippine industrial sector.

To implement the policy conditions for the loan, the Bank turned to allies in the ministries of Industry and Finance. Quietly bypassing the import-control office within the Central Bank, the World Bank hammered out import liberalization and tariff reduction policies with the Ministry of Industry. Exchange-rate policies were expected to pass through the Central Bank; yet here the World Bank finalized de facto devaluation measures with the finance minister.

While the IMF was privy to the Bank's maneuvers (indeed, it was the Bank's behind-the-scenes coach), the Central Bank was struggling to retain its rightful policy domain. It was the World Bank's conscious strategizing to link forces with sympathetic Philippine transnationalists and thereby surmount the once powerful economic nationalists within the Central Bank that enabled the ministries of Finance and Industry to play their new parts so well. As the World Bank (and the IMF behind it) discreetly circumvented the Central Bank by amassing a potent group of transnationalist allies elsewhere, it tilted the domestic power struggle in favor of transnationalist over nationalist factions.

Philippine officials of all persuasions agree that the period of the negotiations marked a critical juncture in the Philippine development path. Tariffs were slashed. Import restrictions that had protected domestic industry were lifted. The exchange rate began a steady and steep devaluation. Strengthened export- and investment-promotion policies diverted resources away from domestically oriented output. New free-trade tax havens, with generous incentives for transnational corporations to exploit low-cost Filipino labor, were set up. Individual light-manufacturing industries (textile, cement, food processing, furniture, and footwear) were slated for restructuring according to World Bank specifications to render them internationally competitive. In sum, the policies spelled one thing: export-oriented industrialization.

The story of the Philippines' transformation into a would-be NIC does not end with the industrial sector. Industrial restructuring was to find a reinforcing counterpart in financial-sector restructuring. This time the vehicle used by the World Bank was a $150 million "apex" loan to the Central Bank, negotiated over the same time period as the industrial sector loan but not signed until nearly a year later.

As the Bank and the Fund well understood, a full-fledged commitment to export-oriented industrialization demanded finance capital. IMF and World Bank officials together fashioned a new vision for the Philippine financial sector, wherein enlarged banks ("universal banks") would be encouraged, if not forced, to undertake major equity investments in industrial enterprises.

Once again, the path to actual policy implementation was not a smooth one. Undisputed reign over the financial sector rested with the Central Bank; there was no feasible way of turning to technocratic allies in other ministries this time. On the surface, the Bank acquiesced in this reality: it opened negotiations over the apex loan with the intransigent and nationalist Central Bank governor who had stymied IMF policy influence in the mid-1970s.

In time, however, it became painfully clear to the powerful at the Central Bank that their authority was in no way immutable. By the middle of the negotiations, the Central Bank hierarchy was no longer an active, informed participant. Instead, Bank missions were spending much of their time coordinating with a new unit that had been created within the Central Bank to oversee the World Bank apex loan. Antagonism from the rest of the Central Bank toward the fledgling "apex" unit was not surprising. In all aspects, it was a World Bank operation: Bank-conceived, Bank-staffed, Bank-trained, Bank-supervised. The Central Bank had been seeded with a potent transnationalist core.

By the time the nationalists caught on to the essence of the Bank's maneuvers, it was too late. By the end of the negotiations, the World Bank had set the stage for the apex institution's expansion. Not only would the first financial-sector loan be channeled through the apex institution into universal banks and, finally, into export-oriented industries, but so too would a growing number of future World Bank loans, future regional development bank loans, and future transnational bank loans.

When the industrial- and financial-sector loans are reexamined together, the role of the Bank and the Fund as policy-making institutions begins to take shape. In particular, three mechanisms of policy influence can be distinguished:

1. Strengthening the role, power, and ranks of technocrats within LDC bureaucracies in policy-making and implementation.
2. Building new institutions within the LDC bureaucracy.
3. Reshaping old institutions to fit with and further the new aims.

The export-oriented industrialization policies that ensued under multilateral institutions' collaboration with segments of the Philippine state had significant ramifications for various sets of international and national actors (see Figure 1). Under the weight of the Bank's and the Fund's successful policy influence from 1979 to 1982, nationalist and transnationalist factions in Philippine state and private institutions experienced their most dramatic transformation to date, in both absolute and relative terms. Within the state, nationalists lost every key foothold of influence on policy formulation, as transnationalists assumed hegemonic control of all major ministries. Within the private sector, economic nationalist factions whose enterprises depended on domestic markets were decimated as a class. As the industrial-sector policy changes left an ever more concentrated industrial sector in their wake, so, too, universal banking undermined all but a small circle of large banks.

These ramifications for state, industry, and finance fed on each other until by the early 1980s the texture of the Philippine political economy had been altered in a pronounced manner. A domestic triple alliance linking the victors in each sector—transnationalist factions of the state to transnationalist bankers to transnationalist industrialists—dominated the landscape.[9] But that domestic alliance rested on a broader one; export-oriented industrialization policies also tightened the bonds of collaboration between TNCs, TNBs, and their respective partners.

New Departures

This examination of external influences on Philippine policy-making was not guided by the rich experience of other researchers, for few have ventured into this policy process. The institutional means by which the Bank and the Fund (either singly or collectively) have assumed key influence in LDC policy-making and implementation have been largely ignored, both in academic and nonacademic literature. But certain traditions within two bodies of literature have laid the foundation on which this work is built: literature on the World Bank or the IMF; and literature on interactions between and within certain of the five sets of institutions presented in Figure 1.

Within the broad-ranging literature dealing explicitly with the World Bank and the IMF, one school consists of traditional or neoclassical analyses. These have brought forward the salient technical features of how multilateral institutions perform their narrowly defined role of fostering longer-run growth and development (for the Bank) or short-run stabilization (for the Fund). Centering their analyses on economic variables, these economists have largely divorced the Bank and the Fund from the realm of political economy in which they function.[10]

Since the 1950s, it has been common parlance within the Bank and the Fund to discuss the institutions' exercise of "leverage" or "conditionality" at a given moment in a given country.[11] In more recent years, a major debate emerged in Fund and academic economic circles concerning what degree of conditionality (none, low, high) should be attached to the various species of loans for different countries.[12] The debate developed in response both to critics from the left and from developing countries attacking the principle of conditionality[13] and to the question of why relatively few LDCs were using Fund facilities. In the context of the Fund's stated objectives, economists John Williamson (of the Institute for International Economics), Sidney Dell (of the United Nations), Bahram Nowzad (of the Fund), and others presented economic rationales behind various interpretations of conditionality. However, although Williamson noted the Fund's role as "giver of policy advice" and Nowzad mentioned its role "of persuading governments of the need for adjustment,"[14] their debate did not touch on the dynamics of policy-making, that is, how the IMF interacts with LDC policymakers to translate conditions into policy. Thus, while the debate offered valuable historical interpretations of the IMF's evolution toward conditionality,[15] it maintained the charade that international economic institutions are somehow divorced from the world of politics and policy-making.

More relevant is a second group of more radical critics of foreign aid. Path-breaking works include books by Teresa Hayter and Cheryl Payer.[16] Piecing together how "multinational corporations and capitalist governments" have historically been the beneficiaries of Bank and Fund advice to LDC governments,[17] Hayter and Payer analyzed the political and economic context in which multilateral institutions operated.

Yet, by concentrating on "the fate of the external economic relations of countries which provide . . . case studies,"[18] these authors bypassed another facet of the larger picture. As Payer acknowledged, what was lost was "a comprehensive picture of a [developing] nation's politics. In such a brief survey the internal factors have to be ignored or slighted."[19] Instead, Payer and Hayter brought the collaborative linkages among the three international sets of institutions to centerstage.

This focus led these radical critics, as a group, to project a black-box analysis of Bank and Fund dealings with LDCs. In a global system structured inequitably, they argued, the Bank and the Fund had the power to influence LDC development paths—and did so to the detriment of the LDC populace at large. But exactly what transpired in that black box of interactions could not be revealed by researchers based in developed countries and working predominantly from written materials (published or unpublished), or even by LDC-based researchers who did not have access to top policymakers.[20] Although the omission was therefore understandable and their work nonetheless an important milestone, it tended to reduce policy-making influence to the level of dictates, leaving readers with a somewhat simplistic vision of LDC states uniformly marching to Bank or Fund orders.

Ever since Lenin put forward his thesis of "solid bonds" existing between global capital and LDC bourgeoisies,[21] a vast literature has been built on the relationships between international and national institutions, of which the dependency school is best known within the tradition of looking at the international or external influence on LDC development paths.[22] For the most part situating their analyses in Latin America, *dependentistas* attempted to uncover the historical roots of the region's continuing "underdevelopment." For them, the critical analytical framework became the distinction between center and periphery. In general terms, *dependentistas* amalgamated the three rays of influence radiating from the international to the national (Figure 1) into one all-powerful, deterministic ray of influence. Thus dependency was presented as lack of autonomy for the periphery.

A major analytical weakness of this school of thought was the derivative position in which it placed the LDC state. In the early work of André Gunder Frank, the fundamental characteristics of underdevelopment induced by external control included the concept of a weak state with no power over the rate or shape of accumulation.[23] In this framework, Frank and other *dependentistas* tended to reduce the relationships between international institutions and the LDC nation as a whole to a mechanistic level, ignoring the growing sophistication of, and divisions within, LDC states and private capital as certain LDCs turned to export-oriented industrialization.

As Paul Baran first tried to turn Marxists' attention from developed countries' class relations to those within LDCs,[24] so too a small group of writers sought to refocus *dependentistas* toward distinctions in the political economy of LDCs that "would condition different responses to the world capitalist system."[25] Often incorrectly grouped within the relatively mechanistic dependency tradition, these theorists have been more accurately labeled the "new dependency" school by one Brazilian economist.[26] Key works here are few: the studies on Brazil by Peter Evans and by Fernando Henrique Cardoso and Enzo Faletto, and on South Korea by Hyan-Chin Lim.[27]

While not pursuing the world-systems level of analysis pioneered by Immanuel Wallerstein,[28] this school built on his distinctions among the different states of LDC dependence or underdevelopment. In particular, they focused on Wallerstein's theoretical construct of the semi-periphery,[29] which could be defined conceptually as those LDCs that have undergone more than minimal industrialization and have in the process gained some control over the surplus created. In this view, the "semi-periphery" would consist of the NICs. Evans, Cardoso, Faletto, and Lim took two of these, Brazil and South Korea, and demonstrated how an LDC within the semi-periphery could achieve levels of industrialization precluded by *dependentistas* and still be termed dependent on core institutions.[30] Cardoso termed this "associated dependent development"; Evans simply called it "dependent development."[31]

In this framework, alliances were central to dependency. Cardoso and Faletto explained:

> Some local classes or groups sustain dependency ties, enforcing foreign economic and political interests. Others are opposed to the maintenance of a given pattern of dependency. Dependence thus finds not only internal "expression," but also its true character as implying a situation that structurally entails a link with the outside in such a way that what happens "internally" in a dependent country cannot be fully explained without taking into consideration the links that internal social groups have with external ones.[32]

Cardoso and Faletto's associated dependent development involved the structuring of a "system of alliances," or links, among "a new kind of oligarchy" of elite representatives from three sectors: local capital, the LDC state, and foreign capital.[33] This represented a significant step forward from earlier dependency theorists' presentation of the LDC state and its dependency. As Cardoso and Faletto stressed: "There is no such thing as a metaphysical relation of dependency between one nation and another, one state and another. Such relations are made concrete possibilities through the existence of a network of interests and interactions."[34]

Peter Evans took Cardoso and Faletto's structure and built on it a ground-breaking work that analyzed in detail "the bases for conflict and cooperation among representatives of international capital, owners of local capital, and the top echelons of the state apparatus" in Brazil.[35] These three interacted to form a "triple alliance,"[36] cemented through overlapping self-interests. Each of the trio was presented as strong enough to strive constantly for a dominant position within the alliance. Evans's work added dynamics to the interactions and brought it far from the *dependentistas'* static world.

Hyan-Chin Lim's work is noteworthy for its attempt to extend the relevance and validity of Evans's "triple alliance" to Asia. One of Lim's main purposes was "to examine the mechanisms of dependent development [in South Korea], with emphasis on the close interplay of the state, foreign capital, and local capitalists under the U.S. security umbrella."[37] Although Lim could be criticized as overreacting to *dependentistas'* weak states by characterizing the South Korean state as enormously powerful,[38] his work nonetheless indicated that concepts developed by Evans and Cardoso had relevance for NICs besides Brazil.

Evans's and Lim's concern for alliances between sets of institutions, however, did not lead to deep analysis of how factions within each set of LDC institutions interact. Both did understand the analytical usefulness and validity of splitting institutions into "class segments" or factions.[39] Indeed, a steady undercurrent in each work traces the existence of what Oswaldo Sunkel has dubbed the elite's "transnational kernel." By that Sunkel meant "a complex of activities, social groups and regions in different countries which conform to the developed part of the global system and which are closely linked transnationally through many concrete interests as well as by similar styles, ways and levels of living and cultural affinities."[40]

With regard to LDC private institutions, the new *dependentistas* built on Baran's concept of a "comprador element of the native bourgeoisie,"[41] or what was later called the collaborating elite. Cardoso and Faletto clearly saw the distinctions between the "national and internationalized bourgeoisie."[42] Evans understood that "local capital cannot be analyzed as a single homogeneous entity. . . . The split between the incorporated elite and the rest of the local bourgeoisie facilitates the functioning of the triple alliance."[43] Yet, overall, the institutional perspective overshadowed the dynamics of conflict as these different factions strove for a hegemonic role.[44]

The present work builds on the work of Cardoso, Faletto, Evans, and Lim, and in particular on their analyses of the alliances that form the basis of LDC policy-making. Had not the new *dependentistas* carefully diagnosed the structural alliances that came with dependent development in the semi-periphery, the analysis of the political economy of policy-making suggested by Figure 1 would not be possible.

Thus, this work attempts to delineate the mechanisms by which the alliance of transnationalist factions in LDC states and bourgeoisies with multilateral institutions helped propel those factions into positions of authority. At the same time, in pushing beyond the dependent development engendered during NIC industrialization, this book seeks to extend the study of dependent development and the alliances it entails for policy-making to the would-be NICs, the group of twenty to thirty LDCs entering stages of export-led light industrialization, and particularly to the Philippines. What emerges is more than a black box of exploitation and coercion. Rather, policy formulation is viewed as emanating from the interaction of interests of local transnationalist classes and international institutions, challenged, with varying degrees of success, by nationalist factions.

The chapters that follow contain three dynamics of action. On one level, this book is a study of the World Bank and the IMF: individually, their mechanisms for influencing LDC policy-making; collectively, their collaboration that enhances the influence. A second dynamic lies in understanding the emergence and direction of the key component of the newest international division of labor, the would-be NICs. On the third and most specific level, the book is a case study of the Philippines, tracing both how it was restructured into a would-be NIC and what maldevelopment has resulted. As this introductory chapter illustrates, these three concerns are linked.

Although most of the events central to the Philippine story fall within the last two decades, the roots of Bank and Fund influence on developing-country policy-making extend from the middle of this century. The next chapter traces that history, from the institutions' founding in the waning years of the Second World War through the present international crisis.

2

Searching for a Role:
The Early Years

Neither the Bank nor the Fund was created to be a macroeconomic policy institution. Neither became a policy institution overnight. Their pivotal roles in the late 1970s Philippines were the result of sweeping revisions of the two institutions' powers and positions in the global economy over the three decades following the Second World War.[1] To review the key historic junctures in these institutions' development opens new avenues for understanding the Philippine economic revolution from 1979 to the present.

Those three decades of the Bank and the Fund can be split into three distinct periods:

1. The founding years of the 1940s under U.S. hegemony.
2. The late 1940s to early 1960s, marked predominantly by LDC import-substitution industrialization and, in the international arena, by stronger bilateral than multilateral aid institutions.
3. The early 1960s to mid-1970s, characterized by LDC export-led growth and the maturing of multilateral institutions.

Origins

In 1944, at Bretton Woods, New Hampshire, before the outcome of the Second World War was certain, final touches were put on what would become the postwar international economic order. At that point, with Europe and Asia devastated by war, the United States was gaining un-challenged hegemony in the global capitalist world in the military, financial, and industrial spheres. Indeed, wartime production had strengthened America's ability to provide abundant global credit and exports.[2]

As historian Gabriel Kolko has convincingly documented, top U.S. leadership spent the war years laying the groundwork for a postwar economic order firmly under its control.[3] U.S. needs were clear-cut: institutionalization of free trade, and reconstruction of Europe and Asia both to import U.S. goods and capital and to export raw materials vital to the United States. At all costs, the "beggar-thy-neighbor" trading policies of the 1930s were to be avoided. Protectionism was to be lowered, and there were to be no more of the 1930s trading blocs, which had excluded the United States, and certainly no more of the U.K. "sterling bloc" and its system of imperial preference.[4]

This U.S.-led geopolitical configuration was reflected at the Bretton Woods Conference (July 1–22, 1944) and related meetings during which blueprints for the World Bank and the IMF were drawn. Although forty-four nations were represented at Bretton Woods (among them the Philippines, still two years away from independence from the United States), the United States was in command. The British, through the renowned John Maynard Keynes, had been exchanging drafts with the United States for the two institutions over the two years prior to Bretton Woods. Keynes and his British colleagues had hoped for a bipolar configuration whereby "the United States and the United Kingdom . . . would be designated Founder States and given a special position."[5] But the Americans, under Assistant Secretary of the Treasury Harry Dexter White, had (as a verse on a scrap of paper from one of the conferences contended) all "the money bags" and different ideas.[6] Just as the voices of nationalist factions in all LDCs carry no real weight at the Bank or the Fund today, in the initial days of the institutions, virtually no delegations challenged the United States.[7]

A case in point was the question of headquarters. There was general agreement that, as the only thriving financial center, the United States should be the host. Keynes and a majority of Bretton Woods delegates had hoped the site would be New York—"sufficiently removed from the politics of [the U.S.] Congress and . . . legations of Washington," as Keynes phrased it.[8] But the Americans closed off any debate with a de facto decree that the site would be Washington, D.C., or there would be no U.S. approval of the institutions.[9] Likewise, it was the Americans who composed the formula for calculating IMF member-country quotas to comply with a U.S. desire to "yield a quota of about $2.5 billion for the United States, about half this for the United Kingdom, and such figures for the U.S.S.R. and China as should assure them third and fourth places, respectively, in the list of quotas."[10] On issue after issue, the United States asserted its control—"railroading," as Lord Keynes termed it.[11]

It was also during these early days that the seeds of the institutions' policy-influencing roles were sown. As Keynes's diaries disclose, what distressed him most about the American architects of the IMF and the World Bank was their insistence that the authority of international institutions could outweigh national authority. Keynes had foreseen international institutions constructed to respect national sovereignty and prerogatives: a Fund offering virtually automatic access to its resources; an adventurous Bank, disbursing all its assets within a decade; both geared to giving nations freedom to choose for themselves the appropriate tools for reaching full-employment equilibrium.[12] The United States wanted the institutions to be far more selective and conservative in their loan disbursements. Again, debate was useless. The United States built its case on what the U.S. Congress would accept, and the British, with a bilateral loan awaiting that congress's approval, were scarcely in a position to argue.[13]

At the end of what Keynes called the Bretton Woods "monkey-house" and a subsequent (March 1946) meeting at Savannah, Georgia, two international economic institutions emerged which the British accepted "without notable enthusiasm."[14] Although the World Bank came into the planning sessions almost as an afterthought,[15] the two were created as adjuncts. "Twins," Lord Keynes christened them;[16] but twins which their founding fathers saw as filling decidedly distinct roles in lubricating the postwar economic order. By the Fund's Articles of Agreement it was assigned six purposes, revolving around currency convertibility and world trade expansion:

(1) to promote international cooperation by providing the machinery required for members to consult and collaborate on international monetary issues; (2) to facilitate the balanced growth of international trade and, through this, contribute to high levels of employment and real income and the development of productive capacity; (3) to promote exchange stability and orderly exchange arrangements and facilitate the avoidance of competitive currency depreciation; (4) to foster a multilateral system of payments and transfers for current transactions and seek the elimination of exchange restrictions that hinder the growth of world trade; (5) to make financial resources available to members, on a temporary basis and with adequate safeguards, to permit them to correct payments imbalances without resorting to measures destructive of national and international prosperity; and (6) to seek reduction of both the duration and magnitude of payments imbalances.[17]

All in all, argued Keynes, the IMF was to be more of a bank than the World Bank,[18] which was to act as a "safe bridge over which private capital could move into the international field."[19] The Bank's founders saw direct lending (from its own resources or sales of its securities) as being appropriate only in "exceptional cases."[20] Rather, "the most important of the Bank's operations will be to guarantee loans in order that investors may have a reasonable assurance of safety in placing their funds abroad. In this way it is expected that the international flow of capital in adequate volumes will be encouraged."[21]

One final note of interest: developed nations were not differentiated from developing ones during the early meetings; no distinction was made between war-ravaged developed economies in need of reconstruction aid and LDCs in need of development aid.[22] It was largely assumed that the institutions would serve both equally, a far cry from their primary emphasis on LDCs by the close of the 1970s.

The Formative Fifties

U.S. dominance in the international political economy, which formed the backdrop to the Bretton Woods Conference, remained largely intact during the early years of Bank and Fund operations. The first fifteen years of the multilateral institutions' infancies—from the mid-1940s through the 1950s—were characterized by the drive to reconstruct Europe and Japan and by the virtually unchallenged supremacy of U.S. institutions in the global capitalist arena.

Overwhelming success at molding the Bretton Woods plans to conform to American needs left the U.S. government imbued with what Richard Gardner, in his study of Bank and Fund origins, called "prevailing overconfidence" in the ability of the multilateral institutions to patch over the havoc wrought by the war years.[23] In an attempt to live up to these expectations, the Bank got off to a quick start in disbursing loans for European reconstruction. Its charter's priorities of guaranteeing loans rather than direct lending and its fairly explicit mandate to treat reconstruction and development with "equitable consideration" were rapidly left behind by the exigencies of the times.[24] The Bank's first four loans were all to developed European states. Moreover, all followed a pattern supposedly reserved for "exceptional circumstances":[25] they were "program loans," general loans broadly destined to finance imports, rather than "project" loans geared to a specific productive investment. All were untied balance-of-payments supports, awarded without stipulations (indeed, almost without discussion), as the four were "developed countries whose general economic policies were presumably acceptable to the Bank."[26]

By 1948, however, it became woefully clear that the colossal task of reconstruction outstripped the reach of the infant Bank. That year the United States launched the Marshall Plan (1948–1952), thereby moving reconstruction operations from a multilateral to a bilateral (that is, government-to-government) basis.[27] Only at that point did the Bank turn to development and project loans.

In the meantime, the IMF, the Bretton Woods twin on which the United States had originally placed its greatest hopes, was finding its mandate difficult to execute. Implementation of its broad and often vague articles (based as they were on the language of diplomatic compromise) proved a tedious task. To say that the IMF played a minor role in LDC policy-making until the mid-1950s is an understatement. Yet, as it slowly moved into action, it established precedents that would have great relevance during its 1960s and 1970s period of widening influence on LDC states.

It is worth noting one such case. By the Fund's Articles of Agreement, it was to provide balance-of-payments loans "on terms which safeguard its interests."[28] There was no mention of specific conditionality as such, no word of jurisdiction over broader domestic financial, trade, or general economic policies. A 1947 IMF loan to Chile, however, translated safeguards into "appropriate fiscal and monetary measures."[29] Conditionality was born, and it evolved over the 1950s as the IMF developed standby arrangements (credit lines whereby the IMF purchases a country's domestic currency) and different "degrees of conditionality" through loans to a number of Latin American countries.[30] In 1952, the IMF officially accepted the conservative U.S. view that conditionality should accompany all loans,[31] and in 1955 it established stepped-up conditionality with a ruling that "the larger the drawing in relation to a member's quota the stronger is the justification required of the member."[32]

Though off to a quicker start than the IMF, the World Bank likewise was weak in the field of development. Both the Bank and the Fund were still totally eclipsed by U.S. initiatives in its bilateral aid institutions and direct U.S. influence on the multilateral institutions themselves. U.S. dominance over IMF actions was so complete that, until at least 1956, before a country would formally request an IMF loan that country would *first* approach the U.S. executive director of the Fund to make certain of his approval and, by extension, that of the U.S. Treasury.[33]

One result of this power was that, almost immediately, Cold War politics were brought into the institutions. The World Bank mandate was explicit that only economic, and not political, considerations were to influence the Bank's decisions.[34] But in 1947 the World Bank suspended consideration of a Polish loan (under pressure from the United States), followed by a political interpretation of this Article of Agreement: "Political tensions and uncertainties in or among its member countries . . . have a direct effect on economic and financial conditions in those countries and upon their credit position."[35] In this case, Poland's relationship with the Soviet Union was seen as construing "political tensions and uncertainties" enough to warrant refusal on what were termed "economic grounds."

U.S. sway over Bank actions was not only channeled through the U.S. government; private institutions too came into play. Given the Bank's reliance on New York financial markets, Wall Street's ratings were a critical determinant of Bank lending policy. As a former Bank official explained, "There was a need to lend to noncontroversial things . . . things that met with the [Wall Street] financial market's desires. So the early [Bank] bigwigs, all investment bankers themselves, got the Bank into economic overhead lending for electric power and transportation [facilities]."[36]

While publicly acting as a project lender, the Bank, even in its infancy, articulated its objectives within the much broader framework of improving the general climate for private (foreign and domestic) investment.[37] Bank officials consciously tried to expand negotiations over project loans into what Eugene Black, Bank president from 1949 to 1963, dubbed "development diplomacy,"[38] touching on LDC states' "economic and financial policies."[39] By its *Tenth Annual Report,* the Bank boasted of "various cases" of success in its "attempts to settle defaulted external debt, to put economic and fiscal policies on a sound footing, and to direct public investment in such a way as to promote, rather than obstruct or displace, the flow of private capital."[40]

Through early LDC lending (small-scale as it was), the Bank began to explore mechanisms of interaction that would mature into means for exerting influence on LDC macroeconomic policy-making during later decades. Two specific mechanisms, highlighted in the Philippine experiment of the 1980s, had their origins in these early days. First, the Bank became an institution builder through its fashioning of autonomous agencies "insulated from domestic political pressures (but responsive, of course, to the nonpolitical pressures emanating from the Bank's own headquarters)."[41] The main agencies born in this period were not necessarily central to LDC policy-making. Most were energy authorities, with relative independence in their ability to set rates and so forth.[42] But in some cases, the Bank successfully created somewhat more important institutions, such as planning agencies in Iran and Thailand, through which the World Bank could make its influence more directly felt on LDC development plans.[43]

Second, the Bank quickly discovered its natural affinity with emerging transnationalist factions of LDC states (the so-called technocrats). Thus, it became established policy for the Bank to stipulate who would staff these autonomous agencies. With the 1955 establishment of its own "staff college" for LDC bureaucrats, the Economic Development Institute (EDI), the Bank sought to assure a steady supply of technocratic counterparts.[44]

Overall relations between developed and developing countries during this early period of World Bank and IMF activity were marked by the continued dominance of government-to-government interactions. But in the arena of multilateral institutions, the Bank assumed a relatively greater role than did the Fund. Both bilateral and multilateral institutions were faced, however, with a general LDC policy climate during this period which was clearly inimical to the overall philosophy of Bretton Woods. Influenced in the 1950s by the ideas of the late Argentine economist Raul Prebisch and the United Nations Economic Commission for Latin America (ECLA), most large LDC states began pursuing some form of import-substitution industrialization policy.[45] These policies spread across the developing world in the years before the Bank and the Fund gained the confidence and power to convince countries to take another tack. The confrontations of ideology would come in the late 1950s and 1960s.

India was the Bank's test case of its ability to fight import-substitution industrialization. Ever since World Bank President Eugene Black's 1952 trip to India had left him "vexed by what he considered India's doctrinaire and unrealistic discrimination against private capital, and its unjustified preference for industrializing through investment in the public sector,"[46] the Bank had begun an accelerating flood of loans to India. (By the early 1960s, India had become the World Bank Group's largest borrower.)[47] The Bank's goal was to win enough "leverage" to transform Indian policies, but it found itself pitted against India's powerful, nationalist finance minister, and its advice went unheeded. By 1958, it became clear that a different tack was needed. In that year the Bank formed a consortium of multilateral and bilateral donors through which it vowed to increase assistance to India if certain policy changes were forthcoming. This signaled the beginnings of a new era of donor collaboration under multilateral institutions' leadership.[48]

Brazil illustrates another case of the Bank's and the Fund's relative impotence during the 1950s. In Brazil, the Bank discovered that its favored policy of "establishing a dialogue" on economic policy and performance would not work if the state was dominated by nationalist factions[49]—as was the case in Brazil from 1954 to 1964. Except for 1958, during which both the Bank and the Fund injected substantial credit into Brazil in the hope of obtaining a foothold for policy leverage, neither institution lent to the nationalist Brazilian government. In a later era, in similar circumstances, the institutions would have been in a better position to search out and bolster transnationalist factions in both India and Brazil.[50]

Both the Bank and the IMF largely steered clear of the Philippines during the 1950s. Independence in 1946 left Philippine exchange and import restrictions under the direct command of the United States.[51] Likewise, Philippine aid and economic policy advice in the 1950s were channeled overwhelmingly through bilateral sources; its first World Bank loan came only in 1957. Although neither the Bank nor the Fund was pleased with the Philippines' environment of import and exchange controls (reluctantly sanctioned by the United States lest the Philippine government collapse), authority to rectify this was not handed to multilateral institutions until the 1960s.[52]

The IMF Takes the Lead

World Bank and IMF roles in the developing world escalated in the 1960s, accompanying several LDCs' shifts from import-led to export-oriented development. These new roles were made possible by two major changes in the international political economy: the reconstruction of Japan and Western Europe, and the rapid decolonization of most of Africa and Asia.

Political stability and economic growth became the norm in Europe and Japan by the early 1960s, leaving bilateral and multilateral institutions freer to devote resources to the developing world. However, the reconstruction effort, coupled with substantial U.S. military grants and loans, took its toll on the U.S. economy: the balance of payments was consistently in deficit after 1950.[53] President Eisenhower's 1958 proposal to augment IMF quotas by 50 percent and the subsequent U.S. policy of relying on the IMF both to finance part of its own deficit and as a "pilot" for aid programs signaled an enhanced position for the IMF.

Independence for the bulk of the developing world helped shift the relative importance of bilateral versus multilateral assistance. By the end of the Bank's first decade, its membership had increased by fifteen; ten of these were Asian countries. Between 1957 and 1967, thirty-two African states swelled the ranks (see Table 1).[54] Once colonies began to sever ties to their mother countries, the Bank and the Fund gained new prominence in promoting export-led growth—particularly during the early-to-middle 1960s in several LDCs where coups, often aided by the U.S. government, replaced nationalist-leaning governments with transnationalists.[55] The 1964 Brazilian military coup, the 1966 takeover of Indonesia by Suharto, the 1961 coup which brought Park Chung Hee to power in South Korea: all these created future top Bank and Fund clients, preaching various forms of economic liberalism.

Economically, European and Japanese reconstruction created the conditions for a booming world market based principally on a more tradi-

Table 1.   Changes in World Bank Membership and Voting Power, 1947–1971

	April 10, 1947		June 30, 1957		June 30, 1967		June 30, 1971	
	Number of Members	Voting Power (%)	Number of Members	Voting Power (%)	Number of Members	Voting Power (%)	Number of Members	Voting Power (%)
Africa	2	1.64	2	1.42	34	7.85	40	8.58
Asia[a]	3	11.66	13	17.49	17	15.13	18	16.15
Australasia	1	2.41	1	2.09	2	2.94	3	2.94
Central and South America	18	8.39	20	9.66	22	8.38	22	8.30
Europe[b]	14	35.72	16	33.99	20	34.35	20	33.79
Middle East[c]	5	2.21	6	2.38	9	3.15	11	3.38
North America	2	37.97	2	32.97	2	28.20	2	26.86
Total	45	100.00	60	100.00	106	100.00	116	100.00

SOURCE: Edward Mason and Robert Asher, *The World Bank Since Bretton Woods* (Washington, D.C.: Brookings Institution, 1973), p. 65.

[a]Includes Israel.

[b]Includes Cyprus and Turkey.

[c]Includes Iran, Iraq, Jordan, Kuwait, Lebanon, Libya, Saudi Arabia, Syrian Arab Republic, United Arab Republic, Yemen Arab Republic, and People's Democratic Republic of Yemen.

tional international division of labor between raw-material-exporting LDCs and manufactures-exporting developed countries. Yet, there were already signs that this division would be shifting. By the early 1960s, seven LDCs—Brazil, Mexico, India, South Korea, Taiwan, Singapore, and Hong Kong—had begun to lay down the preconditions for industrialization for export. In varying combinations and intensities, their drives toward export-oriented industrialization were underpinned by aid, investment, and technology licenses from U.S., Japanese, and British sources. Several of these NICs warmed to Bank and Fund lending and advice over the 1960s; by the mid-1970s all (except India) became models held up by these multilateral institutions for the next group of would-be NICs (the Philippines among them).

As the Bretton Woods twins turned greater attention to the developing world over the decade and a half after 1960,[56] the Fund's role in LDCs rapidly surpassed that of the Bank. The official IMF history labeled the mid-1960s as the time of "growth of responsibilities."[57] The Fund's authority to supervise exchange rates had been established early on, but an escalation of consultations with member-states in 1960 magnified the practice. By the early 1960s, the Fund had achieved recognized jurisdiction over trade policies;[58] by mid-decade, its jurisdiction expanded further:

> The Fund's annual consultations with members began to shift away from the subject of restrictions, and an ever-widening range of financial and economic topics became primary. Increasingly, consultations aimed at assessing members' monetary and fiscal policies and the effects of those policies on the member's own balance of payments position and on the world's financial situation. . . .
>
> Consultations . . . began to cover more fully the consequences of economic development efforts, both in the short run and in the somewhat longer run, for prices, production, monetary and fiscal policies, and the balance of payments; problems of joblessness and measures to increase employment opportunities; the size and servicing of external indebtedness; and members' relationships with regional organizations, as the latter multiplied in number and strength.[59]

Concomitantly, the breadth and range of IMF facilities were extended.[60] What were accepted topics for IMF consultations became the foundation on which the by then fairly routine (although still hotly debated) loan conditions could be built. The institution was then in a position to actively promote its preferred model of export-led growth. "The Fund," explained development expert Dragoslav Avramović, "always had an ideology, but only turned this ideological preference for a specific model of development into a firm, obsessive ideology in the 1960s as the Fund grew into a tightly controlled and hierarchical institution."[61]

Already during this period, as an IMF staff member noted in 1982, "the Fund had a number of stand-by programs that were catalytic . . . in strengthening the technocrats . . . within national governments."[62] It became an initiation rite of sorts for transnationalist LDC regimes to open their administrations with IMF-sponsored "stabilization" programs— Argentina under a military government in 1965, and Uruguay in the mid-1960s, among others.[63] The case of Brazil, 1964–1967, illustrates the supportive role of the IMF (backed by the Bank) in the transformations of the NICs.[64] When a transnationalist (military) faction under Brazilian General Castello Branco toppled the nationalist João Goulart, the IMF quickly resumed loans under conditions that speeded the country's shift toward export-oriented industrialization.[65]

To bolster the position of its LDC allies further, the IMF took the lead from the Bank's EDI and in 1963 opened its own technocratic training center for finance ministry and central bank staff, the IMF Institute.[66]

Both the Fund and the Bank supplemented direct action in the 1960s by presenting their perspective to academics and policymakers in books and articles. By attempting to bill themselves as centers of finance and development thinking, they hoped to enhance the stature and legitimacy of LDC technocrats who shared their ideas. Voluminous Fund and Bank country reports date from this era, as do special topic reports. Thus, when the Bank decided to turn "its attention vigorously" to the problem of import-substitution industrialization in the mid-1960s, it did so by undertaking a long series of scholarly reports documenting the pitfalls of that model, both theoretically and through a fourteen-volume attack on India's economic policies.[67]

For the most part, the Bank operated in the shadow of the IMF during this period in its role in LDC policy-making. There were, however, notable exceptions, particularly India, where the World Bank made "serious efforts in the mid-1960s to influence economic performance."[68] Implementation of Pakistan's 1964 and 1965 import liberalization policies was assisted by the Bank's support for the transnationalist Ministry of Finance over the opposition of the nationalist Central Bank.[69] Such experiences as these set a precedent for how the Bank might best establish a foothold in LDC policy "dialogues" where no transnationalist faction was firmly in command—a key mechanism in the Bank's late 1970s and early 1980s Philippine work. Thus, a World Bank official told Teresa Hayter in 1962: "The Bank's diplomacy . . . was [often] conducted in secrecy, with usually only a few high government officials, hopefully sympathetic to the Bank's point of view, involved in the negotiations."[70]

But the limited focus of the Bank's project lending still constrained the potential reach of its loan-related policy dialogue in most cases. Although agricultural loans became a Bank priority in the 1960s (at the bidding of a "very high official in the U.S. government"), the World Bank loans to LDCs predominantly continued to fund electric power and transport infrastructure.[71] Another trend in Bank lending persisted: freewheeling program loans were (almost without exception) reserved for developed countries.[72] Bank management clearly approached the developed and the developing world on very different terms. A case in point was the IMF's November 1967 standby loan to the United Kingdom, a loan whose size and virtual lack of conditionality greatly upset certain of the IMF's LDC members.[73]

Collaboration between the Bank and the Fund entered a new stage during this period. After an initial few years of fairly close interaction in the mid-1940s, the two institutions separated during the 1950s into a state of "rather distant reserve."[74] By the mid-1960s, however, as both institutions became secure with their respective identities and as the relative decline in importance of bilateral aid conferred added prestige and responsibilities on multilateral aid efforts, a new era of more explicit cooperation regarding LDC work began.

Coordination of Bank and Fund aid and advice with bilateral efforts was institutionalized through consortia and consultative groups. What began as an experiment for India in 1958 evolved (under U.S. support) in the 1960s and 1970s into consultative groups of bilateral and multilateral donors.[75] Between 1962 and mid-1971 alone, fifteen consultative groups were formed under Bank sponsorship, each with the IMF as an active participant.[76]

Outside the consultative groups, new forms of more intense collaboration between the Bank and the Fund also developed. From late 1966, this collaboration was steered by parallel memoranda of agreement from IMF Managing Director Pierre-Paul Schweitzer and Bank President George

Woods.[77] While careful to lay out the distinct "primary responsibility" of each institution, the memoranda emphasized "how large is the area of common interest."[78] The goal was to "avoid contradictory or inconsistent advice," by systematizing procedures whereby (1) factual information on countries would be exchanged; and (2) field missions would collaborate.[79]

In 1970, as each institution moved "to increase . . . mission activities substantially,"[80] the Bank and the Fund reviewed collaborative efforts to seek (in the words of the official Fund history of this period) "ways to work together still more closely."[81] From this emerged a 1970 joint memorandum by the managing director of the IMF and the president of the IBRD, with a detailed plan for formalizing measures "to reduce to a minimum the risk of inconsistent policy advice."[82] Mutual briefings and debriefings were to proceed and follow each mission; draft and final documents were to be exchanged for information and feedback. But, as the Philippine case study reveals, by the late 1970s such collaboration would reach still greater heights.

Over the decade and a half after 1960, coups were not always the mechanisms that put transnationalist factions into power. The 1962 election of Diosdado Macapagal in the Philippines, for instance, brought to power an administration pledged to terminate a decade of import-substitution industrialization protected by exchange and import controls.[83]

Through emissaries dispatched to Washington, D.C., Macapagal prepared to cushion certain immediate effects of his promised decontrol by approaching the U.S. government for bilateral aid.[84] President John Kennedy pledged a total of nearly $100 million on one condition: IMF participation.[85] As Macapagal recalled years later, "I did not have, in particular, the idea [to approach the IMF] myself. I just went along with whatever President Kennedy suggested."[86] The U.S. State Department lost no time in quietly placing pressure on the IMF to meet Macapagal with a set of precise conditions (a lobbying effort that at least one non-Western IMF official tried unsuccessfully to resist).[87] In the end, the Philippines received a joint U.S./IMF stabilization fund, totaling almost $300 million, and a fairly typical packet of IMF conditions: (1) devaluation of the peso against the dollar; (2) abolition of import controls and exchange licensing; (3) extension of incentives to foreign capital; and (4) tightening of domestic credit.[88]

In the Philippines, as in most other LDCs, World Bank influence on aggregate economic policy during this period was felt on a decidedly lesser scale, predominantly through assistance in elaborating economic development plans. In this case, the Bank sent Economic Staff member Dragoslav Avramović to Manila in the summer of 1961. President Garcia, with his nationalist theme of "Filipino First," was still in power in the Philippines, but the 1961 election was expected to usher in the transnationalist Macapagal. Avramović's goal was "to put together an overall investment or development program" and, based on this, to launch the Philippines in its first venture in economic planning to encompass more than input-output analysis.[89] Significantly, this endeavor meant that the World Bank was subsuming and amplifying what had previously been the domain of U.S.-Philippine interactions.[90] Although Avramović in later years recalled no collaboration between his efforts and concurrent IMF work, the Bank, like the Fund, was preparing for the election of Macapagal.[91] Top officials of Macapagal's administration, moreover, were clearly left with the sense that the two missions were related.[92]

Avramović's plan was published as an appendix to Macapagal's *Five-Year Integrated Socio-Economic Program* (which, by the president's own admission, "was not original," but was built on World Bank work).[93] Of perhaps more significance than the plan (which was never seriously implemented) was the Bank's coterminous attempt at institution-building. The Program Implementation Agency, formed at Avramović's suggestion to implement the plan, became a counterbalance to the already existing government economic body still headed by nationalists whose views carried over from the 1950s "Filipino First" era. Avramović's agency later evolved into a central domestic economic and planning institution.[94]

Another IMF stabilization package for the Philippines in 1970 (then under Ferdinand Marcos, elected to his first term in 1965 and his second in 1969) exemplified the ascendency of that institution over the decade. This time, no initial approach was made to the United States; all business was conducted directly with the IMF. Unlike the situation in 1962, when the Macapagal government wrote its own decontrol and delicensing circulars (with IMF approval), the entire 1970 program "was dictated by the IMF."[95] The 1970 loan followed a 1969 foreign-exchange crisis, complicated by the phenomenon, new to the Philippines, of external debt.[96] As former Program Implementation Agency head Armand Fabella explained, "When you are hard up, the IMF is nasty. In 1970, the Philippines was hard up."[97] "We wanted to tighten our belts instead of devaluing . . . but we were at the mercy of the IMF," maintained economist and former Development Bank of the Philippines official Armado Castro.[98]

The agreement was sealed at the highest levels: IMF representatives met directly with Philippine President Ferdinand Marcos. As a result, in February 1970 the peso was floated against the dollar (stabilizing at 6.50 pesos to the dollar, far above the 5.00 or 5.20 to 1.00 predicted by IMF officials).[99] Salient parts of the package were liberalization of foreign investment legislation and the removal of import controls (which had been reimposed over the course of the 1960s). Within the year, a Philippine Consultative Group was established. It was all part of the IMF program—a program, according to then Central Bank official Benito Legarda, "not of our own design."[100]

The World Bank hailed Marcos's 1970 float and accompanying policies as "a commendable act of political courage."[101] Given that the policy changes occurred less than two years after the nationalist-dominated Philippine Congress had passed the "Magna Carta of Social Justice and Economic Freedom," which rejected development based on free trade and TNCs,[102] Marcos's act represented a major victory for the transnationalist aspirations of the Fund and the Bank. In this sense, the Philippine case was typical of the policies the IMF forged in several countries in the early 1970s. Tensions often ran high, as technocratization was still in its formative stages in most LDCs. Therefore, by the close of this last historical period, the IMF's "successes" had left it in the somewhat awkward position of not only being opposed by LDC nationalists but, in certain cases, also being resented by LDC transnationalists for the political tensions exacerbated through IMF influence.

It is striking that at a major 1982 conference of the prestigious U.S. Institute for International Economics, just a dozen years after these developments, more than one participant noted that the Bank was achieving "more good with less friction" in economy-wide adjustment than the Fund.[103]

3

Maturation: Bank and Fund Centerstage

Over the three-decade span between 1944 and the mid-1970s, the roles of the World Bank and the IMF in LDC economic policy-making evolved slowly, though consistently, in the direction of greater involvement. Since the mid-1970s, their roles have expanded far more rapidly, and the Bank's has undergone a qualitative change. The IMF's relative effectiveness in influencing LDC economic policies had been definitively established in the 1960s, but the Bank's capacity in this regard was realized only from the late 1970s onward. At that point the Bank changed from an institution dispensing funds largely through individual project loans to one targeting its operations increasingly at broad structural changes.

The most dramatic manifestations of these shifting roles can be witnessed among the twenty to thirty LDCs that the Bank and the Fund have helped guide into varying stages of export-oriented light manufacturing, constituting a major component of what has been termed a "new international division of labor." One member country of these would-be NICs that has sustained among the most rapid and far-reaching changes has been the

Philippines, substantially assisted in its transformation by major industrial-sector and financial-sector loans from the World Bank. To varying degrees in all these countries, the Bank and the Fund have nurtured and been assisted in these policy shifts by growing corps of technocrats, who have orchestrated legislative initiatives speeding their countries toward export-led industrial growth.

International Political Configuration

Two interrelated phenomena contributed to thrust multilateral institutions, particularly the World Bank, into prominence by the mid-1970s. First was the relative decline of U.S. supremacy in the world—militarily, economically, and politically—as the Vietnam War escalated. Second was the ascendency of a Third World political voice, backed up by OPEC's newfound clout after 1973. Both reshaped the U.S.-dominated postwar international political configuration.

A number of factors contributed to the U.S. decline. As Europe and Japan industrialized rapidly, their growing exports to the United States began a slow yet steady erosion of the U.S. trade surplus.[1] Even more disruptive were the economic dislocations born of the United States' involvement in Indochina. In the ten years between 1965, when U.S. troops first set foot in Southeast Asia, and 1975, when the U.S. ambassador to "South Vietnam," Graham Martin, was removed by helicopter from the roof of the U.S. embassy, the global role of the U.S. economy was shaken.[2] The total bill for U.S. military expenditures during the war was $150 billion.[3] Two American political scientists summed up the war's impact: "The Vietnam War has placed extraordinary stress on the national economy, increasing imports, rendering exports less competitive, and setting off a spiralling inflation."[4]

It was inevitable that the cornerstone of the postwar global monetary order, the U.S. dollar, would suffer the aftereffects of such unrestrained military spending, and 1971 witnessed the first dollar devaluation. That devaluation set in motion the decline of the U.S. dollar as the sole international reserve currency (although it remains the principal one) and provided the first shock to the Bretton Woods monetary system and the paramount position the United States had held within it. It was a shock from which the system has yet to recover.[5]

Vietnam did more than simply weaken U.S. economic and political power and clout. A psychological blow was also dealt to certain U.S. leaders, a realization, for a short time at least, that saturation bombing and the strongest military machine ever assembled had failed. A significant component of a state's political power is a sense of how that nation is perceived in the world. Already in 1968, the Vietnamese Tet offensive revealed to most observers that the United States was not winning the war and that fighting might drag on for years without victory.[6] Followed closely by the U.S. invasion of Cambodia, this left growing numbers of Americans dissatisfied with their country's foreign policy. Gabriel Kolko wrote of Vietnam, "No other event of our generation has turned such a large proportion of the nation against its government's policy or so profoundly alienated its youth."[7]

Partly as a result of the psychological and financial strains of the war, the U.S. economy failed to match the dynamism of certain major allies over the postwar period. As the U.S. share of global exports dropped from 17 percent to 11 percent between 1950 and 1980, the combined share of Japan and West Germany rose from under 5 percent to over 16 percent during this period (see Table 2). Similarly, in the two decades from 1960 to 1980, U.S. transnational corporations' share of the total sales of the world's top two hundred TNCs dropped from 73 to 50 percent, while corporations from Japan and France fared better. The number of Japanese TNCs among the top two hundred rose from five to twenty over this period; the number of French from seven to fifteen (see Table 3). By the end of the Vietnam War, the U.S. share of the total OECD production (Organization of Economic Cooperation and Development, the leading twenty-four industrialized countries) stood at two-thirds of its World War II level.[8]

Thus the bipolar global configuration that had characterized the period from the end of the Second World War until Vietnam increasingly gave way to a trilateral alliance of the United States and the fully reconstructed nations of Japan and Western Europe. As economist William Branson noted in his intensive review of U.S. trade and investment in the postwar period, "The United States has moved from a position of dominance to being one of several roughly equal centers, with increasingly tight economic interconnections among them."[9] The war and its psychological and economic repercussions had left the U.S. government (and people) less willing or able to play a major bilateral role in the developing world. Part of its role as

Table 2.   World Exports: Geographical Breakdown, 1950–1980

	1950	1960	1970	1980	Annual Growth 1950–1980 (%)
	\$ Billion				
Developed countries	36.8	84.9	222.9	1,258.0	12.1
USA	10.2	20.4	42.6	216.7	10.4
FRG	2.0	11.4	34.2	193.0	15.9
Japan	0.8	4.1	19.3	129.3	17.8
UK	6.1	10.2	19.4	115.4	10.0
LDCs	19.8	29.3	58.4	563.4	11.4
OPEC	3.4	8.0	18.1	303.6	15.6
Non-OPEC	16.4	21.3	40.4	160.0	7.3
Centrally planned economies	4.0	12.7	30.5	164.4	12.7
World	60.6	126.9	311.8	1,985.8	11.9
	Percentage[a]				
Developed countries	60.7	66.5	71.1	62.9	
USA	16.8	16.0	13.6	10.8	
FRG	3.3	8.9	10.9	9.7	
Japan	1.4	3.2	6.2	6.5	
UK	10.0	8.0	6.2	5.8	
LDCs	32.7	23.0	18.6	28.2	
OPEC	5.6	6.3	5.8	15.2	
Non-OPEC	27.1	16.7	12.8	13.0	
Centrally planned economies	6.6	9.9	9.7	8.2	

SOURCE: Data from UNCTAD secretariat databank, 1982.

[a]Some columns total slightly less than 100 percent due to rounding.

LDC economic disciplinarian and policy influencer could be turned over to multilateral institutions.

Major political and economic change was not restricted to the developed world. The second event jolting the international political configuration was the rise of OPEC, an ascension marked by the quadrupling of oil prices in 1973 and 1974. For the first time in post–World War II history, a

Table 3. Changing Profile of the Top 200 Industrial Corporations, 1960–1980

	1960			1970			1980		
	Number	Sales ($ billion)	Percentage of Total Sales	Number	Sales ($ billion)	Percentage of Total Sales	Number	Sales ($ billion)	Percentage of Total Sales
USA	127	144.6	72.7	123	313.5	66.0	91	1,080.4	50.1
FRG	20	13.4	6.8	15	34.6	7.3	21	209.0	9.7
UK	24	19.6	9.9	17	39.2	8.2	16.5[a]	199.5	9.2
France	7	3.5	1.8	13	19.8	4.2	15	161.0	7.5
Japan	5	2.9	1.5	13	28.1	5.9	20	155.2	7.2
Netherlands	3	6.4	3.2	3	15.0	3.2	5	89.6	4.2
Italy	3	1.9	0.9	5	9.6	2.0	4.5[a]	69.5	3.2
Canada	5	2.6	1.3	2	2.4	0.5	5	32.5	1.5
Switzerland	2	2.0	1.0	4	6.4	1.3	4	31.9	1.5
Belgium	1	0.5	0.2	1	1.3	0.3	2	14.5	0.7
Sweden	1	0.4	0.2	1	1.0	0.2	2	11.0	0.5
South Korea	—	—	—	—	—	—	2	10.0	0.5
Others	2	1.1	0.5	3	4.4	0.9	12	91.1	4.2
Total (excluding USA)	73	54.3	27.3	77	161.8	34.0	109	1,074.8	49.9
Total	200	198.9	100.0	200	475.3	100.0	200	2,155.2	100.0
Global GDP minus centrally planned economies		1,126.2			2,489.0			7,548.0	

SOURCE: Calculated from *Fortune*'s listings of leading industrial corporations, in John Cavanagh and Frederick Clairmonte, *The Transnational Economy: Transnational Corporations and Global Markets* (Washington, D.C.: Institute for Policy Studies, 1983), p. 11, table 1. Note that countries are ranked according to 1980 sales.

[a] Corporations owned by interests in two countries are counted as .5 for each country.

group of nations outside the traditional power centers exerted substantial economic pressure and, by doing so, were able to amass collective political power.

OPEC's gains quickly overflowed the organization's geographic boundaries, engendering hopes for a unity of purpose among the so-called South or Third World in international forums. Between 1960 and 1970 alone, forty new states had achieved political independence, adding more voices to the demands for a new international economic order. After OPEC's rise, this articulation could be translated into a far more unified developing-country agenda.

LDCs voiced their new international economic order platform at a series of international conferences, beginning at the sixth and seventh special sessions of the United Nations General Assembly in 1974 and 1975.[10] These and subsequent international forums were of decisive importance in giving voice to demands of LDC elites, both transnationalist and nationalist. The demands would include new responsibilities for the IMF and the World Bank.

Although these political shifts were necessary preconditions for recasting IMF and World Bank policy-related roles, they were not in themselves sufficient to dictate economic redirections of LDC policy that the Bank and the Fund would help effectuate. Transnational corporations and banks were the other significant movers in reshaping the international division of labor.

Shifting International Division of Labor

By 1970, a century-old international division of labor between developed countries as manufactures producers and developing countries as raw-materials exporters was in the throes of transformation.[11] Concomitant with the early 1970s rise of OPEC was a gradual move by TNCs, supported by their home governments, to concentrate more sophisticated capital-intensive manufacturing in developed countries and less complex light manufacturing in certain LDCs, including the Philippines.

Although TNCs' global extensions had been spreading since the Second World War, the 1970s marked a period of unprecedented expansion.[12] Fueled by rapid increases in mergers and acquisitions, TNCs achieved remarkable growth rates: compared with world GNP, total sales of the world's top two hundred corporations increased from 18 to 29 percent from 1960 to 1980.[13] The leading TNCs worldwide emerged from the ranks of "the Big Five"—the United States, Japan, West Germany, the United Kingdom, and France, in that order.

By the late 1970s, corporations in some sectors found themselves with substantial amounts of capital available for investment in LDCs, where returns on investment were often far higher than in their home country.[14] Direct foreign investment by the United States in LDCs totaled $19.2 billion in 1970; nine years later the number had soared to $47.8 billion.[15] By the mid-1980s, it scaled $60 billion. The upshot was a growing transnationalization of corporate operations, concomitant with an enhanced ability to oversee and manage production processes in numerous countries.[16]

The tempo of TNC takeovers and investments could never have attained its present pitch without the participation of TNBs on a large scale. A perusal of the world's top one hundred banks dramatizes the awesome power of the TNBs (see Table 4). Their combined assets of $4.4 trillion were the equivalent of more than half the global gross domestic product (GDP) and almost double the combined sales of the top two hundred industrial corporations.

As TNCs and TNBs expanded, so did the amounts they poured into research and development, underpinned in most developed countries by government subsidies.[17] More than any other single factor, a major revolution in technology helped launch this new international division of labor. Computer and satellite technologies quickly spanned the globe, allowing nearly instantaneous communication everywhere, vastly reducing inventories, and greatly facilitating global planning by corporations. The revolution magnified Adam Smith's pin factory to global dimensions by doling out the complex production processes of certain major industrial sectors to several countries before final assembly in a country near the intended market.

These technological advances made possible such creations as the "global car," a final product pieced together from components produced all around the world. *Fortune* magazine dubbed it the "global game," the complex and sophisticated strategies corporate planners created "to break down production steps by geographic areas, turning out large components and subsystems in plants scattered in key industrializing countries around the globe."[18] Among the variables considered as TNCs entered this global

Table 4.   Profile of the Top 100 Banks, 1981

	Number of Banks	Assets ($ billion)	Percentage of Total Assets	Profits ($ billion)	Percentage of Total Profits
Japan	24	1,097.6	25.1	88.4	20.8
USA	12	650.7	14.9	91.2	21.4
France	8	509.2	11.6	35.8	8.4
FRG	11	464.3	10.6	45.9	10.8
UK	5	344.5	7.9	42.1	9.9
Italy	8	258.1	5.9	28.6	6.7
Canada	5	240.6	5.5	34.5	8.1
Netherlands	4	160.4	3.7	2.5	0.6
Switzerland	3	141.9	3.2	12.8	3.0
Belgium	4	100.2	2.3	12.2	2.9
Spain	3	67.5	1.5	6.7	1.6
Brazil	1	65.1	1.5	5.3	1.2
Sweden	3	64.6	1.5	3.1	0.7
Australia	3	60.0	1.4	7.1	1.7
Hong Kong	1	52.1	1.2	—	—
Iran	1	23.9	0.6	1.1	0.3
India	1	20.5	0.5	1.9	0.5
Israel	1	19.2	0.4	4.2	1.0
Mexico	1	18.4	0.4	—	—
Austria	1	18.2	0.4	1.7	0.4
Total	100	4,377.0	100.1[a]	425.1[b]	100.0

SOURCE: Computed from *The Banker* (June 1982), in John Cavanagh and Frederick Clairmonte, *The Transnational Economy: Transnational Corporations and Global Markets* (Washington, D.C.: Institute for Policy Studies, 1983), p. 12, table 2.

NOTE: Countries ranked by assets.

[a] Slight variations in totals due to rounding.
[b] Profit figures not provided for certain banks in the following countries: France (3), Hong Kong (1), Netherlands (2), Japan (1), Italy (1), UK (1), Sweden (1), Mexico (1).

game were wage rates, exchange rates, risk factors, growth rates, inflation rates, trade policies, and market locations.[19]

As far as LDCs (and the Philippines in particular) were concerned, technological revolutions in electronics and textiles and apparel assumed the greatest significance. The silicon-chip revolution in the electronics field actually began in the 1960s (built on an earlier decade of work with transistors), but the microprocessor phase of the 1970s vastly extended the efficiency and range of applications.[20] Microprocessor production lines consist of knowledge-intensive processes, largely located in developed countries, as well as a labor-intensive component. The latter, requiring only a rapidly trained, semiskilled labor force, was best located where labor was relatively cheap.[21]

As a result, semiconductor production was internationalized, as the largely U.S.- and Japan-based industry spread its subsidiaries to Hong Kong in 1961, Taiwan and South Korea in 1964, Singapore in 1969, Malaysia in 1972, Thailand in 1973, and Indonesia and the Philippines in 1974.[22] The phenomenal rate of change in the electronic field's international division of labor was reflected in developed-country imports of integrated circuits and related products, which quadrupled in value between 1972 and 1976.[23] From 1970 to 1978, semiconductor imports to the United States alone jumped more than tenfold, from $139 million to almost $1,479 million.[24] Over 95 percent of this offshore production was concentrated in six countries, all but one of them Asian.[25]

Microprocessors found applications across practically the entire realm of industrial and service sectors, and technology in many other industries became increasingly sophisticated as well. The textile industry, which, along with apparel, is the leading developing-country industrial sector, proved no exception. With textile machinery's rapid technological innovation and speed increases, the traditionally labor-intensive textile industry gained in capital intensity.[26] Its downstream apparel sector, without a comparable shift in technology, remained labor-intensive. The combination led logically to a global division of output where developed countries carried out the most capital-intensive spinning, weaving, and knitting stages, often relegating the apparel stage to certain LDCs. In 1965, developing countries had only an 18.6 percent share of world apparel exports; by 1977, that portion had expanded to 36.7 percent.[27]

Within this schema, there are important refinements: although the textile industry is capital-intensive in comparison with the later stage of apparel production, capital invested per employee is still relatively low on the overall spectrum of manufacturing sectors.[28] This relative labor intensity by global standards was a major factor behind the export of textile machinery, often financed by Japanese capital, to certain LDCs, primarily three of the Asian NICs—Taiwan, South Korea, and Hong Kong. These three, together with the four remaining NICs—Singapore, Brazil, India, and Mexico—accounted for well over 70 percent of all LDC manufactured exports.[29]

By the end of the 1970s, a second stage in this new international division of labor began to evolve as the NICs sought to break into higher stages of production. With World Bank and IMF support, the labor-intensive stages of certain industrial sectors began to be shifted to many of the next group of twenty to thirty would-be NICs. The shift was also related to other factors, including rising wages in South Korea and Singapore, growing environmental restrictions in Japan, and the opening of the People's Republic of China to assembly-line production.

Whereas LDC apparel, electronics, and other light-manufacturing products were seldom marketed in the industrial economies in the mid-1960s, by a decade later thousands of factories in the developing world were producing precisely for that purpose.[30] The Philippines proved a case in point. From next to nothing in the early 1970s, apparel and electronics swelled to more than half of Philippine manufactured exports in 1979.[31] That same year, overall LDC (excluding OPEC) manufactured exports reached a pinnacle of sorts by surpassing in value traditional LDC exports of raw materials.[32]

Aiding this fragmentation and globalization of certain production processes were advances in the efficiency of transportation. Although these advances were admittedly on a less grand scale than the transport innovations of the late 1800s (which saw steamships bring a new dimension to international trade), transport became cheaper, easier, and faster over the decade of the 1970s.[33]

For LDCs, these TNC-financed technological innovations had a devastating impact on the very nature of industrial policy formulation. In the 1960s and early 1970s, before global transformation of certain production processes was technically feasible and economically viable, LDCs that aspired to industrialization were compelled to set up entire industrial sectors (such as shipbuilding, textiles, steel) where most or all value was added in the LDC.[34] Whether financed internally or by TNCs, industrialization in the NICs was integrated and extensive.

But in the wake of technological innovations, the second rung of LDCs, the would-be NICs, was never offered a similar package. The new export-oriented light manufacturing instead required resources to create free trade zones, industrial estates, and other institutional arrangements whereby TNCs could locate factories for minor operations in a global production process.[35] For the IMF and the World Bank steering LDCs toward export-oriented light-manufacturing industrialization in the mid-1970s, the task was much easier than it would have been a decade earlier. The qualitative difference between NIC industrialization and the equivalent process in the would-be NICs meant that genuine industrialization in the latter was in no way assured.

New Bank and Fund Roles

The changed international political, economic, and technological configuration of the 1970s had profound direct and indirect effects on the Bank and the Fund, three aspects of which are relevant to their interactions with LDC policymakers:

- The United States' shift in priorities from government-to-government bilateral aid to multilateral aid
- The Bank's and the Fund's assistance in stimulating LDC policy changes within a new international division of labor
- Initiatives launched by both the Bank and the Fund that propelled the two institutions to new heights of collaboration.

For decades, U.S. foreign military and economic policy was the predominant external influence in many LDCs' policy frameworks, and the former U.S. colony of the Philippines was foremost among those so influenced. The shift from bilateral to multilateral aid had begun in the 1960s, but it was Vietnam and the eclipse of the United States' global economic hegemony in the 1970s that marked the erosion of direct U.S. influence on LDC policy-making.

A U.S. foreign policy that demanded a more indirect American role was first officially verbalized in 1969 as the "Nixon Doctrine," a call for decreased U.S. military presence abroad, to be compensated for by increased economic aid.[36] By the end of the Vietnam War in 1975, there was an even stronger desire to back off from blatant displays of strength in the developing world and to channel economic and political pressures onto LDCs through subtler conduits.

One significant result was a shift in U.S. economic development funding. In the 1970s, aid was increasingly funneled to LDCs through multilateral, rather than bilateral, institutions. As a 1979 U.S. Congressional Research Service study noted, the United States wielded "substantial informal influence within the multilateral development banks." [37] Therefore, as the U.S. Treasury Department emphasized in its annual appeals to Congress for funding for these institutions in the late 1970s, the World Bank and the other international financial institutions provided the United States with "an unusually effective means" to "carry out programs that will effectively implement our wide-ranging interests." [38]

With the Carter presidency, strong voices emerged in favor of cutting off aid to repressive regimes, a position supported by an estimated 87 percent of the American public in 1975, the year before Carter's election. [39] Although human rights issues came to the World Bank symbolically (Congress required the U.S. executive director of the Bank either to vote against or to abstain on loans to human rights "violators"), the Bank did not get as bogged down in the debate as did the U.S. Congress. [40] Rather, it took a pragmatic approach. In 1976, after the World Bank had constantly denied lending to Allende's socialist Chile during the period from 1970 to 1973, [41] World Bank President Robert McNamara defended a controversial loan to Pinochet's authoritarian Chile in terms that built on the Bank's and the IMF's historic camouflage of political actions: "This institution [the Bank] tries to assist countries to advance economically, with benefits for its people . . . there is no room for political considerations in that type of situation." [42] In planning its five-year lending program for certain repressive regimes, the Bank took into account that pressure from congressional liberals would likely lead to symbolic U.S. bilateral aid cuts that would have to be compensated for by increased multilateral aid. [43] By the late 1970s, the top ten recipients of Bank loans included several major human rights violators: Brazil, Turkey, Indonesia, South Korea, Thailand, and the Philippines. [44]

Just as the decline of the U.S. bilateral presence enhanced Bank and Fund roles, so too did the growing Third World voice in these institutions. World Bank and IMF responses to the South's demands began in the IMF. There, the Committee of Twenty filtered the new international economic order demands into less threatening requests for more lending within the confines of the existing system. [45] In 1974, acting on the final recommendation of the Committee of Twenty, the IMF created its "extended fund facility," permitting countries to borrow up to 140 percent of their quotas over three years, with a ten-year repayment period. [46]

Crucial to the new facility were the onerous conditions that accompanied it, bringing three years of strict IMF supervision over a recipient

LDC's economic restructuring. In keeping with the IMF's usual formula, funds were disbursed in "tranches" over the three-year period, each "slice" dependent on adherence to the agreed-upon policy program. These were "high-conditionality facilities," noted monetary specialist John Williamson, and, as such, they were unpopular.[47] As U.N. economist Sidney Dell explained further, "In the first few years after the introduction of the facility, there were relatively few EFF [extended fund facility] drawings because of the difficulties in reaching agreement on the programs to be implemented by the governments concerned."[48] By 1979, almost half a decade after the extended fund facility came into existence, only 548 million special drawing rights (SDRs) had been borrowed from its coffers; nearly half of that total went to the Philippines alone.[49]

The early years of the extended fund facility represent an important instance of the Fund's acknowledging certain demands from the South and at the same time enhancing the organization's role in LDC policy formulation. By the early 1980s, most LDC representatives at the IMF embraced a more transnationalist worldview and thus tolerated "high conditionality." Hence, when Saudi Arabia's quota to the IMF doubled as a result of its May 1981 loan to the Fund, giving it a permanent seat on the IMF's Executive Board, the Big Five overseers of the financial system welcomed the strengthening of the voice of the South. Arab financiers and IMF delegates have proven as conservative as their Western counterparts. After more than a decade of investing in dollar-denominated assets, they came to share the United States' belief in the dollar's sanctity and to scorn demands from certain LDC representatives for a substitute international currency. Furthermore, Saudi Arabia's $9.5 billion loan to the Fund has made it a major creditor to the organization, which helped Saudi Arabia's IMF spokesperson to appreciate the Big Five's insistence that strong conditionality continue to be imposed on borrower nations.[50]

For domestic political consumption, many LDC representatives in the Fund, however, invariably downplayed their transnationalist interests in public forums, substituting instead sweeping Third World rhetoric. Marcos's finance minister, Cesar Virata, for example, during his stint as chairman of the Group of 24,[51] articulated the new international economic order demands in a way that suggested he was speaking for the South's vast and highly differentiated constituency. The stock phrases blurred class distinctions within LDCs and allowed such an authoritarian ruler as

Ferdinand Marcos to stand unabashedly as one of the South's spokespersons at the 1981 North-South meeting in Cancún, Mexico. But the policies LDC Fund representatives pushed, such as the extended fund facility, clearly favored the transnationalist elite and enhanced the Fund's ability to coordinate with that faction in formulating new LDC policies.

In many LDCs, however, the strengthened IMF role was not received enthusiastically by economic nationalist factions. In this sense, certain LDC states' reluctance to approach the Fund—even after the creation of a longer-term facility—came as no great surprise. It had evolved from a growing (and well-grounded) awareness that an application to the Fund potentially spelled "IMF riots" and government upheavals. Even LDC elites whose orientation tended to be more transnationalist than nationalist (Marcos and certain of his ministers among them) at times delivered inflammatory anti-IMF speeches to appease the politically powerful nationalist elements back home.

The World Bank, in a far more subtle move, fared better. As LDC awareness of the IMF grew, so did the size and stature of the World Bank. Its loan volume increased tenfold during Robert McNamara's thirteen-year presidency, from 1968 to 1981.[52] Aside from scattered demands for new economic institutions (demands that have largely been ignored), what most representatives of the South asked of the Bank was to do more of precisely what it was already doing. Yet beneath the Bank's superficial semblance of at least minimal compliance with LDC demands, a significant change was taking place: while the IMF was bearing the brunt of the South's criticisms, the World Bank was subsuming the IMF's role in a number of LDCs by extending its function as policy adviser on economywide matters.

Part of the Bank's enhanced presence resulted from its extremely skillful creation of a "basic human needs" image. Much of this was the work of one person: Robert McNamara, the man who had directed the systemic bombing of Vietnam in the mid-1960s. President Johnson's secretary of defense, McNamara had finally turned against Johnson's management of the war in a 1967 memo bluntly asserting that bombing did not and could not work—a memo in which the roots of McNamara's later "basic needs" strategy of development assistance can be found.[53]

McNamara belatedly learned that a regime that fails to meet even the most basic needs of its poorer majority will never be stable. This instability had been a chronic problem for the regimes the United States created in South Vietnam. Growth-oriented strategies, McNamara concluded, needed to be accompanied by loans targeted at the poor. Hence, over McNamara's term as Bank president, lending for agriculture and rural development jumped from 18 to 31 percent of total loans; most loans contained a "small-farmer element or component."[54]

At the core of the antipoverty rhetoric of basic needs lay the concept of "defensive modernization." Analyst Robert Ayres put it succinctly:

> Was there an underlying political rationale for the World Bank's poverty-oriented work under McNamara? This question was put to many World Bankers at all levels of the institution. Their collated responses suggested that there was. The underlying political rationale for the Bank's poverty-oriented development projects seemed to be political stability through defensive modernization. Political stability was seen primarily as an outcome of giving people a stake, however minimal, in the system.[55]

Political stability could be created in rural areas by engendering a smallholder class closely linked with the national economy—in theory, at least. Export processing zones, strategically placed, would provide enough employment to diffuse discontent. Urban slum upgrading was similarly planned "to palliate urban dissatisfaction."[56] Although some officials within the Bank may have believed in less opportunistic versions of basic needs, by the time these antipoverty project proposals worked their way up the Bank hierarchy, "basic needs" became little more than a trickle-down theory of growth, embellished in new development rhetoric.[57] Growth was the key to defensive modernization, and each project's goals were clearly defined in terms of output, income, and productivity. Rhetoric to the side, World Bank money overwhelmingly funded its traditional, pre–basic needs sorts of projects.[58]

Despite the reality of the Bank's version of "basic needs," transnationalist segments of LDC states could use the rhetoric to rally important segments of their constituencies behind giving a greater role to the Bank. Part of this new role was in the realm of what were termed "structural adjustment loans." Billed as a modern version of the World Bank's program loans, structural adjustment loans were a totally new species of loans, quite unlike the freewheeling program lending bestowed on developed countries in earlier decades. Structural adjustment loans were to be geared to an entire sector of a developing economy—industry, finance, agriculture, energy, or some combination thereof. Each structural adjustment loan was to serve as a catalyst for substantial restructuring according to World Bank specifications. The World Bank would designate the policy adjustments to be pushed through, in much the same manner as the IMF did traditionally. Once these policy changes were initiated, the Bank would provide a multimillion-dollar loan, an incentive to help the recipient country over the initial economic dislocations inherent in the painful restructuring process.

However, the Bank's public posture regarding its structural adjustment lending carefully fostered an entirely different impression of what the new loans entailed. They were officially announced at the 1979 annual meeting of the governors of the World Bank and the IMF. It was a meeting made memorable because the United Nations' Group of 77, in an attempt to bolster its impact as LDC pressure group on the IMF, had gathered in its own ministerial meeting in Belgrade immediately beforehand.[59] Days later, when McNamara formally presented the Bank's newest facility to the full house of governors, the idea was sheathed in language suggesting a concession to LDC demands.[60]

In the narrow sense that the loans were grouped under the rubric of program lending, structural adjustment lending could be interpreted as a response to oft-repeated developing-country calls for "substantial expansion of programme lending by existing institutions."[61] *South* magazine, for example, usually highly critical of the Bank and the Fund, viewed the move to structural adjustment loans as the World Bank buckling under the weight of the LDCs:

> Southern borrowers . . . have been concerned that for most of its history [the Bank] has limited its loans to "project" lending. . . . Lately, the World Bank has acknowledged this problem and has arranged some "programme" loans.[62]

As the Philippine case study reveals, this enhanced lending was a victory for transnationalist segments of LDC elites. Overall, the $800 million of structural adjustment lending in 1980 (and the Bank's five-year goal of channeling one-fifth of all its lending into such loans) led an ambitious move within international financial institutions for the Bank to more effectively augment the Fund in certain countries and to substitute for it in others.[63] The IMF, in its extended-fund-facility experiment, had tread on what was seen as conventional World Bank territory: "supervision of a program of structural change involved Fund intrusion into questions of invest-

ment priorities, microeconomic efficiency, and the structure of incentives."[64] Half a decade later, with structural adjustment loans, the Bank was
stepping onto traditional IMF domain. To quote Williamson:

> In any particular case, the Bank, in association with the borrowing country,
> picks out a number of key areas where it judges policy to be particularly defi-
> cient or misguided and negotiates a set of policy reforms to correct those weak-
> nesses. In so doing, it finds itself involved in areas that have traditionally been
> the Fund's prerogative because, for example, import liberalization, tariff reform,
> and the provision of export incentives cannot be discussed sensibly without also
> covering exchange rate policy.
>   Thus, the former distinctions between the roles of the Fund and the Bank—
> macro versus micro, demand versus supply, adjustment versus development, fi-
> nancial versus real, program versus project loans, short term versus long term—
> have been severely eroded.[65]

But it was not simply that, as Williamson contended, the "division of
labor became blurred after 1974."[66] That blurring had a historical foundation in the institutions' shared birth and in the mutual interests they represented. Even more to the point, the erosion of more distinct functions was
the logical extension of the Bank's and Fund's history of collaboration. As
the institutions acknowledged confidentially in 1980 when they revised
their memoranda on collaboration, "intensifying and ameliorating" such
collaboration was urgent, "because the world is changing and circumstances demand this increase in activity."[67]

With these newfound powers and instruments, the Bank actively promoted LDC development paths that meshed with the emerging international division of labor.[68] Much of this effort focused on helping steer
the would-be NICs into export-oriented industrialization of light manufacturing (or, as the Bank and the Fund dubbed them, "nontraditional exports"). Bank economist Bela Balassa called it the "stages approach" to
comparative advantage.[69] His work provided the appropriate intellectual
rationale behind Bank policy influence in the would-be NICs:

> At the same time, in accordance with the "stages" approach to comparative ad-
> vantage, changes would occur in the product composition of the manufactured
> exports of the developing countries as they proceeded to higher stages of indus-
> trial development. . . .
>   It follows that it is in the interest of the newly-industrializing developing
> countries to upgrade and to diversify their exports in line with their changing
> comparative advantage. This is also in the interest of countries at lower stages

of industrial development, since they can replace exports of unskilled-labor-intensive commodities from the newly-industrializing countries to industrial country markets.[70]

The conclusion for Bank (and Fund) work in countries like the Philippines was clear, as Balassa explained elsewhere: "Developing countries are therefore well advised to learn from the experience of Taiwan and Korea in applying export-oriented policies."[71]

Thus, McNamara delivered a call to the 1979 United Nations Conference on Trade and Development (UNCTAD) for the "international community" to assist "developing countries that undertake the needed structural adjustments for export promotion in line with their long-term comparative advantage." In particular, he referred to those LDCs that "seek to upgrade their export structure to take advantage of the export markets being vacated by more advanced developing countries." There was more: putting export-oriented industrialization in the context of an anti-poverty strategy based on growth and development, McNamara intimated that the Bank was preparing to move to the forefront of this new "program of action."[72]

In this context, structural adjustment loans were the missing ingredient. "Project loans," geared to individual projects such as hydroelectric dams or highways, did not confer on the Bank nearly enough leverage for the necessary restructuring. Structural adjustment lending sought to hasten the realization of the new international division of labor. For a country like Senegal, that meant an agricultural-sector loan promoting groundnuts export. In the Philippines, as in Guyana, Kenya, and Turkey, the Bank noted with satisfaction in its 1981 annual report, structural adjustment lending brought "improvements in institutional support to nontraditional exporters."[73]

Conditions for the loans, according to Williamson's summary of the Bank's late 1970s and early 1980s experiences, "typically involve four elements: the rationalization of prices or 'restructuring of incentives,' covering price policies, tariff reform, taxation, subsidies, and interest rates; the revision of public investment priorities; budgetary reform; and institution building."[74] The World Bank would be careful to portray these policy initiatives as LDCs' own inducements to TNC-led light-manufacturing export industrialization. Yet, in country after country, the Bank was the catalyst.

While the Bank was at the forefront in light-manufacturing export strategies, the policies it was backing were recreating a central role for the IMF, precisely during the high point of its unpopularity in certain countries. For export-oriented industrialization had a corollary: purchase of costly energy-intensive infrastructure and capital goods contributed substantially to soaring LDC debts. And lenders increasingly turned to the IMF to discipline the borrowers.

As the debt piled up, its composition changed. In the early 1970s, commercial banks provided about one-fourth of LDCs' foreign financing requirements. Over the decade, that share more than doubled, to reach almost 60 percent in 1980,[75] and by 1986 private banks held as much as 80 to 90 percent of the debt in many Latin American countries.

Just as debt was concentrated in two to three dozen banks on the creditor side, it was equally concentrated on the debtor side. Of the trillion-dollar debt accumulated by 1986, one-fifth was held by the top two debtors, another fifth by the next five. Indeed, the debt became concentrated in precisely those LDCs pushing export-oriented industrialization. In the mid-to-late 1970s, nearly half of all commercial loans to LDCs, in any single year, converged on five countries—Brazil, Mexico, Argentina, South Korea, and the Philippines[76]—a trend that has continued to the present.

As early as the mid-1970s, the need to maintain an IMF "certificate of good standing" (as Arthur Burns, chairman of the Board of Governors of the U.S. Federal Reserve System, dubbed it in 1977),[77] was a fact of life for LDCs caught in the debt web. As the 1977 report of the U.S. President's Council of Economic Advisers explained:

> Banks now seem to favor lending to countries operating under IMF suggested surveillance. Because banks cannot attach macro-economic conditions to their loans, or in any event monitor them, they apparently feel more comfortable with debtors operating under IMF conditionality.[78]

This explanation is important in understanding the lines of collaboration between the sets of international actors depicted in Figure 1. Whereas TNCs and TNBs will occasionally intervene in LDC policy-making through their chambers of commerce, business councils, or personal contacts,[79] they generally remain on the sidelines of policy formulation and, instead, channel their influence through multilateral (or bilateral) agencies.

Since the 1970s, TNBs have looked to the IMF for this purpose. As dozens of countries have faced balance-of-payments problems in the years since 1982, the role of the IMF rose dramatically. In addition, World Bank structural adjustment loans, noted the World Bank's 1980 annual report, were becoming the certificate of good standing of the not-too-distant future.[80]

The State Role

TNBs and TNCs provided the finance, technology, and management expertise to underpin the Bank, the Fund, and LDC governments in the shifts toward a new international division of labor, but core states also played an important role. U.S. tariff laws offered increased incentives for TNCs to fragment the production process by contracting the most labor-intensive phases to lower-wage LDCs, an operation called "subcontracting" or "outward processing."[81] Such government inducements shifted $250 million of apparel manufacturing annually from the United States to countries such as Costa Rica, Honduras, and Mexico during the late 1970s. Subcontracting was also the phenomenon behind the growing stream of Western European textiles destined for further processing in plants in the Mediterranean states. "Subcontracts" may be signed with the TNC subsidiaries, joint ventures, or wholly owned LDC firms (the specifics have varied from country to country, industry to industry). In almost all cases, TNCs control the marketing and final processing and direct the transplanting of industrial processes.[82]

This series of moves by actors on the international side—state, private, and multilateral—would have been virtually meaningless without close collaboration with LDC states, primarily through ministries headed by sympathetic factions. Free trade zones (FTZs) are the most widespread manifestation of the broad institutional incentives offered by LDCs. In these specially delineated areas, imported goods are stored in warehouses, then processed or assembled, then exported duty-free. Initially established in Ireland with the 1958 Shannon International Free Trade Port, free trade zones spread rapidly, with Asian versions first set up in Taiwan and India in 1965. By the end of the 1970s, the free trade zone had become an extensive LDC phenomenon: seventy-nine zones operated in twenty-five countries throughout Asia, Latin America, and Africa. By the early 1980s, at least that number were under construction or stood as priority items in LDC development plans.[83]

Enclaves within host countries, resting beyond national law, FTZs flourished, and during the 1970s they spawned export processing zones (EPZs). Set up to service the new international division of labor, EPZs extended beyond the FTZs' customs-free privileges by providing subsidized infrastructure and plant buildings explicitly geared for transforming imported raw materials and intermediate goods into manufactured exports.

Relatively cheap labor remained the main attraction. Thus, designated territories were transformed into largely foreign-leased (or, at times, foreign-owned) enclaves of a country's industrial economy, catering specifically to the processing of apparel, electronics components, footwear, and the like, entirely for re-export.[84]

Exactly why LDCs themselves were setting up inducements that so precisely complemented the shifts in the international division of labor is a complicated but important question. The impact of the changing global political and economic setting on the World Bank and IMF roles provides the beginnings of an answer. The Philippine case study supplies a more detailed response.

4

Negotiating Adjustment: The Industrial Sector

Over the decades, it has become established procedure for the IMF and the World Bank each to deal principally with one of two select and nearly mutually exclusive groups of LDC ministries (Figure 2).[1] Whereas IMF loans, including the extended fund facility, are negotiated and implemented primarily through central banks, the World Bank often spreads responsibilities across a broad range of ministries. In addition to its primary contact with planning agencies, the Bank can also work through finance, trade, industry, agriculture, and other ministries responsible for sectors receiving specific loans. In these interactions, Bank and Fund interests usually become inter-reinforcing with those of the transnationalist factions of the various ministries with which they deal. Ministries that successfully negotiate major loans with multilateral institutions often gain substantial prestige, enhancing the stature of the transnationalist faction overall.

When the World Bank entered the economic policy realm on a major scale with the late 1970s advent of structural adjustment loans, the combined power and flexibility of the Bank and the Fund were heightened. If

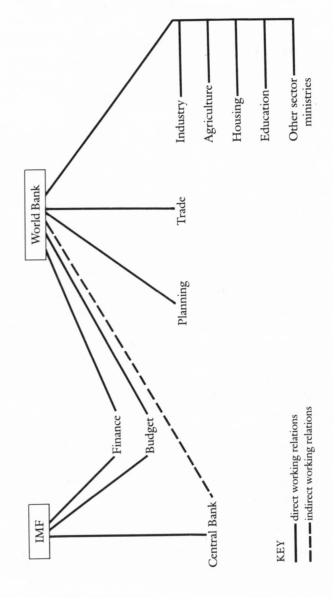

Figure 2. Contacts with LDC Ministries

IMF

World Bank

Finance

Budget

Central Bank

Planning

Trade

Industry

Agriculture

Housing

Education

Other sector
ministries

KEY —— direct working relations
      --- indirect working relations

the IMF faced a hostile central bank dominated by economic nationalist interests, it could turn economy-wide policy work over to the Bank. And if the World Bank faced an unfriendly planning ministry, it could turn either to the Fund or to powerful transnationalist technocrats in other ministries involved with the loan.

A Faltering Facility

Through yearly recourse to the IMF during the 1970s, by mid-1980 the Philippines had become the LDC most indebted to the Fund. Worldwide, its $1.6 billion IMF debt that year was second only to the United Kingdom's.[2] A substantial portion of this Philippine debt was contracted during its three-year extended-fund-facility (EFF) arrangement with the IMF, which began in April 1976.[3] The IMF deployment of the EFF in certain other countries has proven quite successful in promoting far-reaching policy reorientation. In the Philippines, despite substantial efforts, the EFF largely failed in the policy arena.

This evaluation is not accepted by all parties involved. High-level officials in both the IMF and the Philippine Central Bank, whose careers are linked to the success of such major undertakings, attempted to label the 1976 EFF a success. For Central Bank Governor Gregorio Licaros, the EFF "was a success because we straitjacketed the economy according to IMF standards, which helped us weather the successive oil price increases."[4]

A more accurate picture can be drawn by comparing Philippine economic performance to original EFF targets. Among the precise conditions the IMF set for the Philippines in exchange for the SDR 217 million (about $250 million) loan were more than half a dozen quantitative targets to be met over the 1976–1978 period.[5] Philippine average annual GNP growth was to reach a minimum rate of 7 percent, and its annual inflation rate a maximum of 7 percent. The balance of payments was to reach equilibrium. Government tax efforts, measured by the ratio of tax revenues to GNP, were to increase over the course of the program from their 13.6 percent level in 1975 to 16 percent. The interest rate and controlled prices were to be allowed to rise to free-market rates. Ceilings were set on domestic and foreign borrowing; a floor marked the minimum foreign-currency reserves the banking system was to hold. In addition, the Philippine government was to allow the peso to float gradually downward in value over the three years.[6]

An examination of the Philippine economy in 1979, at the end of the three-year exercise, reveals that the IMF targets were not met. Inflation was higher than projected, growth rates substantially lower, and the balance of payments still in deficit, well short of the targeted equilibrium. Tax receipts (at only 13.9 percent of GNP in 1978) were far shy of their target, and import restrictions had not been lifted to any noticeable degree. After the three years of IMF guidance, the government's commitment to phasing out protective tariffs, "vigorously" using the exchange rate (i.e., devaluing the peso),[7] and increasing interest rates remained little more than promises on paper. None of the original ceilings on domestic and foreign borrowing or the floor on reserves was met. All told, the failure was serious, not just the few "marginal quantitative elements" that an IMF staff person intimately involved with the Fund's Philippine work argued were not met.[8]

When pressed about these discrepancies, certain government and IMF representatives persisted in labeling the extended fund facility a "successful exercise."[9] Their stubbornness derived not only from self-interest but also from their criteria for success. The IMF, through its constant dialogue with Central Bank officials, had a sense that the country was moving in the desired direction, unmet targets aside. Above all else, their perception of the extended fund facility's success rested on the government's establishment of a "nontraditional" manufactured-exports drive (which increased in value by 30 percent per annum in real terms, from a very small base in 1972 to 1979).[10]

Success for them was also measured in the Central Bank's new institutional initiatives, which responded to the program's demands for more rigorous economic and financial monitoring. Foremost among these was the IMF–Central Bank Inter-Agency Committee for the EFF (later the Committee for Financial and Economic Programming), which continued to meet into the 1980s to monitor the Philippines' economic performance in relation to targets set.[11]

But as the unmet targets piled up, so mounted the IMF's frustrations: the underlying Philippine-IMF relationship was not a smooth one. Longtime government officials such as Central Bank Deputy Governor Escolastica Bince readily avowed that, compared with the situation in the 1960s and early 1970s, IMF missions had taken on a "less dictatorial and patronizing" style.[12] Governor Licaros confessed that he found "some IMF representatives . . . helpful as advisers."[13] Yet such praise did not camouflage a feeling of impropriety, especially among nationalists in government offices, that had begun when IMF influence was first felt in the Macapagal years: why should a mere IMF staff member be telling a high government official what to do? A more pervasive undercurrent of distrust confronted the IMF representative who had been posted at the Central Bank since 1970 when he entered nearby offices in search of statistics and reports to relay back to Washington. Undoubtedly, that IMF representative, through his access (however begrudgingly granted) to all the Central Bank's files and desks, had compiled a more comprehensive statistical snapshot of the Philippines than most top government officials, stymied by interagency secrecy, ever could. Yet, staff members of both the Ministry of Finance and the Central Bank admitted hiding from him "because he asks too many questions."[14]

The principal problem facing the Fund in implementing the EFF was that most senior officials in its domestic counterpart, the Philippine Central Bank, did not share its transnationalist perspective. Despite successful IMF efforts to instill that perspective in certain lower- and medium-level officers at the Central Bank, they made little headway at the top.

Neither Western-educated, nor young, nor perfectly fluent in English, Central Bank Governor Gregorio Licaros was a breed apart from his technocratic colleagues. "I am a practical man, not a technocrat," Licaros admitted somewhat proudly.[15] Yet for more than a decade, beginning in 1970, he had occupied a post where both the World Bank and the IMF needed a close ally. In the earlier years of the 1970s, Licaros's philosophy on growth and development had meshed well enough with the Bank's and the Fund's: "I am expansionary in my ideas. The more money they [the Bank and Fund] bring in here, the better."[16] That outlook was in large part responsible for the massive escalation of Philippine external debt, from $1.3 billion in 1969 to $17.4 billion by the end of 1980.[17] But when it came to strict EFF policy conditions that threatened Licaros's private domestic allies, the governor refused to make changes.

IMF effectiveness was in this instance further stymied by IMF callousness toward rising tensions within the Philippine national entrepreneur community, which made EFF conditions extremely sensitive politically, as well as toward accumulated Philippine suspicion about the decades-long

IMF history of strong policy activity, often surrounded by what was perceived as undue secrecy.

By the mid-1970s, it was widely (albeit surreptitiously) acknowledged within the Central Bank, as well as without, that the IMF was an "interfering agency,"[18] "more vocal and controversial than the World Bank,"[19] with a tendency to use its economic "models like Bibles."[20] "We've all read *The Debt Trap*," explained one former deputy governor.[21] And though all certainly did not share the analysis of its author, Cheryl Payer, even Central Bank technical adviser and special assistant to the governor, Edgardo Zialcita (normally extremely reticent on the subject) acknowledged agreement on certain points:

> The problem with the IMF is its secrecy in its methodology. Even in technical discussions [with us], the IMF just shares its final figures, the targets. . . . [It] doesn't say how it arrived at them. And sometimes, even if we [at the Central Bank] know what model [or formula the IMF is using], we get a different answer . . . a different projection. . . . But there's no discussion on this level. . . . The IMF does not want to be shown up; they want to be smarter [than the Philippine negotiators].[22]

In this atmosphere of general resentment and suspicion, the Central Bank and the IMF often played cat-and-mouse games. The issue of restrictive import licenses was a case in point. After years of harping on the need to liberalize Philippine import restrictions, the IMF included the policy change as part of the EFF program. The relevant Central Bank office complied by splitting the existing restricted categories into subdivisions and then liberalizing only a handful of these new less-inclusive groupings. For every item liberalized, it seemed another ten appeared in the restricted category.[23]

In fact, throughout the EFF period the protective sheltering of domestic industries continued, even as the new light-manufacturing exports were promoted through export incentives. The IMF fully realized that this dualism was condoned by Marcos himself for political reasons: abandoning protection meant losing the support of national entrepreneurs. Although generally viewing those domestic businessmen as expendable, the Fund was not prepared to risk shattering its history of general success in the Philippines by a major confrontation with Marcos. Nor was it able to reach him through the nationalist Central Bank, which also condoned the dual industrial policy.[24] As the EFF drew to an end, an IMF staff member on the Philippine mission admitted to then IMF Alternate Executive Director Ernest Leung that they would rather not go through a similar exercise in the Philippines again.[25] Maybe a decade earlier the IMF could have carried its program off with aplomb, but in the late 1970s its goals could not be achieved without drawing daggers. Therefore the IMF made way for the World Bank and its structural adjustment loan for the industrial sector.

An Escalating World Bank Presence

Signed in September 1980, the Philippine industrial structural adjustment loan (SAL) must be viewed in the context of almost a full decade of World Bank and IMF initiatives in the Philippines. It was Ferdinand Marcos's declaration of martial law on September 22, 1972, that moved the archipelago centerstage as far as the World Bank and the IMF were concerned. Marcos's declaration not only assured him the presidency for more than the maximum two terms, but it also brought an end to the Philippines' two decades of competitive two-party politics, a system that had seen frequent changes of power among the elites in terms of both party and region.

Privately, Bank and Fund officials viewed the authoritarian regime from a perspective that glorified efficiency above all else. The martial-law state, in Bank terms, became a "public sector assuming a much more important and dynamic role," and authoritarian decrees, promulgated by a stroke of Marcos's pen, were referred to as "legislation."[26] In this, the technocrats' world, democracy of the pre-1972 Philippine vintage—especially the heightened factional struggles of the late 1960s—was to be frowned on for the "political and economic constraints on economic and development management" it had engendered.[27] In its place, the "New Society" (Marcos's favored term for his martial-law regime) held out the promise of "considerable progress."[28]

By 1976, the Philippines had climbed into the ranks of the World Bank's top ten loan recipients, with a promise of another five years of Bank largesse at a level "higher than average for countries of similar size and income."[29] As the Bank's Philippine division chief, Michael Gould, acknowledged confidentially that year, the archipelago stood with distinction as a Bank "country of concentration."[30] Or, as Philippine government officials phrased it somewhat proudly, martial law had transformed their country into a Bank and Fund "guinea pig," a "favorite testing ground,"[31] a "ripe field" in which to push development, "free from the endless legislative debates" of a democracy.[32]

A presidential decree, issued just three days after the declaration of martial law, merged the descendant of the transnationalist planning agency built by the Bank in 1962 with a less powerful nationalist government economic agency to form the National Economic and Development Authority (NEDA). NEDA's designation as the highest economic planning and policy authority suggested that the formalized long-term planning historically nurtured by the Bank would have an even more important place in the mid-1970s Philippines.

When the World Bank's Russell Cheetham was posted in-country for a year to draw up a "basic economic report," he worked out of NEDA.[33] In keeping with the Bank's practice, the all-encompassing economic report was strategically timed to serve as a key input to the Philippines' 1978–1982 five-year plan, which emerged from that same government office in 1977, one year after Cheetham's report. Cheetham's work was only one of several references used by NEDA, but the resulting five-year plan, as the Bank has noted ad infinitum in subsequent documents, was "broadly consistent" with the report in almost every respect.[34] Undoubtedly this consistency was enhanced when the draft plan was sent to the World Bank for comments.[35]

The five-year plan was drawn up in the context of a ten-year plan (1978–1987) as well as a long-term plan to the year 2000, and these also became "broadly consistent" with the Bank's basic economic report. The World Bank was left on fairly safe ground when it asserted in its own 1976 confidential five-year lending plan for the Philippines that the government had accepted the basic economic report's "broad framework for future development . . . as a basis for its future economic plans."[36]

This statement must be interpreted with care. In the Philippines, as in many LDCs, five-year plans—let alone ten-year or twenty-five-year plans—do not usually mean much. But the Philippines' 1978–1982 plan did provide an indication that, overall, the country's economic advisers were aiming at what the World Bank consultant to NEDA wanted: "take off" based on foreign loans and investments that would flow into labor-intensive export-oriented industries once domestic impediments to a free market were removed.[37]

By the end of the decade, the stage was set for the Bank to move from reports and plans into explicit policy formulation and implementation. By then, NEDA, the planning ministry, headed by officials sharing the Bank's transnationalist perspective, was joined by the no less technocratically oriented ministries of Finance and Industry. It was only a matter of waiting for the right moment to launch the SAL.

On August 12, 1980, less than a year and a half after the Philippine government's three-year experiment with its first and only extended fund facility had officially terminated, Marcos's finance minister, Cesar Virata, sent a letter to World Bank President McNamara. There was nothing unusual in such correspondence per se. Minister Virata and Governor Licaros had drafted many such letters to the Fund's managing director as part of the established regimen initiating new standby arrangements. Indeed, all over the world, LDC finance ministers and central bank governors had penned and would continue to pen analogous dispatches to the Fund. But this one was to be delivered across the street—to the Bank.

On the surface, Virata's note was a formal but friendly communication to share with the Bank's management the Philippine government's new directions for the industrial and financial sectors. Assuming these policies met with McNamara's approval, the letter requested a SAL to help defer financial costs. Lest the policies be misunderstood, they appeared in triplicate: first, outlined generally in Virata's letter; next, presented in the context of a broader statement on Philippine industrial policy for the 1980s (a twenty-page, single-spaced attachment); and, in a last attachment, meticulously chronicled in terms of specific legislation, past, present and future. The government's policy-reform commitments emerged distinctly in five areas: (1) lowering protective tariffs; (2) liberalizing import restrictions; (3) taking action to promote and facilitate exports and investment in export-oriented industries; (4) following a "flexible exchange-rate policy . . . to reflect basic market forces"; and (5) restructuring specific industrial sectors to integrate them with the overall export effort.[38]

Here was the Philippine state announcing its intention of implementing a policy package combining many initiatives similar to those that went unheeded when affixed as conditions to the IMF's extended fund facility. But this time, what was involved was much more than simply sharing good intentions. Many of the new reforms were already underway, and a precise implementation timetable to cover the rest was attached.

Virata's letter to the World Bank was part of a larger, carefully preconceived plan. Although both parties went to great lengths to camouflage it, those policy changes emanated from the Bank itself and, by the time of Virata's letter, stood as de facto World Bank directives. Buried in a government file, a working draft of Virata's second attachment provides a clue. Written in late 1979, its original title was less benign than the *Industrial Development Program* chronicle that landed on McNamara's desk: *Measures/ Steps Taken by the Government in Connection with the Industrial Policy Recommendations Contained in the World Bank's Industrial Sector Report.*[39]

The government's acceptance of suggestions it had vigorously rejected when they had been packaged by the IMF was neither as sudden nor as shocking as it may appear. Virata's letter followed years of intense "policy dialogue" between the Bank and top government officials, as well as vigorous sparring among those top government officials themselves. The framing of what eventually evolved into the industrial SAL dates back to 1976 and the EFF.

At the time of the mid-1970s drafting of the Philippines' EFF, there had been a commitment within the Bank to concentrate on agricultural lending in the Philippines. To a certain extent, the Bank agreed to leave broader policy parameters involving industry and finance to the Fund and its EFF.[40] But by no means did the Bank totally leave the formulation of industrial policy to the IMF. In broad terms, the Bank outlined a framework for industrialization in its basic economic report. More specifically, the Bank's confidential 1976 five-year lending plan for the Philippines (the 1976 *Country Program Paper*) reveals that even then the Bank had quite explicitly defined its list of necessary "major changes in the existing policy framework": removing import restrictions, restructuring and lowering tariffs, overhauling the investment incentive system. There was no mistaking the Bank's priorities: "rapid growth in labor intensive exports" stood as "the most important goal."[41]

But the Bank, like the Fund, realized that simply enunciating the desired industrialization strategy for the Philippines was only a first step. As the EFF's first year progressed and sticky "problem areas" emerged, the Bank began to look beyond its overall agricultural and rural development thrust. It launched "a series of sector and special studies," with topics to include export potential; effective protection; labor-intensive, regionally dispersed manufacturing; and, later, the financial sector.[42]

The World Bank effort was closely paralleled by the University of the

Philippines School of Economics' research project on protectionism and industrial-promotion policies (July 1977 to March 1979). Although the official word was that the Philippine government commissioned the study, the research was aided considerably by American economist John Power, who joined the University of the Philippines' team through the aid of a World Bank education loan. The resulting *Industrial Promotion Policies in the Philippines,* published in book form by NEDA in 1979, provided a mathematical analogue to what had been the Bank and the IMF argument all along: poor industrial performance was rooted in the highly protective trade regime and the capital-intensive bias of investment-promotion policies. With the book's publication, certain top government technocrats—including such staunch believers in these reforms as then Economic Planning and Policy Minister Gerardo Sicat (now at the World Bank)—were able to hold up the policy changes as suggestions emanating from the Philippines' own prestigious university, which in turn were simply accepted by the World Bank.[43]

Although the results of the University of the Philippines' exercise would prove useful in the ensuing negotiations, the World Bank by no means planned to wait for the final calculations. A midsummer 1977 Bank mission was posted in-country for two weeks to prepare the Bank's semiannual *Country Economic Memorandum* for the Philippine Consultative Group.[44] Launched by the World Bank in 1970, the Consultative Group brought together all the Philippines' major bilateral and multilateral aid donors to discuss and coordinate strategies and policies for that country, as well as to review past official-development-assistance initiatives with Philippine government representatives. Each annual gathering has a special focus which, according to a NEDA official who attended almost half of the first decade of meetings, was "usually requested by the U.S. government."[45] Subsequent foci would include poverty, energy, and population; in 1977, Bank mission chief Lawrence Hinkle and his crew of four Bank staff members were instructed to pay particular attention to industrial development.

Their report pinpointed impediments to a "freer trade regime" as the root of Philippine industrial-growth problems. But the report did more than just point fingers; within the main text and its special appendix on labor-intensive, export-oriented industries (garments, handicrafts, electronic components, wood products, and nontraditional agricultural and food products including bananas, seafood, and unroasted coffee) appeared policy suggestions that would return to the Philippine government in more detailed form in later negotiations. Paramount among them were cutting nominal tariff rates to an across-the-board average of 20 to 30 percent, removing all import restrictions, modernizing textile plants, and setting up trading houses.[46] Fueled by that report (and by the strong convictions of many participants), the December 1977 Consultative Group issued a call from Tokyo for "intensive efforts" to set Philippine industrial-sector reform in motion.[47]

By 1978, with the EFF in midstream and the stalemate between the Fund and the Philippine government fairly obvious, a World Bank reappraisal of its role in the Philippines led to an official (if confidentially stated) change in strategy following on the heels of the Consultative Group initiative: "Industrial and financial policy improvements should be the major objective of future Bank lending."[48] This would require a great turnabout. Previous Bank loans to the Philippine industrial sector totaled a mere $398 million, and the value of actual loans to agriculture and rural development for fiscal years 1976–1980 was three times that of industry. However, by FY1981–1986, the two sectors were programmed to assume approximately equal billing, each bringing in about one-third of the World Bank's Philippine program.[49]

In late 1978, with the Philippine extended fund facility almost completely drawn down, a World Bank industrial policy adviser in the Industrial Development and Finance Department, Barend de Vries, was dispatched to Manila to confer with the Ministry of Industry on a preappraisal mission of the industrial sector.[50] Three months later, in February 1979, he returned with eleven colleagues for a full-fledged industrial-sector-appraisal mission. Several high government officials and Bank staff members insisted that this mission had been requested by the Philippine government; others conceded that it grew out of "shared concerns" between the two parties. However, in light of the new twist given to the Bank's Philippine program a year earlier, it seems most likely that the Bank's Washington office played a fairly pivotal role.[51] The mission's invitation, for formality's sake, was happily extended by NEDA chairman Gerardo Sicat and his core of technocrats battling the Central Bank.

Whatever the circumstances of its birth, the mission's mandate was clear to both parties. As the minister of industry told a local newspaper, "The study team will determine what changes the country can adopt so it can better achieve broader and more rapid industrial growth, generate more employment . . . and promote exports."[52] Exactly what de Vries had in mind as he evaluated the industrial policies and incentives became unmistakable in a press conference at the end of the three-week mission. Because of "very competitive wages," he announced, preliminary findings had indicated that Philippine exports could replace those of Korea and Taiwan "due to the changing economic structure of these countries."[53] His words were splashed across Manila's tightly controlled media in stories that did not fail to add that the mission was relying heavily on the University of the Philippines' study.

More than a year later, in May 1980, the World Bank published in red-book form (that is, available to the public) what was ostensibly the product of the three-week mission: a three-volume set entitled *Philippines: Industrial Development Strategy and Policies.*[54] Unknown to the public, the mission's report had reached the "restricted distribution" stage by October of 1979, which meant that a "confidential" industrial report had been drafted and discussed earlier with the Philippine government.[55] Rather than offering new insights, the Bank used the mission to put down on paper the ideas concerning the Philippines' role as a light-manufactures exporter in a new international division of labor, ideas it had been developing over the previous three years. As the mission wrote, "The greatest Philippine comparative advantages lie in labor-intensive and resource-based products."[56] In less than six months, de Vries and his colleagues had integrated all recent Bank and Fund work into a coherent overall industrial-policy proposal that became the basis for negotiations over the SAL.

Those negotiations and the initial discussion of a possible SAL through which the policy changes would be implemented began in August of 1979, when a four-man Bank mission traveled to Manila. Again headed by de Vries but this time including 1977 mission chief Hinkle, the mission arrived with a definite goal: to attain "a comprehensive understanding . . . at the highest levels on the objectives that could be reached through a series of staged industrial policy reforms, the initial stage of which could be supported by a structural adjustment loan."[57]

In setting up the mission, the Bank vice-president for East Asia and the Pacific, Shahid Husain, had acted on his understanding that "structural adjustment loans do go to the heart of the political management of an economy." Husain had instructed the mission team that the Philippines was a prime candidate for the first industrial SAL.[58] Thus charged, the ten-day mission began policy dialogues with a wide range of top government officials on the need for "greater freedom" and more competitiveness in Philippine export operations. These officials included representatives from five ministries and an equal number of other high-level public institutions.[59] Among the relevant powers in the Philippines, only the Central Bank, the "fortress" that had constantly frustrated similar IMF endeavors, received an unmistakable and deliberate snubbing.[60] The Philippine Central Bank was too central an institution in this policy realm for its exclusion to have been simple oversight.

More of what a SAL might entail was unveiled to the government at this time. For individuals in certain ministries who did not press the point, the Bank mission tended to fall back on references to an initial $200 million loan (and a possible series of loans totaling $1 billion) for "program-type assistance."[61] This term was undoubtedly chosen to please the Philippine government, which had been denied in both its 1975 and 1976 unofficial requests for the Bank's old-style program lending.[62] It is understandable that the concept of structural adjustment lending was somewhat foreign to Bank clients, as McNamara's official announcement of the new loans was still a couple of months in the future.

These years of meticulous preparation for the SAL by the World Bank were in large part responsible for the speed with which the loan was subsequently disbursed. Preparation, however, was only one step in the operation; achieving a sufficient degree of harmony and consensus within the relevant Philippine ministries was the other.

SAL: The Consensus

The actual SAL would have two components. First, the loan would be a reimbursement scheme for Philippine imports and would finance about 5 percent of the country's total merchandise imports in 1980. When Philippine companies imported goods, they would pay the Philippine Central Bank the import price in pesos, and the Central Bank would pay for the items in the foreign currency required (usually dollars). The World Bank would then disburse part of the $200 million loan to the Central Bank for these foreign-currency payments.[63]

A second stage of the loan would involve placing the pesos paid by local businessmen for imports into a Central Bank "peso counterpart fund" to be used to "finance economic development expenditures" for industrial development.[64] Throughout the negotiations this was touted as an indication that the Philippine government—and not the World Bank—would maintain discretion over the final utilization of the $200 million peso-equivalent. However, that seemingly open-ended field for domestic control was whittled down by an agreement that "high" priorities for the fund be threefold: (1) energy generation and plant conversion to nonoil fuel sources; (2) the domestic engineering industry; and (3) the industrial estate/EPZ program.[65] Moreover, the Bank was adamant that authority for determining precisely where that money be channeled rest exclusively with the office of Finance Minister Virata. Virata's position as the Bank's closest Philippine friend and confidant suggests there was good reason behind this particular negotiation stance.

Like all Bank-borrower face-to-face negotiations, the outcome of the August 20 to 31, 1979, "discussions" was encapsulated in a mission "aide-mémoire," a brief and unpolished synopsis drafted for the benefit of both the Bank management and the Philippine government.[66] Little, if anything, had changed in the Bank's position over the period since the appropriate reforms were first spelled out in the mid-1970s. This fact was made apparent not only through the aide-mémoire's actual policy outline but also in its observation that the negotiated reforms "would be consistent with the macro policies . . . supported by the . . . IMF's Extended [Fund] Facility."[67] But the mémoire revealed a breakthrough in the IMF-Philippine government deadlock: "The discussions concluded that graduated action by the Government to implement industrial and financial policy improvements would provide the basis for substantially expanded World Bank support for the industrial sector over the next few years."[68]

Progress had, indeed, been made. Yet, though the main body of the Bank's mémoire proceeded step by step through the policy announcements that would be forthcoming from the Philippine government, a "Checklist of Items Requiring Philippine Position" was attached. The checklist, in effect, covered *all* the policies, indicating that what was worded as a fait accompli in the text was still probationary.[69] Philippine government participants in the negotiations recalled the August meetings as the time at which it became evident that the SAL would be "difficult because it required lots of [policy] changes from the government."[70] Neither verbal nor written pledges for future policy reforms would do this time. "The World Bank laid it on the line," confessed another high-level NEDA participant in these early discussions: the loan would not be final until the government made a "serious commitment to the reforms." That is, "no policy announcements . . . no new legislation, no loan."[71]

Just a year later, in August 1980, a confidential World Bank document reviewed the past year's policy reforms with approval:

> To date, the Government has acted promptly and in a well-coordinated manner to implement this [industrial development] program. Most of the reforms discussed during the review of the industrial report are either satisfactorily accomplished or progressing as rapidly as could reasonably be expected.[72]

There was no question that the twelve-month period had been marked by a barrage of new policy initiatives. Only one month after the August 1979 meetings, Marcos (in the words of his minister of industry, Roberto Ongpin) "rallied the country to rise to the challenge of confronting the economy" by announcing a new industrial-development policy.[73] By the December 1979 Consultative Group meeting, Bank Philippine desk chief Michael Gould, industrial-sector report and latest economic memorandum in hand, felt secure enough to applaud the progress of the Philippines. He did so by announcing to the Philippines' other major creditors that Bank industrial "lending is . . . likely to increase significantly to support the Government's efforts to expand rapidly economic growth, exports and employment."[74]

The Technocrats: Transnationalist Allies

By no means was the transformation from World Bank policy suggestions to domestic legislation a mechanical or simple process. "Actually," admitted a highly placed NEDA official, "we—that is, both NEDA and the Ministry of Industry—have wanted to move into the area of industrial protection for a long time. But there's always been such a great resistance . . . from vested interests."[75]

Resistance from exactly whom? Bienvenido Noriega, a NEDA economist directly involved with the SAL since the start of the technical discussions with the Bank, shrugged off the question: "There was lots of resistance from different quarters of the government."[76] "Even in the Philippine Cabinet there were different views," explained a NEDA colleague. "It took several years until all parties in the Cabinet were convinced of the structural adjustment's worth."[77]

Gerardo Sicat, economic planning and policy minister, had been a staunch reformist voice in transnationalism for perhaps a decade.[78] Only in July 1979, with the Bank's industrial work in progress, did Sicat gain a strong ally, when Industry Minister Roberto Ongpin was convinced to leave the private sector. The World Bank also pinpointed 1979 as a key transition period from Philippine rhetoric toward action: "Although the Minister of Economic Planning had long advocated industrial policy reform, a cabinet consensus in favor of fundamental reform emerged only in 1979, following a major Philippine study of the incentive system and a Bank sector report which built upon it."[79]

This high-level resistance was overcome in good part because of the corps of Western-educated technocrats who underpinned Marcos. It was these "young graduate-educated administrators brought in by Marcos" (to use the Bank's words) that enabled the Bank to wield as much influence as it did in Philippine economic policy.[80] They were the World Bank counterparts on the inside. They thought like World Bank economists; they shared the philosophy that progress and growth lay in foreign investment and abundant foreign loans. They spoke the same language of mathematic formulas. In brief, they composed a powerful, but not yet hegemonic, transnationalist faction of the Marcos government.

"The World Bank did not make us do anything we didn't want to," claimed Wilhelm Ortaliz, Ministry of Industry liaison to the Bank for the SAL.[81] He had a number of supporters in government on this point, among them ministers Sicat, Ongpin, and Virata, as well as a newer battalion of mid-level bureaucrats like himself and Noriega working on the SAL negotiations and policy changes. Although the claims of these officials that they controlled their own policy were, in part, true, they were misleading. The Bank, consorting with precisely that corps of technocrats who already shared its general outlook, helped tilt the Philippines' domestic power configuration heavily in favor of the transnationalist faction in the late 1970s.

Most of these allied Filipino technocrats clearly recognized the resulting mutually beneficial situation. "That's why the World Bank moved into program loans [that is, SALs]," explained one of NEDA's highest officials. "It strengthens the power of technocrats and helps make the work of the IMF and the World Bank easier. If they had to work with politicians, their batting average would be much lower."[82] NEDA's Bienvenido Noriega concurred: "We're using the World Bank [structural adjustment] loan as leverage . . . to do things NEDA has wanted to do, but hasn't been able to. . . . With this World Bank backing, NEDA has more strength vis-à-vis other ministries."[83]

NEDA's assistant director-general for programs and projects was more blunt: "I use the Bank as a club."[84] "Even when we want to undertake a policy ourselves, sometimes it's hard to stick to our economic priorities without political interference," explained Central Bank Deputy Governor Bince. "After all, you can't be a prophet in your own country. It's easier when it's more than just a national commitment . . . when there's IMF or World Bank help."[85] Minister Sicat, a longtime advocate of industrial reform, phrased it simply and concisely: "We are using the World Bank to add gravy where we need it."[86]

The Bank, in turn, acted on a deep understanding that its weight could tip the scales of domestic power. As early as 1976, a confidential World Bank document surmised that an "active Bank presence" in the Philippines would have the effect of "strengthening the position of the highly capable technical leaders in the Government and helping them to achieve policy objectives, which we endorse."[87] If this held for Bank project loans in general, it was especially true for structural adjustment lending. Mission chief de Vries, trying to generalize on the applicability of the Bank's Philippine SAL experience, did not fail to stress this critical component: "The Ministry of Industry, Board of Investments . . . and other government agencies have built up a competent technical staff, which makes it possible to pursue a comprehensive and rational industrial policy."[88]

Policy dialogues based on sector work lay at the core of the Bank's structural adjustment initiative. But, as confidential documents reveal, "highly effective loan-related dialogue,"[89] according to the World Bank, required interaction with domestic counterparts who "have not been neutral in their policy preferences."[90] These were the transnationalists such as Wilhelm Ortaliz of the Ministry of Industry, who could say with conviction, "We don't like to think of them [the new tariff laws and other policy changes] as conditions. They are our own development thrusts, just helped along by the World Bank's belief in them [the conditions] and commitment to us [the technocrats]."[91] By the late 1970s, Bank dialogues with technocrats like Ortaliz were characterized by a meshing of interests entirely absent from IMF debates with old-school Central Bank guardian Licaros.

From the start of the SAL, the Bank strategized its moves carefully, consciously gravitating toward a strong alliance with the Ministry of Industry. There, as in NEDA, the top bureaucrats were *kumpadres* (to borrow directly the Filipino term used by one of the deputy ministers of industry to explain his ministry's collaboration with the Bank).[92] The Ministry of Industry also presented a better vantage point than NEDA when Central Bank opposition had to be overcome, for an alliance with the ministry carried increased leverage. As the Bank itself noted in this regard, the as-yet-untarnished Ongpin was more than just the minister of industry: he was a member of both the cabinet's five-person highest standing committee and the Central Bank's governing Monetary Board. Furthermore, one of Ongpin's deputy ministers simultaneously held a pivotal post as chairman of the government's Development Bank of the Philippines (DBP), from whose coffers came most long-term domestic industrial finance.[93]

From the Ministry of Industry locus, the World Bank spread outward to other Philippine ministries, in line with Bank Vice-President William Clark's 1978 comment that the Bank managed to find approval for its programs (even in countries without identical priorities) by "constant dialogue," talking not only to planning and finance ministers but also to "other key men in the governments."[94] In October 1979, copying an experiment initiated during the EFF, an interagency committee was set up. Chaired by the Ministry of Industry, the committee included representatives from almost every ministry dealing with economic development. According to member Ortaliz, it was entrusted with using the World Bank industrial-sector report as an "outline" to delineate the Philippines' new industrial reform.[95]

The Bank, however, was not content simply to leave its report as a springboard for policy discussions. It continued to maintain a direct role in the domestic reform process. A Bank mission was sent in November and December 1979 "to help work out the initial package of reform measures to be supported by the proposed loan."[96] In its wake, export promotion, tariff reform, and trade policy initiatives all jumped to the forefront of the legislative slate (a slate tightly controlled by Marcos himself).

For what were considered the more difficult areas of reform—primarily the topics of investment incentives and industrial restructuring that the Bank's industrial report had not detailed sufficiently—the Philippine government was given a $50,000 advance on the loan to subsidize the cost of foreign consultants. These advisers were to base themselves at the Ministry of Industry and chronicle the necessary policy changes. In keeping with its established procedures, the Bank possessed veto power over the Philippine government's choice of consultants.[97] Indeed, for all the talk of amiable policy dialogue, the World Bank still held the more powerful negotiating position; it reminded its Philippine counterparts of this inequality from time to time through statements making it clear that should the industrial policy reform falter, so would Bank funds.[98]

Why, it may be asked, was the World Bank succeeding where the IMF had failed? The answer is complex. Whereas the IMF had dealt almost exclusively with a Central Bank not yet dominated by new technocratic elements, the World Bank turned its back on these "old boys." Instead, it focused on strengthening the positions and furthering the viewpoints of sympathetic technocrats in ministries that could be played off Licaros's Central Bank.

Furthermore, the Bank learned from the IMF's mistakes and consciously strove for a different sort of image in the Philippines. Pervasive among government officials was the feeling that the IMF stood as a "watchdog disciplinarian," to be approached with caution.[99] In contrast, World Bank missions moved in and out with ease, maintaining relative freedom to contact whomever they wanted directly without seeking highest-level Philippine government approval first—and vice versa.[100] At any given time, went the standard joke among Philippine technocrats, there were at least five World Bank missions somewhere in-country, but "who knows doing what, where, or why."[101]

A feeling of camaraderie permeated the SAL negotiations, making them, according to participant Ortaliz, "quite reasonable. Our assumption is that the last thing the World Bank wants to do is screw up our economy."[102] This showed in interagency committee member Noriega's recounting of who comprised the Bank's team at the negotiations:

It's quite a good group, who established a personal rapport with us. . . . There was Hinkle. He acted almost like an Asian, very patient—although according to [another Bank staff member], he assumes a very different role at the Bank. . . . You can see that different people in the mission seem to have specific roles to play. For example, the leader of the mission plays the good guy. You can see this with Chrik Poortman. Before, when he was just assistant [mission] head . . . he was the bad guy. But when he became the team leader, he changed his style, and . . . a German took over Poortman's former role—you know, playing the pushy type. . . . You can see this sometimes: now when Poortman wants to bring up a negative point, another on the mission brings it up for him.[103]

Such amicable role-playing was widely accepted by Noriega and the other Philippine technocrats, their alliance with the bank cemented. Noted Noriega lightly, "We know their roles are all learned in negotiation courses conducted by the Bank for its missions."[104]

Further facilitating the ease of negotiations was the sense of self-importance and confidence with which the Philippine technocrats were able to approach the meetings. The feeling existed that much as they needed the World Bank, these Bank staff members needed them as well. Structural adjustment lending, government participants realized from the start, was an experiment. With tensions growing between the Bank's established project and new program divisions, professional futures within the Bank were staked on the first few structural adjustment loans. So, contended Ortaliz, "when the mission got a bit pushy here, wanting us to include more policy changes than they originally asked for, wanting us also to realign indirect taxes right away [and so on] . . . it was only because they [were] really in need of a successful program loan"[105]—"successful" in the sense that significant domestic policy reform was forthcoming, which the Philippine government was made to understand had not been the case with the World Bank's first three SALs. This heightened sense of importance allowed Philippine technocrats to accept what Ortaliz admitted were the Bank's "at times unreasonable demands."[106]

Throughout the negotiations Wharton-trained Minister Virata, respected in international financial circles through his 1976–1980 chairmanship of the Bank-Fund Joint Development Committee (after which point he was made chairman of the Group of 24), played a critical role. "If it had not been for Minister Virata, there wouldn't have been quite that kind of relationship between the World Bank and the Philippine government," surmised Noriega.[107]

As the negotiations entered their final lap and as ticklish issues cropped up in the somewhat more public interagency committee meetings, Virata, Husain, and McNamara were sequestered to iron out the wrinkles.[108] Such behind-the-scenes activity was more frequent than usual for a Bank loan, but all the participants were accustomed to these private tête-à-têtes. De facto conditions for the granting of IMF and World Bank loans are often hammered out behind closed doors by senior participants in advance of the final negotiations and, therefore, never find their way formally into the written contracts.[109] The beauty of the arrangment was that it allowed people such as Central Bank Deputy Governor Bince to sidestep inquiries into whether the industrial-sector policy changes stood as conditions for the SAL with a curt "You'll never find that in writing."[110]

In midsummer 1980, a Philippine technical team traveled to the Bank's Washington, D.C., headquarters for what was to be the last in this long series of negotiations. The unusually high-level presence of Ministers Virata and Ongpin among the group at this stage of talks was striking testimony to the fact that SAL mediations were above those of normal project loans.[111] At the end of the "technical discussions," the Bank's Hinkle and the Central Bank's special negotiator Soliven dispatched a joint telegram to Deputy Industry Minister Jose Leviste detailing "steps to be completed for distribution of Loan Documents to the [Bank's Executive] Board." Final approval by the Bank management (who would then transmit the loan papers to the Board for a rubber-stamp vote) hinged on fulfillment of three conditions.[112] The Bank management would wait until the government had "(a) enacted a law to implement the [agreed-upon] first three stages of tariff reform, (b) adopted a policy . . . liberalizing commodity import procedures, and (c) sent a letter to the Bank outlining Philippines Industrial Development Policy."[113]

Within a month these last obstacles vanished. Virata's letter bore the date August 12, 1980. Less than two weeks earlier, on August 1, President Marcos issued Executive Order 609, declaring a comprehensive reform covering three-quarters of the items in the Tariff Code. Although eventually geared to bring nominal tariff rates down to the range of 20 to 30 percent (and thereby meeting the Bank's 1977 call for rates in this range), the reform concentrated on three initial stages of a five-year tariff reform program effective January 1, 1981.

Phase I would reduce most current peak nominal rates to a 50 percent (ad valorem) ceiling by January 1, 1982.[114] Phases II and III would concentrate on realigning fourteen important industrial subsector rates over five years to achieve broad uniformity. Under phase II, the average effective rates of protection for food processing, textiles and garments, leather and footwear, and pulp and paper were to be slashed from 158 percent to 30 percent. Phase III was then to reduce the average effective rate of protection from 53 percent to 18 percent for ten other key industries.[115] In addition, a fourth phase was to be proclaimed by January 1981 and was to cover the 25 percent of the Tariff Code not included in the phase I peak-rate reductions or phase II and III sectoral tariff reform.[116] In sum, the four-phased reforms, according to Bank calculations, would "reduce overall effective rates of protection for the economy from 36 percent to 23 percent and for the manufacturing sector from 44 percent to 29 percent."[117] Accompanying this tariff change was the requisite import liberalization, removing the prior-approval requirement on restricted import categories (the Central Bank's "nonessential consumer" and "unclassified consumer" lists of so-called luxury goods).[118]

The rest was fairly pro forma. Upon reading McNamara's final report on the loan (recommending the board's countenance), the executive directors learned that the Philippine government had "implemented nearly all the recommendations on export promotion made in the Bank's industrial sector report," including "the most important and difficult actions required."[119] McNamara's report was quite explicit in enumerating how the obligatory tariff reform related to the Bank's export-oriented industrialization goals for countries like the Philippines:

> The reduction in higher rates of protection afforded to some industries should lead to increases in competitiveness and efficiency and help strengthen the linkages between home and export industries. . . .[120]
> Tariff reform and the liberalization of import licensing should push Philippine effective protection significantly closer to those of Korea and Taiwan which have experienced rapid industrial and export growth. . . .
> They [the reforms] will place home industry in a much more competitive environment and encourage productive resources to be allocated to areas in which the Philippines has an existing or potential comparative advantage. These reforms are likely to mark a turning point in Philippine trade policy as important as that of the early 1970s [when martial law was declared]. . . .
> Nontraditional manufactures would play a central role in sustaining the country's export drive.[121]

The signing of the SAL in September 1980 was marked by victory celebrations on both sides. In the Philippines, ironically, some viewed the approval as a triumph over the dominant U.S. power on the Bank's board. The United States' historical disdain for broad-based program loans to LDCs was no closely guarded secret. "We half expected a U.S. veto on the loan," admitted more than one Philippine technocrat.[122]

But structural adjustment lending was not the same as the relatively unencumbered program lending, as the September 1980 accolades within the executive director's chambers revealed. There, the structural adjustment loan was heralded as a "vehicle" for "overcoming policy constraints." Indeed, the executive directors were so enthralled with McNamara's new tool that they seemed to have only one complaint: why had the Bank not attempted to use its previous Philippine industrial *project* loans as leverage "to have an effective dialogue?" To which the (unnamed) chairman could only reply that the "environment" had become "more sympathetic," "more conducive to dialogue" of late, adding that there were plans for "continuing and expanding" that dialogue "to embrace other issues."[123]

5

Adjustment in Action

With the signing of the SAL, claimed the Bank news release on the loan, came "the implementation of a comprehensive development program designed to accelerate industrial growth, expand employment and maintain the rapid growth of nontraditional exports. . . ."[1] The implementation is a study in World Bank–LDC transnationalist collaboration at its best.

Tariff Reform

Of all the policy changes linked to the industrial SAL, indicated high-level Philippine technocrats deeply involved in the broad interagency discussions, tariff reform and its accompanying import liberalization captured the Bank's primary interest.[2] Indeed, they stood as the cornerstone of the Philippines' new industrial-development designs. This chronicle of policy intervention demonstrates the growing skill of the Bank and its transnationalist Philippine allies in effectively neutralizing an important social class, the national entrepreneurs, during the molding of a new tariff policy.

Items targeted for tariff reform fit a clear pattern: almost 80 percent of the product lines covered by tariff changes were raw materials and intermediate (producer) goods destined mainly for export-oriented, labor-intensive industries such as textiles and apparel, electronics, leather and footwear, and food processing.[3] Complementing the tariff changes was a subsector-restructuring program, partially financed by Bank project loans, to integrate these light-manufacturing industries all the more deeply into the newly enhanced export effort.[4] Consumer goods accounted for the remaining 20-odd percent of the revised tariff lines, with major cuts applied to imported goods similar to those the Philippines would now be exporting, including textiles and apparel, electrical and electronic equipment, furniture, wood products, and processed foods (as well as motorcycles and bicycles).[5]

In other words, opening the Philippines to the Bank's prescribed freer trade regime fostered greater reliance on consumption of imported Western finished goods and on import-dependent export production of goods within the same industry, sometimes even at the same stage of production.[6] The Bank and the Fund rationalized this as accelerating domestic industrial growth and efficiency. National entrepreneurs did not view it in quite the same light.

For all the Bank's insistence that its outlook and work remain strictly within economic parameters (and notwithstanding its critics' complaints that the Bank ignores its policies' political ramifications), political analysis is not unknown to the World Bank. In the case of the Philippines, Bank officials fully understood that implementation of the prescribed tariff reform carried the distinct possibility of a domestic uproar, especially among the fragile but influential class of Filipino entrepreneurs who still retained a share of the domestic market (particularly in consumer goods). Tension with this class had existed ever since the partial dismantling of protection in 1962, when President Macapagal, under IMF guidance, had reversed his predecessor's "Filipino First" policies.

In fact, as the SAL negotiations neared completion, final touches were being put on a Bank report assessing the Philippine political scene. This so-called Ascher Memorandum laid bare the Bank's ultimate concerns. Whether Marcos stayed or went was secondary; what was relevant was reducing the "vulnerability of the 'technocrats' in retaining their economic management positions."[7] Technocrats, not Marcos, were perceived as key to the success of the economy-wide transformations. As the memorandum revealed, Bank officials foresaw that the new policy shifts toward export-oriented industrialization would pit the Marcos regime more squarely against the national entrepreneurs. In such a politically charged atmosphere, Marcos would be tempted to shove aside his transnationalist advisers and yield to political pressures from the deeply entrenched national entrepreneurs.

Therefore, in light of "the scope and complexity of structural adjustment programs [in the Philippines and elsewhere], as well as the political issues to which they give rise,"[8] the Bank borrowed an old IMF practice and set a new Bank precedent. It split its SALs into "tranches" (usurping the IMF's French term for its installments).[9] For the Philippine SAL, there were to be two tranches, with the second contingent on tenacious adherence to the policy reform timetable outlined in Virata's letter. Release of the $100 million first tranche came soon after the loan was signed,[10] that is, once the government had announced phases I to III of the tariff reform (and the accompanying initial phases of import deregulation). Proclamation of phase IV and compliance with the phase I to III reforms "on or before January 31, 1981," were preconditions to the Bank's granting release of the $95 million second tranche.[11]

Rather than resenting this strict World Bank "conditionality," Virata and his corps of technocrats welcomed it (although they did agree that domestically, at least, this facet of the SAL had to be kept confidential to save them possible embarrassment).[12] In fact, one of the Philippine government participants in the SAL negotiations even insisted that the tightening of Bank surveillance was strongly pushed by Virata to strengthen the government transnationalists' position vis-à-vis nationalists in the Philippine private sector. Industry Ministry's Ortaliz was unequivocal on this point: "Virata felt the private sector would do lots of things to stop this policy reform. The tactic was to give us, the technocrats, a weapon against political pressures from the more vocal elements" among the national entrepreneurs.[13] At a later date, Ortaliz repeated these sentiments, adding emphatically, "I couldn't fight these people without the World Bank loan."[14]

Installments provided the Bank with strong leverage should promised policy changes not be forthcoming. How forcefully that leverage could be used soon became apparent. Leery of the growing antigovernment stance of some of his onetime supporters among the national entrepreneurs, toward the end of 1980 Marcos succumbed to "direct pressure by [certain members of] the business sector," confessed NEDA's Noriega.[15] His capitulation took the form of slowing down tariff reductions by amending Executive Order 609, which dealt with tariff reform phases I to III. It seems this was done so hastily that the amended executive order stood wrongly numbered on the books. The new rates (as amended by Executive Order 632A; no Executive Order 609A exists) did decelerate tariff reductions, but did not change or realign the final 1984 rate.[16] Rather, Executive Order 632A bought some of the most vocal domestic businessmen more time and more hope.[17]

In slowing down tariff reductions, however, Executive Order 632A displeased the World Bank. Hinkle and Soliven's July 1980 cable to the Ministry of Industry had made it clear that the original Bank conditions left little room for any such changes: the second tranche would be forthcoming only if "any modifications made in these [reform] measures since their adoption would be consistent with objectives and timing of their original measures."[18] Moreover, by early 1981, according to Noriega, Marcos "felt that the private sector was really up in arms against us" and had a mind to renege on the promised phase IV altogether.[19] Playing its trump card, the January 1981 World Bank review mission promptly refused to sanction the SAL's second tranche.

Despite their harsh public stance, mission head Poortman and his staff understood the domestic power jockeying and sympathized with the technocrats' bind, especially after Minister Virata privately explained Marcos's perception of the current impasse.[20] As it was, under pressure from the U.S. government and the World Bank, Marcos was planning to lift martial law and to hold a presidential election of sorts, both politically difficult steps to execute.[21] The slight opening of the political debate implicit in elections was dangerous for Marcos. It provoked embarrassing scenes such as that of former Senator Jose Diokno, one of the most nationalistic of the elite opposition, standing up before a Rotary Club meeting in Manila and explaining that the national entrepreneurs' death knell came on World Bank orders. Even Marcos's technocrats understood these domestic tensions and were able to communicate to the Bank the fear that the SAL was "unfairly being used to fuel opposition charges against our government's leadership."[22]

As a result, the Bank did comprehend the worrisome political possibility that national entrepreneurs might join more radical forces in opposition to the policy changes—and to Marcos and his technocrats. Indeed, the November 1980 Ascher Memorandum had carried these insights:

> In what ways could the local industrial sector oppose the economic program? While their opposition to further eliminations of protectionism is certainly ex- pected, local industrialists' capacity to oppose effectively has been eroded by their own economic decline due to the concentration of economic power in the hands of the state, multinationals and Marcos' circle.[23] Yet, . . . they are now using the nationalist argument to criticize the government's policy, thereby find- ing common ground with the more ideologically-oriented opposition at the universities. . . .
>
> In addition to trying to influence policymaking, the business sector can join in the political opposition activities designed to remove Marcos along with his economic approach. Business-sector support for the opposition press (albeit subdued), opposition movements in exile, and even the recent bombings have been attributed to elements of the local business sector.[24]

Such an understanding, however, did not alter the program of action. The Bank simply stalled the second tranche, during which time, admitted Ortaliz, "it was suggested" that government officials caucus with national entrepreneurs to appease their growing antigovernment stance.[25] In the meantime, even Bank confidential documents presented the quagmire in euphemistic terms, noting unobtrusively that the second tranche was being "temporarily delayed to allow the Government additional time to finalize and adopt the final phase of the tariff reform and trade liberalization program."[26]

Government calendars for March and April of 1981 carried a full agenda of the prescribed government-business consultations, including hearings on the phase IV tariff reform. The masterstroke was a two-day meeting held by Manila's newspaper *Business Day* on April 22 and 23, 1981, in the five-star Mandarin Hotel. Full-page advertisements geared to Manila's business world announced the "policy conference on tariff reforms" weeks in advance. Smaller print, indicating that the conference was being spon- sored "in collaboration with" the government Tariff Commission,[27] sug- gested that the actual event might not prove as objective as the advertise- ment seemed to imply.

Moreover, the $100-a-day admission fee revealed that the government sought to explain the policy changes to only the wealthier, and potentially more troublesome, nationalist businessmen. As expected, the conference brought forth an audience composed of high-level executives from many well-known, domestically oriented industries, and a rostrum adorned by those very technocrats who had been involved with the SAL negotiations (among them, Ortaliz and Noriega). Four Cabinet members were slated to address the gathering, a clear indication of the importance the government attached to this event.

Quite cleverly, the government used the forum to steer the debate away from political issues and back to a traditional economics domain where its technocrats could reign supreme. In response to questions concerning accelerating bankruptcies, unemployment, and inflation following the tariff changes, the government spokespersons (admitting quite cryptically that "adjustment pains are inevitable,"[28] and that "we expect some dislocations in industry"[29]) launched into what for the majority of the audience was the mystifying domain of economic formulas. University of the Philippines economics professor Norma Tan (who had contributed to the university's research project on the industrial sector) argued that tariff reductions were a painful though necessary precondition for Philippine competition in world markets. Reduced tariffs would guarantee the country's best utilization of its "comparative advantage" through light industrial exports. At the end of her exercise, Tan congratulated her audience on "sacrificing in the short run for promised returns in the long run."[30]

Other less mathematical presentations complemented Tan's. Minister Sicat chastised the group for standing in the way of Philippine survival.[31] After reading Minister Ongpin's prepared speech, Deputy Industry Minister Tordesillias called on the national entrepreneurs to leave self-interest behind and realize that the tariff changes were being implemented so "that investment in the future will be channeled only to those areas where the Philippines has substantial and *permanent* comparative advantage."[32]

Four general reactions were voiced by conference participants. To begin with, they thought Sicat sounded defensive when questioned about the World Bank's role. Second, to most Professor Tan's formulas were unfathomable, but they were willing to believe in their scientific validity. Third, even those who understood some economic jargon did not grasp the concept of a permanent comparative advantage. Finally, the general response was one of begrudging acceptance that they as national entrepreneurs could do little at this point to shift the priorities of a transnationalist-dominated government.[33]

The atmosphere of confrontation somewhat diffused, Marcos pushed forward. Within half a week, the government technocrats had finalized phase IV of tariff reforms. Soon after, the SAL's second tranche began to arrive.[34] And Ortaliz could confidently conclude that this "coddled class" would not "stand in the way of our plans for progress anymore."[35]

Lifting the Import Restrictions

Whereas the ministries central to tariff reform were all controlled by technocrats, this could not be said for the SAL-related commodity import liberalization. Import licensing restrictions were controlled by the same Central Bank whose governor created so many problems for the IMF's extended fund facility. With talk of import licensing liberalization, a heated interministerial debate flared into an open contest of power.

By mid-1980, the Philippine government had adopted a phased plan for removing the Central Bank's import licensing restrictions. Of the 1,304 consumer items protected in 1980 either to shield domestic industries or to conserve foreign exchange, 263 became freely importable in 1981. The remaining items were scheduled to achieve that status in 1982 and 1983.[36]

Import liberalization was important, because the impact of tariff reform would have been greatly weakened if widespread nontariff barriers to entry were allowed to stand.[37] The World Bank was adamant in this regard: "Central Bank licensing . . . is an obstacle toward product improvement, greater competition, and the provision of supplies to export industries."[38] In particular, the Bank asked rhetorically, how was the Philippines' non-traditional-export drive going to take off if yarn for the apparel industry and cans for the food-processing industry were on the restricted lists?[39] Without these additional barriers to competitive imports, the Bank reasoned, an influx of cheaper, better products would force some companies to collapse and others to modernize and merge. This would spur dynamic growth.

Finance Minister Virata, Ongpin, and that allied group of transnationalist technocrats readily agreed with the scenario and turned their attention to the culprit responsible for the expansion of the import restrictions over the years: the Central Bank under Gregorio Licaros. But Licaros refused to view the SAL as anything but a full-fledged, no-strings-attached program loan; he wanted the money for the Philippine economy, but he was not about to abandon import licensing in return. To compound matters, he understood neither the Bank's exigencies nor the textbook economic formulas; concerning import licensing liberalization, the line of reasoning of the Bank, the Fund, and the Philippine technocrats totally escaped him. Nor did he seem to have the desire to understand any of this. He looked down on those whom he called the "young technocrats," those "who think they already know a lot but there are many things that cannot be learned from the books. Experience is still the best teacher." [40] His view was the pragmatist's rather than the transnationalist's, and it buttressed the interests of domestic-oriented entrepreneurs: "A government should have the right to restrict certain imports, especially luxury goods. If not, how are we to keep our balance-of-payments problem under control?" [41]

With this philosophy, Licaros sanctioned the continuing recalcitrance of the Central Bank's import-control office, which had repulsed IMF pressure for import liberalization during the heyday of the EFF feuds. Allegiance to national entrepreneurs protected by import restrictions was one motivation. It was also a question of power. As a prominent former Central Bank deputy governor admitted, the more items on the restricted import list, the more powerful the import-control office and, thus, the Central Bank as a whole.[42] Seeking to keep the Fund and now the Bank at bay, import-control office head Alita Martel and Licaros stood together, backed by the nationalist faction within the Central Bank.

The Bank, however, had shaped its new approach with the Licaros/Martel obstacle in mind. In retrospect, one of the SAL's masterstrokes was overcoming a well-entrenched enclave of the nationalist elite without applying direct Bank force. Instead, the Bank used its alliance with others among the transnationalist elite to enter areas that were the Central Bank's rightful domain. Not the Bank itself, but the SAL interagency team took on Licaros's Central Bank. Noriega, an interagency member, retraced the events:

> Ministers Sicat, Virata, and Ongpin all ganged up versus the Central Bank. And all of them are on the Monetary Board. . . . It was no contest. They had the interagency committee's pressure to back them up. . . . And then suddenly, because of all the pressure we applied on the Central Bank, they [the Central Bank] gave in.[43]

Licaros's Central Bank did not take its erosion of power lightly. Martel, Ortaliz recounted, was "furious" and declined what the victors viewed as a conciliatory gesture, an offer of membership in, and even the chairmanship of, the interagency committee finalizing import liberalization reforms.[44] "Actually," surmised Noriega with hindsight, "her refusal to have anything to do with the committee at that time only made our work easier and faster."[45]

Even as the reforms neared completion, Martel sought to regain her office's power and status, charging that the interagency committee "did this behind her back after she had held the IMF off for so long."[46] According to Ortaliz, the committee finally consoled her with a compromise: "We said we would take this move as a five-year experiment," and if "things turned out badly" and the balance of payments widened considerably, the policy could be revoked. "The move, we explained to them [at the Central Bank], should not be seen as irreversible."[47] But this was not the World Bank view. As McNamara's final report on the SAL explained: "Reimposition of . . . [import] restrictions will be resorted to only as a last resort and would require approval by the IMF."[48]

By early 1981, SAL reforms in place, technocrats in the Ministry of Industry, NEDA, and associated ministries saw little reason to concern themselves with the threat of Central Bank disapproval. Domestic power configurations among government officials had shifted noticeably. Seeing these changes, Martel had retreated, finally throwing her weight behind the interagency committee and assuming its vice-chairmanship.[49] To ensure the continuing subservience of the old import-control office's dominant personalities, control over the residual import restrictions (those requiring licenses for national security or consumer protection reasons) was removed from Central Bank jurisdiction. At the World Bank's "urging," wrote a Manila newspaper, the import licensing function was to be transferred to the Trade Ministry, which shortly thereafter was combined with transnationalist Ongpin's Ministry of Industry.[50]

On January 12, 1981, Manila's most talked-about power play in these maneuverings was carried through. Buckling under the combined weight of domestic and international antagonism to his reign, Governor Licaros submitted—on request, according to unofficial sources—his premature resignation.

Licaros's fall was provoked by several events, but high on the list was his obstinacy in the face of the World Bank, the IMF, and his fellow technocrats. They searched for evidence of improprieties on his part, improprieties they might use to push him out. The opportunity came in January 1981 when Licaros was linked to a scandal involving a Filipino textile businessman of Chinese origin who fled the country with millions of dollars of bad debts.[51]

In Licaros's seat was placed World Bank friend and technocrat Jaime Laya. Some years earlier, in 1979, the World Bank had honored Laya by offering him the highest position it had ever extended to a Filipino (as an executive director for Asia and Latin America). Then Minister of the Budget Laya, considered indispensable at home, had been forced to turn the offer down. That Laya's outlook would be more conducive to the exigencies of the times was obvious to everyone concerned. As Ortaliz said, summarizing the switch, "Laya is of the same mindset as us."[52]

World Bank officials did more than mesh working relations with technocratic elements in the ministries of Finance and Industry. The Bank was also instrumental in advancing—directly or, in certain cases such as this, only indirectly—technocrats with whom they worked well. Marcos and his top advisers (Virata in particular) replaced Licaros with Laya largely to boost international approval, most notably from the Bank and the Fund.

De Facto Devaluation

Tariff and import policy shifts required substantial World Bank finesse, both in appeasing strong economic interests and in circumventing the Central Bank. Policy intervention on the exchange rate provides another model, this time of blunt utilization of power in conjunction with a close and powerful transnationalist ally, the minister of finance.

Historically, of all the snags in IMF negotiations with LDCs, the most widely acknowledged has concerned domestic exchange-rate devaluation. Reductions in the exchange value of a nation's currency have, on several occasions, resulted in rampant inflation in food and other vital industries and a drop in real wages, leaving urban riots, if not government upheavals, in their wake. Indeed, certain high Philippine officials could recite the list of governments thus weakened.[53]

Therefore, of all the suggested policy reforms, it was devaluation that evoked a nearly uniform response among both nationalist and transnationalist factions of the Philippine political and economic elite. Unlike tariff reform, which split Marcos from his technocratic administrators, and unlike import licensing reform, which pitted the Central Bank against technocratic policymakers, devaluation provoked a loud, synchronized chorus of "no" from almost all government offices, a cry that echoed among national entrepreneurs and middle- and lower-class workers and consumers alike.

Yet, in November 1981, U.S. Acting Deputy Assistant Secretary of State for East Asian and Pacific Affairs Daniel O'Donahue took the opportunity of testimony before the U.S. Congress to commend the Philippines on initiating an exchange-rate policy that "will probably translate into a decline in peso value against the currencies of the Philippines' major trading partners." It was, he acknowledged, one of several "economic reforms pressed on the Philippine Government" by "international financial institutions."[54]

Philippine exchange-rate policy, in theory at least, was formulated in the Central Bank, although the broad interpretation of the Bretton Woods agreements made it a legitimate domain for IMF (but not World Bank) proddings. Governor Licaros was accustomed to this pressure:

> Off and on over my eleven years as governor, the IMF has been pushing devaluation. . . . When IMF people look at the exchange rate, they are easily disturbed. They look at figures, formulations, especially the "purchasing-power parity" formula which I personally don't understand. My approach is more pragmatic.[55]

Inside and outside the Central Bank, Philippine technocrats shared Licaros's resentment of the IMF's overwhelming reliance on what Deputy Governor Bince called "the same formula for all countries in all situations."[56] This included even some of the more transnationalist-oriented among them. A prestigious special consultant to Finance Minister Virata, Benito Legarda (who moved on to become alternate director of the IMF and then a consultant to the World Bank) summarized the general irritation:

> Of course, in relying on this magic formula, the IMF seems to forget that it is only valid *if* there was equilibrium in the base period . . . and also inflation has to be over. Neither of which is true in the case of the Philippines. . . . But every [IMF] mission always includes one person from the IMF's Exchange and Trade Relations [Department] who acts as the [exchange-rate] specialist on the mission to give the "party line" on exchange rates.[57]

Annoyed Central Bank officials explained their strong objections time and time again to IMF missions.[58] In turn, the IMF obstinately insisted that its calculations uncovered a "fundamental disequilibrium" in the Philippines, the Fund euphemism for situations requiring devaluation.

But, added Legarda, "that's a vague concept . . . and they would not even tell us what a 'fundamental disequilibrium' is."[59] Then, without explanation, the IMF retreated, and, as Legarda disclosed, "the IMF mission's last report to the board didn't harp on devaluation."[60]

This opened the field for others. As Legarda recollected, it was now left to the U.S. executive director of the Fund "to harp on devaluation."[61] At the October 1980 meeting of the GATT, the United States stressed that "purchasing-power parity" results underscored the indispensability of devaluation if the Philippines wanted to retain a competitive edge in the world market.[62]

The United States brought up the subject at international forums, but it was the World Bank, using the new platform provided by its SAL policy dialogues, that enunciated directly to the Philippine government the need for a higher peso-dollar exchange rate. The Bank clearly bowed to the Fund's expertise in this area by channeling its draft proposals for Philippine exchange-rate reform through the relevant Fund office for approval.[63] All these interactions were quietly executed behind the scenes in Washington, leaving the World Bank's Philippine missions free from the IMF's stigma.

Still, the interagency committee seemed no less adamant in its refusal to devalue. Behind the refusal stood a standard rationale, voiced by government technocrats and nontechnocrats alike. "What advantage do we get from changing the exchange rate?" asked Licaros. "The price and volume of sugar, coconut, copra, et cetera, depend on what is happening in the United States and Japan, not on our exchange rate."[64] As for the rest of Philippine exports, Deputy Governor Bince explained that "at the moment, there is no export we cannot sell due to an overvalued exchange rate. Our manufactured exports have been growing and growing . . . so they must be *already* internationally competitive."[65]

Experience from the 1970 devaluation led Philippine government officials to generally acknowledge that while consumer goods imports might decrease in the wake of a devaluation, oil imports would not be affected.[66] With mineral fuels and lubricants accounting for about 23 percent of 1979 imports and consumer goods only about 8 percent, "we can't expect a devaluation to solve our balance-of-payments problems," commented a Ministry of Finance technocrat. "In fact, it would probably worsen our problems."[67]

In a controversial and confidential draft of a report on Philippine poverty written after a summer 1979 Bank mission to the Philippines, another department of the World Bank issued a stronger condemnation of the 1970 devaluation. There the Bank claimed that in the Philippines devaluation had exacerbated the plight of the lower classes.[68] This insight was nowhere to be found in the Bank's confidential SAL documents, written over approximately the same period as the poverty report. Instead, the Bank's SAL analysis was succinct: tariff reform and trade liberalization would "probably generate some additional import demand" and, therefore, "a flexible exchange-rate policy" was needed "to offset the possible adverse" balance-of-payments effects.[69]

Philippine technocrats involved in the interagency committee insisted that on the issue of devaluation the Philippine negotiating stance did not budge from opposition. "Although the World Bank hinted that we might want to consider devaluation," stressed one participant, "the Philippine government told them no. And they listened."[70] Added Ortaliz, "Minister Virata told the Bank that the exchange rate was not negotiable. The Bank asked us to please keep an open mind and study the issue. . . . But we explained the problems with devaluation. And that was really that."[71]

Yet nowhere in the set of World Bank internal documents on the Philippine industrial-sector loan was there even tacit acknowledgment of disagreement over an appropriate exchange-rate policy. Indeed, the May 1980 public Bank report on the loan suggested otherwise, noting that the Philippine government "regards maintenance of an appropriate exchange-rate policy as crucial to stimulating the necessary expansion of exports"—a clear reference to devaluation.[72]

Was the World Bank simply employing ambiguous but suggestive language to camouflage an area of policy disagreement? Or, at some point in private meetings, did Minister Virata, himself billed by domestic media as a staunch opponent to devaluation,[73] capitulate to demands from his Bank friends? Virata's special consultant Legarda was asked whether the Philippines would devalue under increased pressure from the Bank or the Fund. Legarda refused to answer directly. "The Philippines," he said circuitously, "needs to borrow as much as it can on the market. Big, large countries— India and Brazil—can break promises to the World Bank and IMF. But we haven't got those privileges of rank."[74]

That promise was hidden in Minister Virata's August 1980 letter to the

World Bank formally requesting the SAL: "We intend to follow a flexible exchange-rate policy that will allow the exchange rate of the peso to reflect basic market forces. . . . Our exchange-rate policy will also be consistent with the objectives and policies outlined in this letter."[75] On first reading, Virata's words appear a purposefully cryptic attempt to circumvent the subject of devaluation. But on second reading, his phrases contain all the concessions over the exchange rate that, as far as many interagency committee members were concerned, never were sealed into the agreement.

Beneath the deceptively noncommittal language, the promise stands clear. No more would the Philippine government maintain what is called a "dirty float" wherein, although the peso was technically free to float, the Central Bank intervened in foreign exchange markets to maintain the peso's value against the dollar.[76] Instead, the float was to be a "cleaner" one. It was not simply a promise on paper.[77] From 1977 to mid-1980, the peso-dollar exchange rate had been sustained in the vicinity of 7.40. At the end of June 1980, with the final Bank deliberations over the SAL on the horizon, it slid to 7.53.[78] By September 30, 1981, the peso's value had deteriorated slowly but steadily to reach 8.00.[79] By the time the SAL's second tranche came up for review in early to mid-1981, Philippine authorities had (according to the IMF) "agreed that a policy of continuing real effective depreciation of the peso would be appropriate."[80]

These step-by-step mini-devaluations avoided the sudden, confidence-eroding jump inherent in a one-step devaluation. Nonetheless, they marked a de facto 8 percent devaluation against the dollar during 1981 alone.[81] The Philippines' highest-level technocrat, Cesar Virata, had, in spite of avowals to the contrary, acceded to Bank demands.

Export Promotion

These three areas of reform inspired by the World Bank—tariffs, import licensing, and exchange rate—provoked the widest debates within the Philippine government. Additional reforms, which can be broadly combined under the rubric of export-promotion policies and incentives, also impinged deeply on other key sectors, including finance, energy, and agriculture. Once again, the Bank played a vital role.

The largely uncontested acceptance of the new export-promotion policies and incentives resulted in large part from the World Bank's and its allied technocrats' skill in presenting the reforms. Crucial to the ease with which the new policies were accepted was that the Ministry of Industry, which had an undisputed position of power in this area, was a stronghold of transnationalist technocrats. Suggested export-promotion policies could be and were outlined as simple extensions of policies to which the Philippine government had been committed for a decade, if not longer. But in amplifying the reforms, the World Bank—and in turn the Ministry of Industry, its Board of Investments, and the Ministry of Trade[82]—also extended them to new domains. In internal documents, the Bank was more truthful about its intentions: existing industrial incentives and promotion policies were too biased toward the domestic market, penalizing export industries. The new policies were to reverse this situation.[83]

One such reform involved creating suitable environments to house the new nontraditional-export industries. On January 15, 1981, Marcos promulgated Presidential Decree 1786, authorizing the release of funds for twelve new export processing zones.[84] The Bank, suggesting that the three existing EPZs were far from sufficient for the Philippines' new thrust, had advocated the move. At least three of the dozen zones were to be to some degree financed through the SAL's peso-counterpart fund.[85]

More EPZs were not all the Bank asked of the Philippine government. As the February 1979 Bank mission advised, "*All* manufactured export industries should be placed on a free trade regime to the maximum extent possible."[86] The goal, as a Trade Ministry official explained, was "to see if we can get the mechanisms of export processing zones, without actually having to move to the zone physically. If this works, we'll have foreign exporters knocking on our door."[87]

The solution proposed by the Bank was to expand another arrangement that had already existed to a limited extent in the Philippines since 1974: bonded manufacturing villages.[88] In these villages, as in EPZs, the government invited TNCs to import all inputs duty-free, provided they were processed entirely for re-export. But with each village being a smaller enclave devoted solely to the export of one product, bonded villages could more quickly dot the entire country. The one hundred such bonded villages planned for the early 1980s stood as testimony to this fact.[89] Once the legislation covering these villages was liberalized according to World Bank specifications,[90] the government could respond more immediately to the shifting needs of TNCs by designating an area as a bonded village. According to a University of the Philippines law professor:

> TNCs here like this new arrangement because you don't need a subsidiary. It's almost all done through contracts with a subcontractor whose whole production is geared to your needs. . . . And it's a much faster way—this bonded warehouse manufacturing—of integrating the whole country with the export drive led by TNCs than are export processing zones.[91]

Such integration was to spell more profound changes for the domestic economy. For although the World Bank billed the nontraditional-export drive as a diversification, it pushed the Philippines to concentrate predominantly on four product lines: apparel, electronics, furniture and wood products, and shoes and other leather goods.[92]

Less than twenty-four hours after the new EPZ decree came a second significant export-promotion reform, the January 16, 1981, Omnibus Investments Code (Presidential Decree 1789), which streamlined and codified all laws related to foreign investment and business in the Philippines.[93] The move, admitted government spokespersons publicly, came in the wake of the Bank industrial mission's finding that foreign investors were confused by the panoply of legislation covering export and investment incentives. Those spokespersons could not help acknowledging further that the timing of the decree was significant. Promulgated by Marcos on the eve of lifting martial law, the act (relayed the local media) represented "the government's assurance to make foreign investors stay in the country and lure in other foreign businessmen."[94]

What the government failed to announce publicly (but what national entrepreneurs soon discovered) was that the Omnibus Investments Code did more than render the existing acts more comprehensible; it embellished them. A case in point was a Bank-suggested removal of the article excluding incentives to companies that experienced a (two-year) nominal profit growth of more than 33 percent, which was said to penalize more efficient foreign firms.[95]

Similarly, the World Bank's desire to further strengthen Industry Ministry technocrats was fulfilled: the code delegated to the ministry's Board of Investments (of which Ongpin was chairman) the final voice in deciding corporate applicants' eligibility for the incentives.[96] That is, the Board of Investments was promoted, from being a mere recommendatory agency subservient to NEDA to a quasi-judicial body. And domestic entrepreneurs lost all right of appeal should they be denied access to the incentives. The entrepreneurs found this state of affairs quite worrisome, given the Omnibus Code's focus on foreign investors exporting nontraditional manufactures and given the transnationalist orientation of those Ministry of Industry officials who would be deciding their fate.

When Trade Minister Luis Villafuerte embarked the Philippine government on an aggressive scheme to launch seven major export projects and seven support projects, the venture was billed as the "seven on seven" export-promotion program for the 1980s.[97] Once again, the World Bank imprint was clear.

Included in the "seven on seven," for example, was the Bank-inspired expansion of the twelve trading houses that had been created in response to the 1977 Bank economic memorandum.[98] With the plethora of late 1979 policies that preceded the SAL's signing, the link between these "twelve apostles of trade" (as they were dubbed in the Philippines) and the nontraditional-export drive was firmly forged.[99] Not just any domestic enterprise could organize these Japanese-style trading companies; the twelve were handpicked by Marcos from, as Minister Ongpin told the 1979 Consultative Group meeting, the "largest business groups in the Philippines." Their "common trait," he emphasized, was that "they were all very well managed, very successful, and very well financed."[100] Indeed, ten of the twelve were affiliated with banking institutions, while the other two were, in actuality, commercial banks.[101] Moreover, as Ongpin noted in an *Asiaweek* interview, all twelve had "international experience."[102] A close working relationship between the trading companies and the Ministry of Trade was initiated, with the latter carving up the globe to assign each group a foreign country or region of responsibility.[103]

Over the same period, Philippine businesses producing for the domestic market were losing privileged ties with government. Acting on Bank advice, the government moved to scrap its decade-long "overcrowded" industries policy whereby new investment was tailored to the domestic economy's capacity to absorb a particular industry's output. That policy, explained Ortaliz (who in July of 1979 assumed the chairmanship of the

Overcrowded Industries Committee), was "seen by the World Bank and us in the Ministry of Industry to be just an import-substitution policy. . . . What about export demand?"[104]

With new investments now encouraged in such previously off-limit industries as electrical appliances, steel products, cement, processed foods, tin cans, soft drinks, and batteries (among others), the arena for TNC investment was considerably expanded. This, as Minister Sicat acknowledged, was part and parcel of the revitalized competition the government sought. The government did not passively wait for foreign investors to take advantage of the liberalization; it actively pursued them, to the extent of requiring foreign partners for new cement plants.[105]

At the same time, Virata's letter to McNamara concerning the SAL revealed that the "government has also started actively dialoguing with 140 of the largest manufacturing companies each having a substantial domestic market base to motivate them to focus more attention on exports."[106] In other words, by redirecting goods once destined for the domestic market toward export markets, the Philippines could, at least potentially, earn millions of dollars in foreign exchange even without new investments— and, in the process, nationalist businessmen could be turned into transnationalists. The government reasoned that such exports could more than offset the foreign-exchange-consuming imports required to satisfy the resulting domestic market shortages.

Above all else, however, the policies' consistency—be they tariff reforms, import liberalization, exchange-rate reduction, or investment and export incentives—was to be found in their focus on nontraditional-export promotion. New industrial investments, vowed the Board of Investments (which itself was reorganized according to Bank specifications), would be labor-intensive.[107] Companies importing capital goods could expect approval of foreign loans only if their production processes were geared to exports, decreed the Central Bank.[108] And such was the trend.

The IMF's Hidden Role

The question was posed to members of the Philippine government's interagency committee for the SAL reforms: was the Fund involved in any way? Most responded that "the IMF was interested in what was going on."[109] That is, "the IMF is always interested in the Philippine government's other involvements. . . . Of course, the IMF has to stick its nose everywhere."[110] Upon deeper probing of perceptions of IMF actual involvement, a fairly unanimous chorus answered: no, this was a World Bank loan, not an IMF loan, so there was no reason for direct IMF involvement.

At this point in most interviews, the textbook distinction between the two institutions was carefully elucidated. One of NEDA's highest officials explained, "The IMF deals only with the Central Bank and deals with short-term balance-of-payments developments and exchange restrictions, whereas the World Bank, which is involved not with the Central Bank, but with specific development projects, . . . has a long-run view of development and structural problems."[111] This official spoke for most Philippine government officials when he asserted that while the two institutions "stand as complementary, not competitive, interests," the SAL "involved the World Bank alone . . . although IMF missions might have occasionally coincidentally overlapped with Bank missions."[112]

Such answers do not seem intent on deception. Indeed, this perception was, for the most part, to be expected, given the Bank's and the Fund's conscious fostering of that image of mutual independence. But in the case of the Philippine SAL, as in others, it was far from the truth. In the area of exchange-rate policy reform, the IMF had stepped out of the limelight, but it was by no means out of the picture. And although the IMF and the World Bank maintained distinctly different concerns in theory, their commitment to collaboration—sealed in the 1966 memorandum and its 1970 revision—was heightened with the advent of structural adjustment lending. As the May 1980 discussions between Bank and Fund managements to update that memorandum of collaboration noted:

> There has been collaboration between the two institutions for a long time. But the importance of intensifying and ameliorating it is certainly present in our minds now, if only because both the Fund and Bank are moving somewhat beyond their customary practices. They are doing so because the world is changing and circumstances demand this. . . . In other words, collaboration is a matter of immediate concern.[113]

Recognizing the need to keep the IMF's imprint concealed, the Bank and the Fund structured collaboration over the SAL in ways that would escape the Philippine government's notice. On one level, the institutions' cooperation simply kept pace with what were already long-established procedures for a Bank and Fund partnership in the Philippines. Given its prominence in both Bank and Fund lending programs, disclosed an IMF official well acquainted with the Philippines, the country had become

> one of our special cases, with lots of interaction because both the World Bank and the IMF have lots of interests in the Philippines. Reports are sent to each other before being published. Questions the other has are cleared up before the reports are issued. . . . So, at any point in time, there is knowledge of what each other is doing. . . . Many contacts between the two organizations exist.
>
> And, of course, as [our] interests in the Philippines increase—as with the Bank's structural adjustment loan—the number of reports increases, so the contact between us increases. . . . It's hard to say if these are formal or informal . . . [it] doesn't matter. What matters is if those contacts work. And here, we're seeing that they do. . . . With the World Bank, the IMF's been quite successful in recent Philippine work.[114]

No longer did Bank and Fund cooperation in the Philippines merely rest on the former memos of collaboration whereby the Bank made use of IMF confidential assessments and reports (and vice versa).[115] No more was what Fund Managing Director de Larosière called the IMF's and World Bank's ability "to move and pull in the same direction" just the result of friendly meetings between the respective departments of both institutions.[116]

The SAL's broadened policy-intervention arena qualitatively changed the level of Bank-Fund collaboration. With the SAL covering the Fund's usual domain of "tariff issues and exchange restrictions—or, rather, the exchange system as a whole," commented the IMF official involved in the process, the loan "required more contact because the World Bank relied on the Fund's views and okay for these parts." In other words, draft reports were not dispatched to the Fund simply for that institution's edification or comments; they were sent for actual approval. "Everything was cleared with the Fund beforehand," declared that IMF official. Fund staff members did not necessarily author these sections of the Bank's Philippine industrial reports, but the relevant IMF divisions certainly provided ample crib notes and comments.[117]

In the final analysis, therefore, SAL advice emanated from both institutions. For the financial-sector restructuring, where the Bank was dealing directly with the Fund's sphere of influence at the Central Bank, the World Bank would go so far as to acknowledge officially that the program rested

on a report of joint Bank-Fund authorship.[118] But there was no such admission for the industrial-sector restructuring program, where the Bank
was striving to expand other ministries' domains to circumvent, if not
usurp, Central Bank powers. In this case, what was clear to both the Fund
and the Bank was that the IMF must not be viewed as trying to extend its
role outside the Central Bank in concert with the World Bank. Any visible
IMF role was perceptively recognized by the sister institutions as potentially triggering suspicions and complications.

Given the IMF's tarnished image in the Philippines, the setup was, perhaps correctly, deemed to be the most effective for getting the Fund's and
the Bank's shared advice heeded by the Philippine government. Even so, a
gnawing question remains: why was the IMF so willing to allow the World
Bank to appropriate its area of expertise? Certain lower- and middle-level
staff members in the IMF hierarchy did seem disconcerted about this.
And, although the Bank's executive directors "welcomed the close collaboration which took place between the Bank and the IMF during the
preparation of the policy reform program" for the Philippine SAL, the
Fund's board understandably seemed more concerned about the need to
retain "separate characteristics, functions, and responsibilities."[119]

But in the offices of the Fund's highest-level management, where it
mattered, there were few such misgivings. Managing Director de Larosière
announced to his staff in mid-1980, "I wish to emphasize my personal,
strong support for close, effective collaboration between the Fund and the
Bank. The importance of achieving such collaboration has increased, taking
into account the Bank's intentions to assist member countries with structural adjustment lending."[120] IMF top management discerned that by
being the actual institution behind so many of the SAL's conditions, the
IMF was certainly not bequeathing its total role to the Bank. If anything,
structural adjustment lending increased each institution's reliance on the
other.

IMF officials also understood that there would come a time in some
countries when the situation would reverse itself and the IMF would move
centerstage again.[121] In the meantime, in keeping with de Larosière's conviction that "it continues to be essential that the Bank and the Fund avoid
giving different analyses or policy advice to member countries" (words
echoed by Bank Vice-President Ernest Stern),[122] IMF standby loans backed
up the policy reforms under negotiation in the SAL. Following the EFF

came a 1979 one-year standby facility that, according to an IMF official, "continued implictly the same conditions as [were] covered by the extended fund facility."[123] On its heels, a two-year standby in December of 1979 built on similar intentions. In the same direction, 1980 IMF discussions with the Central Bank emphasized the need for policies including "measures to promote exports, to strengthen and expand the industrial sector," as well as "measures aimed at containing the rate of increase in prices and wage policy."[124]

The IMF also continued to engender allied transnationalist interests in the Central Bank, by training mid- and low-level bureaucrats. Together, the World Bank's Economic Development Institute and the IMF Institute initiated a corps of non–Western-educated Philippine bureaucrats in the technocratic conception of development.[125] Non–Central Bank employees typically traveled to EDI, and Central Bank personnel to the IMF; both destinations were considered a distinctive mark of status. Just a month or two of study in Washington, D.C., not only often brought a promotion upon return to the Philippines but also usually created strong sympathies with the exigencies of the Bank or the Fund. "Now we understand the IMF's language," summarized one Central Bank participant in a two-month IMF course. "So we work much better with the IMF."[126]

Simultaneously, a growing number of Philippine technocrats, after a stint of a few years of service within a Bank or Fund department, were welcomed by the Philippine government at higher secondary posts. Among these was Romeo Bautista who, after heading the University of the Philippines industrial protectionism study, spent more than a year at the World Bank before returning to the Philippines as a deputy director-general of NEDA. Thus, the clamor among low- and mid-level bureaucrats to be chosen for training in the Washington, D.C., world of international financial institutions grew. And with good reason: as the Bank's Ascher Memorandum noted, Philippine "bureaucrats who cannot claim the status of 'technocrat' face . . . [job] insecurity."[127]

In sum, although it was the World Bank that actively pursued policy dialogues with the Philippine government over the SAL reforms, success was greatly enhanced by the IMF's collaboration. At that moment, however, that collaboration could not be publicly acknowledged.

6

Slicing the Economic Pie

Just as different alliances of international and domestic public and private forces coalesced to determine LDC aggregate economic policies, so were these and other sets of actors affected in different ways when the policies were implemented. It is already clear that technocratic elements in the Philippine government were strengthened during the late 1970s shift in export-led growth from primary commodities to light manufactures. They were but the beginning of a long list of gainers and losers.

"Unquestionably, the impact of the policy reforms is far more important than the benefits of direct resource transfer," commented a World Bank assessment of the first year of structural adjustment lending.[1] An important part of this impact involved a highly unequal distribution of gains. Bank industrial mission chief Barend de Vries acknowledged the significance of this level of inquiry:

> Political and social objectives do . . . have a legitimate place along with economic efficiency. Who receives what portion of the economic "pie" can be as

important as how rapidly the pie grows. There is no way to escape the interaction, at the margins, of economics and politics.[2]

From the start, the World Bank foresaw such unequal impacts and, moreover, acknowledged their desirability. "Viability of the economic liberalization reforms," the Bank confided in its Ascher Memorandum (written around the time the SAL was signed), depended on the government's "political and administrative capacity . . . to implement the program without provoking highly destabilizing reactions" from those groups whose interests were forfeited.[3] Indeed, the Bank knew where those negative reactions were likely to arise, and winners and losers were at no point obscured. As the 1979 aide-mémoire warned both the loan's donor and its recipient, "The components of the policy package need to be packaged and presented in a manner and at a time that is most likely to evoke positive response from the private industrial sector and representatives of labour so that [the reforms'] objectives may be more rapidly achieved."[4] It was no secret that the toll was to fall disproportionately on the national entrepreneurs (the Filipino industrialists whose primary interest was local accumulation) and on the industrial wage-earners, whereas the transnationalists in the national arena stood to gain.

The Bank understood that poverty and income-distribution factors would be secondary to growth and efficiency as objectives of structural adjustment lending. The Bank's Bela Balassa wrote of SALs in 1981:

> To begin with, growth objectives will need to be given greater weight as compared to the income distributional objectives. This is because the shocks suffered impose limitations on the ability of the government to pursue several objectives simultaneously, and economic growth is necessary to provide the wherewithal for the alleviation of poverty.[5]

Bank economists recognized that there might be short-term differential impacts from the loans, but they failed to ask the next logical question: what precisely would be the effects of such loans on the poor? By 1983, they admitted as much *internally* with respect to the policy dialogues that are the centerpiece of SALs:

> Poverty issues have seldom featured significantly in such dialogues, and the analysis of structural adjustment programs has rarely considered who will carry the heaviest burdens of adjustment. . . . The Bank has often failed to raise, at

the highest levels, politically sensitive issues of the impact that efficiency adjustments have on poverty.[6]

Such a failure is particularly serious in a country where an estimated 46
percent of the population lived below the poverty line in 1975. By 1986,
after another decade of heavy Bank and Fund lending, that figure reached
an astounding 70 percent.[7]

Sections that follow delineate the Philippines' shifting class configuration in the manufacturing sector in the wake of the SAL reforms. These
sections draw most heavily on the experience of the textile and apparel sectors, areas that were central to SAL industrialization. Although the focus is
on the losing groups, those who gain must also be brought into perspective.

National Entrepreneurs

As the SAL reforms fell into place in the summer of 1980, three years before the assassination of Benigno Aquino, Manila was rocked by a wave of
bombs thrown by the so-called bourgeois bombers. No one made any attempt to pretend that the targets were chosen randomly: they were businesses closely linked to Marcos, his wife, and foreign capital, and they
responded with the purchase of security guards and the latest explosive-
detection devices. The alleged perpetrators: a frustrated, elite fringe of the
Filipino national entrepreneurial class, radicalized into admittedly terrorist
acts by what they viewed as their government's concessions to foreign corporations, foreign goods, and foreign markets. "Our country has been sold
out to foreign interests," accused one of the suspects some months later,
from his prison cell.[8]

The national entrepreneurs (or economic nationalists) are a difficult
group to identify specifically in the Philippine context. Roughly, they can
be divided into two groups: tens of thousands of small-factory owners and
entrepreneurs, and a few dozen large, domestically oriented conglomerates.
The former have traditionally served as the backbone of the consumer-
goods sector, producing textiles, clothing, shoes, processed food, and
other items behind the protection of tariff barriers and import restrictions.
Operating on small margins, they were highly vulnerable to the tariff and
other reforms of structural adjustment. The larger conglomerates were more
resilient. Many had their roots in the Chinese capital that had become cen-

tral to the internal Philippine economy during the centuries of Spanish colonial rule, and many grew rapidly during the import-substitution industrialization years of the 1950s.

As early as 1934, several of these economic nationalists had banded together to form the National Economic Protectionism Association (NEPA).
In subsequent years, increasing numbers united behind the association's
efforts in "protecting and promoting the interests of the Filipino entrepreneurs and professionals, by espousing economic nationalism, so that the
Filipino shall be Sole Determinant and Principal Beneficiary of this nation's economic development, which can be properly and sooner achieved
by an All-Out Industrialization based on an expanded 'Filipino First' policy."[9] On the eve of the Second World War, NEPA boasted 38 provincial
chapters and 160 municipal and barrio chapters. Through the years, it has
served as a research, lobbying, and public relations organization of national
entrepreneurs.

It was the large conglomerates that the World Bank and the Philippine
Tariff Commission had targeted in their April 1981 conference on tariff
policy. Some would not survive the early 1980s shakeout; others would
make it by forging transnational links.

Part of the difficulty in offering precise breakdowns of national entrepreneurs is that their ranks began to be depleted in the 1960s by the other
major faction of Philippine industrialists, the transnationalists. Link-ups
with transnational corporations began as early as the nineteenth century,
but really took off in the 1960s. Link-ups through partial foreign ownership
or joint ventures proliferated until, by 1971, only one-third of the top 250
manufacturing companies in the Philippines were fully Filipino-owned.[10]
The giant Ayala corporation, for example, was tied up with Mitsubishi,
Mitsui, Sanwa, and Toshiba in eleven Japanese-Filipino joint ventures.[11]
Other firms linked up with TNCs through franchise and licensing agreements. The Philippines' largest private firm, San Miguel, became one of
the leading distributors of soft drinks in the archipelago under license and
franchise agreements with Coca-Cola to bottle and distribute Coke, Sprite,
and Fresca. Other firms joined the transnationalist faction as loan recipients from transnational banks during the borrowing spree of 1970–1982.

Among the most vocal transnationalists—and the biggest recipients of
foreign bank loans—were Marcos's so-called cronies, especially Herminio
Disini, Eduardo Cojuangco, Jr., and Ricardo Silverio. In addition to being

heavily favored in government contracts, these men created empires in large part through transnational ties. Disini netted millions of dollars from Westinghouse in his role as agent for the Bataan nuclear-power-plant deal. Silverio made it big by winning the Philippine franchise to assemble Toyota cars. Cojuangco, who created a virtual coconut monopoly, depended on diverse transnational links to market his coconut products abroad.

The categories nationalist and transnationalist are not strictly demar-cated; numerous entrepreneurs operated in both realms. Cory Aquino's trade minister, Jose Concepcion, ran businesses primarily for the domestic market. Yet his Republic Flour Mills had licensing agreements with four U.S. companies.[12] There are other complications: the transnationalist Cojuangco was staunchly opposed to the World Bank demand that, in the interests of efficiency and competition, the Philippine coconut monopoly should be ended. He would agree with the Bank, however, on most other points.

The rise of transnationalists in the private sector had weakened national entrepreneurs by the early 1980s. The SAL reforms were akin to dropping a match on dry kindling. It was this turbulent atmosphere that impelled the World Bank management to initiate Ascher's assessment of "potential problems that could affect the viability of the Bank's approach and opera-tions in the Philippines" (to quote Ascher's own summary of the memo-randum).[13] Ascher affirmed that, with the SAL-supported attack against some of the last "bulwarks of the precarious local private entrepreneurial sector" underway, the "local business community has several mutually re-inforcing reasons to try to undermine the policy directions of the current government."[14] As Peter Evans notes in the case of Brazil, the exclusion of the majority of local entrepreneurs from the benefits of dependent devel-opment "makes practical sense but it also weakens the political foundations of dependent development."[15] Thus, the Bank armed itself and its allied technocrats lest the Philippines' "industrial program based on foreign in-vestment . . . come under *strong* attack."[16]

By the early 1980s, there was no camouflaging the fact that the new economic restructuring scheme held few niches for national entrepreneurs (that is, if they hoped to continue production geared to local accumula-tion). Even the one plank of the 1980s Philippine industrial strategy that seemed to cater to national entrepreneurs had been sharply pared down under World Bank and IMF pressure. This was the $6 billion package of eleven capital-intensive, basic heavy industries, the "major industrial projects."[17] Ever since assuming office in mid-1979, the Harvard-educated Minister of Industry Roberto Ongpin had proclaimed the Philippines' resolve to march forward into basic capital-intensive industrialization. The package of eleven was his brainchild, and he proudly presented it to Marcos for use in stirring, nationalistic speeches. Ongpin felt so strongly about the projects that in late 1980 he barred from Ministry of Industry press conferences a Manila business columnist who had cited critical opinions of some of the eleven.[18]

When announced by Marcos in September 1979, the major industrial projects seemed custom-tailored to suit some of the national entrepreneurs' more pronounced demands for an industrialization strategy that, as nationalist Alejandro Lichauco phrased it, "launches us into the Machine Age."[19] As former president of the Philippine Petroleum Association, Lichauco had watched closely the saga of the first Filipino-owned oil refinery, Filoil, in the late 1950s and early 1960s. Filoil's planners had envisioned it as an all-Filipino endeavor, but lack of technological expertise and access to oil had led them to approach Gulf Oil as a minority partner (30 percent equity). Finally, in the aftermath of the 1962 IMF liberalization program, they had sold out completely to Gulf Oil. This and related events transformed Lichauco into one of the most vocal nationalists among domestic businessmen.[20] During the 1970s he wrote a series of lengthy manuscripts that charged the government with stooping to external demands and betraying domestic businesses. His deep disdain for light-manufactured export priorities led him to support the idea of major industrial projects (his disapproval of the eleven was for other reasons):

> An underdeveloped country attempting to develop its economy . . . should be concerned with something much more than simply increasing its output of beer, ice cream, soft drinks, cosmetics, toiletries, textiles, food products and other consumer items, essential and nonessential. . . .
>
> *An underdeveloped country striving to graduate into developed status should be concerned primarily with changing the structure of its productive mechanism* so that instead of being able merely to turn out consumer goods, it will be able to manufacture the machines and industrial plants, which it still has to import, that turn out these finished goods. It should develop the capability to transform its iron ore into steel ingots, instead of exporting these ores as raw materials only to import them in processed form; to manufacture its own tractors and farm and agricultural implements, produce its own machine tools, precision in-

struments, engineering and the host of other capital equipment which it still imports, and for the supply of which it remains dependent on the productive mechanism of the developed countries.[21]

At first, the major industrial package—including a petrochemical complex, heavy engineering industries, an integrated steel mill, aluminum smelter, and so on—appeared to satisfy Lichauco's criteria. Indeed, Ongpin couched the idea in terms that could have been Lichauco's own: "If only labor-intensive industry is developed, we would have an imbalanced industrial structure which would be forever vulnerable and without sound foundation, because it must rely on imports of basic raw materials. We would be merely a country of sweatshops, processing through our cheap labor the produce of the industrialized countries around us."[22]

Although the Philippine government tended to lump the major industrial package with the rest of the SAL reforms for domestic publicity purposes, neither the World Bank nor the IMF was pleased with the government's attempt to pursue projects that (according to the Bank) did "not harmonize well" with the overall SAL policy thrusts.[23] "The orientation of industry must necessarily be labor-intensive," wrote industry mission chief de Vries publicly, in clear rebuttal of the eleven.[24] Before bestowing its blessing on Philippine industrial restructuring, the Bank demanded what it termed "clarifications."[25]

In December 1979, only a couple of months after the Philippine government had inaugurated the idea of the eleven projects with great fanfare, Minister Ongpin stood before the World Bank–led Consultative Group to explain away the doubts. It was a meeting from which the Philippine government hoped to garner financial and verbal backing for its overall industrial restructuring. Ongpin's defense of the major industrial package totally betrayed the concerns of the national entrepreneurs. To the maximum extent possible, he vowed, the projects would be foreign-owned—indeed, up to 100 percent so—and export-oriented.[26] "Now the government's chatting away about major industrial projects that will do nothing for Philippine development, as they'll be controlled by foreigners," lamented Lichauco. "So much for basic industries . . . and we'll continue to import hand tools. It's the same old thing: make way for foreign corporations; push domestic business aside."[27]

Continued remonstrances by the World Bank and the IMF against the set of eleven necessitated even further capitulations. "Our mistake was in announcing the eleven as one package," alleged a top NEDA official in late 1980. "Because now if the government should come to believe that maybe a few should be postponed, how can we back down without losing face at home?"[28] Why the government might want to back down was clear: although the World Bank approved of Ongpin's two new caveats as far as some of the projects were concerned, it was exerting heavy pressure on the Philippines to scuttle others, especially the steel mill and the petrochemical complex—both, in the view of nationalists such as Lichauco, critical for autonomous Philippine industrialization.[29]

Again the Philippine government retreated. "What my minister [Ongpin] meant when he said [in September 1979] we were going to implement the eleven major industrial projects," offered Ortaliz in January 1981, "was that economic and financial feasibility studies would be undertaken. Project implementation begins with [determining] feasibility."[30] Conveniently ignored were earlier documents and announcements on the major industrial projects that had cited completed, favorable feasibility studies for the whole group.[31] Thus, although Ongpin's rhetoric remained firm, by November of 1981—almost halfway through the original implementation timetable for completion of the eleven—Minister Virata was able to voice his forebodings that feasibility studies would disclose some of the projects not to be "viable." High on the list for scrapping, he intimated to the seventh annual Philippine Business Conference, might well be the petrochemical complex. Moreover, that listing was likely to have more than one entry.[32]

Virata's late-1981 premonitions were buttressed by Marcos himself, who took the opportunity at the same gathering to reiterate the need for "world competitive" industrial projects "based on comparative advantage."[33] It was quite a contrast to his "strategy to survival" speech unveiling the eleven projects two years earlier. Then he had warned, "If we don't shift gears today and get on the . . . fast track, I am concerned that we won't be able to catch up and that we shall be left in the dust of those we follow."[34] Something more consequential than shifting feasibility projections had recast that speech. As Marcos told it, "Only fools don't change their minds."[35] One of Virata's staff members explained the policy change somewhat more convincingly: "Without World Bank support [for specific projects], we had no chance of getting [private Western] bank loans. And without bank loans, there was no chance of going ahead with the $6 billion package. We had no choice."[36]

As far as national entrepreneurs were concerned, the World Bank's power to influence economic policies that in the end affected their survival was ominous. Shattering national entrepreneurs' dream of domestically owned and oriented basic industries in the face of the exigencies of a government that needed the Bank's seal of approval was only a first step. It coincided with increasing numbers of national entrepreneurs falling into bankruptcy as a result of Bank-prompted reforms that opened the door to foreign investment and goods. The World Bank's influence in deciding domestic fates became all the more obvious as the institution carved itself a direct role in setting the future course of industrial development in individual subsectors. Included on the Bank's list of priority subsectors to realign were textiles, food processing, furniture, leather and leather products, and mechanical engineering [37]—all related to the nontraditional-manufactured-export drive and all increasingly to be under foreign corporate control through TNC investment and subcontracting.

Although most of this subsector work was scheduled through individual Bank project loans, the restructuring was part and parcel of the Bank's SAL program. [38] "Directly related to the SAL," Ortaliz confirmed, "will be the rehabilitation and modernization of the textile industry . . . which will demonstrate an industry-specific restructuring program . . . involving shifting emphasis away from protection [through the decreased tariff rates] . . . and then financing [the equipment for] those firms that can be competitive in the world market." [39]

Although the impetus for the textile restructuring had come from the Bank's SAL work, the Philippine government had expected that it alone—without the World Bank—would take over this program once the SAL reforms were in place. But the Bank had no intention of giving the government sole command. As Ortaliz added later, "The Bank insisted [on helping] through a project loan. And, of course, we don't mind a little extra help—financial and otherwise." [40] Why had the Bank been so insistent? Noriega offered a hypothesis based on his experience with Bank missions: "I think they just wanted to make sure we'd use the new environment [of tariff cuts, etc.] to the fullest. You know, it's sometimes hard for them just to sit back and watch us make the decisions." [41]

After one month in-country, an April 1980 World Bank team formulated a master plan for the textile-sector restructuring. At the Bank's discretion rested such key decisions as "the most economical size for local textile mills, the most appropriate locations and types of products to be produced—among others," disclosed Minister Ongpin.[42] To ensure that the restructuring would not deviate from the Bank's suggestions, a $157.5 million textile project loan was promised.[43] That amount was modest in relation to the estimated $600 million total cost of the imported spinning, weaving, and finishing equipment that the program envisaged.[44] But it was enough to sanction the Bank's continuing direct oversight.

In early January 1981, Dewey Dee, a dominant corporate actor in the Philippine textile and apparel sectors, fled the country, leaving in his wake a tangled web of unpaid debts amounting to nearly $90 million.[45] Some contended that the plunging textile tariffs provoked Dee's downfall. Whatever the catalyst, the businessman's hasty flight presaged a rough period for domestic textile entrepreneurs. As a senior government official admitted:

> Actually, Dewey Dee made it easier for us to weed out the firms that we'll help modernize from those that we won't. . . . Restructuring means that we'll see firms collapsing, merging, and modernizing as they're forced to export. . . . The Dewey Dee caper only got this off to a head start.[46]

Of the hundreds of textile mills engaged in spinning, weaving, knitting, or finishing nationwide, about twenty possessed large, integrated operations. Only these and a few others were big enough to potentially survive the rigors of the World Bank's blueprint for restructuring, with its stringent requirements concerning management, rates of return, potential for increased equity, past as well as potential export performance, and—most difficult of all to meet—the requirement that they purchase one-quarter of the new machinery with their own resources.[47] Complained an executive from one of the outcast firms:

> Look, we've been making cloth that Filipinos have their tailors make into clothes. Now the government lets in similar cloth cheaper . . . and, as if that weren't enough, it tells us we've got to specialize, we've got to export . . . or produce cloth for exporters [of apparel]. Then, if we can prove we can cut production costs by 40 percent, and pay for a good chunk of the machines ourselves . . . we can get a loan for the rest. . . . We can't. Certainly not after the Dewey Dee affair. But I doubt we could have anyway. We don't have those [necessary] banking or international connections. So we can't. . . . So most of the companies like ours will die. . . .
>
> Some of us have been talking about boycotting the program. But if the biggest textile mills, with their international interests, are able to comply, a boycott's not likely to do us much good. . . . Either way, it seems, we smaller guys producing domestically are on the way out.[48]

No one denied that the restructuring was intended to buttress the handful of largest, most modern mills and to weed out the rest quickly. According to Ramon Siy, president of the thirty-two-member Textile Mills Association of the Philippines, the textile industry was to "go through a process of elimination."[49] That is, smaller mills were being forced to merge with the larger ones or "die a natural death. . . . The weaker ones will have to close down."[50]

Siy's glibness came as no surprise. Among the beneficiaries of the restructuring was likely to be his Unisol Industries and Manufacturing Corporation. Using imported raw materials and boasting a fully automated range of the most modern West German and Swiss machinery, Unisol produced knitted fabric, under order from Hong Kong. The rest of its output was further processed by the apparel industry and exported.[51] A sign of things to come in the Philippine textile industry, Unisol's 37,000 spindles turned twenty-four hours a day, seven days a week, under the supervision of four hundred laborers. (For that same number of spindles, the soon-to-be liquidated older mills would have employed two and a half times that number of workers.)[52] As a 1981 United Nations Industrial Development Organization study of the global semiconductor industry noted, it was not simply "low overall labour costs" that led to the relocation of export-oriented industrial production processes to countries like the Philippines. A second factor was "greater machine utilization made possible by the longer annual work hours characteristic for countries with high degrees of internal repression and severely constrained trade union movements."[53]

Unisol was not merely surviving; it was expanding further into the export market with a new weaving mill whose sheet and shirt fabrics were likewise destined for completion overseas.[54] Said Siy, such "staple items" were being phased out in Hong Kong and Taiwan, which, with their higher labor costs, instead "enter[ed] into making the high-priced, high-fashion items." This, he continued, left a gap to be filled by firms such as Unisol.[55]

Joining Siy among the healthy survivors of the textile-sector shakedown was likely to be another textile group whose reach was widening, with the government's blessing: the Patricio Lim group. Upstream in the production process, Lim's Filipinas Synthetic Fiber Corporation (Filsyn), a joint venture organized by Japan's number-two textile company (Teijin) and Japan's largest cotton trader (the general trading company Toyo Menka Kaisha), began operations in the early 1970s. Taking advantage of the favorable climate offered by the recent rationalization drive, in 1981 Filsyn acquired its sole competitor in the polyester staple-fiber and filament-yarn field. At that point, producing an estimated 70 percent of the textile industry's total fiber and yarn inputs, Filsyn held a quasi-monopoly. Making the most of the situation, Filsyn raised its prices more than 60 percent above the world market level, leaving its affiliated mills in a position to take over nonaffiliated mills floundering not only from the restructuring but also as a result of the higher fiber prices.[56]

When asked whether Filsyn's cornering of that fiber market might put Lim's textile mills in a monopolistic position, a Philippine Securities and Exchange Commission commissioner stressed the "need for bigness" in certain sectors if the Philippines was to achieve "faster economic growth."[57] Those sentiments were repeated, in the context of Philippine economic restructuring as a whole, by another ranking government official: "It's all part of the general concept of greater exposure to competition—we shake industries to make them more competitive. Letting firms go under if they can't survive competitively, while the surviving few get bigger and bigger, is good for us."[58]

In other words, under the catchword "competition," World Bank–conceived restructuring meant liquidation for some textile firms. For others, it entailed selling out to TNCs or to one of the two dozen or so transnationalist Philippine business groups, such as Lim's, that dominated local affiliations with TNCs.[59] Competition, however, must be understood for what it was. Whatever else Bank economists had in mind with their call for "efficient and competitive" structures, in neither the industrial sector nor the financial sector was restructuring geared to fostering competition among those that prevailed.[60] Export potential and past performance stood as preconditions for inclusion in the Bank-funded textile restructuring program—and thus, as preconditions for survival. But once this benchmark of international competitiveness was passed, the benefits were to be distributed in an orderly fashion: the Ministry of Industry's Board of Investments (with the help of Bank-funded consultants) would decide which particular products each of the mills accepted into the program would produce.[61]

Ironically, the textile loan was stalled for four years and was eventually scrapped. Thirty-one firms qualified for the program by 1982, but, ultimately, none could come up with adequate financing for the 25 percent of new equipment costs they were expected to cover themselves. Hard hit by declining tariffs and stagnant markets, in the early 1980s the industry went into a tailspin from which it has yet to recover. In March 1986, textile mills were running at only 40 percent of capacity.[62] Yet a few firms—among them Unisol and Filsyn—were not only surviving but were doing quite well.[63]

As the SAL-related economic restructuring proceeded, the "bourgeois bombers" took the offensive. But most Filipino businessmen producing for the domestic market responded through poorly organized protests aimed at self-preservation. The Nationalist Economic Protectionism Association petitioned against the reforms, charging that with the bankruptcies would come accelerated foreign control.[64] Filipino producers in the Philippine Chamber of Commerce and Industry accused the government of dislocating local industries.[65] As the Bank's policies pushing concentration and rationalization worked synergistically with stagnation in the global economy after 1980, the "few highly visible plant closings" the Bank had predicted began,[66] and the complaints escalated. But, after a time, as the Bank statement implied, the closings became less visible: only boarded doors and windows of small, domestically oriented firms in Manila's textile, shoe, and garment districts stood as testimony.

In private, members of the national entrepreneurial class complained that they had no hope of survival. With Virata elevated to the post of prime minister in July 1981, the economic changes seemed cemented in place; no more was to be gained from public condemnations and protests. By and large, they talked as broken and desperate people with little choice but to await domestic demise as the five-year reform schedule ran to its close.[67]

Among the national entrepreneurs, the main bursts of activity emanated from the richest and best connected, such as millionaire Hilarion Henares, Jr., who attempted to use influential friends to obtain the necessary documents and loans for converting their production processes for the export market. Henares, whose name called forth the epithet of "nationalist," was known as one who disdained transnationalists and who professed to have kept his hands clean of involvement with foreign corporations and foreign markets. But by early 1980, he claimed, there was no other way—it was a matter of "export or perish":

> It's a tragedy. The Philippines is importing a perfect substitute for what I will be exporting [coconut-based alcohol]. . . . The multinational corporations controlling that sector here—Procter and Gamble, Unilever, Colgate, . . .—are all

importing it. . . . But with all the loans and tax exemptions reserved solely for exporters, how can I afford not to export?

I believe it is our duty to produce for the domestic market. But I don't want to perish.[68]

In November 1980, Ascher translated into writing the World Bank's fear that because industrial restructuring had opened the doors for more than five times the foreign investment in 1980 than the annual average for the previous decade, the Bank's "imprimatur on the industrial program runs the risk of drawing criticism of the Bank as the servant of multinational corporations and particularly of U.S. economic imperialism."[69] Fear of retaliation from "bourgeois bombers" even prompted Bank officials to hastily shift the site of the January 1981 Philippine Consultative Group meeting from Manila to Paris.[70] Over the course of the next year, however, that worry subsided considerably. Responding to a November 1981 U.S. congressional inquiry on the effects of the Philippine "economic reforms" on "political stability," a U.S. State Department spokesperson summed up the national entrepreneurs' plight:

> We do not think the political dislocations created . . . will seriously test [the Philippine government's] ability to manage [the reforms]. . . .
>
> We believe that the . . . [reforms'] application . . . will create some political difficulties that are transitory, manageable, and worth the pain. The most serious political effect would be created by the failure to pursue the reforms—which would affect confidence in the future. But the economy's management is held in high regard and we don't see that happening now.[71]

As Ascher had hazarded to guess, the "capacity" of local industrialists to oppose the reforms effectively had been "eroded by their own economic decline."[72] Henares, the nationalist being forced into world markets, agreed: "Maybe I can survive by exporting, but, as a whole, we domestic businessmen are a dying breed."[73] Nor, at the other end of the social spectrum, were industrial wage-earners faring any better.

Industrial Wage-Earners

Both the World Bank and the IMF have external-relations departments and both know the value of public relations and careful packaging of their products. At times, industrial-sector reforms implemented through the

SAL have been billed as a strategy of "poverty redressal."[74] "For the poorer of the population groups," emphasized de Vries in a 1980 article based on the Philippine experience, "industry can lead the way to higher incomes, since its jobs are productive and rewarding."[75]

Five years earlier, the IMF had offered the hypothesis that investment in Philippine export-oriented industries would render moot the distributional question by generating "sufficient economic growth to increase the demand for labor and ultimately to raise real incomes."[76] That same trickle-down theory of alleviating urban poverty was echoed in the Bank's assessment of Philippine poverty (the so-called Poverty Report). There it was forecast that the new mix of reforms, by increasing "the growth of output," would "cause overall tightening of the labor market [that] should directly benefit the lower income classes through increased real wages."[77] In other words, at different times the World Bank and the IMF both postulated that industrial wage-earners would reap rewards from export-oriented industrialization in one of two ways: either through higher wage levels, or through increased employment opportunities.

If both institutions were sincere in their beliefs, it seems unreasonable for the Bank to have feared destabilizing reprisals from representatives of labor. In actuality, however, their conjectures regarding wage levels and employment rates were negated by a wealth of evidence to the contrary, derived not only from the unraveling of the new Philippine industrial order but also from the pages of Bank and Fund reports.

Export-oriented industrialization was constructed with the concept of "comparative advantage" in a new international division of labor at its core. Through the SAL, the World Bank prodded the Philippine government to take advantage of its precious resource: cheap labor. "The idea is simple, and it's working," explained Central Bank Deputy Governor Bince. "We have lower labor costs than in other countries. . . . And so now that we are providing the proper environment, plants are moving here because of our lower costs of labor."[78] By the early 1980s, the TNC influx certainly had accelerated under the SAL's lucrative export incentives. Relocating from South Korea, Malaysia, and Singapore, "U.S. electronics manufacturers are rushing into the Philippines as an alternative," confirmed *Business Week* in mid-1980.[79]

To generate an even greater TNC response to these lower wages, the World Bank industrial mission had proposed international subcontracting

to Philippine small-scale and cottage industries as having "excellent potential for expanding the production of labor-intensive manufactured export
items and for increasing the productivity and employment of the urban
poor."[80] Hence, according to Minister of Industry Roberto Ongpin, the
Philippine government took it upon itself to do more than just "provide
the facilities for large multinationals to come in and do the more labor-
intensive aspects of their operations in this country." As he elaborated, "We
know that we have a substantial labor cost advantage in the Philippines and
we would like to capitalize on this by making an arrangement with the
large multinationals whereby they would . . . subcontract the more labor-
intensive aspects of their operations to us in the Philippines."[81]

Indeed, the flexibility of such subcontracting arrangements often seemed
to TNCs as good as, if not preferable to, implanting wholly owned subsidiaries. In the late 1970s, over half of Philippine apparel exports resulted
from international subcontracting.[82] In the other leading export-oriented
industry, electronics, two or three big Filipino-owned companies, producing under subcontract for U.S. and Japanese electronics firms, dominated
the sector.[83]

To some extent, foreign corporations' preference for subcontracting arrangements derived from an uneasiness about Philippine political stability.
More than that, however, it emanated from an awareness that the Philippines' "comparative advantage" might not (with lower wages available in
China, Sri Lanka, and elsewhere) be a permanent phenomenon. For the
time being, however, several foreign-owned firms relocated labor-intensive
production operations (such as Mattel's Barbie doll-making) in Philippine
EPZs either directly or indirectly through subcontracts. This was, the local
press announced to the Filipino people, because "the country is excellent
for the purpose. For within ASEAN [Association of Southeast Asian Na-
tions], the level of wages here is the lowest."[84]

Minister Ongpin elaborated exactly how low was "lowest" at the December 1979 Philippine Consultative Group meeting, as he sought to mus-
ter additional international approval for Philippine development initiatives:

> Our labor cost is competitive. . . . A recent survey by one of the big three in the
> U.S. electronics industry, and one of the big three in the world, points out the
> following. The effective cost of labor in the Philippines, including fringe bene-
> fits in addition to the basic wage, is 49 US cents an hour. In Singapore it is
> 95 US cents an hour; in Taiwan 85 US cents per hour; and in Hong Kong al-
> most three times as high as the Philippines, $1.41 US cents [sic] per hour.[85]

The truth was that Philippine wage levels were not simply low: they had actually declined substantially in real terms over the decade—a fact corroborated by separate findings of the World Bank and the U.N. International Labour Organization (see Table 5).[86] By one Bank analysis, real wages fell by 25 to 30 percent between 1970 and 1980, and erosion continued after 1980.[87] Although the confidential draft of the Bank's Poverty Report termed "the phenomenon of an almost 50 percent drop" in Manila-area real wages over the fifteen-year period from 1960 to 1975 "startling and . . . the source of moderately high incidence of poverty among wage earners,"[88] Bank development strategy was based on precisely that phenomenon. "The Philippines is in a strong position to continue expanding its nontraditional exports," the 1979 Bank industrial appraisal mission observed. And it was very explicit as to the reason: "Philippine wages have declined significantly relative to those in competing and customer countries."[89]

In analyzing this decline, the two versions of the Bank's Poverty Report are not always consistent. The revised "restricted" version of the original "confidential" draft[90] placed most of the blame on the Philippines' protectionist tendencies. An application of the 1941 Stolper-Samuelson theorem, it asserted, proved that tariffs, by increasing the relative price of the Philippines' more capital-intensive imports, would simultaneously exert a downward pressure on real wages.[91] The implication was unmistakable: economic liberalization would reverse the situation.

But the original report, while acknowledging this explanation, gave credence to a slightly different interpretation of that tenet of traditional international economics. The Bank argued there that because Philippine nontraded goods were relatively labor-intensive, imports were capital-intensive, and exports were natural-resource-intensive and land-intensive, "we would therefore expect that a fall in the relative price of the most labor-intensive (i.e., nontraded) commodities would for the reasons emphasized by Stolper-Samuelson lead to an unambiguous decline in the real wage rate."[92] It was, this analysis continued, such policies as the "large devaluation of 1969" that triggered the plunge in real wages, by bringing "massive rises in the prices of traded relative to nontraded goods."[93] It was devaluations—the IMF's standard remedy—and not tariffs that were deemed the worst enemy of maintaining real wages.

However, in the final analysis, the whole debate was peripheral to the Philippines at this historical moment. For even if Stolper-Samuelson re-

Table 5.   Real Wage-Rate Index of Skilled and Unskilled Laborers in Manila
            and Suburbs, 1954–1978 (1972 = 100)

	Skilled Laborers[a]	Unskilled Laborers[a]	Salaried Employees	Wage-Earners
1954	140.1	113.4	118.1	109.5
1955	141.5	117.8	123.5	113.8
1956	138.1	116.6	121.7	112.3
1957	135.7	113.4	122.2	114.2
1958	135.6	110.3	124.6	111.5
1959	139.5	112.2	131.5	117.3
1960	133.4	107.9	133.5	119.3
1961	131.2	108.8	134.4	117.8
1962	125.5	105.9	131.0	113.0
1963	122.3	105.6	128.2	108.1
1964	115.1	98.6	121.0	104.3
1965	115.2	102.7	119.3	107.8
1966	114.9	104.8	119.0	112.8
1967	113.1	103.2	113.8	112.3
1968	119.4	112.1	116.8	110.3
1969	123.3	115.2	119.9	112.7
1970	114.4	111.6	109.7	105.9
1971	105.1	104.1	103.0	99.9
1972	100.0	100.0	100.0	100.0
1973	92.4	90.0	96.6	89.4
1974	75.6	72.8	79.5	73.5
1975	72.7	72.9	82.4	76.1
1976	71.2	72.3	86.7	82.3
1977	72.9	70.4	—	—
1978	76.1	68.4	—	—

SOURCE: World Bank, *The Philippines: Poverty, Basic Needs, and Employment: A Review and Assessment,* draft of Report 2984–PH, n.d., p. 113A, table 4.3.

[a] Real wage-rate index has been obtained by deflating money wage-rate index by the consumer price index (1972 = 100) in Manila.

sults did indicate that labor's wages should rise in the aftermath of the SAL policy package, the Philippine government, the Bank, and the Fund had agreed that this would not happen. As early as 1974, Marcos had given his vow: "We intend to see to it that our export program is not placed in jeopardy . . . by a rapid rise in wage level."[94] How this promise was translated into policy was illustrated in April and September 1979 minimum-wage and cost-of-living increases from which labor-intensive, export-oriented industries—among them, electronics firms—were exempted.[95] The high inflation rates that had prompted the government's acquiescence to the general increase in the first place meant that in these specially designated industries real wages had actually fallen. Such policies won accolades from the foreign corporate community. As Business International reported in 1980, "Philippine labor remains among the cheapest in the world. . . . The [relevant] minimum wage has less than doubled in the last seven years and only tripled since the sixties."[96]

Given such an enthusiastic response, the Philippine government, under different circumstances, might well have willingly initiated this iron-fisted wage policy on its own. But, this time, it came on the imperative of the IMF and the World Bank. Cautions about the necessity of holding down wages so as not to "introduce undesirable distortions in the economy" appeared in IMF reports,[97] while Bank reports spoke of wage restraint in positive terms.[98] Such advice permeated the SAL discussions, according to a Philippine government participant in those policy dialogues:

> The [Bank] mission warned us that if wages rose, nothing would work. We have to grow . . . we have to compete with other countries' low wages. The answer, we agreed, was not to redistribute income through higher wages. It is better to grow and to keep wages artificially low.[99]

Building rationalizations on Stolper-Samuelson calculations and the like, the Bank and the Fund have consistently denied their role in furthering repressive wage structures in countries like the Philippines. Instead, the blame is pushed onto others. Displaying this inculpable attitude, Gloria Scott, head of the Bank's Women and Development Program, claimed the institution's innocence: "It is not our responsibility if the multinationals come in and offer such low wages. It's the responsibility of the governments."[100] An IMF official agreed with those sentiments: "It's the governments that must make such political judgments about the appropriate wage levels, not us. We simply provided an economic program for economic stability and development."[101]

But responsibility for the plight of wage-earners cannot be so easily dismissed. As part of the 1980 and 1981 two-year standby program for the Philippines (developed in the context of the SAL reforms), an IMF report noted succinctly, "Wages are expected to lag behind the increase in prices."[102] It was a seemingly successful exercise in this regard. "During the course of [SAL] negotiations," revealed Ortaliz, "the [Bank] mission expressed satisfaction that our level of wages was appropriate."[103]

What stands as "appropriate" from the Bank and Fund perspective is shocking from other viewpoints. In late 1980, according to the Philippine Wage Commission, the average Filipino family of six required a 50.46 peso daily wage to reach a minimum subsistence level. At that date, the minimum daily wage (P18) plus cost-of-living allowances (P17.17) for non-agricultural workers fell far short of the target.[104] According to a later study by the Bank, in 1979 the average daily wage in urban areas was one and a half times the poverty threshold. By 1983, it had fallen to just above the poverty line.[105]

In many factories, the true wage story was even more dismal, putting even two-wage-earner families below the minimum subsistence level. Compliance with the minimum wage could never be taken for granted, and full payment of the various cost-of-living allowances—from which firms could exempt themselves by pleading financial distress[106]—was more the exception than the rule. According to a University of Pennsylvania researcher, "The most common violation of [Philippine] labor laws involved the non-payment of minimum wage and wage supplements."[107] That author contended that an estimated 40 percent of Manila's workers did not receive the minimum wage; a Manila newspaper reported in March 1981 that the minimum-wage law covered only 15 percent of the labor force.[108] The Employers' Confederation of the Philippines offered the startling revelation that a mere 10 percent of the business community had complied with the wage and allowance minimums since 1976.[109]

With such a spectrum of divergent statistics, a precise description of the industrial wage-earners' plight is difficult. But, as a Manila social worker suggested:

> Right now it's questionable whether low-skilled industrial workers' wages are even up to the Marxian level of "self-reproduction." Look at workers in export processing zones. . . . We're seeing lots more protein deficiency . . . malnutrition among these families. What food they can buy with their daily wage keeps shrinking. . . . Once they probably could have bought enough fish and rice . . . to fill stomachs. Now it's often just rice (even if the children are also working). Stomachs are no longer full. . . . And we're very afraid for the mental capacities of the next generation. . . . We just can't live and reproduce at these wage levels.[110]

Helping to hold down the low industrial wages was government emasculation of labor rights. "Trade union activity itself has remained restricted in recent years which . . . allowed the [labor] market to operate more freely and prevented any significant increase in the earnings of any specific labor groups," the Bank's draft Poverty Report noted approvingly.[111]

A gap in enforcement of antistrike legislation between the January 1981 lifting of martial law and the June 1981 presidential election, therefore, worried the World Bank, foreign investors, and government technocrats alike.[112] "Filipinos take advantage of these freedoms, you see," explained a ranking technocrat during that period. "With the current strike a day, how can export-oriented 'vital industries' compete worldwide?"[113]

Yet, in the first four months of this six-month span, of the 138 strikes reported (52 of them in the so-called vital industries),[114] almost all were wage-motivated, in reaction either to noncompliance with minimum wage and allowance pay schedules or simply to the general decline of wages in the face of inflation.[115] Moreover, even during this period, strike activity was far from unhindered: at least four strikers were brutally murdered as they walked picket lines.[116]

In any case, soon after Marcos's election victory, he reneged on his campaign promise to restore strikers' rights. Cabinet Bill 45 returned the labor climate to that of martial-law years. High on the lengthy list of industries where strikes were, in effect, banned were those within EPZs. These industries, it was argued, were crucial to "national interests."[117] *Whose* "national interests" was becoming increasingly clear.

Of the two principal facets of the industrial wage-earners' plight, low wages and low employment levels, the draft Poverty Report had ascribed more weight to the first in concluding that poverty was worsening: "What appears to explain the level of poverty among wage earners and, at least partly, the increase in poverty over time is the level and movement of real wages."[118] However, in January 1981, when Minister Sicat stood before the Consultative Group to explain his government's perception that poverty was declining, he built his defense on employment trends. He attacked the leaked Poverty Report's central focus on plunging wage levels, arguing instead for a wider analysis that included the steps the Philippine government was taking to fight poverty. Paramount among these, he claimed, was offering increased employment opportunities through the labor-intensive, nontraditional-export drive.[119]

Sicat undoubtedly knew he was on fairly safe ground in this line of defense. Whatever the allegations of the confidential poverty assessment, the stated rationale of the IMF and the World Bank for export-oriented industrialization tended to focus heavily on a resulting increase in employment levels. As the expurgated, restricted version of the Poverty Report had explained, because the Philippines' new industrial development strategy "might" bring new employment opportunities to one million families, it was to be lauded as a "poverty alleviation" policy for the working class.[120] Part of the reason for the wage restraint was to allow for just such an expansion in the industrial labor force, Fund and Bank missions had emphasized throughout the 1970s.[121] In other words, the theoretical argument went, if employment rose, even falling real wages could be equated with a higher total wage-income level.

Unfortunately, this was not the case with Philippine labor-intensive industrialization. A 1976 World Bank *Country Program Paper* estimated that Philippine industrial policy, to be "reasonably successful" in employment terms, had to provide "at least 75,000 new jobs a year" by the early 1980s.[122] By comparison, the Philippines' three operating EPZs boasted a total employment force of 22,988 in 1980, 22,644 in 1981, and only 21,125 as of mid-1986.[123] Yet mission chief de Vries intimated in 1980 that by creating 360,000 new jobs by the year 1985, the Bank's export-oriented industrial thrust for the Philippines would be able to meet those severe stipulations.[124]

There were major problems in the Bank's employment projections, however. First, the figures were based more on the public-relations needs of the moment than on solid economic analysis.[125] A more critical problem was what the figures omitted: unemployment emanating from the industrial restructuring and rationalization was left unmentioned. The latter the industrial mission tossed aside as "insignificant" in comparison with the 600,000 or 700,000 additional job-seekers each year and, therefore, irrelevant to the calculations at hand.[126]

Indeed, the industrial mission's employment projections were even challenged by another department within the Bank—internally, of course. The draft Poverty Report contained a scathing indictment of the industrial mission's sloppy economic analysis—if not outright whitewash—in this regard:

> The recommendations [for the SAL reforms] . . . are based largely on examination of manufacturing activities as reflected in establishment surveys and cen-

suses, which is about a third of total employment in the [manufacturing] sector. The bulk of sectoral employment (that is "establishment" employment in units with less than five workers . . .) remains largely outside their focus. . . . Further investigation of the structure and organization of this sector is necessary; otherwise a macroeconomic policy can have an undesirable side effect . . . of eliminating a lot of jobs.[127]

This was more than just a hypothesis: it was substantiated by the poverty mission's own analysis of the Philippines' shift toward nontraditional-export manufacturing over the course of the 1970s. That transformation, it concluded, "represents a modernization trend, but . . . has entailed displacement of a large amount of employment in smaller units."[128] "Large" was not used loosely. A prominent example was the apparel sector, which in 1970 employed nearly four-tenths of all workers in manufacturing.[129] In apparel, the document charged, "a shift to imports and to a more capital-intensive and large-scale production for exports which spilled over to the domestic market" had undercut domestic-oriented tailoring and dress-making shops. The net result over the first half of the decade: by 1975, one-fifth of workers in the clothing/footwear sector had lost their jobs. In one sector alone, then, nearly 110,000 jobs—almost one-third of de Vries's employment-creation goal—were erased.[130]

That loss, the draft Poverty Report continued, was magnified by similar patterns in small-unit employment within other key manufacturing sectors, including textiles, metal products, electrical and nonelectrical machinery, wood products, and furniture. A consistent pattern had emerged: the Bank's labor-intensive, export-oriented schemes were *less* labor-intensive than the mode of production they replaced.[131] As early as September 1977, key Bank officials involved with the Philippine experiment had been forewarned in a confidential memo that this would be the case:

Will this then go some way toward solving the employment problem[?] My guess is not very far. Why? Because although there will be a steady increase in modern . . . industry employment, this is likely to be more than offset by declining employment in the cottage industry subsector. This is an almost inevitable result of the development of a modern . . . manufacturing sector under Philippine conditions. . . .
This then leaves us with quite a large residual for the service sector to employ or of course to remain unemployed.[132]

By the early 1980s, as the SAL restructuring took root and as the international economy stagnated, this employment debacle was only too clear.

In the first nine months of 1980, one of Licaros's last economic reports to Marcos disclosed, record layoffs shook the manufacturing sector.[133] Over the next year this trend accelerated, leaving an "increasing number of jobs . . . terminated as a result of shutdowns and retrenchments," according to *Business Asia*.[134] As former Philippine Senator Benigno Aquino, Jr., revealed in testimony before the U.S. Congress, 300,000 Filipinos—a staggering figure—joined the ranks of the unemployed during the first nine months of 1981 because of factory shutdowns and layoffs.[135] By the end of 1982, overall manufacturing employment levels had dropped to 90 percent of 1980 levels; in textiles, to as low as 68 percent.[136] Three years later, even these dismal figures would look high.[137]

That Philippine industrial wage-earners had been transformed into the country's "comparative advantage" was a case of bitter irony. An industrialization policy based on what the Bank called "exploiting its advantages of wage"[138] would not even guarantee Philippine workers their existing jobs, let alone improved employment opportunities. "Give us time," responded one high government technocrat when pressed to explain these contradictions.

> It's an economic law that . . . development must at first worsen the income distribution. . . . In the longer run, we'll see rising wages and more jobs. You've just got to wait. . . . Right now, it's a matter of triggering higher growth rates. . . . And after that, there'll be better and more [job] opportunities.[139]

Instead, as Cardoso and Faletto had suggested, "the 'marginal groups' . . . are growing in number because of the form assumed by capitalist development in the periphery. Actually, the modern industrial system increases marginalization."[140]

With structural adjustment lending, remarked a Bank official in early 1981, Bank President McNamara had fashioned "the World Bank's best weapon yet for resisting LDC pressures toward self-sufficiency and protectionism."[141] The Philippine industrial SAL has provided an excellent case study of the force of that new "weapon." Gravitating toward, and strengthening, already high-level technocratic allies within the Philippine government, the Bank was able to establish a synergistic relationship with them. Together, these technocrats and the Bank—the latter with the quiet collaboration of the IMF—were able to circumvent a hostile Central Bank, at one point a fortress of strength in the Philippine government. The result: a molding of new transnationalist power centers in the government and a reorientation of the economy away from serving domestic needs.

Remolding and reorienting did not stop with the industrial sector or with ministries outside the Central Bank. Export-oriented industrialization required comparable transformations within the financial sector—the subject of the next two chapters.

7

Industrialization and the Financial Sector

Shifting the Philippines to export-oriented light manufacturing had to extend beyond the confines of industry to be successful. It required effective mobilization of domestic and international finance, and hence a transformation of the Philippine financial sector. Unavoidably, this involved extensive dealings with the locus of nationalist power in the Philippine government: the Central Bank.

That such radical restructuring was well underway by the early 1980s is evidence of the World Bank's skill, as well as the experience gained in the SAL negotiations. Aided by constant advice from the IMF, the World Bank injected a tight cell of technocratic transnationalists into the larger organism of the Central Bank.

Through a $150 million loan, new legislation, and careful co-financing arrangements with transnational banks, the cell expanded its domain until it was able to push the entire Central Bank in a transnationalist direction. For the World Bank, this represented a resounding success in the simultaneous deployment of its major tactics of influence: the training and strengthening of technocrats, the reshaping of LDC institutions, and the creation of new institutions.

During 1981, keeping abreast of the flurry of activity in the Philippine financial sector proved no simple task. At centerstage, a wave of consolidations and mergers rippled through the sector, the largest commercial banks linking formally with the biggest investment houses. On the sidelines, Philippine depositors watched the mergers nervously, and many transferred their funds from smaller banks to those larger banks that boasted TNB backing. These transfers only added to the merger flurry. Then the government made its move, employing government-owned banks to infuse equity into the merging banks, which were, in turn, encouraged to channel funds into export-oriented industries through equity participation. Against decades of established Philippine financial policy, each stage of this rapid transformation stood as an aberration. And, event by event, each stemmed from the World Bank's financial-sector loan to the Philippines.

Taken in sum, the changes foretold a tighter working alliance between the Philippine state, big export-oriented industrial concerns, and large financial institutions. Fostering that close relationship became part of the World Bank's and the IMF's strategies for more effectively and fully restructuring the economies of relevant LDCs toward export-oriented industrialization. Whereas the Bank's industrial SAL prompted the intermeshing of the Philippine state with the bigger Philippine export industries, the Bank's and the Fund's financial-sector reforms remolded the crucial third element, the banks, and brought the three together.

Fathering Domestic Legislation

In May 1981, the World Bank and the Philippine government sealed an agreement for what was termed the "apex loan." Just as the SAL marked the Bank's pioneer venture into an overall Philippine industrial-sector loan, so too the apex loan stood with distinction as the Bank's "first financial sector loan" for Philippine industrial financing.[1]

Step by step along the path toward this final agreement, the interactions between the Bank and the Philippine government closely paralleled the pattern already narrated for the SAL negotiations. (See Figure 3's timeline.) The March 1979 financial-sector mission followed on the heels of the February 1979 industrial-sector mission. A June 1979 draft financial-sector report was discussed with the Philippine government along with the draft industrial report in August 1979.[2] This marked the commencement of "policy dialogues" that, within the year, carried a series of financial

Figure 3. Timeline: Industrial- and Financial-Sector Negotiations, January 1979 to July 1981

Financial		Industrial
	1979	
		– – – IBRD industrial-sector appraisal mission
IBRD-IMF financial mission – – – –		
Three-year IMF EFF completed – – – –		
		– – – – IBRD economic mission
IBRD-IMF financial-sector report – – – –		
		– – – R. Ongpin becomes minister of industry
Philippine "Financial Reforms Committee" set up – – – –		– – – IBRD mission discusses draft reports with Philippine government; identifies proposed SAL; aide-mémoire written
		– – – Interagency committee for SAL set up
		– – – Preappraisal mission for SAL
IMF mission on annual November review – – – –		– – – Consultative group meeting
	1980	
IMF approves two-year standby arrangement – – – –		– – – SAL appraisal mission
ECB signed into law; Villanueva spends month at IBRD – – – –		– – – IBRD textile mission
Public version of IBRD financial report – – – –		– – – Public version of IBRD industrial report

Villanueva starts at ADFU and meets with IBRD team - - - -   - - - - SAL negotiations completed

- - - - Comprehensive tariff reform; Virata formally requests SAL

Villanueva meets with IBRD team - - - -   - - - - SAL approved

- - - - Ascher memorandum

Villanueva and Licaros meet with IBRD team - - - -

1981

Dewey Dee flees; Licaros resigns; martial law lifted - - - -   - - - - IBRD review mission; SAL second tranche stalls; Omnibus Investments Code and new EPZ decree

First commercial bank to become an ECB - - - -   - - - - IBRD textile mission

Virata leads team for financial-sector negotiations; - - - - Virata formally requests apex loan   - - - - Business Day hosts tariff reform conference

ADFU set up; apex loan approved - - - -   - - - - Presidential "elections"

- - - - Marcos picks Virata to be prime minister

reforms onto the Philippine legislative slate. Once again, the germ of each reform was to be found in the Bank's report.[3]

With the reforms in place, Virata could dispatch his requisite letter (March 13, 1981) to the Bank. Just as Virata's industrial policy letter of eight months earlier had been skillfully drafted to camouflage the Bank's leading role in domestic legislation, this letter feigned total Philippine government autonomy in recent major financial policy changes.[4] Then, and only then, was the apex loan sanctioned in Washington.

Given the mirrorlike pattern of interactions over the two loans, detailed elaboration of the apex loan's chronology analogous to that presented for the SAL in Chapters 4 and 5 is unnecessary. Rather, this section will highlight key maneuvers and debates in Bank, Fund, and Philippine government interactions over the financial sector and will bring some critical questions into perspective:

1. How did the two sectoral loans work together to further common aims? Why were they conceived as separate loans rather than one loan?

2. What was the IMF role in this Bank loan? How did the loan shuffle the boundaries of Bank and Fund historical roles?

3. Why did the Bank deem it necessary to move inside the Central Bank for this facet of its Philippine policy dialogues? Could it not have been assured greater success if it had concentrated on its alliances in ministries outside Governor Licaros's realm?

4. How was the Bank able to surmount strong domestic opposition to the enumerated reforms?

Just as Philippine government officials often slipped into more comfortable references to the industrial structural adjustment loan as a program loan, so they tended to refer to the apex loan as either a structural adjustment loan or a program loan.[5] For World Bank purposes, this was not so: the apex loan never reached the "nonproject" loan classification in which structural adjustment loans (the Philippine SAL among them) are categorized.[6] The confusion among Philippine government officials is, however, understandable, for in the Bank's quest to restructure the financial sector, it deployed the apex loan in the same all-encompassing fashion as a structural adjustment loan: it pinpointed a sector and helped reshape it according to Bank specifications. If the apex loan was not a sector-specific structural adjustment loan in name, it certainly was in essence.

Part of the mistaken terminology on the Philippine side undoubtedly also grew from the two loans' shared birth. At the outset, the Bank framed its Philippine restructuring as one package of "industrial and financial policy improvements" that would "provide the basis for . . . World Bank financial support for the industrial sector."[7] By the time of the August 1979 aide-mémoire and the commencement of policy dialogues, the Bank was willing to concede that a single packet might not be the most efficacious: "Changes in the financial sector could be introduced either simultaneously with or independently of industrial policy measures as deemed most effective for achieving the acceptance and objectives of both."[8] As the Bank's structural adjustment experience grew worldwide, so did its realization that the magnitude and complexities of the reforms it demanded were such that the programs were better spread over a period of years.[9] By late 1981, it became established Bank policy to bifurcate structural adjustment programs to achieve maximum leverage. The split was accomplished, a Bank official explained, "either by sector, as in the Philippines, or by stages . . . as was done in Turkey."[10]

Traditionally, the World Bank had left all lending geared toward financial-sector restructuring to the IMF. Still, in addition to technical assistance on such matters as capital-market development and local-savings generation, the Bank had managed to leave its imprint on LDC financial sectors in one area: the fostering of national development finance companies. It had entered this activity by an ingenious route. The Bank's desire to fund certain private enterprises in LDCs was greatly restricted in practice by a statutory requirement that all such loans to nongovernment entities be guaranteed by national governments. LDC governments often shied away from this activity, to avoid accusations of favoritism to individual enterprises. A further restriction on deeper involvement was that only the International Finance Corporation within the World Bank group and not the overall Bank could undertake equity investments.[11]

To circumvent such criticism and limitations, the Bank had found it could underpin private enterprise instead through project loans to provide (in its own words) "catalytic support for either the creation or reorganization" of development finance companies that, in turn, pumped equity or loans to the private businesses.[12] Such Bank loans served the dual role of aiding private industry and strengthening financial institutions that the Bank felt could play a more central role.[13] Until the late 1970s, these institutions stood as the World Bank's main contribution to LDC banking systems worldwide.

The Philippines had been no exception to this institutional practice. From 1962 to 1980, the World Bank had channeled its limited lending for the Philippine industrial sector through three development finance companies, molding and strengthening these institutions in the process. As of 1978, the Bank had allocated ten loans, totaling $225 million, to the government-owned Development Bank of the Philippines, fostering what Bank officials termed "heavy involvement" and "close dialogue" with that institution.[14] Referring to a second beneficiary, the foreign-backed Private Development Corporation of the Philippines (PDCP), the World Bank bragged of its "considerable impact" on the corporation ever since it had been created in 1963 at the urging of the Bank itself.[15]

In 1978, a Bank assessment of its Philippine industrial support admitted to "increasingly serious misgivings" about the level of industrial development supported through its development-finance-company loans.[16] It was simply not meeting the growing needs. In order to accelerate the transformation of the Philippine economy toward export-oriented industrialization, then, the World Bank resolved that

> future loans to financial intermediaries would concentrate on the resolution of major financial sector policy issues. In order to widen the institutional coverage of Bank financing and address sector issues more effectively, industrial lending to financial intermediaries will be channelled through an "apex" unit in the Central Bank. . . . Such "apex" lending would replace conventional finance company lending.[17]

Switching to the more centralized "apex"-type loans was a careful strategy to shift the World Bank from the periphery to the center of financial-sector decision-making. As the Bank reported elsewhere, "The most important justification for the loan is that it would enable the Bank to work closely with the Government on policy issues concerning the country's financial sector."[18]

The Bank decision ushered in a third stage of external influence on the Philippine financial sector during this half-century. In the 1940s, in line with the pattern of U.S. dominance over Philippine macroeconomic policies, a U.S. mission had fabricated the grand designs for a new Philippine financial sector, legislated through the General Banking Act of 1948.[19]

With the 1963 creation of the IMF's Central Banking Service, the pre-eminent role in remodeling banking systems in the Philippines and other developing countries had been transferred to the IMF.[20] For newly independent African nations, this meant relying on the IMF to chisel the outlines of central banking systems and to supply senior officials to staff the infant central banks' highest offices. For countries like the Philippines, with a financial infrastructure already in place, the IMF's role entailed advisory missions offering technical advice on both central and commercial banking.[21]

Therefore, when the Philippine General Banking Act was amended in the early 1970s, the reforms built on IMF recommendations. Following a pattern initiated by the United States nearly three decades earlier, the official formulation of the proposed reforms was presented as the culmination of a six-month study by a Joint IMF–Central Bank Banking Survey Commission composed of three representatives from each side.[22] But there was never any question as to who was in command. As Armand Fabella, a Filipino Commission member, recollected, "It was called the IMF-CBP [Central Bank of the Philippines] Commission and not the CBP-IMF Commission for good reason. On these matters in which we in the Philippines have little expertise . . . we defer to the greater experience and wisdom of the IMF."[23]

"Coincidentally," Fabella continued, "if I'm not mistaken, our ninety-nine recommendations were published officially in September of 1972, the month martial law was declared."[24] Mistaken Fabella was not; nor was it coincidence. With martial law in place, the translation from suggestions into domestic law proceeded smoothly and expeditiously, unencumbered by the nationalistic debate over the banking sector that had rocked the Philippine Congress immediately prior to that month.[25] In order to facilitate matters even further, the commission took it upon itself (in the words of then Central Bank Governor Licaros's cover letter to the September 1972 report) to draft "bills for the suggested reforms which require legislation" and to prepare "plans or programs for the implementation of recommendations which need only administrative action."[26]

Thus, in the first years of martial law, the financial sector was overhauled in accordance with IMF proposals. Minimum capital-base levels for commercial banks were hiked fivefold, from a long-standing P20 million to P100 million.[27] Room was thus conveniently created for the 40 percent

Figure 4. The Philippine Financial Sector Prior to the 1980 Reforms

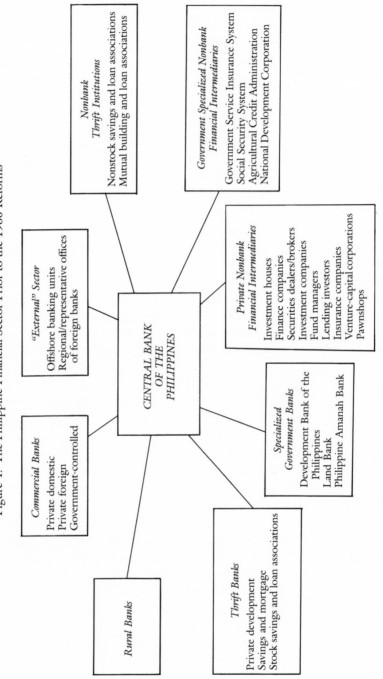

Nonbank
Thrift Institutions

Nonstock savings and loan associations
Mutual building and loan associations

Government Specialized Nonbank
Financial Intermediaries

Government Service Insurance System
Social Security System
Agricultural Credit Administration
National Development Corporation

"External" Sector

Offshore banking units
Regional/representative offices
of foreign banks

Private Nonbank
Financial Intermediaries

Investment houses
Finance companies
Securities dealers/brokers
Investment companies
Fund managers
Lending investors
Insurance companies
Venture-capital corporations
Pawnshops

CENTRAL BANK
OF THE
PHILIPPINES

Commercial Banks

Private domestic
Private foreign
Government-controlled

Specialized
Government Banks

Development Bank of the
Philippines
Land Bank
Philippine Amanah Bank

Rural Banks

Thrift Banks

Private development
Savings and mortgage
Stock savings and loan associations

SOURCE: Adapted from figure in Ibon Databank, *The Philippine Financial System—A Primer* (Manila: Ibon Databank, 1983), p. 8.

TNB equity presence newly allowed in domestic banking institutions, a policy that reversed a historical Philippine de facto prohibition against foreign-equity participation in banking.[28]

The reforms also included provisions that would be rethought in the 1980 banking reforms. The 1972 decree reinforced and further delineated the separation of functions among the various types of financial institutions originally outlined in the 1940s legislation. Mirroring the 1933 U.S. Glass-Steagall Act, investment banking—that is, underwriting of government and corporate securities,[29] stockbroking, and buying and selling securities—was split off from the normal functions of deposit-taking commercial banks. This left a financial sector dominated by commercial banks (both domestic and foreign) with an array of other banking and nonbanking financial institutions performing specialized functions (see Figure 4 and Table 6). This was not so much a new move as an attempt to update statutory distinctions and to cover more thoroughly the new banking activities for which demand had evolved over the decades.[30]

Finally, in keeping with the centralization of power inherent in martial law, the early 1970s reforms sought to strengthen the hand of the Central Bank, enlarging its domain to encompass nonbank financial institutions as well as banks.[31] The Philippine Central Bank summed up the rationale: "The pressures in 1972 were related to the consolidations of the banking and non-banking sectors of the financial system under the supervisory and regulatory powers of the Central Bank so that the primary responsibilities of maintaining domestic and external monetary stability could be more effectively discharged by the Central Bank."[32]

Opening the Floodgates

In 1972, a strong Central Bank was perceived as an important component in modernizing the banking sector. Before the decade was out, however, the strengthened Central Bank under Licaros began to plague the World Bank and the IMF. For, as these two institutions understood, there was no conceivable way to circumvent the Central Bank in consolidating the banking sector so that it could serve as a drive wheel in export-oriented light manufacturing. Unlike the industrial sector, which lay under the multiple supervision of the Central Bank, NEDA, the Ministry of Industry, the Ministry of Trade, and others, the Central Bank's jurisdiction over the financial sector had become unambiguous and comprehensive.

Table 6. Total Assets of the Philippine Financial System Prior to 1980 Reforms

	Amount (Million Pesos, End-of-Year Figures)			Percentage of Total		
	1974	1976	1978	1974	1976	1978
Banking institutions	54,142.8	79,989.7	121,164.7	72.3	69.6	74.5
Commercial banks	42,424.8	58,730.9	89,798.6	56.7	51.1	55.2
Thrift banks	1,666.9	3,024.5	5,602.8	2.2	2.6	3.4
Private development banks	296.3	482.1	759.7	0.4	0.4	0.5
Savings and mortgage banks	1,159.9	2,043.1	3,896.8	1.6	1.8	2.4
Stock savings and loan associations	210.7	499.3	946.3	0.3	0.4	0.6
Rural banks	2,110.7	3,017.7	4,037.0	2.8	2.6	2.5
Specialized banks	7,940.4	15,216.6	21,726.3	10.6	13.2	13.4
Development Bank of the Philippines	6,758.0	12,779.8	18,209.7	9.0	11.1	11.2
Land Bank	1,182.4	2,384.4	3,446.1	1.6	2.1	2.1
Philippine Amanah Bank	—	52.4	70.5	—	0.1	—
Nonbank financial institutions	20,714.2	34,923.6	41,553.6	27.7	30.4	25.5
Investment houses	3,839.9	4,824.7	4,762.5	5.1	4.2	2.9
Finance companies	2,306.7	4,644.6	7,365.7	3.1	4.0	4.5
Investment companies	689.0	3,751.4	4,651.1	0.9	3.3	2.9
Securities dealers/brokers	882.1	1,091.8	1,119.8	1.2	1.0	0.7
Pawnshops	100.8	149.0	192.3	0.1	0.1	0.1
Fund managers	1,951.5	3,302.0	834.4	2.6	2.9	0.5
Lending investors	24.9	16.9	18.5	—	—	—
Nonstock savings and loan associations	71.2	112.1	191.8	0.1	0.1	0.1
Mutual building and loan associations	24.7	23.5	21.4	—	—	—
Private insurance companies	3,468.0	5,230.1	7,273.9[a]	4.6	4.6	4.5
Specialized nonbank	7,355.4	11,777.5	15,122.2	9.8	10.3	9.3
Government Service Insurance System	4,144.5	6,303.6	7,833.3	5.5	5.5	4.8
Social Security System	2,388.9	3,841.4	5,499.4	3.2	3.3	3.4
Agricultural Credit Administration	451.5	709.9	751.3	0.6	0.6	0.5
National Development Corporation	370.5	922.6	1,038.2	0.5	0.8	0.6
Total	74,857.0	114,913.3	162,718.3	100.0	100.0	100.0

SOURCE: World Bank and IMF, The Philippines: Aspects of the Financial Sector, World Bank Country Study, May 1980, p. 3, table 1.

The dilemma then was clear-cut: new reforms could come only from the Central Bank, traditionally IMF territory. Yet the IMF was in no position to conduct amiable policy dialogues with Licaros. That left the World Bank. Admittedly, the Central Bank was not totally alien territory for the World Bank. On occasion, when no other suitable national financial conduit had existed (and when it was not deemed necessary to inspire the creation of an appropriate institution), the World Bank had channeled its loans through the Central Bank.[33] But this had been done as a matter of convenience, rather than with an eye to major financial-sector reform. By the late 1970s, however, the virtual handcuffing of the IMF vis-à-vis Licaros necessitated its replacement by the World Bank.

Easing the World Bank into the IMF's historical domain at the Central Bank without provoking suspicion and tainting the Bank's unsoiled reputation required time and finesse. Financial-sector missions in 1979 were joint efforts, composed of members of both the IMF and the World Bank, but a Bank official was placed at the head.[34] In this way the IMF could introduce the World Bank to the Central Bank without the World Bank appearing to overstep its bounds. Then the IMF could move into the background, still sharing technical advice but deferring to the World Bank in the actual process of negotiation.

Although the combined effort behind the financial reforms was clear,[35] the World Bank's apparent domination left most Philippine government officials emphasizing its role. Reinforcing this perception was a logical deduction: "What was at stake with the reforms was a World Bank loan," reasoned Carmelita Areñas of the Central Bank. "Therefore, the World Bank [not the IMF] had the upper hand."[36] Government technocrats who saw through the joint mission setup framed it in their own terms. A top NEDA official, for example, offered his explanation:

> They had to do this . . . jointly, you see. The IMF deals with the Central Bank, so the World Bank had to include them [the IMF]. . . . But, after that, we [the Philippine government] were really talking to the World Bank. We were negotiating with the World Bank. . . . By having a joint mission . . . it was good for us too. . . . [We were] able to get around the usual IMF stubbornness . . . [and] its patronizing attitude.[37]

It was important, however, that the IMF's public posture not be erased altogether, as had been done with the SAL. Given the nature of the desired reforms, it would have seemed strange to have only the Bank exacting policy changes in areas mandated by the IMF less than a decade earlier. This was especially true because the new reforms strove to undo some of the very characteristics of the Philippine banking system that had been created according to IMF (and, earlier, U.S.) specifications. To leave the IMF out at this juncture would have provided an already recalcitrant Licaros with the perfect excuse for charging the World Bank with trying to overturn policies sanctioned by the IMF and not budging an inch during the policy dialogues. As an IMF official with years of experience in dealing with the Philippines explained further:

> Now we see the need for long-term lending by domestic banks to export enter-prises. That fact wasn't always so clear . . . ; it wasn't in 1972. Times change . . . needs change . . . demands change. What the IMF helped do with the financial sector in 1972 was critical. We're not saying it was a mistake. What we are say-ing is . . . demands on LDC financial sectors are different now. . . . But right now, it's easier to have the World Bank in on this, to pass the buck a little.[38]

Thus, one rationale for splitting the financial-sector loan from the SAL was to allow IMF and World Bank collaboration in the area where it was essential and to let the World Bank go in alone where an IMF presence might have proven a liability. Another motivation for the loans' separation was the far greater complexity of and resistance to the financial-sector com-ponent. The Fund's and Bank's maneuverings vis-à-vis the Central Bank on the financial-sector loan were more uncertain and the loan-related policy dialogue dragged on more hesitantly. By purposefully circumventing the Central Bank as much as possible, the SAL negotiations advanced more expeditiously. Explained SAL interagency committee member Noriega, "The apex loan made lots of problems for the World Bank . . . because it can be so difficult working through the Central Bank. Not like the SAL work with us, where we're moving along quickly and satisfactorily."[39]

Foremost among the banking system restructurings that the Bank and the Fund sought to implement through the apex loan was what Governor Licaros described as "letting any bank [or nonbank financial institution] do what any other can do."[40] Slated for obliteration was the enforced spe-cialization between commercial and investment banks that the IMF (and the United States) had built into Philippine banking law. Instead, what the Fund and the Bank called for was a variation of the German and Swiss models of universality in banking. Combining the full domestic and international banking functions of commercial banking with the underwriting, securities dealership, and equity investment powers of investment houses, "universal banks" (or, as the Philippine government preferred to term them, "expanded commercial banks") would be created. That title would be bestowed only on those banks that were able to meet specific criteria regarding past performance, enlarged capital base, and technical expertise.[41] As Licaros recalled, "The World Bank had it in mind that we would consolidate our banking sector into superbanks, each offering a supermarket of services."[42]

The expansion of commercial banks into equity participation in corporations would open up vast and unprecedented opportunities for the enlarged banks. As before, expanded commercial banks (ECBs) were to be encouraged to control up to 100 percent of the voting stock in most categories of allied enterprises—that is, other banks and associated businesses. But there was more. In nonallied enterprises—agriculture, manufacturing, public utilities—ECBs could hold up to 35 percent ownership.[43] As the Bank and the Fund viewed the proposal, it would have two major consequences (when taken in conjunction with the increased capitalization requirement):

1. Domestic savings flows—and thus the amount available for loans and investment—would be expanded.

2. Increasingly, this lending would be done on a long-term basis (over five years in the Philippine context), complementing ECB equity investment.[44]

An elaborate legal foundation for expanded commercial banking was written into Philippine statutes through seven April 1980 amendatory laws and four July 1980 circulars of implementation, hailed by government and media as a crowning achievement of Governor Licaros's eleven years in office.[45] Yet, once again, this was but a well-orchestrated ploy to shroud Bank and Fund initiatives in the vocabulary of Philippine nationalism. At the time the universal banking idea was first launched by the 1979 joint mission, Governor Licaros was not among its proponents.[46] Joining him in firm opposition to the move were certain officials within the Central Bank—some of whom would later share Licaros's public billing as motivating forces behind what were dubbed the "magnificent seven" pieces of legislation and their accompanying "gang of four" circulars.[47]

What expanded commercial banking boiled down to was a scheme for funneling more domestic resources into export-oriented industrialization or, as the World Bank euphemistically phrased it, into meeting "the country's long-term development needs."[48] A successful nontraditional-export drive, the Bank had counseled the Philippine government repeatedly since at least 1977, required "larger credit reserves" as well as a firm commitment that none of these would be squandered on national entrepreneurs' more capital-intensive, import-substitution projects.[49]

As Virata reiterated in his August 1980 dispatch to McNamara, the financial reforms were being geared to "improve the efficiency of financial intermediation for export-oriented and labor-intensive industrial development."[50] With expanded commercial banking in place, applauded a Bank staff appraisal of the apex loan, "important milestones . . . in mobilizing and channeling resources to meet the financial needs of the Government's new and ambitious industrial policy" were reached.[51]

The export-oriented industrialization motivation behind these changes, however, was hushed up, given the controversial climate surrounding other Bank and Fund industrial restructuring, particularly the late-1970s tariff reductions and import liberalizations. Instead, a different, less controversial rationale was articulated: the need to further economic efficiency. Larger banks resulting from consolidations of commercial banks into universal banks, it was claimed by the Bank, the Fund, and certain key Philippine technocrats (among them Virata), would achieve significant economies of scale.[52] Expanded commercial banking would "open up" and "strengthen" the Philippine banking sector.[53]

Armand Fabella, chairman of the late-1970s Central Bank Banking Survey Commission, was a staunch convert to this line of reasoning: "The aim of expanded commercial banking is to take advantage of scale economies by permitting growth on the argument that the bigger you are—and the more diversified, too—with the ability to amass more assets, the faster you grow. . . . [With the reduction in enforced bank specialization], with more competitive financial conditions, your more efficient private banks would manifest themselves more vigorously."[54] Eight years earlier, as Filipino cochairman of the comparable 1972 IMF-CBP Banking Survey Commission, Fabella had echoed the IMF's previous contention that exactly the opposite was true: compartmentalized banking of the U.S. genre was more suitable for the Philippine context.

Key non–Central Bank transnationalists such as Minister Virata underwent similar transformations, for they could readily perceive the crucial role of such a banking revolution in underpinning Philippine light industrial exports. To many Central Bank officials hostile to complete reliance on such a path of industrialization (among them, Licaros and Deputy Governor Legarda), however, the 1972 legislation was still far more prudent.[55] One of these high-level officials countered the Bank's and the Fund's rationale, expressing a different philosophy of development: "Some of us have a feeling there are actually diseconomies of scale. Big banks with lots of tie-ups to big industry probably have passed the point of economic efficiency, and now favoritism takes over."[56]

These hesitations Fabella disclaimed as "the nationalistic drivel of small-business fanatics" or the thinking of "nonscientific pockets remaining in the Philippine bureaucracy . . . that do not understand that we must acknowledge that the IMF and World Bank can conduct superior empirical investigations."[57] Fabella, a transnationalist with close ties to ministries outside the Central Bank, understood the benefits of bowing to that superiority. Indeed, ever since the early 1960s, when Fabella had headed the government agency overseeing the implementation of the IMF's 1962 packet of economic reforms, the Program Implementation Agency, his reputation had been wedded to his role as skillful translator of external advice into domestic policy. In this sense, confided an IMF official, Fabella was a perfect "liaison. He knew how to work with us, and he accepted the World Bank's new dominance here."[58]

Was there empirical evidence to support the economies-of-scale argument? Since the Bank's and the Fund's rationale for the financial reforms was based on the benefits redounding to export-oriented industries, and not on the economies-of-scale argument, they made no further effort to give substance to their assertions. Instead, in a footnote toward the end of their report, they passed the responsibility back to the Philippine government, in the process destroying Fabella's justification for why advice had been sought from these institutions in the first place: "No empirical research could be carried out to support this [economies-of-scale] contention. Most data needed for such an exercise are available to the research department of the Central Bank who should be encouraged to carry out the studies."[59]

Neither side conducted any such studies. Yet in the introduction to the

July 1980 Central Bank circulars accompanying the expanded commercial banking legislation, the relationship had miraculously become conclusive: "economies of scale *would* result" from the 1980 financial reforms, the Filipino public was informed.[60]

"What It Means to Be a Guinea Pig"

The question of economies of scale was only one of a number of issues surrounding universal banking that provoked controversy inside the Central Bank. Although by the late 1970s Licaros found the idea of interacting predominantly with the World Bank over the financial restructuring rather than with the IMF "a welcome change," his first choice was clearly that both institutions stay out of any major Philippine financial-sector activity.[61] Why, he argued, should his Central Bank have anything to do with a World Bank loan destined for industry? Carmelita Areñas of the Central Bank echoed him: "Our position initially was that the World Bank should just lend to industry . . . like it has all along. Why should we commit our whole financial sector to either the World Bank or the IMF?"[62] Let the World Bank give its loan to the Development Bank of the Philippines, suggested one Central Bank official.[63] Or, offered another, pass it along to the government-owned Land Bank of the Philippines.[64]

After the joint Bank and Fund mission of March 1979 detailed its suggested reforms, the debate within the Central Bank halls rose in pitch. An October 1979 internal Central Bank memorandum provided an indication of how vehemently some ranking Central Bank officials opposed the reforms. Signed solely by Licaros's special assistant Arnulfo Aurellano, the nine-page memorandum continually lapsed into the "we" form, revealing that it voiced the objections of others besides Aurellano, Licaros undoubtedly among them. Fears of economic concentration and collaboration between big banks and big industries were strong. Aurellano wrote, "We have strong reservations" concerning: (1) equity involvement of banks in non-allied industries; (2) direct equity financing by banks through underwriting; (3) mergers between commercial banks and other types of financial institutions; and (4) deposit taking by nonbank financial institutions. In other words, although the memo was too diplomatic to say so directly, the objections covered every key facet of the universal-banking concept.[65]

If all the Bank and the Fund sought was more long-term financial backing for industry, the memo argued, that could easily be accomplished through broader incentives geared to encouraging commercial banks "to provide medium and long term funds for industry via loans or bonds," rather than equity. Indeed, Aurellano charged, recent tax and interest incentives had already elicited "positive results" in amplifying commercial banks' long-term funding bases. Why, then, call forth the specter of a handful of unwieldy universal banks "which may be able to dominate the financial system" and were likely to cater discriminatorily to the "requirements of larger and well established firms"? [66]

Even the six-man Central Bank Banking Survey Commission whose task it was to "coordinate with the joint . . . mission on the report . . . and proposals arising therein" [67] was hardly unanimously in favor of the universal banking reforms. One panelist represented the Investment Houses Association of the Philippines, an organization whose members feared that universal banking would spell their demise as independent entities. The substantially larger commercial banks had an uncontestable head-start over investment houses in reaching a universal bank's requisite minimum level of capitalization. That was one likely negative vote. [68]

The other private-sector panelist represented the likely commercial bank beneficiaries, but even his constituency had doubts about the full financial reform package. Memories of the rash of mergers and foreign partnerships that had followed the 1972 financial reforms were still fresh. Seven years later, only the biggest banks wanted to gamble on an even more deadly round of such mergers and foreign partnerships that were likely to be precipitated by universal banking and its further expanded capital-base requirements. Such overall hesitations and conflicting views among the commercial banks led to what was called a "noncommittal" sentiment on the part of this representative of the Bankers' Association of the Philippines. [69]

Among the Central Bank deputy governors who joined Fabella to round out the committee, at least two were negatively inclined toward the proposals. Deputy Governor Gabriel Singson had strong forebodings about this new World Bank role vis-à-vis the Central Bank, reservations that had to do with his own power base at the Central Bank. [70] Perhaps the deepest antagonism came from Deputy Governor Legarda, as was explained by NEDA's Noriega:

> Legarda said it was ridiculous. Every time the IMF had a new whim or fancy as to how our financial sector should look . . . were we supposed to switch around

every time that view changed? We've done enough for the World Bank and IMF in the past—that's what Legarda said, and why he felt we should do as little as possible for this loan now.[71]

Credit for transforming these hostilely predisposed committee members and the overall Central Bank into financial-reform advocates was attributed to various phenomena. Noriega, whose view was shaped by what his Bank "friends" on the SAL missions confided to him, credited the World Bank's skill at sensitizing its apex team to the delicate situation at hand:

> The World Bank wasn't oblivious to Legarda's negativism. It reacted by trying to adjust its team to the needs of its [Philippine] counterparts. . . . It is much better . . . than the IMF at this. . . . So you had on the mission an Indian guy who was very patient . . . a good listener. . . . His job was to listen and listen to Legarda's [and others'] complaints . . . and to win confidence.[72]

Fabella, however, insisted that no such persuasion of the Philippine committee was necessary. As he recounted it, the Bank and the Fund were the ones coaxed into compromise, while the Philippine government never acquiesced to the full IMF and World Bank prescription:

> The decisions were exclusively the Philippine Panel's decisions. . . . The IMF was pushing for a stronger recommendation, more similar to the German universal-banking system. . . . We didn't think German universal banking would fly in the Philippine setting, so we picked out the good parts [of the joint financial-sector report] and toned down the not-so-desirable aspects—or not-proven aspects—into expanded commercial banking.[73]

In theory, there was a distinction. Expanded commercial banking gave each specialized financial institution a choice: to remain as it was, or to increase its capitalization, in the process taking on an even wider range of responsibilities. Finally, at the P500 million milestone, the title of ECB would be bestowed, placing all financial functions under the auspices of one bank.[74] Under strict universal banking, implied Fabella, no such options existed: all banks, by law, had to become P500 million ECBs or cease operations. "But we believe in the free-market philosophy of choice, not compulsion," emphasized Fabella.[75]

Yet, in reality, little distanced these two financial-sector setups that time would not erase.[76] Even Fabella himself conceded that his "successful" scenario for Philippine expanded commercial banking visualized "a club of big boys . . . a handful of banks . . . controlling the financial sector" within a matter of years.[77] Like small Filipino textile enterprises, many small specialized banks not "choosing" to broaden their capital bases and expand their repertoire of functions would eventually be liquidated or taken over.

Fabella's semantic charade may initially have soothed a few fears and quelled some debate, but it certainly was not the deciding factor in the Central Bank's eventual obeisance. In due time, Fabella's terminology was transformed into a joke among Philippine government and banking circles (by both friends and foes of the financial-reform package)—a laughing reference to "universal banking, or, as Armand Fabella wants us to say: expanded commercial banking."[78]

Other factors beyond the patient Indian's proddings softened the objections of Licaros's Central Bank and the rest of Fabella's committee. Above all else, it was a matter of pragmatism, an understanding of the enormous power these multilateral institutions wielded with the Philippine government, as well as of the declining importance of the Central Bank vis-à-vis certain other transnationalist-dominated ministries that were being upgraded in importance as the SAL process unfolded. Legarda was asked why he finally came around to seeing the merits of the financial-sector reforms. There was no lengthy explanation, no admission that he ever doubted the wisdom of universal banking, just a simple and direct, "You have to see this in its proper perspective: it is a matter of our own involvement with the World Bank. . . . Ours is a good relationship, with lots of loans."[79] Echoed Licaros:

> It does not matter whether I originally wanted it or not. . . . That's what it means to be a guinea pig. We keep having to experiment with new ideas the IMF and World Bank might have. . . . It's not always easy. Sometimes it's like a straitjacket. But it is necessary.[80]

In Licaros's case, the reason for his final submission was also rooted in his maneuverings to survive. By late 1979, said one of his confidants in the Central Bank,

> You could see his power slipping . . . and Virata taking over. [Licaros] realized he should have played along better before . . . in the past. It was silly in a way: he was so stubborn . . . over little things. . . . He thought Marcos would always need him for . . . his skill at the negotiating table . . . but Marcos needed Virata's closeness to international circles more.[81]

Licaros faced a World Bank whose concurrent SAL work involved many policy changes he disapproved of, at a pace he could barely keep up with, and with ministries he had no control over. The most he could do was to make some last futile efforts to regain his standing as policy innovator at the helm of the Central Bank. And so he took up the banner of universal banking and brandished it as his own. But it was too late: when the Central Bank's governing Monetary Board approved these amendments to the banking laws in early 1980, board member Virata, not Chairman Licaros, was handed the accolades.[82]

By April of 1980, just one year after the World Bank and the IMF set the process in motion, the seven universal banking laws stood on the books. President Marcos had given the rubber-stamp Philippine legislature exactly two weeks to turn the Central Bank proposals into law. If not, Marcos vowed, they would be passed as presidential decrees.[83] In this fashion, what critics in the Central Bank continued to deride as "the seven shotgun amendments to the existing bank laws" were born.[84]

As comprehensive as the financial reforms of 1980 were, they were only one component of what the World Bank and the IMF sought to implement through the vehicle of the Bank's apex loan. Institution-building stood as a major element of the Bank's and the Fund's blueprint for reshaping the Philippine financial sector to better fit the Philippines' shifting role in the new international division of labor of the late 1970s.

Seeding the Central Bank

On August 15, 1980, the Apex Development Finance Unit (ADFU) of the Philippine Central Bank formally came into existence.[85] About a month earlier, in Washington, D.C., Minister Virata and his entourage had ironed out the final details of the agreement for the Philippines' first structural adjustment loan. A month prior to that, the government-owned Philippine National Bank (PNB) had signaled the commencement of a new era in Philippine banking by applying for the first ECB license.[86] The three events were all firsts. And they were all closely interrelated.

While the Philippine press paid homage to Virata's international renown and to PNB's farsightedness, the ADFU opened without much ceremony. There was little fanfare from either Central Bank Governor Licaros or his six deputy governors in welcoming ADFU head Eduardo Villanueva, fresh from intensive training in the Bank's Washington headquarters,[87] to the Central Bank ruling team. As far as the rest of the Central Bank employees were concerned, the new ADFU staff seldom opened their doors or their work to outside scrutiny. Only the frenzied activity in the ADFU suite of rooms on the Central Bank's prestigious top floor revealed the existence of new life within the bureaucracy.

As the months passed, little more than a skeletal outline of the activity filtered out from that suite, even to other Central Bank offices. Employees from these other offices who requested an explanation from ADFU personnel had to settle for a vaguely worded circular containing less substance than many of the rumors floating through Central Bank corridors.[88] Even top Central Bank officials tuned in to the apex loan negotiations were reluctant to divulge activities underway inside the ADFU.

Ironically, approaches to Central Bank officials outside Villanueva's dominion to learn more about ADFU invariably ended in requests: "You find out what's going on [in the ADFU] and tell us. . . . You're an outsider; you don't work here . . . so it's easier for you . . . to find out [than for us]."[89]

When presented with the paradox of a Central Bank unit that stood as an enigma to the vast majority of Central Bank staff, ADFU head Villanueva offered no apologies. There was no reason, he argued, not to let "the quizzical attitude about what it's all about" remain as it was.[90] And while Villanueva admitted that the January 1981 inauguration of a transnationalist Central Bank governor ushered in "a friend" privy to "all our secrets,"[91] the secrets were not shared with those below new Governor Laya. In Central Bank offices other than Laya's—from that of the senior deputy governor on down—great bitterness and resentment toward the ADFU festered.[92]

Why all the mystification and evasion? Part of the answer lay in the need to distance the creation of the ADFU as much as possible from the billing it rightly shared with the controversial universal-banking reforms as preconditions to the flow of apex loan money.[93] It also reflected a decision by the ADFU staff, who understandably had a vested interest in the loan being signed, to say little so as not to jeopardize the final months of negotiation.

These were reasons enough in themselves, but there were still others. Apex lending through the ADFU, it turns out, was a pivotal piece in the puzzle of the World Bank and IMF strategy to reshuffle power in the

Philippine government while assisting the country's shift toward export-oriented industrialization. When Bank officials decided to experiment with this "new approach to industrial lending in the Philippines,"[94] the move was engineered to circumvent a number of problem areas in one swift maneuver.

In the World Bank's own words, the creation of the ADFU was a central component of what it termed its "major justifications of the [apex] loan": "the broadening of the Bank's institution-building assistance to cover not only the three development finance institutions financed by the Bank in the past, but also other institutions in the financial sector, *including the Central Bank.*"[95] Rather than entangling itself directly in a cumbersome recon-struction of the *whole* of Licaros's Central Bank, the Bank had embarked on a much simpler form of institution-building—that deceptively small Apex Development Finance Unit. As a local newspaper explained in the most general terms, the "ADFU is intended not only to be a trend-setter, but an activist institution that will play a critical role in helping implement the government's industrial development strategy and would provide leadership."[96] The ADFU represented even more. By constructing this new in-stitution inside the Central Bank, the World Bank sought to realign the traditional nationalist power centers there.

To what extent Licaros and his six deputy governors sensed that the in-stitution-building component of this $150 million World Bank loan was conceived with an eye toward rendering many of them superfluous is not clear. According to Licaros (who was in office for much of the negotia-tions), he and his deputies were willing to allow the ADFU "to handle exclusively this World Bank loan," but they were not willing to "let it grow or take on more functions."[97]

To Licaros and others at the Central Bank, one worrisome aspect of the ADFU was the Bank's insistence on its autonomy.[98] Prior to the ADFU, the Central Bank hierarchy had been well demarcated: five "sectors" or groups of departments, each headed by a deputy governor on whom the governor kept tabs through a single senior deputy governor.[99] From the outset the ADFU stood as a unit, outside the bounds of any sector and beyond the reach of any deputy governor. It achieved what the Bank called "maximum operational autonomy," for, although it reported directly to the governor, the Central Bank's Monetary Board exercised authority over operational procedures.[100] This arrangement gave transnationalists outside the Central Bank the deciding voice. As Villanueva told it: "The World

Bank and the governor of the Central Bank [Licaros] agreed it would be best if [the ADFU] were permitted to develop on its own, . . . to be rather autonomous because of the unusual character the World Bank wanted it to have."[101]

The ADFU's unique position in the bureaucracy immediately distanced it from other Central Bank departments. But what elevated it above them was the status its staff members carried. This was no accident; precise staffing specifications formed a critical component of the World Bank's institution-building blueprints and hence of the Bank–Philippine government negotiations.[102] As Governor Licaros recalled, "The World Bank felt strongly that [the ADFU] should not be organized according to the normal ways the Central Bank is organized."[103] The contrast was striking: traditionally enormous Central Bank rooms spilling over with a swarm of lower-level bureaucrats, versus Villanueva's sedate suite with its initial dozen high-level staff members.[104]

To lead the unit, Villanueva was recruited from one of the highest executive positions in the Philippines' largest and most prestigious accountancy and auditing firm, SyCip, Gorres, and Velayo (SGV).[105] With him came his SGV assistant, who explained that the World Bank wanted a core of ADFU staff members to come from the private sector.[106] Having its top executives transformed from transnationalists in the private sector to key transnationalists in the Philippine state was nothing new for SGV. Indeed, at the time of the ADFU's formation, SGV boasted an impressive list of such alumni, most notably former senior partners Virata, Laya, and Roberto Ongpin.[107]

It was no secret that the World Bank was kindly disposed toward SGV. Many World Bank loan contracts with the Philippine government specified that the project auditor could be none other than SGV (an arrangement undoubtedly facilitated by the closeness SGV's Washington, D.C., office maintained with the Bank).[108] When queried about this bias, a Bank official explained that the more likely auditing candidate, the Philippine government's Commission on Audits, was, "by definition, not an objective auditor."[109] The result, bemoaned an inside observer, was that "there's an SGV mafia in the government today. It's a good part of our problem . . . for these are systems people . . . technocrats . . . without a feel for the national interest."[110] To the World Bank, these were laudatory epithets, descriptions of potential and real transnationalist allies.

For the potential allies, the World Bank added a training component to the loan, transforming a willing SGV (and associated) team into a Bank team. During Villanueva's intensive Bank training, he learned to "lean heavily" on World Bank insights and advice gained then and in a number of subsequent expeditions to Washington.[111] Another staff member spent two or three months studying at the Bank's Economic Development Institute, a sojourn that earned him the prestigious title of "EDI fellow" in the Philippine press.[112] Further training sessions for the other ADFU professionals became part of the apex loan agreement.[113] The World Bank went a step further to ensure transnationalist standards: at the Bank's suggestion, a United Nations Development Program (UNDP)–financed, but World Bank–recommended, foreign consultant would be dispatched to oversee the first two years of ADFU operations.[114]

Trained by World Bank personnel to employ World Bank criteria and evaluation methods, the ADFU staff was originally mandated to conduct a single operation: processing the industrial loans to be financed through the Bank's apex money. Almost immediately, however, the ADFU began to emerge as a key domestic institution that would play a central role in the economy-wide restructuring. Both the industrial rationalization (stimulated by the Bank and the Fund through the SAL and associated loans) and the concomitant financial rationalization (with its origins in the Bank's and Fund's universal-banking reforms) were to be sustained and amplified by the ADFU. Just as the IMF had earlier ducked into the wings to cede to the World Bank the leading role in their combined restructuring efforts, so now the Bank was to employ the ADFU as a Philippine shield to deflect attention from the Bank.

To further financial-sector restructuring, the ADFU spent early 1981 examining the soundness of local financial institutions to determine which merited accreditation as suitable conduits for the apex loan. Applicants, the Bank staff appraisal report for the apex loan affirmed, would be judged against the following criteria (criteria, Villanueva's assistant added, that had been set by the Bank itself):[115]

    a. sound financial position and performance and a healthy portfolio;

    b. sound operating policies and procedures, and a development-oriented strategy for future operations;

    c. an organization, management, and staff with the requisite expertise to undertake term lending operations including the technical, economic, and financial appraisal of projects and their supervision.[116]

"After an initial review with the World Bank on how you should look at an organization," Villanueva explained, "we assess the [financial] institution before its accreditation . . . and can suggest some minor changes."[117] "Minor" was not quite the best description. Given a sweeping mandate in this endeavor, the ADFU was empowered to stipulate conditions covering capital structure; operating policies, strategy, and planning; organization and staffing; and dividend and reserve policies, among others—certainly an open-ended, if not all-encompassing, list.[118] Indeed, the ADFU wielded power enough to demand step-by-step restructuring of nearly all facets of both public and private financial institutions.

Bank confidential documents confirm that even before the apex loan was signed the Bank and the ADFU had agreed on a list of candidates to be put through the ADFU institution-building regimen. Names filling the roster, according to Villanueva's assistant, came "at the World Bank's suggestion."[119] In addition to the three earlier recipients of Bank loans (DBP, PDCP, and the Philippine Investments Systems Organization [PISO]), the "most promising channels for the proposed Bank loan" included an impressive array. Eight of the existing twenty-six large private Filipino commercial banks (the eight included the six largest commercial banks and together controlled 42 percent of the total private commercial bank assets) as well as four of the ten remaining investment houses (all four with minority foreign ownership, and together shouldering nearly half of all investment house assets) were the first candidates.[120] An ECB license was not an ironclad prerequisite for accreditation by the ADFU, but the Bank clearly understood that it had selected fifteen institutions among those most likely to evolve, through mergers, consolidations, and TNB equity infusions, into the ECBs of the near future.[121] And as the ADFU began its process of accrediting "participatory financial institutions" in the early 1980s, this was exactly what happened: of the eight accredited institutions, by 1986 only one was not a universal bank.[122]

In other words, the ADFU accreditation process accelerated concentration in the financial sector and a buildup of the leading financial institutions. But there was a deeper significance to what the Bank acknowledged as reliance on Villanueva and his technocratic team as a means of "broadening . . . the Bank's institution-building assistance to cover . . . commercial banks."[123] Over each ADFU step, it must be recalled, the Bank exercised control and veto power ("not necessarily forever," explained Villanueva, "but at least for the first year or two, just to help us get the feel of things").[124]

Not only had the Bank and the Fund set the Philippine universal-banking reforms into motion, but also, through the ADFU, the World Bank hoped to shape the growth of the universal banks.

There was still another step in the apex loan disbursement. Under the coverage of this World Bank loan, the ADFU—and the World Bank behind it—extended into the industrial sector. Here, ADFU operations took over certain traits of the Bank's traditional loans to development finance companies. Once accredited by the ADFU, the "participatory financial institutions" would select industrial enterprises with projects deemed worthy of the apex loan money, primarily to finance the foreign-exchange cost of improving plants and equipment.[125]

Although Villanueva emphasized that the definition of worthwhile projects was open-ended and "a matter of ADFU discretion," there were definite bounds.[126] Indeed, only "export-oriented" and "labor-intensive" industries with total assets between P15 and P50 million (then $2 to $6.7 million) could send their project proposals to the participatory financial institutions for consideration.[127] The World Bank publicly claimed that such a range covered medium- and large-scale industries, and a scrutiny of the then top 1,000 Philippine corporations revealed about 550 eligible firms in the 300-to-900 range.[128] As many of the top 300 had foreign equity participation and experienced little difficulty in raising loans, the upshot of these eligibility requirements was to buttress large (but not the very largest) nontraditional exporters. The Bank estimated that the apex loan, if lent in full, could be stretched to assist some 170 such labor-intensive, export-oriented industries in their "establishment, expansion or rationalization."[129]

"The export-oriented and labor-intensive guidelines . . . are the same guidelines that have been used by the World Bank in the past," noted Villanueva's assistant proudly.[130] That was not fortuitous—these specific guidelines and priorities were agreed upon during the loan negotiations.[131] As the Bank's final report and recommendation on the apex loan emphasized, the ADFU would "closely monitor" the disbursement to ensure that funded projects furthered the government's "industrial policy . . . of encouraging industries which have an inherent comparative advantage and need minimum protection . . . or can compete effectively in the export market."[132]

"The Apex loan," boasted a Philippine newspaper in mid-1981, just prior to the signing of the loan, "is in line with a new World Bank concept, and the Philippines has been chosen as the most suitable country for the demonstration of the concept in Asia."[133] All indications were that by World Bank standards it was to go down as a successful demonstration. The SAL and apex loans were to become self-reinforcing. Between them, they bestowed on the Bank and the Fund astonishingly broad leverage to build, reshape, and buttress Philippine economic institutions.

Beyond the Apex Loan

The World Bank had longer-term visions for the ADFU; the $150 million was only a beginning, merely seed money. When the loan agreement between the Philippine government and the World Bank was sealed, the ADFU was given control not only over the Bank's $150 million but also over a $100 million "co-financing" fund to be supplied by transnational banks for the same apex operations.[134] Co-financing with TNBs was a 1974 innovation by the World Bank aimed at increasing its reach and—at no cost to itself—the funds available for its projects.

Such channeling of TNB loans to augment specific World Bank lending had been a rarity during the 1970s. But the opportunity to benefit from the World Bank's nearly flawless default record and its expanding economic role through its nonproject lending changed that: co-financing operations increased from one $55 million loan with just one TNB in 1975, to an average $200 million a year through the rest of that decade, to $1.8 billion with twenty TNBs by 1980.[135]

Recognizing that its co-financing arrangements still covered only a small, albeit growing, percentage of TNB lending to LDCs, the World Bank was now moving to use its policy-based loans to further extend its collaboration with TNBs—especially in what the Bank called the "higher-income" LDCs.[136] The Bank viewed its co-financing arrangements as ideal for the thirty-odd industrializing (and more debt-ridden) LDCs. Included were not only the seven NICs but also the next group of would-be NICs being groomed by the Bank and the Fund to take over as labor-intensive locations for TNCs' global production lines.

Moreover, to facilitate the shifting international division of labor, the World Bank steered its TNB co-financing into export-related sectors of these countries. For the Philippines, therefore, the Bank in 1980 pin-

pointed financial and industrial restructuring as top among the "particularly appropriate vehicles for co-financing," the amount of which "would
increase significantly in the next several years."[137] Thus was born the apex
loan's companion TNB loan.

In the case of the apex loan, co-financing not only placed $100 million
in TNB lending under the World Bank "umbrella," but it also amplified—
indeed, nearly doubled in monetary terms—the ADFU domain. As such,
it was a move not warmly received by Licaros's Central Bank during the
months of policy dialogue.

The altercation over whether the apex loan would include a co-financing
component was one of the rare debates that could be followed by reading
between the lines of Manila's newspapers. In November 1980, the media
announced (under the attention-grabbing headline of "WB Plan Spurned")
that although the World Bank "wants [the proposed apex loan] to be
funded through a co-financing arrangement," Licaros's Central Bank was
not "in favor of raising [the then-discussed] $50 million counterpart."[138]
By the end of that year, Licaros's oppositionist stance was reported to have
hardened further. The Central Bank, relayed the newspaper reports, "does
not intend to increase" the ADFU loan fund by $50 million in co-financ-
ing, but "will make do with the proposed loan" of $150 million.[139]

Making do, however, turned out not to be an option. As Licaros recollected events, sometime before he vacated office (just weeks after these
newspaper reports depicted his firm opposition), he finally acquiesced to
co-financing upon realizing that the "World Bank people were dead set on
this matter."[140] With Laya as governor, the World Bank easily increased the
co-financing requirements, doubling the stakes from the original $50 mil-
lion to $100 million. Even then, however, the Bank took no chances: an
April 1981 confidential report revealed that co-financing had become one
of the "special conditions" to be met before the apex loan was signed. Indeed, the Central Bank had until July 31, 1981, to secure $100 million
from TNBs for the apex project.[141]

This requirement proved among the easiest to fulfill of the whole array
of Bank and Fund conditions accompanying the SAL and apex loans. As
World Business Weekly explained to its predominantly business audience, the
$100 million appeal was answered rapidly and on extremely favorable
terms from the Philippine government's perspective. This was, in large
part, because co-financing with the World Bank "had a special attraction to

banks" because they "know the World Bank is a stickler for prompt repayment" of both principal and interest.[142]

This—and an optional cross-default clause ensuring that the Bank would employ its "good offices" should repayment problems arise—was an important catalyst for the TNBs' largesse.[143] A 1976 World Bank booklet on co-financing provides a somewhat more exhaustive picture of why a consortium of TNBs might so readily accept the Bank's Philippine proposition. Among the general advantages cited were the following:

> The Bank, with the consent of the borrower, provides them [TNBs] with information on the country and the project. This aspect of the co-financing relationship is very important for private investors, who are usually not in a position to conduct as comprehensive an analysis of the projects for which they make loans. They also benefit from the regular supervision of the project by the Bank's staff.
>
> The World Bank assumes certain administrative responsibilities in respect of the private loan, such as assisting in its disbursement and acting as a channel for service payments by the borrower. . . .
>
> Commercial banks also have investment quotas for the countries in which they do business. . . . Some of the bankers have expressed the view that co-financing arrangements with the World Bank might enable them to make some additional funds available to a country even where their lending quota for the country was virtually exhausted. Whatever the possibilities for some of the higher-income developing countries to tap the longer-term, private institutional market in the United States, they are likely to be greatly enhanced if the private loans are arranged on a co-financing basis with the World Bank.[144]

Co-financing was also a way to set the stage for a growing proportion of Philippine borrowings from TNBs to be funneled through the ADFU. According to Villanueva's assistant, the ADFU expected to be the recipient of "higher and higher amounts of World Bank money after the first two years,"[145] a point reinforced in Bank and ADFU documents that made reference to apex loans rather than to a single apex loan.[146] Beyond the Bank loans, disclosed Governor Licaros, "the World Bank wanted part, if not all, of our [foreign] commercial loan borrowing to be channeled through the ADFU."[147]

Licaros elucidated his objections to the proposal:

> I did not agree to this, because the ADFU will be controlled by World Bank policies and reviewed by the World Bank. . . . My thinking is that the more money the World Bank channels to the Philippines through ADFU, the better. And if those World Bank loans involve co-financing, that too can go through

ADFU. But no more. . . . Having all our [international] commercial borrowing go through ADFU as a general rule would subvert approval of all our borrowing to World Bank conditions and evaluations . . . but I wouldn't be surprised if Governor Laya thinks differently.[148]

Less than three months after Licaros's dismissal, his intuition was borne out by an April 7, 1981, World Bank staff appraisal report. In assessing whether or not the Philippine government had adequately implemented the array of financial reforms on which subsequent approval of the apex loan hinged, the report noted:

The guidelines approved by the Monetary Board were generally satisfactory but some modifications were necessary to bring them in line with the basic philosophy of the proposed Bank financing, as are some additions, to make them more comprehensive. First, instead of being restricted to administering foreign exchange funds obtained from the Bank and ADB [Asian Development Bank], ADFU should have the capability of mobilizing and administering funds raised from other sources including foreign commercial banks. This is needed not only for raising the overall resources required for the project [i.e., for cofinancing], . . . but also for the long-term development of ADFU. . . . The Central Bank agreed to incorporate the necessary amendments in the operating policy guidelines and has since obtained Monetary Board's approval to the revised guidelines.[149]

Before the month of April drew to a close, precisely such expanded authority for fund-raising operations was bestowed on the ADFU by the Philippine government.[150]

When earlier that same month World Bank staff drew up a statement delineating the ADFU's "operating policy guidelines," there was no pretension that the apex loan stood as the ADFU's main mission. At the top of the list of the ADFU's "major functions" came the much broader role of administering "financial resources provided/loaned to the Central Bank by international lending agencies and other sources . . . for financing the medium- and long-term needs of the Philippine industrial sector, all in accordance with national economic priorities."[151] This, explained the Bank elsewhere, "should improve the Central Bank's institutional capacity as an onlender of funds for development purposes."[152] It was as Licaros had feared.

The World Bank's ADFU venture arrived none too soon for TNB lending to the Philippines. By 1981, as Philippine export growth dwindled, external debt spiraled, and a spate of bankruptcies shook the industrial sector, international bankers saw hazards ahead.[153] "In general, but especially in times like these now," explained an IMF official with special reference to the Philippine scenario, "the more influence the Fund or Bank . . . has on an economy's development path and . . . on making sure money is used rationally . . . to economically viable end uses, the better it is for other foreign lenders and investors."[154]

International bankers seemed only too happy to accept a new structure whereby the majority of their loans would be channeled through a transnationalist-controlled, domestic institution operating on World Bank specifications and under World Bank oversight. From their perspective, such a setup greatly enhanced the chances of repayment. And as far as the World Bank and the IMF were concerned, this latest attempt at institution-building opened new vistas, for with it came a guaranteed structure for funneling loans, to the maximum extent possible, into export-oriented industrialization. If co-financing had, in the Bank's words, "prompted more efficient and economic use of the total external resources available," how much more effective would the ADFU be in ensuring the Philippines' strict adherence to Bank and Fund priorities.[155]

Another indication that the World Bank had built the ADFU with an eye to extending the Bank's and Fund's domestic control came in early 1981, months before the apex loan agreement was sealed. The official story was as follows: the January 1981 revelations of fugitive businessman Dewey Dee's huge debt default generated severe apprehensions among Philippine industrial creditors. Fearing that Dewey Dee was but a symptom of a deeper economic malaise, most local and international lenders halted short-term lending, and some began recalling past loans, leaving Philippine industries in a potentially deadly credit crunch. To "keep the whole economy from crumbling until the Dewey Dee mess was sorted out,"[156] the Philippine government threw together a $650 million (P5 billion) "industrial finance fund" (more commonly referred to in Manila as a "rescue troubled companies fund"). The government office slated to administer the rescue operation was none other than the World Bank's spin-off, Villanueva's ADFU.[157]

Placing the blame on Dewey Dee's shoulders was easy, but it was not quite the whole story. A year and a half before the Dee default broke into the headlines, Bank and Philippine government officials had agreed that precisely such an "assistance program" (above and beyond the other SAL-related "rationalization/rehabilitation programs") might well have to be initiated for companies in the industrial sectors hardest hit by the "tariff reduction program."[158] Dee's textile sector would certainly have been high on the list. In other words, although Dee's departure sharpened the crisis, it was not the root cause. Salient among the causes of the ensuing credit squeeze were the strict, IMF-imposed restrictions on the growth of domestic credit and money supply, which exacerbated the tightness of short-term funds in late 1980.[159]

But the Dee caper provided the ideal rationale to broaden the ADFU focus. The ADFU described its task in administering the industrial finance fund in words that seemed to come out of the apex loan documents: "The fund is aimed to be used to provide basic structural changes in the financial make-up of a qualified company accompanied by required changes in the management, ownership and organizational structures of the enterprise."[160]

Not just any enterprise could avail itself of the largesse. On this point, the industrial finance fund's statement of policy left no ambiguity: only "industries and specific enterprises" playing "a critical and crucial role in the national economy"—gauged by the "economic importance of the industry" and, in turn, the "relative importance of the enterprise to the industry"—were eligible.[161] Indeed, Governor Laya himself whittled the list down to a choice "13 companies/Groups" to be aided.[162] "An important criterion for assistance," explained a government official, "was, of course, the company's actual or potential foreign-exchange earnings. This way we can use the fund to further our other development goals."[163]

The ADFU's reach through the industrial finance fund extended beyond the industrial sector to the newly created universal banks. As with the apex loan, industrial rationalization was undertaken by the ADFU through what was basically a subset of its accredited financial institutions—either potential or actual universal banks, or the major institutional shareholders of such banks. In turn, these financial conduits were encouraged to go about their task by purchasing equity in the troubled companies.[164]

Indeed, Villanueva and his staff put their World Bank training to good use in resuscitating and reshaping a select group of major transnationalist Filipino-owned conglomerates with international business ties. As headlines of international magazine articles noted, the rescue operation was a classic case of "A Little Help for Some Friends," a "Helping Hand" for the "Sweetheart" firms.[165]

In the process, those who had come to be known in the Philippines as Marcos's cronies—whose companies had grown rich and powerful over the previous decade more as a result of favored positions than of business acumen—were (at least for the moment) to be saved from a fate the ADFU admitted was "eventual insolvency and bankruptcy," as long as they put up with the requisite remolding.[166] It was necessarily a painful process for the cronies, but the adjustments were certainly preferable to the uncushioned bankruptcies plaguing the smaller, unfavored nationalist entrepreneurs.

Once again, the World Bank was playing a critical role in exacerbating the concentration of economic and political power in the Philippines. But this time, the Bank perfected a way to work from afar through a domestic institutional substitute. Creation of the ADFU allowed the Bank to continue its and the Fund's program for restructuring the Philippine economy toward export-oriented industrialization while maintaining the illusion of unsoiled hands.

8

Reshaping the Philippines' Political Economy

Like the SAL, the apex loan and its concomitant reforms wrought far-reaching changes in certain institutions and social groups. The financial reforms reinforced the industrial restructuring's squeeze on national entrepreneurs and industrial labor. But the ramifications of the financial reforms did not stop there. More than had the SAL, the apex loan precipitated a reshaping of the entire Philippine political economy and of the ways major institutions and social groups within it meshed. By the early 1980s, the potency of the financial reforms could be clearly seen in the enhanced concentration within and interactions among institutions of finance, industry, and government.

This metamorphosis can be traced graphically (see Figure 1). During the early 1980s, the transnationalist factions of both the Philippine state and the private sector (finance and industry) expanded, encroaching further on economic nationalist factions. Repercussions of state policy on private institutions also grew, as the Marcos government assumed functions previously held by the private sector. Finally, collaboration between private international and transnationalist domestic actors deepened, as loans and investments between the two grew in size and number.

162

"Separating the Men from the Boys"

Concentration of economic power invariably generates apprehensions from several quarters; Philippine financial-sector concentration was to prove no exception. In the perceptions of those Central Bank high-level officers who shared Governor Licaros's views, a nightmarish vision loomed of the financial sector emerging from the banking reforms conceived by the World Bank and the IMF. Licaros's special assistant Aurellano put it into writing: the specter of "very large financial institutions, large by our standards, . . . able to dominate the financial sector."[1] A meticulously researched article on universal banking, written by a Central Bank bureaucrat, appeared in the magazine of one of the Philippines' most prestigious universities (known to be a center of nationalist thinking) and echoed Aurellano's charge, expanding it into a concern felt by the growing student movement.[2] The subject found its way into sermons preached by some of the more socially active members of the Philippines' powerful Roman Catholic Church.[3] And in the business and financial world, executives of smaller banks and investment houses, when asked about universal banking, voiced deep-seated fears about the impending concentration and their own futures.[4]

Philippine technocrats as well as World Bank and IMF financial missions tried to head off such concerns, arguing that they had framed the changes with built-in safeguards. As the authors of the legislation explained in an introduction to the universal-banking rules and regulations, "the dangers of declining competitive conditions or of increasing oligopoly have not been overlooked." Specifically, they insisted, they had been mindful of the "dangers . . . in which one or a few large banks dominate the financial system, with all its social implications and to the detriment of maintaining effective conditions of competition."[5] Similarly, the Bank and the Fund acknowledged in their joint report on the Philippine financial sector that "these dangers are the possibility of increased concentration of market power, and potential conflicts of interest. Concentration in the financial sector tends to create excessive market power for a few institutions."[6]

By admitting such dangers, these Bank, Fund, and Philippine government officials implied that they had shaped the financial reforms cautiously, with an eye to avoiding adverse repercussions. Indeed, these three sets of technocrats went a step further: they insisted that universal banking was structured to destroy what Minister Virata argued was an already existing financial "oligopolistic system," by forcing "active competition" onto the banking sector.[7] Thus, the groundwork for the implementing rules for universal banking was carefully laid out by rationalizations, claiming that one of the "main objectives" of the 1980 financial reforms was to stimulate "increasing competitive conditions with resultant greater efficiency."[8]

Elsewhere, however, the Bank and the Fund gave a slightly different twist to the likely scenario:

> The implications for the financial system would be far reaching in that a new division of labor will emerge on the basis of comparative advantage. While it is unlikely that the changes will be swift and dramatic, some institutions may well change their character, or disappear over time. The changes are bound to cause some unhappiness to those who have interests in the present system. From the authorities' point of view the criterion of change should be whether it contributes to the long-run efficiency of the system, consistent with the maintenance of a stable monetary system.[9]

Philippine financial reforms, echoed a confidential IMF assessment, "are expected to promote a rationalization of the structure of the financial sector through mergers and acquisitions and, hence, to make for a more efficient system of financial intermediation.[10]

Philippine technocrats' words also conveyed this altered nuance: through the financial reforms, these officials admitted, a group of banks was being groomed to "assume an even more influential role in the banking sector."[11] This change was being wrought by (among other means) deeming "mergers or consolidations . . . a desirable policy" and relaxing the former "absolute rule that no person shall be allowed to be concurrently a director of one bank and an officer of another."[12]

If the scramble among banks to attain universal-bank status, with its attendant bankruptcies and takeovers, can be called "competition," then the financial reforms represented competition in its highest form. That the resulting economic formation would be characterized by an oligopoly consisting of an exiguous number of large banks with close ties to the largest industrial firms was not mentioned. Nor were the adverse effects of this oligopoly on competition (and hence potentially on efficiency) popular topics with the Bank and the Fund.[13] Once again, the World Bank, the IMF, and their transnationalist domestic allies masked the implications of their policies with words chosen to soothe the fears of their domestic critics.

Bank and Fund documents and officials made no attempt to clear up the contradiction between the "active competition" they publicly professed to be facilitating and the likely oligopolistic outcomes of the new policy.[14] Philippine technocrat Armand Fabella—who coined the phrase "expanded commercial banking"—was more candid. Fabella's central role as liaison with the Bank and the Fund over the reforms and the noticeable reluctance of his colleagues to pursue the subject in interviews make it worthwhile to quote him at some length:

> The name of the game was increasing competition in the financial sector, . . . a specific type of competition: expanded commercial banking is a technique for separating the men from the boys, so that your more efficient private banks would manifest themselves more efficiently. . . . The philosophy behind expanded commercial banking is how much competition to [allow], . . . because competition can be very expensive. And some bigness can be very useful. You need bigness for economic growth. . . .
> [With ECB] it is possible to build up a financial conglomerate. . . . That's the whole name of the game. You put out a carrot to separate . . . the men from the boys. And then you sit back and watch the race. . . . That's what I'm doing now: crossing my fingers. . . . As long as the men don't form an exclusive club, there's no problem. . . .
> And if they do? . . . And, if they do, well, that's a problem for the future— hopefully. Hopefully, because if things go well, as we hope, we should have the problem of bigness. . . . If things go poorly, we won't have the problem of bigness. We'll be poor, and I don't buy the poor-but-happy argument. I'd rather see the former [the problems of bigness], and then deal with the rationalization. . . . Hopefully we will have to deal with the problem in the future, because it will mean we are doing well.[15]

Fabella was careful to convey that his vision was shared by the Fund and Bank officials who hammered out the reforms with his Banking Survey Commission. "We were all in this one together," he stressed. "In fact, our friends from the World Bank and IMF wanted to move in this direction even faster than I thought prudent . . . or possible."[16]

By the onset of universal banking in 1981, the Philippine financial sector was already relatively highly concentrated. Although 2,653 financial institutions existed in mid-1981 (1,209 of them banks), 121 of them accounted for 56 percent of the assets of the top 1,000 Philippine corporations (see Table 7). The leading thirty-one commercial banks accounted for 72 percent of total financial-sector assets. These giant commercial banks and a handful of large investment banks stood to gain the most from

Table 7.   Banks and Financial Institutions in the Top 1,000 Philippine
            Corporations, 1981

	Number	Assets[g]	Gross Revenues[g]	Net Income[g]
Commercial banks	31	161,286	20,390	1,436
Government/semi-government[a]	3	52,663	6,539	259
Private domestic[b]	24	92,231	11,110	993
Branches of foreign banks[c]	4	16,392	2,741	184
Private development banks[d]	2	659	86	12
Savings and mortgage banks	5	5,860	541	(65)[e]
Offshore banking units	18	35,230	4,474	147
Nonbank financial intermediaries	65	21,139	7,535	450
Insurance companies	45	8,183	5,471	311
Investment houses[f]	8	7,518	904	87
Financing companies	10	5,098	978	32
Investment companies	2	340	182	20
Total	121	224,174	33,028	1,980
Top 1,000 corporations	1,000	402,533	212,030	2,387
Banks and financial institutions as percentage of top 1,000	12.1%	55.7%	15.6%	82.9%

SOURCE: Ibon Databank, *The Philippine Financial System—A Primer* (Manila: Ibon Databank, 1983), p. 34.

[a] Includes Philippine National Bank, Philippine Veterans Bank, and Republic Planters Bank.

[b] Includes banks taken over by the Philippine government in 1981. Also includes Family Bank (formerly Family Savings Bank).

[c] Bank of America, Chartered Bank, Citibank, Hong Kong and Shanghai Bank.

[d] PDCP not included.

[e] Includes Union Savings & Mortgage Bank (now Union Bank), which incurred a net loss of P94 million in 1981.

[f] PDCP included.

[g] Expressed in millions of pesos.

the reforms. It was the more than 1,000 tiny rural banks, the thrift banks, and the smaller investment houses that faced takeover or liquidation.[17]

From the time the race for universal-bank status began, events spoke for themselves. By early 1982, five out of the thirty-three (public and private) commercial banks had reached that goal—all five having already occupied prominent positions among the top ten of the banking sector.[18] That trend continued into 1982 as the number of ECBs among the top fifteen commercial banks grew to nine by mid-year. By the end of the year these nine were joined by what had been the Philippines' largest savings bank.[19] By 1983, the ten ECBs were off and running. Their net incomes grew by 40 percent that year, as against 19 percent for other commercial banks. The four TNBs with fully owned branches in the Philippines fared even better, registering a 60 percent growth in net incomes in 1983, following a 72 percent growth in 1982.[20] Meanwhile, smaller banks fought for survival.[21]

Merger waves in the early 1980s stood as further testimony to the tightening financial oligopoly. Far East Bank and Trust Company (partially owned by Mitsui Bank and Chemical International Finance, each with 12.5 percent) merged with the World Bank's old conduit, PDCP.[22] The wealthy Ayala family's Bank of the Philippine Islands (the third largest commercial bank as of 1978, in which both the Philippine Roman Catholic Church and J. P. Morgan have substantial interests) and the Commercial Bank and Trust Company of the Philippines (whose largest stockholder is Chase Manhattan, with 30 percent) joined forces.[23] American Express's Bancom Development Corporation, an investment house, was taken over by the Bancom Group's Union Savings Bank, which then merged with the government's Land Bank of the Philippines.[24] The race was on.

Interlocking directorates provided another indication of the biggest banking groups' tightening hold over the sector. Pre-merger Bancom and Far East Bank and Trust, for example, shared five directors on their respective boards, yielding what were termed "closely integrated" operations.[25] Yet, in spite of expectations to the contrary, they chose not to merge with one another. Instead, the union of Far East Bank and Trust with PDCP brought to the former the benefits of the latter's interlocking directorates with the first two universal banks.[26]

As Minister Virata acknowledged in the aftermath of these friendly mergers, the days of the investment houses "are now numbered."[27] Whereas eight investment houses ranked among the top 1,000 Philippine corporations in 1981, only five remained two years later.[28] What Virata failed to add was that the days of Fabella's "exclusive men's club" were already upon the Philippine banking sector.

"Bring in a Foreign Partner"

Domestic banks were not the only institutions to feel the impact of the Bank's and the Fund's financial reforms. Transnational banks and corporations stood in the ranks of the major gainers. As such, they were often principal targets of the harangues against the financial-sector reforms heard inside and outside the Central Bank in its nationalist-dominated days.[29] When elite opposition to Marcos denounced the 1981 "paper lifting" of martial law, they deplored the fact that "Filipino banking and financial institutions" were being "put . . . at a disadvantage with the multinationals and foreign institutions" in the wake of the financial reforms.[30]

In this context, the IMF-prompted financial reforms of the early 1970s provided a microcosm of how TNBs stood to gain from the reforms. "It was felt," summarized a knowledgeable source close to the Central Bank, "that following the precedent of the 1972 . . . financial reform which led to merger and consolidation [of Philippine commercial banks] with foreign banks, the foreign presence in banks will only increase with universal banking."[31]

The historical evidence was unambiguous: between 1972 and 1976, under the Central Bank exhortation to "put up the money, merge, or bring in a foreign partner," the private domestic commercial banking sector had been transformed from one in which foreign participation was prohibited to one in which foreigners controlled nearly a third of total equity.[32] In all, a dozen TNBs had come to the rescue of the third of Philippine commercial banks that were unable to expand to the increased requisite P100 million capitalization minimum on their own. Of the twelve, six were American, three Japanese, two Canadian, and one British; each acquired between 10 and 40 percent investment in a local bank.[33]

Nearly half a decade later, none of universal banking's proponents made much attempt to deny the likelihood that the 1980 minimum capitalization increase would entail an intensified replay of earlier events. An IMF official involved in Philippine work tried to be noncommittal about whether greater TNB participation was purposely built into the IMF and World Bank plans: "No one would be too surprised if Western banks took advantage of the opportunity we're creating."[34] Another indication was provided by the Fund's and the Bank's joint report: "The openness of the economy makes it necessary for commercial banks to develop international links."[35]

TNBs did respond. In 1983, the Philippine research organization Ibon Databank chronicled the equity participation of twenty-one transnational banks in large Philippine financial institutions: the United States (twelve), Japan (four), the United Kingdom (three), and Germany and Canada (one each).[36] In all but three cases foreign equity participation exceeded 10 percent, and it rose as high as 40 percent. These shares were put in perspective by a former official of the U.S. Federal Reserve System's Regulation and Supervision Division: a mere 10 percent interest, according to him, sufficed to give a U.S. bank "substantial say in the management policy of the foreign institution."[37]

There might have seemed little reason to complain about the enlarged domestic banking resources if this increase in long-term lending and equity investment was to be channeled into strengthening domestically oriented industries and services. But just the opposite was to be the case. As Licaros's special assistant Aurellano warned, "If the banking institutions, through merger and integration with related financial intermediaries, become larger, it may be even more difficult [than it was before universal banking] for the smaller borrowers to obtain financing since it has been observed that the larger institutions have shown preference for servicing loan requirements of larger and well-established firms."[38]

Verbal attacks leveled by Licaros and his associates were even more specific.[39] For, as was elucidated by *Asian Finance* magazine, "Multinationals have been the traditional borrower-clients of the [Philippine] local banking system, a fact which Filipino bankers seem to welcome and the populace, as a whole, to abhor."[40] A failing national entrepreneur, decrying the framers of the 1980 industrial and financial reforms, was somewhat more emotional about the matter:

> If our machinery is old . . . it's because we often could not avail ourselves of loans. If you're big, . . . a multinational, . . . well, that's no problem for you here then. But they [the TNC subsidiaries or joint venture operations] soak up the funds. We wait in line, . . . but, by then, it's gone.[41]

In the case of the Philippines, the phenomenon of TNCs borrowing more capital domestically than they bring across the border into host LDCs has been well documented, leading to historical (but unheeded) demands by nationalists for "filipinization of credit."[42] According to a mid-1970s Manila Jaycees' report, TNCs operating in the Philippines had, at that point, borrowed what amounted to a startling three-quarters of domestic banks' combined capital accounts.[43]

That universal-banking reforms were destined to exacerbate this imbalance was undebatable. As part of the financial-reform package, noted a confidential IMF report, "guidelines on domestic borrowing by foreign firms engaged in export-oriented activities were liberalized" even further.[44] For every 40 cents an exporting TNC carried in from abroad, 60 cents could now be tapped from local sources.[45] Explained a Central Bank official with access to the relevant accounts:

> Nontraditional exports demand less capital investment per worker. . . . But that's a deceptive statement for a country like ours . . . [because] what we're seeing is that . . . multinationals supply even *less* capital on their own and rely on us [domestic banks] for an even greater percent. . . . In fact, we [the Philippine government] encourage them to do so. . . . It might be insane from your view, but, to us, it makes sense. If not, they'll go somewhere else. . . . So it makes sense that we're being encouraged to increase our domestic bank assets if our growth strategy relies on this [export-oriented industrialization].[46]

Benefits that the Bank- and Fund-conceived financial-reform package held for transnational banks and corporations did not revolve solely around the expanded capitalization and lending capabilities of the enlarged domestic banks. TNBs and TNCs were also catered to through the ADFU-led restructuring in both its facets: TNBs, via the requisite reshaping of domestic banks prior to accreditation; TNCs, via the apex loan's and the rescue operation's industrial remolding.

A quick recounting of TNBs' experiences after their 1972 influx into the Philippine domestic banking sector is again helpful to grasp the 1980 implications. Overall profit rates for U.S. direct foreign investment in Philippine banking ranged between 28 and 41 percent from 1977 to 1980, dwarfing overall Philippine profit rates for U.S. firms, which ran from 13 to 15 percent over this period.[47] Individual banks reported impressive figures: Bank of America's wholly owned Manila branch, for instance, was disclosed to be one of its top ten most profitable overseas branches.[48]

The ADFU's 1980s oversight role in reforming certain bank structures and policies prior to accreditation was attractive to TNBs and TNCs for another reason. Corrupt practices endemic to the Philippine banking sector had, over the course of the late 1970s, led to severe dissatisfaction among certain TNBs. "Many of the foreigners found the cosiness, the sometimes lackadaisical attitude and the lack of professionalism in some Filipino banks more than they could stomach," noted *Euromoney* magazine rather bluntly.[49] One foreign banker phrased the dilemma somewhat more euphemistically: "There is quite a lot of 'paternalism' in Philippine banking practices. There is a lot of 'paternalism' in banking management too. This turned off the foreign bank partners."[50]

In TNCs' industrial undertakings, similar dissatisfaction was often expressed. "Of all the country's problems, the one that most seriously undermines the confidence of international bankers and investors is the high-level corruption that pervades Philippine life like jungle rot," affirmed *Fortune*.[51]

Until 1980, corruption was practically unavoidable, for it was precisely the most corrupt of the transnationalist-oriented Philippine businessmen, Marcos's cronies, who boasted the tightest links to the domestic power centers. As Peter Evans noted in the case of Brazil, "Foreign groups with [local] partners embedded in the local social structure have a special competitive advantage over those who lack such partners."[52] In the Philippines, the cronies were the most logical choice for TNCs' partners in joint ventures; indeed, those TNCs with the best crony connections were winning the choice deals from the Marcos administration.

For TNCs, however, the payoffs required by the domestic partner could rise only so high before the entire venture became of dubious profitability.[53] Enter the World Bank–trained ADFU. It was precisely such a nominally independent institution that was in the best position to force the necessary changes onto the erring enterprises. As the ADFU guidelines revealed, Villanueva's official mandate in the industrial arena covered this terrain ably: "Professionalization of the Management and Management Reorganization," it was called.[54] Licaros's replacement, Governor Laya, aptly phrased the ADFU's task as overcoming existing "defects in management."[55] A similar concern pervaded the ADFU's financial accreditation work.[56]

When Ferdinand Marcos called representatives of the foreign business community to the presidential palace in February 1981, it was no secret that he was seeking to reassure them of the post–martial law regime's belief in "foreign investment," "private enterprise," and "stability."[57] But his reassurances went beyond the traditional litany. One TNC executive based in Manila recapitulated Marcos's promises in words that bring the ADFU restructuring to mind:

> We're going to see more of . . . [a] businesslike atmosphere around here now, . . . more professional managers of Western sensibilities. . . .
>
>   I suppose you could say there's been a bit of pressure, . . . a bit of pushing (if you will) on Marcos. . . . Yes, I suppose you could say there's been some pressures pushing him to restructure his cronies to reassure us foreign investors.[58]

But it was neither the TNCs nor the TNBs that had to do this "pushing." The Bank and the Fund, with their enhanced leverage, served the purpose well.

The Triple Alliance

Only when the impacts of the industrial and financial restructurings are considered jointly does their full significance emerge. It was not just industry that was being restructured. And it was not just industry and finance. The change was far broader. The entire Philippine political economy was being reshaped toward a well-coordinated meshing of industry, finance, and state—what could be called a triple alliance.[59]

In this sense, the transformed political economy brought the Philippines several steps closer to the Japanese model of tight collaboration among these three sectors.[60] The difference is that the Philippine alliance remained closely tied in with, and dependent on, large foreign banks and corporations. In the case of the Philippines, this entwinement among major economic and political institutions was being stimulated by the Bank and the Fund, in the name of creating a structure that could compete better on the global market.

A major factor in these overall shifts was the evolving symbiosis between the newly emerging concentrated structures of finance and industry. The strengthening of this industrial-financial alliance should come as no surprise. It was a natural extension of a reform that encouraged expanded commercial banks to hold up to 35 percent of an industrial corporation's stock. The bonds were being tightened by bank actions, but industry was also a catalyst. As an IMF official with years of experience in the Philip-

pines acknowledged, "You could say that our universal-banking reforms
. . . add to the logic of big industrialists going into commercial banking."[61]

It must be stressed that the 1980 financial reforms were only strengthening an alliance that had existed for decades. For almost all private Philippine commercial banks, there is an industrial group or foreign enterprise
that effectively owns it or dominates its board.[62] Long before universal
banks, directors crisscrossed between industry and finance, sitting together at a board meeting of an industrial enterprise one week, of a bank
the next, and of another corporation soon after. A late-1970s study of such
"interlocking directorates" revealed that the directors of a sample dozen
Philippine banks reappeared as board members of "305 financial, manufacturing and commercial enterprises" and that eighty-one Filipino families,
spread across ten banking groups, had become dominant actors in the economy.[63] To take another example, all of the twelve Philippine trading companies selected by the government to launch the export drive shared their
directors, if not major stockholders, with at least one financial institution.[64]

Universal banking pulled the network much closer together. It was
precisely the owners or directors of the largest commercial banks—the
emerging universal banks—who controlled the vastest industrial (and
agricultural) holdings: Lucio Tan of the tobacco industry, Ramon Siy of
textiles, the Ayala-Zobel family with their sixty-odd corporations, the coconut industry's Eduardo Cojuangco, and Herminio Disini, among others.[65]
In other words, the gainers from the industrial and financial restructuring
did not simply intersect; they reinforced one another.

Central Bank officials involved in regulating the pre-1980 banking sector had no trouble presaging that the equity investment arena thrown open
by the universal-banking reforms would "result in concentration of too
much economic power in the hands of a few individuals."[66] Large banks
had always favored lending to the larger corporations. With the big getting
bigger in each of these sectors and with the stakes extended to include
equity participation, excessive concentration and widespread conflict-of-
interest situations could be expected. As Licaros's special assistant Aurellano
argued in his 1979 anti-universal-banking memorandum:

> When a bank acquires equity in a private corporation, the probability of abuse
> in the extension of credit to that corporation would be increased. The bank may
> not be able to evaluate objectively the application for loans of a corporation in

which it has acquired equity. The bank may even be practically forced to support the said corporation even if its credit standing does not warrant additional loans in the bank's desire to help the corporation if it is in difficulties to protect its investment. At present, supervisory authorities already have a problem in controlling loans granted by banks to directors, officers, stockholders and related interests (DOSRI). The history of banking in the Philippines shows that management of banks have not always exercised objectivity in processing loan applications of firms with special relationships with the bank. In a majority of bank failures, one of the common principal causes was overextension of credit to DOSRI. We feel that to allow banks to acquire equities of private corporations would give rise to similar or perhaps more difficult problems.[67]

Officially, the Bank, the Fund, and their allied Philippine technocrats insisted that "safeguards" were built into the 1980 financial reforms to ensure that (in Armand Fabella's words) "things stop short of financial-industrial conglomerates as you see in the extreme in Germany."[68] An ECB's maximum total equity investment in all undertakings was limited by law to 50 percent of the ECB's net worth; a single investment, to 15 percent.[69] Furthermore, the combined investment of all banks in a given "non-allied" enterprise had to remain a minority.[70]

"Safeguards" was perhaps a misnomer in this case. What the big bankers had petitioned for during the pre-reform debates was legislation that would ensure them an effective minority veto in major decisions of industrial enterprises.[71] The 35 percent equity ceiling bestowed on them ample opportunity to realize precisely this. No one was asking for "absolute control," yet Bank, Fund, and Philippine government officials flaunted their "guard against absolute control" of industries by banks as a sign that the reforms were framed with the intent to prevent "undue concentration of power."[72]

At other times, Bank and Fund officials twisted the rationalization a bit differently by arguing that the "already close informal links between banks, business groups and other financial institutions . . . might well tend to become more formal and thus more visible and controllable" in the wake of the reforms.[73] But a more logical inference turned the Bank and Fund rationalization on its head—for the reforms sanctioned broader links, which led to an even less controllable environment. As this May 1980 Bank and Fund report itself continued, "The closer association of banks and industries need present little conflict of interest . . . because growth and profitability of banks and industries would be of mutual interest to both groups."[74] This statement was closer to the point, encapsulating the Bank's and the Fund's vision of the oligopolistic structures that had to be forged within and between the Philippine industrial and financial sectors if the demands of export-oriented industrialization were to be met.

Facilitating this industrial and financial cohesion was the enhanced role the Philippine state assumed, under World Bank and IMF prodding. An attachment to Virata's August 1980 letter to McNamara included a promise of "closer cooperation . . . between the government and the private sectors in the . . . implementation of the industry policies and program."[75] As events of the early 1980s unfolded, that cooperation slowly emerged as a strengthened role for the state—the third member of the industrial-financial alliance—an ideal partner for facilitating the requisite transformation of the other two.

Government activities expanded to mesh with the Bank's and the Fund's molding of enlarged enclaves for transnationalist allies both inside and outside the Central Bank. High-level government technocrats were by and large reluctant to admit as much, but the ADFU industrial rescue fund did serve, in part, as a scheme for more tightly weaving the state in with the private sector. Ailing firms, whose survival might rest with ADFU loans, were required to accept the possibility of government equity participation.[76] Government equity was even infused into many of the emerging private universal banks, a practice that was to spread in the depression months following the 1983 Aquino assassination. As a result, billions of government pesos flowed into key enterprises in the financial and industrial sectors, so much so that new net credit to the public sector for 1981 represented 52 percent of the expansion of total domestic liquidity, an all-time high.[77] (That figure was almost four times the 1979–1980 average of 14 percent.)[78]

In such periods of crisis, private-sector links with the state are usually not entered into reluctantly. Evans's observations on this score point up important benefits:

> The ability of state enterprises to enter into alliances with both the multinationals and the national bourgeoisie arises in part from the recognition by the private partners that the state's contribution is valuable to them, not only in terms of the actual capital provided but also in terms of security. Partner-

ship with state enterprises usually improves relations with the rest of the state apparatus.[79]

In the Philippines, as in Brazilian "dependent development," most of the local capitalists who survived did so through alliances not only with international capital but also with the state.

By the beginning of 1982, the face of the Philippine economy had been reshaped. Although "private" commercial banks still retained that billing, they no longer necessarily lived up to it. Government-owned PNB, itself a universal bank, became the major equity shareholder of crony Ricardo Silverio's Pilipinas Bank.[80] Similarly, the government's Land Bank of the Philippines, in conjunction with another government entity (whose main task was supposedly to provide social security to the public sector), bought up almost all of the newly merged Union Bank's stock.[81]

Government ownership spread, particularly to enterprises dominated by crony connections. In late 1981, after crony Disini's International Corporate Bank absorbed his two insolvent finance companies (Atrium Capital and Asia Pacific Capital), the Development Bank of the Philippines became 70 percent owner of the surviving financial institution.[82] Similarly, in the industrial sector, PNB and another government entity acquired 30 percent of crony Rudolfo Cuenca's Construction and Development Corporation of the Philippines (CDCP).[83] Each passing month only lengthened the ledger and magnified state involvement—and, in some cases, partial government ownership widened into a full bailout.

Growing entanglement between public and private sectors went beyond ownership per se. Ownership rights brought inflated powers for Philippine government technocrats, who were transformed into financial controllers and board members of these major private institutions. While Cuenca retained CDCP's presidency, in 1982 Industry Minister Ongpin assumed the company's chairmanship.[84] PNB took over five of the eleven seats of Silverio's Delta Motor Corporation's board.[85] Into the post of Pilipinas Bank chairman stepped PNB president Pamfilo Dominga.[86]

As these developments suggest, it was the transnationalist faction of the state that rose to the top of this new government, industry, and finance triple alliance, a logical culmination of earlier institutional shifts accompanying the World Bank and IMF reforms. As early as mid-1981, Marcos announced, "I'm going to sit back and let the technocrats run things" as a follow-through on World Bank suggestions that its favored technocrats be accorded hegemonic positions—political as well as economic.[87] As a high-level government official had freely speculated beforehand, "Marcos will make his [mid-1981] appointments in an attempt to please international creditors."[88]

Appropriately, the Bank's and the Fund's closest confidant, Finance Minister Virata, assumed the concurrent post of Philippine prime minister. Placido Mapa, Jr., fresh from a two-year stint as a World Bank executive director, became the Philippines' new economic planning minister. Joining these two were other Bank and Fund allies, including Alejandro Melchor, Jr., whose appointment as presidential adviser pulled him from the Asian Development Bank into a cabinet-rank position. Rounding off the transnationalist corps controlling key policy-making positions were less well-known Bank- or Fund-connected technocrats appointed to secondary positions. Roy Zosa, for example, brought his experience as regional manager for East Asia of the World Bank Group's International Finance Corporation to his new station as a DBP governor.[89]

In sum, the World Bank and the IMF catalyzed the transnationalist faction of the Philippine state into its more hegemonic position over both the public and private sectors in the early 1980s, via three well-tested techniques: (1) elevating technocrats; (2) building institutions; and (3) recasting the role of existing institutions.

It is impossible to state definitively whether total realignment of the Philippine political economy stood as a primary goal of all Bank and Fund officials as they fashioned the comprehensive Philippine export-oriented industrialization strategy. But, overall, Bank and Fund officials and their Philippine technocratic counterparts well understood in advance that this would be the logical result of their Philippine structural adjustment experiment in the late 1970s and early 1980s. Realignment toward a concentrated and self-reinforcing triple alliance of transnationalist factions (which, by 1982, held hegemonic reign throughout the country's state, industrial, and financial sectors) created the necessary institutional basis for the Philippine effort to advance nontraditional exports as the leading sector of the economy.

9

Export-Oriented Industrialization: An Assessment

From the early 1960s to the mid-1970s, the Philippine economy could have been characterized as an open dual economy, with a large rural sector engaged in traditional agriculture and a "modern" export-oriented sector based on agricultural exports (coconuts, sugar, bananas) and extractive industries (copper, logs). From the mid-1970s onward, the World Bank and the IMF contributed—through loans, training, institution-building, and their close ties to TNCs and TNBs—to creating a far more sophisticated dual economy, with the modern sector consisting of both an agricultural/extractive component and an equally important light-manufacturing component.

This chapter speaks to the wisdom of such a transformation. Based on their knowledge of domestic and international economic realities, did the World Bank, the IMF, and Philippine transnationalists in the late 1970s and early 1980s push aggregate economic policies that were likely to foster development in either the short or long run?

Events during that period suggest that this question should be grappled with on two levels:

1. Did the Bank and Fund adequately take into consideration the dangers of a development strategy based on export-led growth in an uncertain world market, one in which global trade began a steady slide toward stagnation after 1979? This must be addressed for the Philippines in a context where the Bank and the Fund were also promoting similar development paths for the other twenty to thirty would-be NICs, further heightening competition for export markets.

2. If the "modern sector" in a dual economy generates high value added and if a substantial proportion of that value added is channeled toward stimulating domestic economic activity, then the entire economy can be pulled forward. If value added and linkages to the domestic economy are low, then the "modern sector" becomes an enclave with a negligible impact on development. It is thus crucial to ask if export-oriented industrialization based on light manufactures in the Philippines was creating little more than a modern export enclave.

The analysis presented in this chapter is based not on hindsight but on knowledge available to the Bank, the Fund, and Philippine technocrats at the time of the industrial and financial restructuring (i.e., through mid-1982). Only in the final chapter will an assessment of Bank and Fund strategies beyond the time of Benigno Aquino and Ferdinand Marcos be offered.

Stagnation on Global Markets

An expanding global economy is a necessary prerequisite for successful export-oriented industrialization. If nontraditional exports were to be the so-called engine of growth for the rest of the Philippine economy, world trade—that is, global demand for these products—had to grow each year. There was no way to escape this logic in the aggregate.

Yet, at the time when the Philippines was induced to embark fully on its nontraditional-export path, these necessary conditions were decidedly absent. Over the decade from 1963 to 1973, the volume of world exports rose at a rapid average rate of 8.5 percent annually.[1] By the years from 1973 to 1980 a deceleration was already evident; the average annual expansion slowed to 4 percent.[2] At the end of that period, the rate faltered even more, advancing only 1 percent in 1980 and stagnating completely in 1981.[3] Moreover, 1981 had the dubious distinction of being the first year since

1958 to witness an actual *decrease* of world trade in current dollar terms, a shrinkage of 1 percent.[4]

Behind these global trade statistics lurked the industrial market economies' domestic stagnation, or what the World Bank in 1979 termed the industrialized countries' "undistinguished performance of the present decade."[5] According to IMF figures, the four years from 1976 to 1979 saw real GNP of industrial countries growing at a tolerable average yearly rate of 4 percent.[6] By 1980, OECD growth crawled ahead at only 1.25 percent; the next year again at only 1.25 percent.[7] By mid-1982, OECD revised its projections for its member countries' 1982 average growth rate down from a late-1981 forecast of 1.25 percent to 0.3 percent, and warned that stagnation would continue well into the following year.[8] Likewise, the European Economic Community (EEC) executive commission shaved its prognosis of an average 1.5 percent 1982 annual growth to 0.5 percent.[9]

Another pitfall facing LDCs' export-oriented industrialization in the late 1970s and early 1980s was that, according to the GATT, fully half of global trade had fallen under quantitative restrictions of some sort.[10] At the same time, despite official encomiums to "free trade," OECD countries barricaded their economies behind what even U.S. President Reagan's Council of Economic Advisers admitted were "neo-mercantile" policies.[11]

These defensive machinations to moderate the recessionary bite at home constituted what has been baptized the "new protectionism," which witnessed a proliferation of American, EEC, and Japanese trade barriers, notably quotas on LDC-manufactured exports. "New" referred to the widespread extension beyond tariff barriers, which had been regulated by the GATT since the Second World War, to a dazzling array of nontariff barriers.[12] As the World Bank and the IMF imposed "free trade" policies on LDCs, the major voting blocs within those institutions retreated from any semblance of "free trade" at home. The retreat became inextricably meshed with the crisis: as OECD growth slackened, quotas were tightened. And the more successful the particular LDC export category, the more restrictive the quota became. With the new protectionism, "we are facing a situation as potentially dangerous as the 1930s," an OECD official said in 1981.[13]

By World Bank economists' own calculations in 1979, the most dangerous of the new protectionist barriers were in the sectors of apparel, textiles, and footwear.[14] Yet it was precisely these sectors—along with furniture, wood products, and electronics—that they and the Fund had pinpointed to head the Philippine engine of growth. With the highly restrictive allotments of the Multi-Fiber Arrangement (MFA), textiles and apparel became perhaps the most heavily controlled sectors in international trade.[15] Trade statistics showed the ominous results: over the early years of the 1980s, LDCs' share of textile and apparel exports began to shrink.[16]

Likewise, talk of a multi-footwear agreement augured poorly for LDC footwear exports.[17] The outlook for Philippine furniture and wood products was not much brighter: a 1981 U.S. exclusion of Philippine rattan furniture (and parts) exports from the generalized system of preferences (GSP) seemed a precursor of restrictions to come.[18] Thus, for the Philippines, a proliferation of tariff and nontariff barriers on imports into developed countries seriously dampened the prospects of expanding its nontraditional exports.[19]

Did the Bank and the Fund adequately address the impact of global economic stagnation on their policy directives? It is clear that, as early as 1974, the Bank and the Fund understood certain pitfalls that the 1970s and 1980s might hold for export-oriented industrialization in general and especially for the Philippine endeavor. That year Bank President McNamara had noted: "The adverse effect on the developing countries of . . . a reduction in economic growth in their major markets would be great. There is a strong—almost one-to-one—relationship between changes in the growth rate of OECD countries and that of oil importing nations."[20] This was especially so, the Bank acknowledged two years later, in the Philippines, "with international trade the equivalent of almost half of GNP."[21] As to the new protectionism, the World Bank clocked it from 1976.[22]

Once the SAL and apex policy dialogues had begun, the Bank and the Fund continued the occasional admissions (both publicly and confidentially) of the incongruity between their favored strategy and prevailing conditions. SAL mission chief de Vries, his Philippine business accomplished, professed that "a genuine concern exists that export growth may be frustrated by protectionism and economic constraints in the industrial countries."[23] And the head of the IMF delegation to the 1979 Philippine Consultative Group meeting commented that in "the period ahead, the emergence of recessionary tendencies and growing protectionism in the industrial countries will make the [Philippines'] adjustment problem even more difficult."[24]

As is highlighted throughout this chapter, however, Bank and Fund officials planning paths for LDC development continually made assumptions that ignored such pressing problems. Their models, grounded in free trade and comparative advantage, depended on the absence of such conditions. Instead they opted for what they termed "one set of reasonable assumptions" concerning the growth of world trade—without explaining what might confer legitimacy on those assumptions.[25] The set of "reasonable" assumptions about trade and protectionism that underpinned the Bank's and the Fund's Philippine structural adjustment reports was some permutation of the following: industrial countries were to grow 4 percent per annum in the 1980s; "worldwide economic recovery" stood on the horizon; there were to be "no major setbacks in major markets."[26]

Most disturbing was the often wide chasm between these assumptions and the private assessments of Bank and Fund officials. Although John Power, a member of the World Bank SAL appraisal mission, privately admitted his personal "doubts" regarding the successful outcome of Philippine export-oriented industrialization, given the gravity of the "world situation," his University of the Philippines background book on industrial restructuring refused to give credence to any such misgivings.[27] In the same sort of contradiction, a 1979 assessment by two Bank economists acknowledged already existing "severe import restrictions" imposed by certain key developed countries and increasingly smaller quotas allocated for up-and-coming LDC manufactures exporters,[28] but a later Bank report argued that there remained "considerable opportunities" for Philippine nontraditional exports.[29]

What the effects of this unsubstantiated optimism might be on the Philippine economy was a question never seriously entertained by the Bank or the Fund. "What else could we do?" was the usual response. In other words, if the economic models did not fit reality, the solution was to filter transnationalist-colored perceptions of reality through the models, not to change the models. Their prescribed development path was transformed into a kind of dogma: "the more hostile the external environment, the more urgent" the need for restructuring.[30] A Bank director, for example, took the floor at the Executive Board's final meeting on the SAL to question the management's scenario of Philippine "dynamic" export-led growth in light of "an adverse environment . . . [including] lower than projected growth rates in industrial countries and increased protectionism."[31] Disguised as quasi-scientific forecasting, the response offered by the unnamed chairman of the gathering epitomized the unquestioning attitude: "If the environment turned out to be more adverse than projected, then the ultimate benefits under the adjustment program would be reduced, but the nature of the adjustment needed would not be changed."[32] But the proof of this was far from obvious, and the conjecture remained unsubstantiated.

It was becoming increasingly clear that the World Bank (and the IMF) had no vision of development in a world economy of vastly reduced growth. That was, in large part, because they equated growth with development. To them, development did not mean providing adequate food, clean water, clothing, housing—in short, offering a standard of living consistent with human dignity. Those were secondary concerns, which would be met through growth. Development meant growth. In the Bank's and the Fund's view, no growth meant no development, and hence could not be seriously considered.

The Bank's 1981 *World Development Report* (as in previous editions) did formally present a quantitative global model incorporating "slower industrial [country] growth" and "increased protectionism." Yet at best the exercise was a questionable one; at worst, it was deceptive. Although admittedly lower than either the accompanying "best case" scenario or previous *World Development Report* estimates, the "low case" scenario for 1980 to 1985 still promised a 2.6 percent annual GDP growth rate for industrial countries and a 3.5 percent yearly increase in world trade volume.

Given the unimpressive performance in GDP and trade arenas in 1980 and 1981, as well as the virtually unchanged outlook by mid-1982, the Bank's "low case" must be seen as another excessively optimistic scenario. This much was practically admitted in the *World Development Report* forecasting attempts: "Still lower growth rates are not considered here, not only because they are thought unlikely, but also because they would be associated with structural changes in trade and other relations between countries that could not be captured in the present analytical framework."[33]

In any event, the "low case" projections were largely ignored in specific country plans and projections. When incorporating global growth estimates in aggregate economic work for various LDCs, the Bank used figures closer to "high case" yields. This was done without any caveat explaining that an alternate set of somewhat less optimistic Bank forecasts existed.[34]

With Bank and Fund officials failing to assess adequately the negative repercussions of global developments on national policy, it should come as little surprise that transnationalist Philippine technocrats generally toed a similar line. The sentiments of many were summed up in Ortaliz's comment: "Bank friends are very optimistic about our future in nontraditional exports, so why shouldn't we be? They certainly have a better, more knowledgeable grasp of the world economic outlook than we tucked away here in Manila can ever hope to [have]."[35] Similarly, as the global economy worsened, transnationalists in the Philippine government joined their Bank and Fund colleagues in digging their heels in deeper in defense of the strategy. Former Planning Minister Sicat put it well: "If you're sick, you don't postpone going to the doctor when the weather is bad . . . or you might be sicker when the weather is fair."[36]

That attitude toward global events would merit objections even if the Philippines had been the only country pursuing this export-led policy. It was not. The Philippines may have been a guinea pig in terms of early Bank structural adjustment lending, but the Bank never viewed its work in the Philippines during the late 1970s to early 1980s as an isolated instance. Quite the contrary—if anything, it was a model. By mid-1982, Bank and Fund officials were already fostering and working with transnationalist factions in many of the other would-be NICs, pushing their economies onto paths parallel to that of the Philippines.

Who were these countries, these thirty-odd LDCs that, like the Philippines, had by the early 1980s begun the transformation toward light-manufacturing exports in hopes of moving from the periphery into the semi-periphery? Table 8 provides an illustrative set of these thirty-one second-tier LDCs. As Tables 9 and 10 reveal, it was largely these would-be NICs who had received the big loans and concomitant amplified attention from the Bank and/or the Fund since the mid-1970s. Indeed, of the twenty LDCs who had received IMF extended fund facilities of over $50 million as of mid-1982, twelve fell into the would-be NICs grouping and two were NICs. Of the ten LDCs who had been rewarded with a SAL of $50 million or more as of mid-1982, eight were would-be NICs and one was a NIC. The remaining country, Jamaica, although not formally a would-be

NIC, was certainly moving in that direction under transnationalist Prime Minister Edward Seaga's rule (since 1980) and heavy Bank and Fund involvement.

Just as the IMF had its model of austerity, so too the World Bank pushed its own brand of structural adjustment on these middle-income countries. SALs were designed to move the balance of payments from the red into the black and thus focused exclusively on trade-related sectors. The Bank's SALs to Kenya, Turkey, Senegal, the Ivory Coast, Thailand, and Pakistan—and its Philippine SAL—all concentrated on improving export incentives and performance.[37]

Take the case of Thailand: in mid-1979, a central bank official had vowed that the Bank's suggested export-oriented industrialization policies, contained in a World Bank report dubbed the Balassa Report by the Thais, would "never be listened to or followed by top people here."[38] But a few years and a SAL later, that country had implemented a set of aggregate economic policy changes almost identical to those of the Philippines.[39] Just as Cesar Virata and his transnationalist team had strengthened (and, in turn, been strengthened by) the Bank's powerful presence, so too Pakistan's Mahbub ul-Haq, Peru's "Dynamo" team led by Manuel Ulloa, Turkey's Turgut Ozal, and other transnationalists finessed the transformation of Bank SAL advice into actual policies. In still other cases, would-be NICs—notably Chile and Indonesia—received the Bank blueprint for an export-oriented development path, which they followed, without a formal SAL.[40]

In other words, the Bank and the Fund, using weapons similar to those deployed in the Philippine experiment, were helping to create the Philippines' competitors in export-oriented industrialization.[41] The result of all this was a battle to offer cheaper, more docile labor forces and more alluring incentives to attract TNC assembly lines away from the other countries. As Teodora Peña, then Export Processing Zone administrator, noted in 1980, "We are in a competitive situation. We are competing with all the countries around for investment."[42] Sri Lanka's 1981 appeal to "expansion-minded manufacturers" said it well: "Sri Lanka challenges you to match the advantages of its Free Trade Zone, against those being offered elsewhere. . . . Sri Lanka has the lowest labor rates in Asia."[43] As variations on that theme were issued by one LDC after another, TNCs found themselves in choice positions from which to bargain the most lucrative investment or subcontracting deals.

Table 8.   The Would-Be NICs, According to Four Classification Systems

	GDP Greater than 16% in Manufacturing (1980)	Annual Growth Rate of Manufactured Exports Greater than 28% (1970–1979)	"Semi-Industrialized" or "Marginally Semi-Industrialized" (World Bank)	"Future Newly Industrialized" (U.S. CIA)
Africa				
Egypt	×		×	
Ivory Coast			×	
Kenya			×	
Morocco	×	×	×	
Rwanda	×			
Senegal	×			
Tunisia		×	×	×
Zambia	×			
Asia				
Indonesia		×		×
Jordan	×	×		×
Malaysia	×	×	×	×
Pakistan	×			×
Philippines	×	×	×	×
Sri Lanka	×	×		×
Syria	×		×	
Thailand	×	×	×	×
Turkey	×		×	

SOURCES: Column 1: World Bank, *World Development Report 1982* (New York: Oxford University Press, 1982), pp. 114–15, table 3; World Bank, *World Development Report 1981* (New York: Oxford University Press, 1981), pp. 138–39, table 3.

Column 2: Oli Havrylshyn and Iradj Alighani, *Is There Cause for Export Optimism? An Inquiry into the Existence of a Second Generation of Successful Exporters,* World Bank Division

The competition was decidedly fiercer in times of stagnant or shrinking global markets, when one country could export only at another's expense. The most that could be hoped for, Philippine technocrats conceded by the early 1980s, was to use a mixture of "offensive and defensive" battle plans to forestall TNC departures.[44] (They said this even as they put the finishing touches on the financial and industrial restructuring.) According to Deputy Governor Bince, "We've got to always be careful now, . . . always watching, on the lookout for other [developing] nations' next moves. . . . And then we've got to make sure we meet their offer and better it."[45]

In the Philippines, as elsewhere, bettering that offer and thereby main-

Table 8.   *(continued)*

	GDP Greater than 16% in Manufacturing (1980)	Annual Growth Rate of Manu- factured Exports Greater than 28% (1970–1979)	"Semi- Industrialized" or "Marginally Semi- Industrialized" (World Bank)	"Future Newly Industrialized" (U.S. CIA)
Latin America				
Argentina	×	×	×	×
Bolivia	×			
Chile	×		×	×
Colombia	×	×	×	
Costa Rica	×		×	
Dominican				
Republic			×	
Ecuador			×	
Guatemala			×	
Honduras	×			
Paraguay	×			
Peru	×	×	×	×
Uruguay	×	×	×	×
Venezuela	×		×	
Other				
Cyprus		×		×

Working Paper 1982–1, January 1982, p. 4, table 1. (Note that this source classifies Argentina as a NIC.)

Column 3: Gershon Feder, *On Exports and Economic Growth,* World Bank Staff Working Paper 508, February 1982, p. 22.

Column 4: United States, Central Intelligence Agency, "Future Newly Industrialized Countries: More Competition?" 1984, cited in John Kelly and Tim Shorrock, "The CIA: Exploiting Economic Discord," *AfricAsia,* no. 29 (May 1986): 48–49.

taining the so-called comparative advantage necessitated labor repression and exploitation; a police state facilitated success. As one Manila-based TNC executive commented quite matter-of-factly:

> We tell the [Philippine] government: you've got to clamp down [on labor rights and wages]. We need to be assured a stable planning horizon, you know. . . . Or we threaten to move elsewhere. And we'll do just that. There's Sri Lanka . . . [and] now China too . . . and there'll be others after those.[46]

Bank and Fund documents sought to downplay the problems associated with the growing competition among NICs and would-be NICs. In a

Table 9.   Extended Fund Facilities over $50 Million as of June 1982
            (listed chronologically by date of country's first loan)

	Date of Approval	Amount (million SDR)
* Kenya	July 1975	67.20
* Philippines	April 1976	217.00
† Mexico	January 1977	518.00
Jamaica	June 1978	200.00[a]
	June 1979	260.00[a]
	April 1981	477.70[a]
* Egypt	July 1978	600.00
* Sri Lanka	January 1979	260.30
Sudan	May 1979	427.00[a]
Guyana	June 1979	62.75[a]
	July 1980	150.00[a]
* Honduras	June 1979	47.60
* Senegal	August 1980	184.80[a]
* Morocco	October 1980	810.00[a]
	March 1981	817.05[a]
* Pakistan	November 1980	1,268.00[a]
	December 1981	919.00
Bangladesh	December 1980	800.00[a]
* Ivory Coast	February 1981	454.50
Sierra Leone	March 1981	186.00[a]
* Zambia	May 1981	800.00[a]
* Costa Rica	June 1981	265.75[a]
Zaire	June 1981	912.00[a]
† India	November 1981	5,000.00[a]
* Peru	June 1982	650.00[a]

SOURCES: IMF, *Annual Report for the Financial Year Ended April 30, 1982* (Washington, D.C.: IMF, 1982), p. 114, table 1.7; *IMF Survey* (January 10, 1983): 7; IMF, *Costa Rica—Request for Stand-by Arrangement,* EBS/82/214, November 23, 1982, p. 1.

[a] Canceled sometime before three-year coverage ended.
* Would-be NIC.
† NIC.

1979 assessment of LDCs' manufacturing export potential, two top Bank economists forecast that "the increasing number of successful competitors may make it increasingly difficult for newcomers to get established" and that the success of a "few" would leave "too little" opportunities for the rest.[47] Regarding the Philippines particularly, McNamara's final report on the SAL acknowledged that "the benefits that will result from the strength-

Table 10.   Structural Adjustment Loans of $50 Million or More as of June
            1982 (listed chronologically by date of country's first loan)

	Date of Approval	Amount ($ million)
* Kenya	March 1980	55.0
* Turkey	March 1980	275.0
	May 1981	300.0
	May 1982	304.5
* Bolivia	June 1980	50.0
* Philippines	September 1980	200.0
* Senegal	December 1980	60.0[a]
* Ivory Coast	November 1981	150.0
† South Korea	December 1981	250.0
* Thailand	March 1982	150.0
Jamaica	March 1982	76.2
* Pakistan	June 1982	140.0

SOURCES: World Bank, *Annual Report 1982* (Washington, D.C.: World Bank, 1982),
p. 40; and information provided by Information and Public Affairs Department, World
Bank, March 17, 1983.

[a] Second tranche canceled.
* Would-be NIC.
† NIC.

ened export incentives will depend very much upon . . . the degree of competition from other developing countries."[48]

However, this concern was never taken very seriously, because it was the
Bank, in collaboration with the Fund, that had set this chain of competition in motion. At one moment, the Philippines was counseled to take advantage of the fact that its "wages had declined significantly relative to
those in competing . . . countries," notably South Korea and Hong Kong.[49]
Almost simultaneously, the Bank helped steer Indonesia onto a parallel
course, advising that "incentives for firms to locate there rather than in
some other Southeast Asian country . . . must be provided."[50] In the
meantime, Sri Lanka received a $20 million World Bank loan to establish a
new offshore production platform for apparel subcontracting.[51] The en-
trance of the People's Republic of China into the competition was aided by
the Bank, with the encouraging assessment that "the outlook is promising,
given the abundance of skilled low-wage labor."[52] Thailand too entered the
arena, followed by some of the Caribbean Basin countries and others.[53]

The Philippines faced additional competition from the nontraditional-manufactures exporters of an earlier era: the Asian NICs of South Korea, Taiwan, Hong Kong, and Singapore. As a United Nations economist explained in 1981, these NICs were not jumping fully from textiles, apparel, and electronics assembly into higher stages of industrialization; their economies "remain firmly rooted in textiles and apparel (accounting for just under a third of South Korea's exports and just over a third of Hong Kong's)."[54] When these "miracle economies" found it difficult to penetrate viciously competitive high-technology export markets, they retreated partially back into their sanctuaries of proven expertise.[55]

Yet even with this flexibility, the Asian NICs were finding it hard to match the stunning average growth rates of 8 to 10 percent they had experienced in the 1970s. In 1982, for example, as world trade stagnated, the NICs found themselves fighting what *Business Week* termed a "double-barreled attack": as they tried to step up into high-tech and more capital-intensive exports, OECD protectionism confronted them; if they fell back into light-manufacturing exports, they had to compete with the would-be NICs' cheaper labor.[56] In this setting, rivalry among the NICs also grew.

Thus, one set of objections to the Philippine shift to light manufactures includes the timing of and competitive conditions surrounding the shift, along with the lack of serious consideration of the timing question by the relevant national and international officials. Another set of objections concerns the wisdom of the strategy even under the best of external conditions.

A Modern Enclave

In assessing whether the leading sector in an open dual economy induces development or becomes an "enclave," Nobel Prize–winning economist Arthur Lewis proposed two criteria: (1) what proportion of the value of exports is domestic value added? and (2) what proportion of domestic value added is spent on buying domestic goods?[57]

Before the late 1970s shift toward light manufactures, several economists and Philippines specialists characterized the island nation as an open dual economy with a land surplus, as opposed to the traditional labor surplus studied by Lewis.[58] The late 1970s and early 1980s shift can be said to have diversified the "leading" or "modern" sector to encompass both agricultural/extractive exports and the new nontraditional light manufactures.

Using Lewis's criteria, it is possible to assess whether the shift facilitated genuine growth and development, as argued by the Bank and the Fund, or engendered enclaves disarticulated from, and with negligible positive impact on, the economy as a whole.

First, the Bank, Fund, and Philippine transnationalist version: in confidential documents as well as public statements, the Bank and the Fund left no doubt as to their firm belief that export-oriented industrialization represented the sole strategy able to bring sustained economic growth to the Philippines (and, it should be added, to address Philippine poverty).[59] Most Bank and Fund documents concentrated on disaggregated technical concerns, shifting to this larger picture only in sweeping—often undocumented—phrases.

In this fashion, the Bank's 1976 five-year Philippine lending plan explained that the outlined export-oriented industrialization strategy "would provide sufficient food for the expanding population, insure a minimum increase in the standard of living and provide the number of jobs necessary to prevent an increase in unemployment" as opposed to "the policies of the 1960s, which if continued would have made it impossible to maintain the momentum of economic growth."[60] World Bank Vice-President Shahid Husain reiterated this stance to the 1978 Philippine Consultative Group meeting: "The Philippines' export-oriented growth strategy provides an opportunity for both more rapid and more equitable growth than does import substitution."[61]

In short, echoed Industry Minister Roberto Ongpin, export trade was "the lifeblood of the economy."[62] A late-1970s advertisement for the Bataan Export Processing Zone brandished the vision shared by the Bank, the Fund, and Philippine technocrats as incontrovertible fact:

> Exports spur development. New jobs are created. Foreign earnings are generated. Trade relations with other countries are forged. And the Philippines is prominently placed in the international trade map.[63]

But data from the Philippines supports not this prognosis but, rather, Arthur Lewis's criteria for enclaves. First, the issue of value added. A prominent feature of the Philippines' light-manufactures-export–oriented industrialization was the gaping disparity between the gross value of industrial export earnings and the value added to the product in the LDC. When brandishing the nontraditional-export strategy's triumphs, the Philippine government (like the Bank and the Fund before it) naturally focused on the far higher of the two figures, the gross value. An Export Processing Zone Authority advertisement, for example, flaunted yearly gross exports of $74 million in 1978 as definite proof of the Bataan EPZ's vast "impact to the economy."[64] Government officials, by and large, were unwilling to concede that this total export revenue concept was delusory as a gauge of the Philippines' share.[65] But it was. Only when stripped of import components' costs does that figure approach the "value added" by the domestic side of production.

With the Philippines importing cartons for its banana exports, cans for some food exports, and a wide assortment of machinery and component parts for its phase of apparel and electronic global assembly lines, value added in most Philippine industries was quite low. Although the public version of the Bank's economic memorandum to the 1979 Consultative Group meeting admitted the aggregate value-added statistic for Philippine nontraditional exports to be "at best only 40 percent," its confidential apex loan staff appraisal report revealed the precise Bank calculation to be a figure of 25 percent.[66] In other words, for every dollar of nontraditional-export earnings, twenty-five cents stayed in the Philippines, with three times that amount siphoned off by import payments.

The individual industrial sectors of course differed in the amount of value added. According to a Manila-based consumers' association, apparel exports' value added, for example, was 44 percent in 1979.[67] As calculated by a Philippine economic research group, the figure remained at 44 percent the following year.[68] World Bank statistics concurred: "Some 60 percent of the value of garment exports lies in imported fabric," its 1979 SAL report alleged.[69]

The Philippine electronics industry was given a wider range in value-added estimates, but no matter which were closest to reality, the domestic gains were far less than in apparel. Using World Bank figures, the 1978 value added for electrical equipment and components overall (mainly integrated circuits) was only 13 percent.[70] United Nations statistics for the narrower standard international trade classification (SITC) 729.3 (thermionic valves and tubes, transistors, etc.) disclosed a comparable 12 percent value added for electronics assembly in the Philippines in 1977.[71] A United Nations report, however, incorporating 1977 U.S. Bureau of the Census data for U.S. electronics assembly in the Philippines, placed the figure at 32 percent.[72] But these numbers do not yet tell the full story of export-oriented industrialization. Inasmuch as a considerable percentage of subcontracted goods flow between a parent TNC and a Philippine affiliate, repatriated earnings represent yet another leakage.[73]

Low value added was a fact of life inherent in the Philippines' position in the new international division of labor. While the Bank described the rapid "growth in payments for raw materials and intermediate goods from $1.3 billion in 1976 to an estimated $2.3 billion in 1979" as "somewhat puzzling," its own explanation was clear. "One factor has been the rapid increase in imports of inputs such as textiles and electronics components for labor-intensive industries," the report continued.[74]

Value added in the apparel industry could be increased through large-scale buildup of the textile sector, but the Multi-Fiber Arrangement offered incentives to the contrary. An Outward Processing Traffic clause granted subcontracted apparel (where cloth is imported and clothing exported) larger quotas in the EEC.[75] And in the electronics industry as well, the overwhelming import reliance was "unlikely" to diminish, as the Bank itself acknowledged.[76]

According to one of the few in-depth analyses of LDC electronics subcontracting, the long-term outlook for the industry in LDCs was even bleaker. As this United Nations report detailed, the percent of value added in new LDC microprocessor production lines rose until 1973, but by 1977 value added in the newest LDC factories had already begun to fall. This was so even as the gross value of semiconductors re-exported to the United States soared tenfold from 1970 to 1978.[77] Of the seven LDCs studied, the Philippines was the last to be launched into silicon chip assembly. Entering on the downswing of the curve, value added in its factories was the lowest of all (see Table 11). In other words, since 1977 an increasing share of the value was being retained in the electronic TNCs' home countries. By the 1980s, the United Nations report emphasized, "as the complexity of circuitry increases, more value added is produced in the early wafer-fabrication stage, i.e., in the U.S., in Japan or in some locations in Western Europe. Furthermore, the more complex circuits require much more complex, computerized final testing, which again is usually done in OECD locations, particularly in the U.S. and Japan."[78]

As the international manager of Motorola's semiconductor group explained to *Business Week* in 1982, it was not that electronics companies

Table 11.   U.S. Semiconductor Imports: Foreign vs. Domestic Content
              (tariff items 806.30 and 807.00, 1977)

	Total 806.30 and 807.00 Imports to U.S. ($ thousand)	Foreign Content		U.S. Content	
		$ thousand	%	$ thousand	%
Malaysia	269,936	120,313	45	149,623	55
Singapore	234,616	108,958	46	125,658	54
South Korea	208,971	81,413	39	127,558	61
Taiwan	72,720	33,286	46	39,434	54
Hong Kong	63,885	35,896	56	27,989	44
Mexico	63,286	21,785	38	41,501	62
Philippines	52,182	16,579	32	35,603	68
Total	965,596	418,230	43	547,366	57

SOURCE: UNIDO, *Restructuring World Industry in a Period of Crisis—The Role of Innovation: An Analysis of Recent Developments in the Semiconductor Industry*, UNIDO/IS.285, December 17, 1981, p. 250, table 6.9, citing U.S. Bureau of the Census, Foreign Trade Data Printouts/TS USA 806/807.

were planning to pack up their Southeast Asian assembly lines (as some scholars contended);[79] it was simply that "those countries will miss out on the growth."[80]

In the process, the problems plaguing the Philippines' nontraditional exports' already low value added could only be aggravated. By United Nations calculations in the early 1980s, LDC semiconductor employment figures were almost universally "stagnating if not declining."[81] Philippine women workers in 1980 were performing only one of the ten major operations of electronics production[82]—a reality that belied conjectures that labor-intensive nontraditional exports would enable the Philippines to construct a vigorous, viable industrial base. The Bank's and the Fund's version of export-oriented industrialization was not engineered to leave much behind in the domestic economy in terms of value added, employment, technology, or capital base. Rather, it was creating a new enclave.

Lewis's other enclave criterion was the proportion of domestic value added that was spent on domestic goods. Theoretically, nontraditional-export endeavors were forged with an eye to enabling an LDC to amass substantial foreign exchange that could stimulate the rest of the domestic economy. What was conveniently underplayed by Bank, Fund, and Philippine technocrats was the paradoxical reverse side of the coin: transforming a given LDC into an alluring location for TNC light-manufactures production required large outlays for modern infrastructure, much of which was imported. Peter Evans had earlier noted a similar trend in Brazil:

> Trade balances are not a problem for the "real" periphery. During the period of classic dependence, Brazil's balance of trade was always favorable. . . . It is when a country begins to move from classic dependence to dependent development that the balance of trade becomes a problem. . . .
> Dependent development is import intensive and cannot be otherwise.[83]

In the Philippines, physical infrastructure for the Bataan EPZ alone cost an estimated $150 million in government funds—to which should be added the nearby $2.1 billion Westinghouse nuclear power plant that was being constructed essentially to guarantee Bataan and Manila industries a power supply.[84] And that was only one (admittedly the largest) of at least fifteen EPZs to which the government was then committed. Indeed, the bill for Philippine infrastructure over the decade of the 1980s was projected to reach a staggering $27 billion.[85] This burden—along with the weight of export-oriented industrialization's ponderous machinery, raw-materials, and intermediate-goods requirements—promised to leave (and, indeed, was already leaving) the Philippines with an onerous inheritance: a massive foreign debt and its attendant balance-of-payments deficit.

By the late 1970s, Philippine debt was spiraling upward. Business International wrote in 1980 that the Philippines' "rate of growth of debt has consistently outpaced expansion of exports."[86] In 1979, while the country's outstanding external debt grew by $1.8 billion, export earning (in gross, not value-added, terms) expanded by only $800 million, less than half the debt increase.[87] In 1980, the current account deficit passed $2 billion, the approximate value of that year's nontraditional exports.[88] Between 1980 and 1981, external debt soared nearly 20 percent, from $17.4 billion to $20.8 billion; export earnings in the meantime dropped 4.3 percent, from $4.65 billion to $4.45 billion, while the balance-of-payments deficit swelled nearly 50 percent.[89] At the end of 1981, that Philippine external debt of $20.8 billion equaled more than half the year's gross domestic product, and the IMF, tacitly acknowledging that the Philippine debt burden would outstrip earlier projections, raised the country's annual external debt ceiling over 70 percent from 1980 to 1981.[90]

The Philippines' annual repayment commitments underwent similar revisions. During the heart of the policy dialogue in 1979, the Bank had forecast that the Philippine debt-service ratio would stabilize at 22 percent annually in the first half of the following decade.[91] That was already above the Philippines' statutory 20 percent limit (and further beyond earlier projections of a 19 percent peak).[92] According to a 1982 IMF assessment, however, the ratio (as calculated by the IMF) would leap to 28.4 percent by the end of that year and would "continue at high levels thereafter."[93] By Morgan Guaranty estimates, in 1982 Philippine debt service, had it been paid in full, would have demanded an astounding 91 percent of earnings from goods-and-services exports, the highest percentage in all Asia.[94]

What these statistics boiled down to was that by 1981 the Philippines had been forced into the no-win situation of taking out new loans simply to repay the old.[95] But as one Bank analyst divulged, the Philippines' ability merely to hold its ground could not be taken for granted; meeting future debt payments was "possible but not probable."[96] Concerning Arthur Lewis's criterion, domestic value added from manufactured-export earnings was largely being channeled into debt service, with only a small percentage buying domestic goods.

Again, the question should be posed as to the Bank's, the Fund's, and the Philippine technocrats' attitudes toward these developments. Confidential reports disclosed that these institutions understood the potential quagmire as early as 1976. In that year the Bank admitted that "failure to reduce the dependence on foreign loans would, in a few years, result in a serious balance of payments problem and economic dislocation."[97] In 1978, another confidential assessment reiterated that the current account deficit "will have to be reduced in coming years . . . in the interest of prudent debt management."[98] Two years later came still another admission: "Without balance of payments adjustment, growth would decelerate to 5 percent or less, thus dimming the prospects for poverty alleviation."[99]

Yet the Bank and the Fund were the very institutions encouraging the Philippines and other potential light-manufactures-exporting LDCs to accelerate investments in energy and industrial infrastructure, with all their attendant debt commitments. In the case of China, for instance, the Bank suggested that the government swell its $3.4 billion outstanding debt in

1980 to as much as $79 billion by 1990 (in 1990 dollars) and onward to $214 billion by 1995.[100] The Fund remained a bit more cautious overall on the question of LDC debt, but concurred that high debt was an "unavoidable" part of the Philippine plan.[101]

One of Virata's staff offered an explanation: "Sure, we're up to our eyeballs in debt, but to 'take off' you have to spend."[102] That was a "basic economic law," said the Central Bank's Zialcita, adding that some of his technocratic colleagues were willing to let borrowing soar exponentially and for an indefinite period.[103] To paraphrase top Philippine technocrats, the dollar amount of external debt was irrelevant, for the loans were being channeled into productive export-oriented industrialization.[104]

But the state of the Philippine economy told another story. Indeed, by the early 1980s, the problems of export-oriented industrialization were becoming too clear for even the Bank, the Fund, and the Philippine technocrats to avoid. "Actual events have deviated somewhat from . . . expectations," World Bank Vice-President Shahid Husain was forced to admit in late 1979 in his assessment of the Philippines' initial years of building a nontraditional-export nucleus.[105] Or, as a confidential Bank report rephrased it a year later, "expectations have been overtaken by recent events."[106] Yet, even as "expectations" continued to be so "overtaken," the Bank and the Fund repeatedly instilled undue optimism in their new statistical forecasts, thereby camouflaging the fundamental weakness of their development strategy and the assumptions on which it was based.

Overall Performance

Thus the culmination of the structural adjustment loan, the financial-sector restructuring, and other Bank and Fund initiatives was to create a few large enclaves of light manufacturing for export. That the enclaves were not generating growth, much less development, was seen by the early 1980s even in two indicators which these institutions consider extremely important: GNP and export growth.

While the Philippine 1978–1982 five-year plan had originally called for an 8.0 percent GNP growth rate in 1980, Marcos and Economic Planning Minister Sicat debated at year-end whether the realized official rate was 5.5 or 4.7 percent.[107] (To play it safe, Industry Minister Ongpin cited the lower as "an excellent growth rate.")[108] As might be suspected, both figures were inflated; independent analysts claimed a more realistic figure to be at best not quite half the initial goal—around 3.7 percent.[109] But whichever of the above statistics is used, the Philippine growth rate for 1980 stood as the lowest of all Southeast Asian nations.[110] Also in that year, apparel exports (the Philippines' leading nontraditional export of the 1970s) actually declined in volume, falling into second place behind semiconductors and electrical appliances.[111]

If the Philippine government refused to divulge the extent of the disarray in 1980, it was even more circumspect concerning the state of the economy in 1981. A mid-cycle revision of the 1978–1982 five-year targets had set 6.3 percent as the goal, with 5.0 percent termed the "unfavorable scenario."[112] It was, however, somewhat more unfavorable than that. Central Bank officials announced a preliminary estimate of 4.9 percent, later clipped to 4.0 percent.[113] An IMF confidential document suggested 2.5 percent (a figure less than the population growth rate).[114] At the IMF's mark, the performance was worse than any other Asian market economy except Papua New Guinea, but a number of commercial banks put the correct figure even lower.[115]

That same year, Philippine exports fell in both value and volume.[116] Central Bank figures disclosed a 1.7 percent drop in value (from $5.79 billion to $5.70 billion), and Chemical Bank recorded a 2 percent drop.[117] Those aggregate figures hid even more ominous trends. Nontraditional exports' growth slowed to half of the previous year's percentage increase.[118]

It was not simply two bad years; the situation looked even grimmer toward the end of 1982. Indeed, at the close of this one more year during which exports tumbled in value and volume, the Philippine government itself was holding out for only 2.4 percent GNP growth.[119]

Looking back, it is remarkable to note in a 1978 World Bank in-house report the forecast for the Philippines that "the desirable annual growth rates . . . for the next decade [the 1980s] may well exceed 8 percent."[120] Just four years later, many top government officials could only predict "things getting a lot worse before they get better."[121]

Add to these figures the escalating bankruptcies of national entrepreneurs, mass layoffs of industrial workers, and the grinding, degrading poverty that permeated Philippine cities and countryside, and the development horizon becomes bleak indeed.

This chapter has assessed the recent Philippine development record through both statistical analyses and the perceptions of the major actors for an important reason. These perceptions, advanced with the utmost confidence by Bank and Fund officials, kept them from developing policy alternatives to export-oriented industrialization and led them to ignore the strong misgivings that had been voiced by at least one World Bank staff member as early as 1977:

> Look at the handicrafts you may say. Indeed I am delighted with the success in this area, but in a fiercely competitive and fickle international market, Philippine handicrafts will be in fashion today, and [gone] tomorrow. The bread and butter market and the basis of a modern manufacturing sector will always be at home.[122]

Neither Bank, Fund, nor Philippine transnationalists had built any safety nets under the Philippine economy as they restructured it. Instead, by acting on their conviction that reforms must be aimed at "increasingly integrating" the domestic economy with "the export effort,"[123] they systematically destroyed whatever safeguards had existed. There was no economic planning for possible alternative scenarios: that OECD growth stagnated; protectionism tightened; competition intensified; and/or nontraditional exports, value added, and employment slipped backward.

This stands as one of the most telling commentaries on Bank and Fund development advice. In brushing aside any uncertainties or incongruities in their chosen strategy,[124] they lumped scarce domestic resources (present and future) in one all-encompassing effort. It was no piecemeal economic restructuring, but a shrewdly strategized package of economic and financial reforms complemented by individual World Bank project loans. Urban loans (in the Bank's own words) were "designed to support" the objective of "increasing employment and productivity in view of . . . the high level of skills, education and low comparative wages of Philippine labor which should enable it to expand exports."[125] Vocational training loans set up manpower training centers in the middle of EPZs (enabling TNCs to forego labor training costs).[126] Education loans strove to downplay the importance of liberal arts education and replace it with training more suitable to the light-manufacturing demands at hand.[127] In the agricultural sector, projects like the so-called "cash crop Mindanao"—furthering what the Bank itself acknowledged was the poverty-inducing impact of commercial export crops on the poorer rural community—became the order of the day.[128]

Furthermore, when a series of leaked confidential Bank and Fund documents in the early 1980s brought a wave of scathing critiques from all parts of the globe, neither the IMF nor the World Bank attempted publicly to defend themselves or their models. Instead, the reaction was to further cloister themselves from public scrutiny—threatening suspected leakers with lie detector tests and tightening top management's control over who said what to outsiders. Rumors spread in the Bank that the FBI had been summoned to plug the leaks.[129] It was not the response of institutions confident that their policies were promoting growth and development in the developing world.

In Manila, Ferdinand Marcos and his ruling New Society party seemed equally impotent to defend the economic policies implemented under Bank and Fund tutelage. When queried about the administration's major economic accomplishments in a first-of-its-kind televised debate one month after the lifting of martial law in January 1981, Marcos's two representatives came up with what can only be termed a feeble reply. As painful gyrations within the early 1981 Philippine economy were too conspicuous for even Marcos's team to deny, they chose the circuitous path of brandishing the World Bank's heightened "confidence" in the Philippine economy as the centerpiece of their response.[130]

More typically, in public and in formal interviews, government technocrats produced a confident (if somewhat vague) chorus of belief in export-oriented industrialization's present achievements and future potential. But in private and informal conversations, many responded differently. They returned to reiterating that there was no choice, given the Philippines' reliance on the international capitalist market:

> Look, we haven't any choice. We rely on Western banks. Without the World Bank and IMF, we won't get any loans. . . . Sure, we could sit back and take a negative view and say: yes, quotas will increase; the world's economic problems will continue, or even worsen. . . . But it's better to have a positive attitude and give it a try.[131]

At that moment, prospects for rejuvenating the Philippine economic transformation seemed grim.[132] The Conference Board predicted that industrial countries' "sluggish demand" would be the story "throughout the

1980s and beyond"; *Business Asia* envisioned continued "weaker demand for Philippine manufactured export items."[133] IMF Managing Director de Larosière himself admitted as much. "There is nothing routine about the present recession," he conceded bleakly in early 1982. "There are, as yet, no convincing signs of an early recovery."[134]

In the next four years, all these warnings would prove to be understatements. Stagnation of trade and rising protectionism would be joined by plunging primary commodity prices and an explosion of the debt crisis. In the Philippines, a political crisis would follow the economic and social crises, leading to the possibility of change.

10

Things Fall Apart: The Rise of Debt, the Fall of Marcos, and the Opportunity for Change

by Robin Broad and John Cavanagh

The prolonged postwar economic boom had suffered downturns before. But these had always been short, and upturns had always followed. In 1982, debt crises erupted across the Third World in rapid succession. This time, the world economy, in a downturn since 1980, did not bounce back. Crisis followed upon crisis. The cycle seemed to have been broken. By 1986, still no upswing appeared and economies that were heavily dependent on the world economy—including even the "miracle" NICs—were in various states of recession or ruin.

As opportunities for profit in the Third World dwindled, transnational banks and corporations refocused their sights back on the developed world. Four years as the lead international institution in this era of debt crisis management left the IMF almost universally despised across the South—and nearly broke. So, the next heir to the international debt and development management throne was anointed: the World Bank, which (with U.S. government blessing) chose structural adjustment of the Philippine variety as its cure-all.

The model Philippines, having been opened up to the world economy

in new and expanded ways in the early 1980s through the structural adjustment process, fared among the worst of the debtor nations. Internal corruption and cronyism combined with collapsing export earnings to plunge
the country into deep economic and then political crisis. Only those Filipinos who managed to salt dollars away abroad through secret and often
illegal capital flight seemed able to avoid the worst of this all-encompassing
crisis.

Indeed, in many respects, the one relic of value that a fleeing Ferdinand
Marcos left his successor was a negative example: a two-decade blueprint
for guaranteed economic disaster. There was much to learn from studying
Marcos's mistakes. For in the failure of Marcos, the World Bank, and the
IMF lay important lessons that might be applied to another approach to
development—one placing people before the market.

The Slide Continues

One of the most tragic commentaries on the state of the world economy
and North-South relations appeared in 1983 and has been a yearly occur-
rence ever since: a net transfer of resources out of the developing world and
into the developed world. This marked a first in postwar history. In the late
1970s and early 1980s, new international private, bilateral, and multilateral lending plus transnational investment had exceeded developing-
country outflows of debt service and investment income by approximately
$40 billion annually (see Table 12). In 1982, however, as debt service pay-
ments leaped to $50 billion, the positive net inflow was almost erased, and
it has grown into an ever larger outflow each year since. By 1985, owing
largely to the retreat of TNBs in extending new loans, the net outflow surpassed $31 billion; Latin America, which boasted nearly all the major
debtors, was the region hardest hit.

Yet, the World Bank and IMF took advantage of this period of decline
and retreat to vastly expand their involvement in economic policy-making
in those developing countries. Each year during this period, the World
Bank's *World Development Report* got prettier, the graphics sharper, the
colors more varied. One thing, however, has remained constant over the
decade of the 1980s: Bank growth projections for both output and trade
have—year after year after year—turned out to be far higher than what
was subsequently achieved.[1] Rather than correcting this annual over-

Table 12. Net Transfer of Resources to Developing Countries, 1979–1985 ($ billions)

	1979	1980	1981	1982	1983	1984	1985[a]
Mediated through all credits[b]							
Net capital flow	47.9	54.2	62.5	50.8	39.7	32.0	13
Net interest paid	-17.2	-23.6	-34.8	-50.0	-48.3	-53.9	-54
Net transfer	30.7	30.6	27.7	0.8	-8.6	-22.0	-41
Mediated through direct investment							
Net flow of investment	10.1	9.8	14.2	12.0	8.9	8.5	9
Net direct investment income	-11.4	-13.7	-13.5	-13.1	-11.6	-11.3	-13
Net transfer	-1.3	-4.0	0.7	-1.1	-2.7	-2.8	-4
Through official grants	12.0	12.7	13.1	10.7	11.0	12.3	14
Total net transfer	41.4	39.3	41.5	10.4	-0.3	-12.5	-31
To Latin America and Caribbean[c]	15.6	11.9	11.4	-16.7	-25.9	-23.2	-30
To sub-Saharan Africa[d]	6.4	6.0	9.5	10.1	7.9	0.8	1

SOURCE: United Nations, Department of International and Social Affairs, *World Economic Survey 1986: Current Trends and Policies in the World Economy*, 1986, p. 74, table IV.4.

NOTE: Net flow of foreign financial resources available for imports of goods and services (i.e., after payment of income on foreign capital outstanding). All flows are inflows minus outflows of residents and nonresidents. Sample of 93 developing countries.

[a] Estimates, rounded to nearest billion dollars.
[b] Includes all official bilateral and multilateral credits, including use of IMF credit, and all private credits, short-term as well as long-term.
[c] Thirty-one developing countries or territories, accounting for about 92 percent of the trade of the region.
[d] Thirty-seven countries, accounting for about 92 percent of the trade of the full group.

optimism, the Bank seems to have realized that few take the time to go back and check whether projections matched reality. To the contrary, the high projections have served admirably to justify Bank policy prescriptions that have continued to urge export-oriented development.

With the exception of 1984, when global output and trade advanced at their pre-1980 rates, the first half of the 1980s has been disastrous for most of the world economy. After a decade (1971–1980) in which output grew at over 4 percent annually and trade barreled along at over 5 percent, the years from 1981 to 1985 were bleak: output grew at an average 2.7 percent per year, and trade at 2.8 percent. These latter figures are far more dismal if Eastern Europe and China are excluded: output over those five years grew only 1.4 percent in developing countries and 2.3 percent in the developed world.[2] The volume and value of developing-country exports actually declined over the period, as did the value of imports; the volume of imports stagnated.[3]

Rising protectionism even affected the fastest-growing NICs: South Korea, Taiwan, Singapore, and Hong Kong. After two decades of nearly 9 percent annual average growth of GDP, these four countries slowed to an average of 2.3 percent in 1985.[4] Hardest hit was Singapore, whose exports of goods and services are twice the size of its GDP; its economy actually shrank 1.7 percent in 1985.

By the mid-1980s, the three factors that had already been identified in 1982 as impediments to the export success of the thirty-odd would-be NICs only worsened: the slowdown of trade, the growth of protectionism, and the proliferation of other would-be NICs competing for the same, stagnating manufactures markets. Malaysia, for example, one of the would-be NIC stars in the late 1970s and early 1980s, was talking about the possible exhaustion of its export-led and import-dependent EPZ-based development path. Its change of heart was based on falling manufactured exports and employment, which, in turn, convinced many remaining workers to take "voluntary" wage cuts of up to 20 percent.[5]

Part of the trade slowdown, particularly among the debt-ridden NICs and would-be NICs, was attributable to the particular brand of debt crisis management engineered by the IMF. The debt crisis exploded onto the financial pages the world over in mid-1982, when the Mexican government announced it could no longer meet debt service payments. Banks refused to lend further without an IMF seal of approval, and between 1982

and 1985, ninety-eight IMF standby arrangements and extended fund facilities were signed with developing countries.[6] IMF agreements invariably
included currency devaluations, which lowered prices of exports (hence
making them more attractive to the buyer) and raised local currency costs
of imports.

Through such policies, the IMF managed to turn a $22 billion trade
deficit for the twenty largest debtor nations in 1981 into a $25 billion sur-
plus by 1985 (see Table 13). This incredible turnabout was not accomplished through an increase in export value; almost all of it reflected a
sharp decline in imports of everything from consumer goods to vital intermediate goods and raw materials for industry. It could convincingly be argued that the IMF's import austerity was undermining the very industrialization that the World Bank claimed to be supporting. Export value
failed to grow in large part because of the inevitable glut effect of more
countries exporting more of the same products. In such circumstances,
prices could only fall. Between 1981 and 1985, world prices of food commodities dropped at an average annual rate of 15 percent; agricultural raw
materials at 7 percent; minerals and metals at 6 percent.[7]

IMF debt management was undeniably disastrous for trade. By the
mid-1980s, however, as the prime mechanism for debt management shifted
from IMF "austerity" to World Bank "adjustment," the Bank claimed that
a revival of world trade was just around the corner. Indeed, already in its
1986 *World Development Report,* the Bank was heralding 1985–1995 as "a
decade of opportunity" that would see world trade grow again at well over
5 percent annually.[8]

Such optimism, however, is likely to prove as far off the mark as the
Bank's annual projections in early *World Development Reports,* for reasons
beyond World Bank officials' purview. For even assuming a miraculous
about-face in debt management, there are, as the United Nations has argued, "longer-term factors" behind the slowdown in world trade—factors
"such as resource-saving innovations, competition from synthetic materials
and shifts in consumer preferences towards services."[9]

A single anecdote typifies these longer-term structural shifts in commodity markets. Before 1981, the single largest consumer of the world's
sugar was Coca-Cola. But that year, in a move rapidly emulated by other
soft-drink giants, Coke stopped using sugar as its sweetener and raw material and instead turned to corn syrup. Two years later, Coke shifted its diet

Table 13.   Trade and Current-Account Balances for the Twenty Largest Debtors, 1980–1985 ($ billions)

	1980	1981	1982	1983	1984	1985[a]
Exports	201.6	209.9	193.2	192.8	212.9	212.0
Imports, f.o.b.	−210.0	−231.7	−207.4	−184.0	−185.6	−187.5
Balance of trade	−8.4	−21.9	−14.2	8.8	27.3	24.5
Net services & private transfers	−30.5	−45.0	−55.5	−42.1	−44.2	−42.0
Current account	−38.9	−66.9	−69.7	−33.3	−16.9	−17.5

SOURCE: United Nations, Department of International and Social Affairs, *World Economic Survey 1986: Current Trends and Policies in the World Economy*, 1986, p. 175, table A.V.10.

NOTE: As of the end of 1981, the debtors were Algeria, Argentina, Brazil, Chile, Colombia, Egypt, India, Indonesia, Israel, Mexico, Morocco, Nigeria, Pakistan, Peru, Philippines, South Korea, Thailand, Turkey, Venezuela, and Yugoslavia.

[a] Preliminary estimates, rounded to nearest half-billion dollars.

soft-drink sweetener to a biotech product, aspertame. These simple decisions by Coca-Cola changed the lives of millions of sugercane cutters
across the Third World. Advances in plastics, synthetic fibers, food chemis-
try, and biotechnology are bringing similar and far-reaching changes in
other markets.

Longer-term trade shifts reach beyond the raw-materials-input stage.
Consider semiconductors, the centerpiece of export-led light manufacturing in many of the would-be NICs. In 1985, the *Wall Street Journal* described a U.S. factory of the transnational corporation Schlumberger. In
a Maine subsidiary of the firm, highly automated machines weld semiconductor chips onto matchbook-sized metal frames. One person moni-
tors eight machines that turn out 5,120 circuits per hour. Just a year
before, a worker in Singapore had performed the same job for the TNC—
producing only 120 circuits per hour. Schlumberger is not alone; United
Technologies, National Semiconductors, and others are following suit.[10]

A year later, the *Journal* reported equally portentous developments in
the other centerpiece of light manufacturing: "a machine that does what
no machine has been able to do before: automatically construct the sleeves
for a man's coat and sew them onto the body of the jacket." The producer
is none other than the corporation that created the last major breakthrough
in apparel over a century ago: Singer of sewing-machine fame. In a parallel
move, Japanese engineers, bankrolled by the powerful Japanese Ministry of
International Trade and Industry, are working toward the following:

> Fashion designers would design fashions on computers, and robots would do
> the rest. Lasers would cut fabric into precise pieces; robots would sort and
> group the pieces; unmanned machines would sew backs to fronts, liners to
> pockets and buttons to sleeves.
>
> Down the line, a robot would pick up a half-finished suit and put it on
> a mannequin; robots with sewing-machine arms would reach over and sew
> on sleeves and collars; other robots would inspect the suit and send it to be
> shipped.[11]

Needless to say, these robotized factories will not be "footloose"; they
will not be located in Malaysia, Singapore, or the Philippines—or any of
the other NICs or would-be NICs. Rather, many global assembly lines appear to be coming home to the developed world.

There were ominous warnings for World Bank industrial structural
adjustment strategies in these new corporate technologies. As more corpo-

rations organize full assembly-line operations in one country, the world market stands to lose a substantial amount of trade in semiprocessed components. Furthermore, the Third World no longer holds as much attraction as it did a decade ago for transnational corporate investment.

At the same time, in the wake of the eruption of the debt crisis, transnational banks—the other major source of private financing in developing countries—have been unequivocal in their abandonment of the Third World. In 1983, international bank lending to developing countries (excluding offshore bank centers) totaled $35 billion. By 1985, a mere $3 billion in new lending trickled in.[12]

For transnational corporations, the decision whether to stay or leave has been more complicated. The low wages, absence of workers' rights, lax environmental standards, and other incentives that have lured corporations into the Third World for over a century remain. Indeed, the competition among developing countries to offer even greater incentives has intensified in the last four years. What has changed is not only automation but also the growth of uncertainty. Foreign investment has been highly concentrated in the NICs and would-be NICs, that is, the major debtors, led by Brazil, Mexico, Malaysia, and the Philippines.[13] As such troubled debtors struggle to meet debt service payments, many have imposed strict foreign-exchange restrictions, making it increasingly difficult for corporations to get dollars out of host countries. TNCs have reacted by cutting back on new foreign investment, although by no means as drastically as TNBs have cut lending. Net foreign investment flows to the developing world surpassed $10 billion for the first time in 1979 and peaked in 1981 and 1982 at $14.2 billion and $12.0 billion, respectively. Since 1983, however, the total has fluctuated in the $8–$9 billion range.[14] For the seven leading Latin American debtors and foreign-investment recipients, net new direct investment reached a $4.5 billion high in 1981 and has hovered in the $2.0–$2.8 billion range ever since.[15]

In sum, the traditional external private sources of capital, transnational banks and corporations, have, at least in the short term, reduced the rapid increase in Third World involvement that characterized their activities in the 1960s and 1970s.

Glory Days?

As the role of private transnational capital diminished over the four years following the 1982 outbreak of the debt crisis, the stage was set for the multilateral financial institutions to play far greater roles than their founders had ever imagined. In 1982, it was the IMF that was to be thrown centerstage in an international financial system in crisis. Postwar Philippine history is testimony to the important role the IMF has long played as a global financial phenomenon, but 1982 ushered in a new era.

It is difficult to summarize briefly the varied currents that flowed into the international debt crisis and why the situation came to a head in so many countries almost simultaneously. The World Bank certainly played a major role throughout the 1970s by encouraging a model of development based on heavy borrowing. Beyond the Bank, the crisis, in simplest terms, is rooted in the sustained overborrowing of the late 1960s and 1970s, which was stimulated by historically low real interest rates and still-expanding markets for Third World exports. After 1979, both conditions tragically reversed. Within eighteen months, interest rates jumped to double digits and rose as high as 20 percent, while world trade foundered.[16] Mexico's announcement in August 1982 that it could no longer service its debt opened the floodgates for dozens of similar announcements in the ensuing four years.

The task the IMF faced was daunting not only because of the number of countries involved, but also because small and medium-sized banks cajoled into the lending spree of the 1970s now saw the handwriting on the wall. Many wanted out, and hence far more of the IMF's energy than had been the case in the past was directed toward harnessing increasingly "involuntary" commercial bank resources.

Not only were IMF agreements more numerous; they were bigger—much bigger. Jumbo IMF loans to Brazil and Mexico skipped beyond the usual several hundred million dollar figures to several billion dollars. By the end of fiscal year 1983, thirty-nine nations had standby agreements, the largest number of IMF clients at one time ever. That year and the next, IMF loans to developing countries surpassed $10 billion.[17]

Glory days, however, these were not. Three problems came into clear focus by 1984–1985: the IMF was growing unpopular across the Third World, it was running out of money, and the crisis was only getting worse.

Table 14.   Extended Fund Facilities of $50 Million or More, July 1982 to
              June 1986

	Year of Approval	Amount (million SDR)
† Mexico	1983	3,410.63
† Brazil	1983	4,239.38
* Dominican Republic	1983	371.25[a]
Malawi	1983	100.00
* Chile	1985	750.00

SOURCE: Information provided by the IMF, July 1986.

[a] Canceled before completion.

* Would-be NIC.

† NIC.

An indication of countries' wariness of the Fund is that only one extended fund facility was signed in the three years after September 1983
(see Table 14). The Fund's "bad guy" image became so pervasive that in
1984 it attempted to refute its critics across the globe by publishing a pamphlet, under the authorship of managing director de Larosière, entitled
"Does the Fund Impose Austerity?"

Cash flow at the IMF became a problem by the mid-1980s because of
the inordinately short repayment schedules demanded by the Fund, which
was, after all, set up to be a short-term lender. Most IMF facilities must be
repaid three to five years after drawing.[18] Hence, the large 1982 drawings
already fell due beginning in 1985. So, from a high of $11.1 billion
in 1983, net flows of IMF lending (new drawings minus repayments)
plummeted to $0.2 billion in 1985.[19] By mid-1986, six countries were so
far behind in repayments that they were declared ineligible for IMF lending.[20] That same year, Third World debt for the first time passed the trillion
dollar mark.[21]

In a last gasp, the IMF created its own "structural adjustment facility" in
March 1986.[22] As against the World Bank's emphasis on would-be NICs,
this facility was "designed to assist low-income member countries with
protracted balance of payments problems adopt medium term macroeconomic and structural adjustment programs to help correct distortions
in their economies."[23] In fact, one could argue that the new facility was set
up to bail the IMF out of a repayments crisis it began facing in Africa in

1985. Between 1980 and 1985, the IMF disbursed over $7 billion to African nations.[24] By 1985, the Sudan, Liberia, Zambia, and the Gambia had fallen into arrears with the Fund; other countries, struggling to make payments, appeared likely to follow.

This increasing realization that short-term instruments were inadequate to meet the problem at hand thrust the World Bank into undisputed leadership in the debt/adjustment arena in late 1985. The World Bank had been moving toward this new role as early as 1980, with its first structural adjustment loans. In 1983, it took two further steps to enhance its capabilities as both crisis and macroeconomic policy manager. That year, it launched a major effort to shore up lagging transnational bank interest in the Third World. Watching World Bank–TNB co-financing operations suddenly drop 50 percent from 1982 to 1983, the Bank revised its co-financing instruments so that either it participated directly in commercial bank loans (with repayments going first to the commercial bank and later to the World Bank) or it guaranteed repayment of later parts of commercial loans.[25] The new co-financing instruments were to prove vital, for example, in convincing reluctant banks to join a billion-dollar financial package from Chile's major creditors in 1985.[26]

In February 1983, the World Bank addressed the immediate liquidity problems facing a number of developing countries by creating a Special Assistance Program to disburse already committed money more rapidly.[27] As was now the usual practice, the program was not without its conditions. In the words of Bank President A. W. (Tom) Clausen: "We will accelerate disbursements only to those countries which indeed take needed policy action to overcome their economic difficulties."[28]

Two significant expansions of World Bank activities followed in 1985. One was the creation of the Multilateral Investment Guarantee Agency (MIGA) to stimulate private capital flows to developing countries. Expanding on the concept of the U.S. Overseas Private Investment Corporation, MIGA guarantees TNC investments against noncommercial risks and also provides technical assistance and information on investment opportunities.[29] Just as co-financing made the Bank an effective catalyst for transnational bank lending, MIGA gave it a foothold for stimulating transnational corporation investment. Expanding in another direction, the Bank created its own Special Facility for Africa, a three-year program with fast-disbursing resources of $1.2 billion, reinforced by the IMF's new structural adjustment facility.

Beyond these new facilities, however, the most significant transformation within the World Bank between 1982 and 1986 did not involve any new legislation or amendment or opening ceremony: it was the rapid rise of the early 1980s Philippine-type nonproject lending from a peripheral activity of the Bank to its most important activity. This involved both the expansion of structural adjustment loans and the rapid increase of sectoral and other nonproject loans with structural adjustment–style conditionality.[30] Indeed, by the launching of the Baker Plan in October 1985, in many developing countries the World Bank was already a more influential policy agent than the IMF or any other external institution.

Structural adjustment loans jumped from $355 million in Bank commitments in fiscal year 1980 to $1,272 million in 1984—or, in percentage terms, from just over 3 percent of total 1980 Bank lending to more than 8 percent four years later.[31] By Bank rules, SALs were not to exceed 10 percent of annual total lending. But as SALs approached this limit in 1985, the Bank, with the blessings of the United States, upped the limit to 20 percent.[32]

Of eighteen SALs equal to or over $50 million approved between July 1982 and June 1986, nine were to would-be NICs, one to a NIC (see Table 15). The loans focused on areas vital to balance of payments: industry, energy, agriculture, and institutional reform.[33] With experience, the World Bank expanded not only the number of sectors covered but also the conditionality attached to each loan. Kenya's first SAL came with nine conditions; its second, forty-five. Turkey's first SAL had eleven conditions to be met; its second, eighty-five.[34]

As structural adjustment loans became multisectoral and more complicated, many developing countries opted for less ambitious sector loans that accomplished the same macroeconomic adjustment goals but on a somewhat smaller scale. Moreover, over the years since the Philippine experiment, SALs had become explicitly linked to IMF agreements, whereas sector loans were not—although the "close collaboration" between the two institutions remained.[35] Sector loans, like SALs, were generally disbursed in tranches so that the Bank could closely monitor compliance with conditions.

From about 4 percent of World Bank commitments during fiscal years 1979–1985, sector adjustment operations shot up to 10.3 percent in 1985. Once again, would-be NICs and NICs were priority countries for sector loans. Some of these stood as follow-ups to SALs, like the $178 mil-

Table 15.   Structural Adjustment Loans of $50 Million or More, July 1982 to
             June 1986

	Year of Approval[a]	Amount ($ million)
Jamaica	1983	60.2
	1985	55.0
*Kenya	1983	130.9
*Philippines	1983	302.3
*Thailand	1983	175.5
*Turkey	1983	300.8
	1984	376.0
Yugoslavia	1983	275.0
*Ivory Coast	1984	250.7
†South Korea	1984	300.0
Malawi	1984	55.0
	1986	99.0
Panama	1984	60.2
*Colombia	1985	300.0
*Costa Rica	1985	80.0
*Chile	1986	250.0
Niger	1986	60.0
Guinea	1986	50.0

SOURCE: Information provided by the World Bank, July 1986.

[a] Year refers to World Bank fiscal year, which begins on July 1 of the preceding year.
*Would-be NIC.
†NIC.

lion loan to Pakistan to continue the reforms begun under that would-be NIC's 1981 SAL. Others were disbursed sequentially, such as Morocco's 1984 and 1986 industrial and trade policy adjustment loans (which were initiated only after negotiations for a single comprehensive SAL fell apart in 1981). Still others were disbursed simultaneously (as in Brazil) or, on occasion, were to build up to a SAL. But in each case, the reforms pushed by the Bank resembled those of a SAL—for example, a $300 million trade policy sector loan to Colombia in 1985 sought to "tilt the economy towards the promotion of exports," while South Korea received an industrial finance sector loan. In effect, these were single-sector SALs, very much out of the model of the Bank's earlier Philippine industrial SAL or its financial-sector apex loan.[36]

By the fiscal year ending in June 1986, fully a third of Bank lending was nonproject, policy-oriented; in Latin America this figure rose as high as

40 percent.[37] The lending was highly concentrated, not in the poorest countries, but in the NIC and would-be NIC debtor nations. In 1985, for example, World Bank lending to the top ten debtors rose 47 percent over the previous year, as against an overall increase in Bank lending of 16 percent.

Where did all this lending leave the would-be NICs? Statistics on the first third of the decade display a dismal record on the trade front. All but one of the thirty-one would-be NICs registered average growth in the value of exports of over 12 percent annually through the 1970s. But only three registered positive growth rates in exports for both 1981–1982 and 1982–1983. Fifteen watched export values drop in one of those years, and thirteen suffered export drops in both years (see Table 16). Still, the Bank pressed on.

Former U.S. Congressman Barber Conable's ascension to the World Bank presidency in July 1986 signaled an intensification of the shift from project- to policy-oriented lending. In his very first news conference, Conable said he expected to change Bank structure and operations to some degree "because of the consensus that the Bank should move more toward adjustment lending and less toward project lending." [38]

The partial vacuum in external finance to the Third World—left by retreating private banks, corporations, and the IMF—was being filled in by the World Bank with gusto and with a strong orientation toward its version of structural adjustment. And there were few indications that the Bank's post-1986 expanded role would be any less devastating on wide strata within the developing countries than its 1980 lending had been on the Philippines.

From Bad to Worse: The Philippines, 1983–1986

If the early to mid-1980s were rough on the would-be NICs in general, they were outright brutal for the Philippines. After one month in office in early 1986, Philippine Finance Minister Jaime Ongpin ticked off item after item to impress his U.S. creditors with the seriousness of the development debacle inherited by the Aquino government: "negative GNP growth rate almost 10 percent for '84 and '85 combined . . . *real* unemployment is probably 15–20 percent and underemployment 35 to 40 percent . . . manufacturing capacity utilization is generally running below 50 percent." [39] And the light-manufacturing industrial sector—the sector that

Table 16.   Export Performance of the Would-Be NICs

	Average Annual Growth in Export Value (% f.o.b.)		
	1970–1980	1981–1982	1982–1983
Indonesia	35.9	−11.3	−5.3
Jordan	34.9	2.9	−23.1
Ecuador	30.4	−7.9	−5.9
Syrian Arab Republic	27.2	−3.7	−6.2
Tunisia	27.0	−19.2	−7.2
Thailand	24.7	−1.3	−8.3
Malaysia	24.2	2.2	17.4
Ivory Coast	23.0	−11.8	−7.5
Venezuela	20.3	−18.3	−8.8
Bolivia	19.9	−8.6	−9.0
Colombia	19.6	4.7	−0.5
Guatemala	19.6	−8.6	3.5
Rwanda	19.0	2.3	−12.2
Paraguay	18.8	11.5	−13.9
Costa Rica	18.3	−13.5	−0.6
Argentina	18.0	−14.7	0.5
Cyprus	17.9	−0.2	−11.0
Honduras	17.8	−13.3	5.8
Uruguay	17.8	−15.8	2.2
Philippines	17.5	−12.3	−0.3
Kenya	17.3	−17.7	−0.3
Turkey	16.2	20.9	0.2
Chile	16.1	−5.0	3.4
Morocco	16.1	−11.3	0.1
Dominican Republic	15.5	−35.4	2.2
Senegal	15.4	7.9	11.1
Peru	14.6	1.2	−8.4
Sri Lanka	13.6	−2.8	10.6
Pakistan	13.3	−16.8	31.5
Egypt	12.9	−3.5	3.0
Zambia	1.2	−1.4	−21.5

SOURCE: UNCTAD, *Handbook of International Trade and Development Statistics, 1985: Supplement* (Geneva: UNCTAD, 1985), pp. 16–20, table 1.5.

was supposed to have brought the Philippines up the development ladder to become a NIC—was in such a painfully battered state that it was sliding backward.

The fact that most would-be NICs experienced slow growth during this period while the Philippines actually slipped into reverse indicates that behind the accelerating decline of the Philippine economy lie not only external but also internal factors. Some observers (including Minister Jaime Ongpin, brother of Marcos's Industry Minister Roberto Ongpin) place most of the blame for the poor Philippine performance on domestic causes—"years of reckless Marcos extravagance and corruption,"[40] topped with capital flight and uncontrolled cronies. This, however, is only part of the story.

Internal factors behind the economic slide find their roots far back in the Marcos presidency when the first favors were meted out to those who would become Marcos's powerful cronies—golfing buddies, old college fraternity brothers, close relatives. Yet, although cronyism exacerbated the inequalities and inefficiencies in the Philippine economy, it was only after the August 1983 assassination of Benigno Aquino on the tarmac of the Manila International Airport that commentators (both domestic and international) began to speak of the economy getting out of control.[41]

A peasant- and worker-based opposition to Marcos had been growing steadily since 1968, but the events of August 1983 set into motion a middle- and upper-class revolt that, by 1986, was also to encompass (and, to some extent, be led by) significant segments of the Roman Catholic Church and the military. And, in 1984, amid rising bankruptcies, layoffs, and corruption, prominent members of the Makati business elite—including future Aquino ministers Jaime Ongpin and Jose Concepcion—joined the ranks of outspoken opponents of the regime.[42] Demonstrations—often more like parties or fiestas—involving ever larger numbers of this new alliance of malcontents became weekly occurrences in major cities.

So too the financial and popular press in the Philippines and abroad began regular chronicles of a related malaise: growing capital flight. Finance Minister Cesar Virata admitted that capital flight exceeded $2 million per day in the third quarter of 1983.[43] Eight months after the Aquino assassination, one Western diplomat estimated that 30 percent of Philippine government spending was being diverted to corrupt purposes, most of it sent abroad—compared to about 10 percent in "normal" developing countries.[44]

But the kiss of death for the Marcos regime can be traced to an external event two years after Aquino's murder: an August 1985 U.S. government interagency meeting at which all participants (State, Treasury, Defense, Central Intelligence Agency, etc.) reportedly agreed that Marcos had to be pressured to share power with members of the pro-American elite opposition.[45] Throughout 1985, a series of Reagan administration special envoys, from CIA Director William Casey to Senator Paul Laxalt, urged early presidential elections on Marcos.

By late 1985, Marcos could no longer ignore the message. The Philippine president, hoping to catch a divided opposition off guard, announced on a November 1985 U.S. television program hosted by David Brinkley that elections would be held in February 1986. The announcement venue was suggested by Laxalt—and, ironically, it meant that U.S. audiences heard the news before would-be Filipino voters.[46]

That the elite opposition laid aside petty and not-so-petty differences and catalyzed their support quickly behind candidate Corazon Aquino surprised almost all observers, as did her apparent victory at the February 7 ballot box. Marcos made a bumbling attempt to doctor the results, but his taste of victory was brief. Two weeks after the "snap election," as the U.S. Congress moved to cut off military aid, segments of a growing reform movement in the Philippine military broke ranks with Marcos and led a four-day "snap revolution" that culminated in Aquino's inauguration on February 25.[47]

The role that the World Bank and the IMF played in the Philippine political economy over the three-year period leading up to February 1986 was particularly intense, as was the popular reaction to it. As a 1985 *Far Eastern Economic Review* special edition on the Bank and the Fund highlighted: "It is rare that an anti-government demonstration ends without some speaker lambasting the World Bank for its 'imperialist' lending practices, citing it as a tool of American economic domination of developing nations. . . . The Bank is also chastised frequently for using the Philippines as its 'guinea pig' for unproven development-lending programmes."[48]

Between 1983 and the fall of the Marcos regime, the IMF extended two standby arrangements, both after longer than usual negotiations, and the World Bank arranged a second SAL, a heavily conditioned agricultural input nonproject loan, and several project loans (see Figure 5). Stagnation in world trade and spiraling Philippine debt service made these years thankless ones for the Bank and the Fund. In this hostile environment for growth, the Bank and the IMF viewed with more and more displeasure Marcos's cronies who, their transnational affiliations notwithstanding, were seen as increasingly uncompetitive and unwilling to shed their special privileges. Although the Fund grabbed the upper hand in debt management between 1983 and 1985 (after having stepped into the background, behind the Bank, during the negotiation and implementation of SAL I in 1979–1982), both institutions collaborated closely in fighting crony monopolies and in pushing institutional reform. During this whole period, "structural adjustment" remained the paramount slogan of both the multilateral institutions and the Philippine technocrats.

What stands out in the IMF's interventions in the post-1982 period is a fourteen-month stretch, starting in October 1983 (when the February 1983 Philippine standby fell apart), of heated negotiations over a new standby arrangement for SDR 615 million. The period spanned five ninety-day moratoriums on repayment of Philippine debt principal, and at least four draft letters of intent to the IMF before final agreement could be reached. Mission after mission from the IMF flew in and out of Manila, grappling with the exchange rate, the capital flight hemorrhage, a Central Bank scandal involving falsified foreign-exchange statements, a shrinking GNP, huge current account deficits, and Philippine government intransigence in dismantling crony-run sugar and coconut monopolies. Creditor banks and the World Bank put their collective muscle behind the IMF demands by dramatically restricting badly needed credit over the negotiation period (see Figure 5). In the end, the Philippine government gave in on all counts. President Marcos gave a television address announcing the long-awaited agreement and calling on Filipinos to "buckle down" and weather the sacrifices that would accompany a further devaluation, new taxes, rising inflation, and higher gasoline prices.[49]

If the mid-1982 to mid-1986 period was grueling and somewhat frustrating for the IMF, it was even more so for the World Bank. In early 1982, the World Bank had great plans for expanding its Philippine experiment: by mid-decade it hoped to have sealed agreement on a total of three SALs (including one focusing on export agriculture) as well as several sector-specific loans following textile- and coconut-sector restructuring work.

Figure 5. Timeline: The World Bank and the IMF in the Philippines

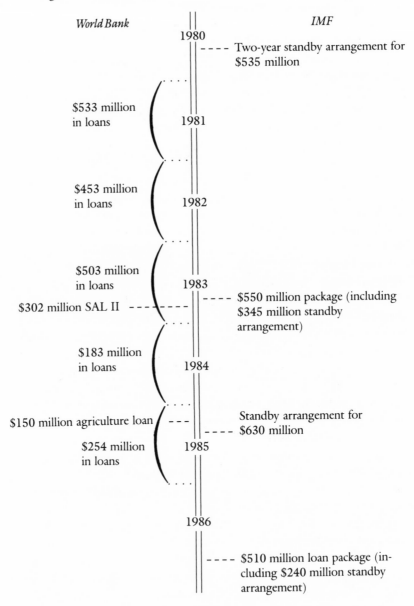

World Bank   *IMF*

1980 ---- Two-year standby arrangement for $535 million

$533 million in loans   1981

$453 million in loans   1982

$503 million in loans   1983

$302 million SAL II ---- $550 million package (including $345 million standby arrangement)

$183 million in loans   1984

$150 million agriculture loan   Standby arrangement for $630 million

$254 million in loans   1985

1986

$510 million loan package (including $240 million standby arrangement)

SOURCE: Information provided by the World Bank and the IMF, July 1986.

Instead, by the fall of Marcos, only two SALs had been completed, the textile-sector loan had been an acknowledged failure, and no other sector loans had passed the tentative stage. These four years of pent-up frustration and discouragement perhaps explain the deluge of 1986 World Bank missions to the Philippines after President Aquino's inauguration. There was a lot of catching up to do.

But in April 1983, when SAL II was signed, the World Bank assessment of the policy changes initiated by SAL I was still rosy: "Despite the international recession and the ensuing domestic economic difficulties, implementation of the program has been good."[50] SAL II was designed to build on this success—in the words of the World Bank, to "extend the guiding principle of comparative advantage" in garments, electronics, electrical equipment, leatherware, and other light manufactures.[51] SAL II included a continuation of SAL I's tariff and import reform and added a new industrial-incentives policy geared "to allow market forces to play a greater role" by compensating export firms for "market imperfections."[52] The loan also targeted certain tax changes, reform of public resource management, and restructuring of the Philippine energy sector.

As recently as February 1984, the Philippine SAL program still received rave reviews, this time from the U.S. government. Looking ahead to 1986–1990, the Manila office of the U.S. Agency for International Development forecast:

> The structural improvements in the allocation and efficiency of resource use should make it possible to restore higher economic growth. . . . This rate of growth will be achieved mainly as a result of improved performance of the manufacturing sector due to the restructuring of domestic industries and the expansion of manufactured exports.[53]

But it would be only a matter of months before the Philippines' dismal economic performance smashed any such hopes. In the midst of the decline, the World Bank indefinitely postponed its third SAL, which was to have initiated a broad range of agricultural-sector reforms to increase cash crop exports and end monopolistic control of key subsectors, as well as to further earlier SAL reforms in the energy sector and in public finance. SAL III was shelved, in part, because the IMF was pursuing similar agricultural-sector reforms in its marathon debt-management negotiations. A further blow to the Bank was sustained in September 1984 when the U.S. executive director (under orders from the Treasury Department) voted against a

$150 million World Bank agricultural-inputs loan to the Philippines as an expression of displeasure at Marcos's footdragging on initiating reforms.[54] U.S. government public apprehension over Marcos dates from this vote, as do the seeds of World Bank doubts that serious policy reforms could continue to be implemented through a Marcos government increasingly inflexible in the face of growing opposition.

Industry and Finance: The SAL Record

Industry-related SAL reforms provide an example of a case where the Bank could rightly claim that many, if not most, of its policy conditions were carried through by the Philippine government. Yet the result, by almost any standard, was disaster.

SAL I was the centerpiece of the industrial-reform effort, reinforced by the textile-sector loan and part of SAL II. Key to these reforms was trade liberalization, through both tariff reform and relaxation of import controls. The first was largely a success—tariff rates on most items were reduced to the targeted range of 0–50 percent, with the average import tariff at 25 percent.[55]

Lifting of import controls was another story. As the IMF negotiations of late 1983 to late 1984 delayed badly needed injections of fresh foreign exchange, balance-of-payments difficulties worsened and a number of stopgap controls (on both imports and exchange) were reintroduced. These, the World Bank understood, "were temporary and necessitated by the exceptional financial situation" and the Bank's mid-term review of SAL II reforms in 1984 still declared satisfaction at the "substantial progress" of Philippine government reform efforts.[56] By 1986, however, there seemed to be a difference of opinion, with one World Bank official arguing that such import restrictions had intensified to the point where they "probably neutralized the effects of tariff reform."[57]

Export promotion, another SAL reform goal, was largely carried out as promised, but efforts to spread export incentives through export processing zones met with only limited success. Blueprints to create as many as a dozen more EPZs or industrial estates across the archipelago were shelved; indeed, only one new zone was opened in the wake of the SALs. This was the Cavite Export Processing Zone, formally opened as one of Marcos's last acts as president in January 1986 with the remarkable claim, "The story of our overall economic performance provides ample proof of the efficacy and validity of the wide-ranging social and economic reforms that we have instituted in the decade just past."[58]

One other SAL reform, a more flexible exchange-rate policy, was bolstered by subsequent IMF negotiations and was a clear success. The initial "free float" that accompanied the SAL was followed by almost yearly devaluations to the extent that a 1980 rate of 7.5 pesos to the dollar eroded to 20 pesos to the dollar by 1985.

Less success greeted the textile-sector modernization loan. Few Philippine textile firms even applied for the loan, owing to a combination of sluggish world textile markets and the firms' inability to raise enough internal company resources to finance the required 25 percent local contribution. After several years of no takers, the World Bank temporarily reprogrammed most of the foreign exchange into short-term loans to finance raw materials for nontraditional-export industries (an act that itself seemed to acknowledge the pitfalls of building an import-dependent export sector) before canceling the loan in mid-1985.[59]

Moving from the Philippine government's performance in implementing the loans' conditions to the resulting performance of the economy, a decidedly more negative picture emerges. Perhaps in only one measure was the drive toward light manufactures a success. Whereas in 1970 light manufactures made up only 9 percent of Philippine exports, their share jumped to 48 percent, or nearly half, by 1983. Electronics rose to 21 percent of total exports and garments to 11 percent, both shoving aside the traditional leaders, coconut oil (with 10 percent in 1983) and sugar (with 6 percent).[60] But successful transformation of apparel and semiconductors into the mainstay of Philippine exports had its down side: as early as 1982, light manufactures began to experience difficulties finding markets. After enjoying growth rates of 32 percent in 1980 and 19 percent in 1981, Philippine nontraditional-manufactures exports skidded to a near halt with only 1.1 percent growth in 1982 and 0.5 percent in 1983.[61]

The years 1984 and, particularly, 1985 were even less kind to light-manufacturing exports. Sales of export-oriented light manufactures declined 11 percent in 1984, 43 percent for apparel.[62] Electronics exports were pummeled the following year as the computer industry suffered flagging sales in the three main markets for Philippine-assembled chips: the United States, the United Kingdom, and Japan. In 1985 alone, Philippine semiconductor exports dove from $910 million to $711 million.[63] It is tragicomic to reread the export projections contained in the economic memorandum that the Philippine government presented to the IMF and 483 creditor banks in 1985. On paper, exports were slated to increase 10 percent that year; instead they dropped 14 or 15 percent—to total only $4.7 billion, as opposed to the $2.8 billion in debt service the Philippines owed on interest alone that year.[64]

The fabled surge in jobs in the "labor-intensive" nontraditional-manufacturing sectors also failed to materialize. Between 1980 and 1985, total employment in export-oriented light-manufacturing sectors fell 1.2 percent—7.0 percent for apparel, 1.4 percent for electronics.[65] After five years of structural adjustment, fewer people were employed in the targeted sectors than when the experiment began—and this despite lavish subsidies and incentives.

Millions of workers were laid off during the first half of the 1980s.[66] The *Far Eastern Economic Review,* for example, reported one survey that claimed that three million people (15 percent of the work force) lost their jobs between January 1984 and January 1985.[67] In the process, hundreds of firms went bankrupt. The Philippine Securities and Exchange Commission reported close to 200 corporate dissolutions both in 1982 and in 1983.[68] The rate escalated in subsequent years: in the first quarter of 1985 alone, 800 of the country's top 2,000 corporations ceased operations, most temporarily, some for good.[69]

Although national entrepreneurs were hardest hit, EPZs did not prove to be the promised showcases of bustling activity. After reaching a peak employment of 27,000 in 1981, the largest zone, Bataan, lost Mattel, Ford, and twenty-seven other firms; employment dropped to 14,000 by 1986.[70] That year, only fifty-eight firms were operating in all the EPZs combined: of these, twenty-four produced textiles and apparel and ten assembled semiconductors and consumer electronics.[71] Only 10 to 15 percent of the supposedly enticing infrastructure facilities in the zones were, then, actually being utilized.[72]

Some transnationals, such as Mattel, vacated the premises as their tax holidays expired, shifting their Barbie dolls closer to Manila as they planned their exodus to neighboring countries and new tax holidays. Others, such as Baxter Travenol and General Motors, left in response to the uncertainty generated by foreign-exchange shortages, labor unrest, and political instability.[73] Still others, unable to transfer dollars out of the Philippines because of strict exchange controls, made the most out of the situation by using their peso profits to expand their Philippine operations.[74] Overall, however, the country was no longer viewed as an attractive spot for new TNC investment.

The sorry state of Philippine light-manufactured exports was communicated by Aquino's new finance minister, Jaime Ongpin, to the World Bank in March 1986. Textiles and semiconductors, Ongpin confided to the visiting mission, "were in such bad shape that they are asking for a government bail-out."[75]

But the World Bank would hear of no such pessimism. Refusing to shoulder any blame for the Philippine economic collapse, the Bank instead took the opportunity of the change in government in 1986 to embark on a "revival" of its industrial-sector SAL reforms. In the words of one Bank official involved in the Philippine mission: "The [early SAL] policy reforms contemplated were . . . largely derailed by the economic and financial crisis which erupted in 1983. The effects of this crisis itself present a new opportunity for reform such that industrial growth can now be re-ignited."[76] Why? The Bank explained elsewhere:

> Paradoxically, there are many features in the current situation which make it a fortuitous time to implement such a revival.
>
> Many of the ill conceived industries that were spawned in the heady 1970s have already met their own natural death. In normal circumstances, phasing out uncompetitive industries is a painful process and usually politically infeasible. Industrial restructuring then becomes difficult to implement. In the Philippines' case, this pain has, perforce, already been borne and it is therefore now much easier to develop a competitive industrial structure more suited to the Philippine comparative advantage. . . . The misfortunes of the last few years have increased the relative real wage difference between the Philippines and its key competitive neighbors . . . —with presumably little change in relative skill composition.[77]

For what it was worth, the World Bank certainly knew how to make the most out of a gloomy situation. And to further convince the Aquino government that a rerun of the SAL I experiment was the way to go, the Bank threw in another one of its rosy, but totally unsubstantiated, projections: "With world GNP recovering, a major expansion of Philippine manufactured exports cannot be ruled out in the medium term."[78]

Shifting from industry to finance, a similarly dismal picture emerges. The centerpiece of the 1980 World Bank reforms had been the secretive, high-level apex unit built inside the Central Bank. The plan for the unit's future had been grand: World Bank and transnational bank loans would be channeled by the apex unit through accredited participatory banks into medium- and long-term loans for industry. But by 1986, only eight financial institutions had been accredited (seven of them universal banks) and less than a fifth of the available $250 million had been borrowed.[79]

Partial blame for the failure lies with the stagnant conditions the industrial sector faced over these years. Another portion of the blame could, however, be placed on the IMF and the World Bank themselves for other policy advice they were giving the Philippine government at the same time—specifically, their insistence on devaluation. Since the apex unit passed foreign-exchange risks on to the final industrial borrower, the steadily depreciating peso made the loans far less attractive and more risky.

The financial restructuring did succeed, however, in speeding up concentration in the sector. The centerpiece of the financial sector was a group of about thirty commercial banks that, by 1983, controlled three-quarters of the banking sector's total assets. By that year, ten of the banks had grown enough—several through large mergers—to amass a capital base in excess of 500 million pesos, which qualified them as expanded commercial banks (or universal banks).[80]

As Bank and Philippine technocrats had intended, the major victims of consolidation were the smaller members of the sector. Between January 1984 and May 1986, 168 financial institutions went under, most of them rural banks.[81] The more than 1,000 rural and thrift banks in 1984 accounted for only 6 percent of bank assets; this share fell to 4 percent in 1985. That year, 543 of the country's 949 rural banks—that is, more than half of them—were reported in trouble.[82] But the downturn was so severe that not only the small were threatened. In early 1984, the *Wall Street Journal* could report that "about 10 of the country's 34 commercial banks have been hard hit. . . . The banks traditionally have made profits by lending to importers who, lacking foreign exchange, recently have had to either cut back or even close down operations."[83]

In the midst of the 1984 slowdown, a new Central Bank governor, transnationalist Jose Fernandez, echoed expanded-commercial-bank overseer Armand Fabella's battle cry of some four years earlier and launched a "crusade" to consolidate and strengthen the financial sector. Virtually the next day, as testimony that no domestic bank was too large for the merger block, one expanded commercial bank (Bank of the Philippine Islands, 20 percent owned by Morgan Guaranty) acquired another expanded commercial bank (Family Bank and Trust Company, which had been the Philippines' largest savings bank). The marriage created the largest private commercial bank in the country.[84]

Throughout this weeding out of the "men from the boys," the four transnational banks with fully foreign-owned branches in the Philippines fared best. A fifth of the growth of assets and deposits of all commercial banks between 1981 and 1984 was accounted for by the four transnational banks among them. These four also registered the highest profit rates, as individual savers and businesses shifted their deposits from smaller banks to the TNBs.[85]

What did the Aquino government learn from the financial-sector reforms? In March 1986 private conversations with the World Bank, new Finance Minister Jaime Ongpin suggested extending the World Bank's apex-type financing of the industrial-export sector to the agricultural-export sector—much as the World Bank had intended with its ill-fated SAL III. Ongpin's plan mimicked what the Bank had done in the early 1980s: he envisioned "an apex institution receiving mostly foreign soft money and Government equity and then using financial intermediaries whose resources would be matched on a 50/50 basis by the Apex's resources and be passed on to agricultural ventures as equity contribution again on a 50/50 basis."[86]

The World Bank also promised the Aquino government a financial-sector mission in fiscal year 1987 to set financial-sector reforms in motion once again. Just as the Bank was serving the Aquino government the same platter of industrial-sector reforms, there were indications that the suggested financial-sector reforms would hold few surprises. For in the financial-sector failure, as in the industrial-sector failure, the World Bank read exactly what it wanted and no more. A Bank official involved in the industry-sector missions put it this way: "Given the depressed state of the economy at present, there is almost no demand for such funds [apex term financing for industry] but as an economic recovery is launched the non-

availability of term finance could become a serious constraint impeding industrial expansion."[87] It was just like a returning door-to-door salesman,
with only one set of wares to sell.

Triple Alliance Revisited

In previous chapters, analysis has focused on two sets of triple alliances
that historically have advanced a transnationalist-oriented model of development. One is a domestic alliance, among transnationalist factions of
government, industry, and finance. The other, first identified by Peter
Evans in his work on Brazil, links transnational capital, the domestic government, and domestic business interests. Both alliances, it was argued,
were strengthened during the structural adjustment drive of 1979 to 1982.
How did they weather the attempted implementation of structural adjustment in a period of international and domestic crisis?

The major readjustment of the domestic alliance involved the rapid decline of transnationalist Marcos cronies in both their financial and their industrial ventures. Built on heavy borrowing and political favors, many of
those ventures collapsed as credit dried up. The collapse began in earnest
in the wake of the 1981 flight of textile entrepreneur Dewey Dee. From
the outset, the Philippine government made the decision to bail out the
leading crony banks and corporations before they sank, often to the tune of
more than one billion pesos. American researcher John Lind studied fourteen Philippine firms and financial institutions that had been merged into
eight larger entities and then "rescued" through major government bailouts between 1981 and 1984. These included such giants as Delta Motors,
the Toyota assembly firm, and CDCP, once the largest construction firm in
Southeast Asia. Of the merged eight, six had been owned by three cronies
alone: Herminio Disini, Rodolfo Cuenca, and Ricardo Silverio.[88]

Most of the bailouts were effected through the government National
Development Corporation (NDC) and three government banks. The
bailouts left the government not only with foundering businesses but also
with responsibility for the corporations' massive foreign debt. Through
the NDC's new equity in four of these eight large bailouts, for example,
the government took on close to one billion dollars in foreign debt.[89]

Many non-crony businesspeople, including transnationalists such as
Jaime Ongpin, then president of Benguet Corporation, grew furious that

government resources were being squandered on obviously "bad assets."[90] Ongpin claimed that Marcos let the cronies hang on to the most profitable companies in their empires: "The government takes all the lemons and lets them keep the plums. But if you're not a crony, the government takes everything."[91] The financial squeeze, in other words, led to a crack in the domestic triple alliance, pushing transnationalist cronies closer to Marcos while pulling non-crony transnationalists into the Marcos opposition. It also created tensions in the other triple alliance, the one involving transnational capital. Both cracks would later contribute to Marcos's downfall.

Evans, in his studies of Brazil, unveiled similar tensions emerging among members of the second triple alliance: "a less beneficial external environment . . . reduced the set of policies consistent with the continued profitability of both transnational corporations . . . and local capital, and brought the contradictory nature of dependent development to the fore much more quickly than might otherwise have been the case."[92]

By 1984, the Philippine situation had gotten so far out of hand that one U.S. banker commented, "I thought 18 months ago that the technocrats were running a first-class operation. I've since learned that they're running a zoo out there."[93] At that point, the World Bank, the IMF, and creditor banks openly lined up with the Ongpin non-crony faction and launched an attack against the worst excesses of "crony capitalism." It was a carefully planned attack: the Fund in the marathon negotiating sessions for its 1984 standby arrangement, the Bank in its agricultural-inputs loan of 1984, and the U.S. government in its "no" vote of that World Bank loan all targeted the sugar monopoly of Roberto Benedicto and the coconut monopoly of Eduardo Cojuangco.

Marcos took several small steps in an attempt to re-cement the cracked alliance and appease his transnational allies overseas. In December 1983, Marcos decreed that foreign investors could hold up to 100 percent of certain domestic industries.[94] Less than a month later, following the discovery of falsified statistics at the Central Bank, Marcos appointed Jose Fernandez as the new Central Bank governor. Fernandez had won the confidence of transnational bankers as president of Far East Bank and Trust Company, a universal bank owned in part by Mitsui Bank and Chemical Bank. Finally, in August of 1984, Marcos partially dismantled the monopoly in sugar trading.[95]

But, in retrospect, Marcos's steps were too little and too late. The efforts

of his growing corps of technocrats in key government posts notwithstanding, in the wake of his crony bailouts Marcos was never to regain the full
confidence of the Bank, the Fund, creditor banks, or the U.S. government.
By mid-1985, these external forces were actively looking for non-crony
transnationalist elements with whom Marcos could be coerced to share
power. Understandably, Jaime Ongpin headed many of their lists.

It was perhaps with this knowledge that President Corazon Aquino
chose Ongpin as her finance minister and quickly sent him on a trip to
Washington. His assurances that the foreign debt would be fully honored
were met with great relief. And whereas Marcos acquired crony companies, the Aquino government sought to sell them off. Trade and Industry Minister Concepcion indicated in June 1986 that the government
planned to liquidate or divest itself of about half of the seventy-nine corporations that the government-owned NDC had taken under its wing.[96]

Who would take the cronies' place in these corporations? Consider the
saga of Interbank, the failing universal bank formed from a merger of
crony Herminio Disini's three financial institutions in the early 1980s.
During the financial crisis, the government-owned DBP had bailed Interbank out, taken it over, and later transferred it to the government-owned
NDC. When the Aquino government put Interbank on the auction block
in 1986, the American Express International Banking Corporation became
owner of a 40 percent share, using as its bid an equivalent reduction in
debt owed to it by the Philippines.[97] In other words, the moves to privatize
would bring the Philippine financial sector—and the Aquino government—closer to a few transnational banks.

Overall, despite pressure from nationalists in her government, President
Aquino in her first year in office demonstrated a willingness to let her transnationalist economic ministers attempt to revive the World Bank/IMF style
of export-led structural adjustment. Marcos had failed in his attempt because of stagnation in the world economy and because of his cronies, but it
is clear that even had he achieved success, it would not have been a victory
for the majority of Filipinos.

The course launched by Aquino's leading economic ministers, Ongpin
and Fernandez, seems similarly destined to fail. Not only does the world
economic climate remain hostile, but also transnational capital—with the
exception of "captive" creditor transnational banks—is no longer interested in new Philippine involvement. In such a brutal external environ-

ment, development strategies desperately demand rethinking. Some of that rethinking is already going on and deserves greater exposure.

Rethinking Development

During the dozens of interviews with Philippine, World Bank, and IMF technocrats conducted in the early 1980s, an implicit view of development continually emerged. Economic growth with political stability, almost all these transnationalists believed, could be achieved through one fairly universal set of policy instruments: free trade and investment. Let free-market forces determine prices. Guarantee that those economic sectors geared to the world market receive primacy in the allocation of state resources. And, accordingly, the global capitalist world's free-market capitalism and technocratic modernization would ensure the ideal environment for these policies—the expansion of world trade.

This, in a nutshell, was the dominant version of structural adjustment— the one path to growth and development—that was seen as a given by those interviewed. The rules were viewed as objective ones. Few doubted that the entire population would benefit from such an approach, perhaps not in the short term, but at least in the end. This approach was presented as a science, and the language the technocrats used to portray policy choices enhanced this aura of objective correctness. Their own market interventions, those promoting exports, became "incentives"; interventions leading in any other direction were called "distortions."

This book has argued, through a case study, that this version of structural adjustment certainly assisted some, just as it certainly hindered others. In particular, the Philippine industrial structural adjustment aided a select group of transnationalist entrepreneurs and hurt smaller national entrepreneurs and industrial workers. The approach was entirely from the top down and involved no participation from those most adversely affected. One person's "incentives" were another's "distortions."

A more global example of this reality surfaced in the mid-1980s when World Bank agricultural-export loans helped propel vast quantities of Third World cash crops—Argentine grain, Malaysian palm oil, Thai rice, etc.—onto world markets. U.S. farmers, hurt as they lost markets to these lower-cost Third World competitors, lashed out against the World Bank loans as "unfair subsidies." Similarly, cheap wages are viewed as an "incentive" by some and as a gross violation of labor rights by others. The diagnosis differs depending on where you stand.

In this sense, it is difficult to judge development experiments as total successes or failures: most tend to help some groups and to hurt others. That many in the Bank and the Fund acknowledged Philippine development to be a failure by the end of the Marcos reign was because they measured it against one indicator: growth. And they blamed the dismal growth statistics not on their own models but on the slowdown of world trade and the excesses of Marcos's cronies.

When pushed on that acknowledged failure, the transnationalists (be they Bank, Fund, or Philippine officials) usually throw back a two-pronged defense: "What? Are you against adjustment?" and "Well, if you're against export-led growth, then you're for import substitution—which didn't work any better and certainly left many more distortions."

The short answer to both charges is no. Of course, there is a need for adjustment of structures. The question is, adjustment for whom? There are no easy answers or universal models—although there are certainly more options than just export-led growth or import-substitution industrialization.

Instead, two principles may be posited on which any version of adjustment that furthers genuine development should be based. First, developing countries should diversify and reduce their dependence on the world economy. Diversification would prevent economic (or political) events in one developed country or region from thoroughly disrupting everyday life and medium- to long-range planning. Reduction does not mean autarky. It means carefully rethinking trade and financial linkages so that they conform to a development logic that is internally consistent, rather than geared to the demands of Western corporations and consumers. This is important not only because we appear to be in the midst of a new era of vastly reduced growth of global markets.[98] It is important also in order to regain sovereignty over national economic events, a goal that political independence granted to very few developing countries. As the world economy has become more integrated, effective sovereignty across the developing world has waned.

Second, people—their dignity, their participation, and their empowerment, as well as the satisfaction of their basic needs—should be the primary goal of any development effort. Given the grossly unequal distribution of wealth and income that characterizes most of the Third World, this means placing redistribution and equity policies at the very top of the adjustment priority list. It also means setting up a development process in which people participate in making decisions and planning projects that affect their lives—where inhabitants of an area decide what kind of projects they want and what kinds they can afford. This is very different from the more typical situation in which those who will be affected sit passively on the sidelines watching World Bank teams scurry in and out of the country, planning with top government officials how to irrigate farmlands, generate electricity, improve road facilities, and so on—changes the majority of the supposed beneficiaries may or may not want or be able to afford. The Bank missions, in their orderly technocratic fashion, have become all-knowing; the people, unconsulted.

Some at the World Bank would argue that they agree with this second principle and, moreover, that the Bank has taken it seriously ever since the 1974 publication of its "semiofficial" volume (produced jointly with the Institute of Development Studies in Sussex, England), *Redistribution with Growth*. That volume concluded that "the cross-section evidence does not support the view that a high rate of economic growth has an adverse effect upon relative equality," and it argued for the twin pursuit of growth policies with projects aimed to increase the productivity, income, and output of the poor.[99] Bank President Robert McNamara immediately picked up on this, steering the Bank toward both export-led structural adjustment and an increased emphasis on project lending for rural development, urban slum improvement, small-scale enterprises, and population planning.

The problems with this approach were plentiful,[100] but two stand out. First, the Bank (particularly since 1979) placed primary emphasis on the export-led structural adjustment policies. Although the World Bank publicly said that a "purpose of adjustment is to establish a policy framework more favorable to growth—which is a prerequisite to the alleviation of poverty,"[101] we have seen how in the Philippines adjustment contributed instead to a substantial rise in joblessness. Only as a secondary priority did the Bank come in with its poverty-oriented projects to patch up the damage already done. People-oriented development must, rather, be the centerpiece—not a hoped-for side effect or an attempt to reduce a potentially troublesome aftereffect.

Second, the Bank seldom seriously consulted the intended local beneficiaries of its poverty-related projects. A fascinating glimpse of this was

afforded by accompanying a disgruntled Philippine mayor through the
World Bank in 1981—in the midst of the Philippine SAL process. He had
come to attempt to extricate his city from a World Bank "slum improvement" loan to which the mayor who preceded him had agreed. The new
mayor found that the majority of the intended beneficiaries had no idea
that the improvements constituted a loan they themselves would have to
repay through increased rents and that, in fact, they would be financially
unable to afford the higher monthly rents. The discovery shocked the
mayor enough to prompt him to go right to the source of the problem: the
World Bank's Washington headquarters. Once there, the mayor was told to
go home: the loan was already signed and the World Bank dealt only with
the relevant national-level housing authority, not with elected mayors. The
slum dwellers would pay those increased rents or face eviction.

The technocrats' other frequently mentioned defense of export-led
growth—the reference to the failures of import-substitution industrialization—is certainly partially true. Import substitution, as practiced widely in
the Third World in the 1950s, was largely inefficient, costly, and rarely
moved beyond production of light consumer goods.[102] Yet, the defense
itself is a sad commentary on both the state of development economics
and the technocrats' visions of development. In many of their minds, developing countries had and continue to have only two choices: export-led
growth, or import-substitution industrialization. If you are against one,
you must be for the other.

Part of the reason for this narrow conception of options is found in the
tragic 1982 reflection on the field of development economics by one of the
giants of development thinking, Albert Hirschman: "The old liveliness is
no longer there . . . new ideas are even harder to come by and . . . the field
is not adequately reproducing itself."[103] Around the same time, development economist Paul Streeten wrote, "At the end of the day . . . we must
confess that we do not know what causes development and therefore lack a
clear agenda for research."[104]

Despite this withering of the development debate in academic circles,
the field is and has long been far richer than a choice between export-led or
import-substitution strategies. Indeed, what is needed is not "new ideas."
What is needed is a revival of the debate over a wide spectrum of analyses
and experiences that have been offered over the past two decades. Many

have brought fresh perspectives to the questions of linkages with the world economy and people-oriented development.

To provide a flavor of some of the offerings, six are mentioned—six among many that should have led to robust debate during the last ten years but instead were drowned by the dominant paradigm of development:

1975–1977: Publications of the Dag Hammarskjöld Foundation in Sweden spell out approaches and strategies for "another development" focused on fulfillment of material needs (employment, habitat, health) and nonmaterial needs (education, democratic rights, spiritual fulfillment) in an ecologically sound and self-reliant manner.[105] The Foundation expands on this in subsequent years, calling for "another development with women."[106]

1978: A debate is launched over the costs and benefits of various degrees of openness to the world economy. Carlos Díaz-Alejandro and others argue the merits of "selective delinking" from the world economy.[107]

1980: African nations meeting in a special session of the Organization of African Unity draft a blueprint for African self-reliance. This Lagos Plan of Action identifies an increase in indigenous food production and distribution as their top development priority.[108]

1985–1987: UNICEF carries out a series of studies on the impact of debt and world economic crises on children. From this evolves the notion of "adjustment with a human face."[109]

1985: The Inter-American Development Bank (IDB, the mini–World Bank for the Latin American and Caribbean region) shocks its major donor, the United States, by using the IDB annual survey on economic and social progress in Latin America to give voice to criticism of the dominant model of structural adjustment. The survey reviews the evolving schools of thought on development in Latin America and argues that a neo-structuralist consensus is emerging which rejects both the short-term policies of IMF adjustment and the longer-term policies of export-led growth.[110] From 1985 on, the debate widens from theory to practice as fledgling democratic governments in Argentina, Brazil, and Peru initiate their own brands of anti-inflationary programs and explicitly reject traditional IMF guidelines and expertise.[111]

1979–1986: The Nicaraguan development experiment provides a tumultuous testing ground for people's participation in development. Local popular organizations and ongoing literacy and health campaigns strive to empower people by involving them in the development process.[112]

In the Philippines, similar debates and experiments are being launched and revived with the new political opening—the *apertura,* as they say in Latin America—that has accompanied the Aquino government's assumption of power. In 1986, both a study by a team of academics and a draft agenda for "people-powered" development by the government's National Economic and Development Authority publicly initiated discussions on the best routes to a new set of goals: generating employment, respecting workers' rights, lowering the debt service payments, alleviating poverty, and ending crony-type abuses.[113]

A resuscitated national press and popular education publications are helping make this a debate among the Filipino people. The Manila-based Ibon Databank research group, for example, has disseminated highly accessible, nontechnocratic summaries, discussions, and critiques of the NEDA plan throughout the country.[114] At the same time, popular organizations representing various social sectors and coalitions have responded with their own development goals. The multisectoral, nationalist coalition Bagong Alyansang Makabayan (BAYAN, or New Patriotic Alliance), for instance, has articulated popular demands for genuine land reform, foreign capital controls, and increased linkages between domestically oriented agriculture and industry. The National Economic Protectionism Association, fairly dormant during the years of martial law, has rejoined the debate with a young generation of economic nationalists joining the old to plot a new path to "Filipino First."

These debates will continue to grow in intensity in the Philippines and across the rest of the Third World. The World Bank and the IMF seem intent on ignoring or attempting to sidetrack these voices for as long as possible.[115] Indeed, the Bank and the Fund will use the pressures of the debt crisis and the desperate need of many countries for external credit to continue to impose their model of development and adjustment. The economic and political power of these institutions is enormous—and daunting. It translates into access to the international press, an ability to dominate establishment development circles, and a strong influence on the popular debate on development.

The challenge that faces the development community is to confront the orthodoxy head on. Each case of structural adjustment must be studied and debated thoroughly. And through this, the questions must be refocused. For it is not a matter of whether or not to adjust. It is, rather, adjustment for whom?

NOTES

Preface

1. Jacques de Larosière, "Adjustment Programs Supported by the Fund: Their Logic, Objectives, and Results in the Light of Recent Experience," *IMF Survey* (February 6, 1984): 46.

2. U.S. Congress, Senate, Committee on Foreign Relations, *Statement by James A. Baker, Secretary of the Treasury,* 99th Cong., 2d sess., May 20, 1986, p. 7.

3. Princeton University's Woodrow Wilson School of Public and International Affairs provided funding for the original research, which was conducted in the Philippines from November 1980 to June 1981 and from July through August 1982. That research was the basis for an earlier version of the present work: Robin Broad, "Behind Philippine Policy Making: The Role of the World Bank and International Monetary Fund," Ph.D. dissertation, Princeton University, 1983. The research also served as the basis for the author's contributions to "Export-Oriented Industrialization: The Short-Lived Illusion," "Structural and Other Adjustments," and "Technocrats Versus Cronies," in Walden Bello et al., *Development Debacle: The World Bank in the Philippines* (San Francisco: Institute for Food and Development Policy, 1982).

4. "Under Attack—And Caught in a Dilemma," *Far Eastern Economic Review* (October 10, 1985): 77.

5. IMF, *Annual Report of the Executive Board for the Financial Year Ended April 30, 1985* (Washington, D.C.: IMF, 1985), p. 96, table 1.2.

6. Stanley Please, *The Hobbled Giant: Essays on the World Bank* (Boulder, Colo.: Westview Press, 1984).

7. World Bank, "Visit to the Philippines for Operational Discussions," memorandum from John Blaxall to David Turnham, May 15, 1986, p. 1.

8. World Bank, "Aide-Mémoire," minutes of meetings between World Bank and Philippine Government ministers, March 17–24, 1986.

9. For details, see *New Philippines Daily Express* (Manila), August 2, 1986, p. 2; and World Bank, "Visit to the Philippines," pp. 1–2.

10. See "The Casino Society," *Business Week* (September 16, 1985): 78–90.

Chapter 1

1. An earlier version of parts of this chapter was published as "The Transformation of the Philippine Economy," *Monthly Review* 36 (May 1984): 11–21. On the Bataan general strike of June 4–7, 1982, see Henry Holland and Mimi Brady, "Le Nouveau Militantisme ouvrier," *Le Monde Diplomatique* (January 1983): 18.

2. The category of NICs does not always include these same countries but varies according to the precise definition used by each author. In this book, the NICs comprise seven LDCs that jointly accounted for well over 70 percent of LDC industrial exports in 1978. See UNCTAD, *Fibres and Textiles: Dimensions of Corporate Marketing Structures,* TD/B/C.1/219, November 19, 1980, p. 185, table 49. All the NICs except India followed export-led growth paths.

3. In this book, "the World Bank" and "the Bank" refer to the International Bank for Reconstruction and Development (IBRD) and its affiliate the International Development Association (IDA, established in 1960). As opposed to a second affiliate, the International Finance Corporation (IFC), the IBRD and IDA have the same staff, guidelines, and procedures (although different funding sources).

4. Immanuel Wallerstein, *The Modern World System: Capitalist Agriculture and the Origins of the European World-Economy in the Sixteenth Century* (New York: Academic Press, 1974), pp. 349–50; and Wallerstein, "Dependence in an Interdependent World: The Limited Possibilities of Transformation Within the Capitalist World-Economy," *African Studies Review* 17 (April 1974): 1–26.

5. *Business Week* (June 6, 1983), quoted in *Ibon Facts and Figures,* no. 149 (October 31, 1984): 3.

6. These were analyzed in what remains the most extensive and well-researched work on the World Bank's operations in one country: Walden Bello et al., *Development Debacle: The World Bank in the Philippines* (San Francisco: Institute for Food and Development Policy, 1982), pp. 9–12, 198.

7. Most Bank mission reports, for example, have a life cycle that, for the purposes at hand, can be reduced to the following: The mission writes a "confidential" report, which may go through a number of drafts. Sometimes this report is discussed with the government concerned. Then that report, minus its more critical or controversial statements, becomes a "restricted" document, which "may be used by recipients only in the performance of their official duties." This version is sent to various member governments and U.N. agencies. Finally, some of these documents are sanitized further and become available to the public (or, at least, to the Western public).

8. See List of Persons Interviewed.

9. The term *triple alliance* is borrowed from Peter Evans, *Dependent Develop-*

ment: The Alliance of Multinational, State, and Local Capital in Brazil (Princeton, N.J.: Princeton University Press, 1979). As is indicated by the book's title, Evans's triple alliance referred to multinational corporations, local private entrepreneurs, and state-owned enterprises in Brazil.

10. Much of this literature came from people connected with the Bank or the Fund as staff or consultants. *Finance and Development,* a quarterly publication of the IMF and the World Bank, is filled with references to such articles and books. Other examples include Judith Tendler, *Inside Foreign Aid* (Baltimore: Johns Hopkins University Press, 1975); and Escott Reid, *Strengthening the World Bank* (Chicago: Adlai Stevenson Institute, 1973). See also the work of the Institute for International Economics in Washington, D.C.

11. See, for instance, Edward Mason and Robert Asher, *The World Bank Since Bretton Woods* (Washington, D.C.: Brookings Institution, 1973), pp. 420–56; and Joseph Gold, *Conditionality,* IMF Pamphlet Series 31, 1979.

12. John Williamson, *The Lending Policies of the International Monetary Fund,* Policy Analyses in International Economics 1 (Washington, D.C.: Institute for International Economics, August 1982); Sidney Dell, *On Being Grandmotherly: The Evolution of IMF Conditionality,* Essays in International Finance 144 (Princeton, N.J.: International Finance Section, Department of Economics, Princeton University, October 1981); and Bahram Nowzad, *The IMF and Its Critics,* Essays in International Finance 146 (Princeton, N.J.: International Finance Section, Department of Economics, Princeton University, December 1981). Williamson's August 1982 work is based, in large part, on a March 24–26, 1982, conference on IMF conditionality sponsored by the Institute for International Economics. Papers from that conference, held at Airlie House, Virginia, were published in John Williamson, ed., *IMF Conditionality* (Washington, D.C.: Institute for International Economics, 1983).

13. Williamson, *Lending Policies,* p. 62.

14. Ibid., p. 35; Nowzad, *IMF and Its Critics,* p. 25.

15. See Chapter 2, below.

16. Teresa Hayter, *Aid as Imperialism* (Harmondsworth: Penguin, 1971); Cheryl Payer, *The Debt Trap: The International Monetary Fund and the Third World* (New York: Monthly Review Press, 1974); and Cheryl Payer, *The World Bank: A Critical Analysis* (New York: Monthly Review Press, 1982). See also Susan George, *How the Other Half Dies: The Real Reasons for World Hunger* (Montclair, N.J.: Allanheld, Osmun, 1977); Denis Goulet and Michael Hudson, *The Myth of Aid: The Hidden Agenda of Development Reports* (Maryknoll, N.Y.: Orbis Books, n.d.); Frances Moore Lappé, Joseph Collins, and David Kinley, *Aid as Obstacle: Twenty Questions About Our Foreign Aid and the Hungry* (San Francisco: Institute for Food and Development Policy, 1980).

17. Payer, *Debt Trap*, pp. xii–xiii.

18. Ibid., p. xi.

19. Ibid.

20. This latter group includes, for instance, Payer, *Debt Trap*; Betsy Hartmann and James Boyce, *Needless Hunger: Voices from a Bangladesh Village* (San Francisco: Institute for Food and Development Policy, 1979); and Ernest Feder, *The World Bank and the Expansion of Industrial Monopoly Capital into Underdeveloped Agricultures* (Quezon City: University of the Philippines Law Center, n.d.).

21. V. I. Lenin, *Imperialism: The Highest Stage of Capitalism* (New York: International Publishers, 1930), p. 85.

22. Included within this school are André Gunder Frank, Teotonio Dos Santos, Guillermo O'Donnell, Colin Leys, Walter Rodney, and Oswaldo Sunkel. See, for example, André Gunder Frank, *Capitalism and Underdevelopment in Latin America: Historical Studies of Chile and Brazil* (New York: Monthly Review Press, 1967); André Gunder Frank, "The Development of Underdevelopment," *Monthly Review* 18 (September 1966): 17–31; Teotonio Dos Santos, "The Structure of Dependence," *American Economic Review* 60 (May 1970): 235–46; Guillermo O'Donnell, *Modernization and Bureaucratic Authoritarianism* (Berkeley and Los Angeles: University of California Press, 1973); Colin Leys, *Underdevelopment in Kenya: The Political Economy of Neo-Colonialism, 1964–1971* (Berkeley and Los Angeles: University of California Press, 1975); Walter Rodney, *How Europe Underdeveloped Africa* (London and Dar es Salaam: Bogle-L'Ouverture Publications, 1972); and Oswaldo Sunkel, "Transnational Capitalism and National Disintegration in Latin America," *Social and Economic Studies* 22 (March 1973): 132–76.

23. See Frank, *Capitalism and Underdevelopment*; and André Gunder Frank, *Latin America: Underdevelopment or Revolution* (New York: Monthly Review Press, 1969). Cf. Wallerstein, *Modern World System*, p. 349.

24. Paul Baran, *The Political Economy of Growth* (New York: Monthly Review Press, 1957).

25. Hyan-Chin Lim, "Dependent Development in the World-System: The Case of South Korea, 1963–1979," Ph.D. dissertation, Harvard University, 1982, p. 27.

26. Marcos Arruda, "A Study of Capitalism in Brazil," *Latin American Perspectives* 7 (Fall 1979): 34. They themselves would perhaps prefer to see their work in the tradition of Raul Prebisch's structural school.

27. Evans, *Dependent Development*; Fernando Henrique Cardoso and Enzo Faletto, *Dependency and Development in Latin America*, trans. Marjory Marringly Urquidi (Berkeley and Los Angeles: University of California Press, 1979); and Lim, "Dependent Development."

28. Wallerstein is of neither the dependency nor the new dependency school. His school of thought focuses on "class conflicts generated by the global relations

of production," rather than on contradictions between nations. Wallerstein "explicitly selects the world capitalist system, and not the nation-state, as the unit of analysis for comparative purposes. He stresses that capitalism was from the beginning an affair of the world economy and not of nation-states" (Arruda, "Study of Capitalism," p. 34).

29. See Immanuel Wallerstein, "The Rise and Future Demise of the World Capitalist System's Concepts for Comparative Analysis," *Comparative Studies in Society and History* 16 (September 1974): 387–415.

30. One of the most influential theoreticians of Third World underdevelopment, who also drew heavily from the dependency school, was Samir Amin. Amin focused on the historical process of how these LDC economies became "disarticulated" by serving external needs. See, for example, Samir Amin, *Neo-Colonialism in West Africa,* trans. Francis McDonagh (New York: Monthly Review Press, 1973); and other works by the same author: *Accumulation on a World Scale: A Critique of the Theory of Underdevelopment,* trans. Brian Pearce, 2 vols. in 1 (New York: Monthly Review Press, 1974); *Unequal Development: An Essay on the Social Formation of Peripheral Capitalism,* trans. Brian Pearce (New York: Monthly Review Press, 1976); and "Self-Reliance and the New International Economic Order," *Monthly Review* 29 (July–August 1977): 1–21.

31. Lim follows Evans's terminology.

32. Cardoso and Faletto, *Dependency and Development,* p. 22.

33. Ibid., pp. 174, 153.

34. Fernando Henrique Cardoso and Enzo Faletto, *Dependencia e Desenvolvimento na America Latina: Ensaio de Interpretação Sociológica* (Rio de Janeiro: Editora Zahar, 1973), p. 140, quoted and translated in Evans, *Dependent Development,* p. 27.

35. Evans, *Dependent Development,* p. 4.

36. Ibid., p. 32. This is a domestic-international triple alliance, to be distinguished from the domestic triple alliance.

37. Lim, "Dependent Development," p. 6.

38. In particular, Lim underestimated the strength of TNCs in joint-venture setups and ignored the strong bargaining position afforded TNCs through their control of technology. Ibid., pp. 44, 88–89, 132, 139, 184, 189–90.

39. Two researchers delved into this kind of "class segments" analysis in their work on Chile. See M. Zeitlin and R. Ratcliff, "Research Methods for the Analysis of the Internal Structure of the Dominant Classes: The Case of Landlords and Capitalists in Chile," *Latin American Research Review* 10 (Fall 1975): 54.

40. Sunkel, "Transnational Capitalism," p. 146.

41. Baran, *Political Economy of Growth,* p. 195; see also pp. 205, 255. Cf. Evans, *Dependent Development,* pp. 282–83.

42. Cardoso and Faletto, *Dependency and Development,* p. 167; see also p. 210.

43. Evans, *Dependent Development,* p. 282. Cf. Lim, "Dependent Development," p. 35. Yet Evans tended to see the distinctions as being big versus small capitalists rather than as transnationalist versus nationalist.

44. In the case of Brazil, Marcos Arruda began to put factional life into Evans's state. As Arruda phrased it, "The question of who controls the state is key for the determination of . . . in which direction and for whose benefit state power is being used." Evans, Arruda argued in 1979, "leaves a doubt as to which interest group is ultimately hegemonic. My position is that a globalist faction of the Brazilian state bourgeoisie is currently hegemonic and controls the core of state power." Neither Arruda nor the others, however, brought the analysis down to the specific ministries through which globalist influences are translated into policy (Arruda, "Study of Capitalism," p. 39; see also p. 33). While Arruda is more correctly placed in the Wallerstein world-systems school, his work has contributed to the theoretical advancement of the new *dependentistas.*

Chapter 2

1. The history of the two institutions is extensively chronicled in the World Bank's semi-official history by Edward Mason and Robert Asher, *The World Bank Since Bretton Woods* (Washington, D.C.: Brookings Institution, 1973); and the IMF's multivolume official histories: J. Keith Horsefield, ed., *The International Monetary Fund, 1945–1965: Twenty Years of International Monetary Cooperation,* 3 vols. (Washington, D.C.: IMF, 1969); Margaret G. de Vries, ed., *The International Monetary Fund, 1966–1971: The System Under Stress,* 2 vols. (Washington, D.C.: IMF, 1976); and Margaret G. de Vries, ed., *The International Monetary Fund, 1972–1978: Cooperation on Trial,* 3 vols. (Washington, D.C.: IMF, 1985). See also the series of articles from *Finance and Development* commemorating the fortieth anniversary of Bretton Woods and republished by the Bank and the Fund in 1984 under the title *Bretton Woods at Forty: 1944–84* (Washington, D.C.: World Bank and IMF, 1984).

2. See, for example, David H. Blake and Robert S. Walters, *The Politics of Global Economic Relations* (Englewood Cliffs, N.J.: Prentice-Hall, 1976), pp. 11–14; Fred Block, *The Origins of International Economic Disorder: A Study of United States International Monetary Policy from World War II to the Present* (Berkeley and Los Angeles: University of California Press, 1977), pp. 33–38.

3. Gabriel Kolko, *The Politics of War: The War and United States Foreign Policy, 1943–1945* (New York: Random House, 1968). See also U.S. Congress, House, Committee on Banking and Currency, *Participation of the United States in the International Monetary Fund and the International Bank for Reconstruction and Development—Report to Accompany H.R. 3314, A Bill to Provide for the Participation of the*

United States in the International Monetary Fund and the International Bank for Reconstruction and Development, Report 629, 79th Cong., 1st sess., 1945, p. 2.

4. Robert Gilpin, "The Politics of Transnational Economic Relations," in *Transnational Relations and World Politics,* ed. Robert Keohane and Joseph Nye (Cambridge, Mass.: Harvard University Press, 1971), pp. 57–59; Block, *Origins,* pp. 32–69; Dean Acheson, *Present at the Creation* (New York: W. W. Norton, 1969), p. 81; Richard N. Gardner, *Sterling-Dollar Diplomacy in Current Perspective: The Origins and the Prospects of Our International Economic Order,* rev. ed. (New York: Columbia University Press, 1980).

5. Keynes's original draft of what he titled the Clearing Union (later called the IMF), cited in Roy F. Harrod, *The Life of John Maynard Keynes* (London: Macmillan, 1951; reprint ed. Harmondsworth: Penguin Books, 1972), p. 655.

6. According to Gardner, *Sterling-Dollar Diplomacy,* p. xiii, this note from one of the Anglo-American meetings on the Bank and the Fund said in full: "In Washington, Lord Halifax / Once whispered to Lord Keynes: / 'It's true *they* have the money bags / But *we* have all the brains.'"

7. Although discussions on the Bank and the Fund were separate, and the Fund commanded the most attention, for the concerns at hand they can be treated together. See U.S. Department of State, *Proceedings and Documents of United Nations Monetary and Financial Conference, Bretton Woods, New Hampshire, July 1–22, 1944,* Department of State Publication 2866, International Conference Series 1, 3; 2 vols. (Washington, D.C.: U.S. Department of State, 1948).

8. John Maynard Keynes, *The Collected Writings of John Maynard Keynes,* ed. Donald Moggridge, vol. 26: *Activities 1941–1946, Shaping the Post-War World: Bretton Woods and Reparations* (Cambridge, England: Macmillan, 1979), pp. 211, 221.

9. Ibid., pp. 221–22; Harrod, *Life of Keynes,* pp. 686, 746; and "Report of the Committee on Site," March 13, 1946, in IMF, *Selected Documents: Board of Governors Inaugural Meeting, Savannah, Georgia, March 8–18, 1946,* 1946, pp. 29–30.

10. Horsefield, *International Monetary Fund,* vol. 1, p. 95. (The Soviet Union signed the agreements establishing the Bank and the Fund, but never ratified them.)

11. Keynes, *Activities 1941–1946,* pp. 212, 222. See also Gabriel Kolko and Joyce Kolko, *Limits of Power: The World and United States Foreign Policy, 1945–1954* (New York: Harper and Row, 1972), p. 85; and Bereket Hable Selassie, "The World Bank: Power and Responsibility in Historical Perspective," *African Studies Review* 27 (December 1984): 35–46.

12. Keynes, vol. 25: *Activities 1940–1944, Shaping the Post-War World: The Clearing Union,* ed. Moggridge (Cambridge, England: Macmillan, 1979), p. 404; and Keynes, *Activities 1941–1946,* pp. 34, 65, 68–69, 109, 223; Harrod, *Life of Keynes,* pp. 686–87; Horsefield, *International Monetary Fund,* vol. 1, pp. 67–73,

101−2; Robert W. Oliver, *International Economic Cooperation and the World Bank* (London: Macmillan, 1975), p. 138. See also David P. Calleo and Benjamin M. Rowland, *America and the World Political Economy: Atlantic Dreams and National Realities* (Bloomington: Indiana University Press, 1973), p. 40; and Sidney Dell, *On Being Grandmotherly: The Evolution of IMF Conditionality,* Essays in International Finance 144 (Princeton, N.J.: International Finance Section, Department of Economics, Princeton University, 1981), pp. 1−7.

13. Harrod, *Life of Keynes,* pp. 753−54. On the loan, see Gardner, *Sterling-Dollar Diplomacy;* and Keynes, vol. 24: *Activities 1944−1946: The Transition to Peace,* ed. Moggridge (Cambridge, England: Macmillan, 1979).

14. Keynes, *Activities 1941−1946,* pp. 41, 42, 63; Robert W. Oliver, *Early Plans for a World Bank,* Princeton Studies in International Finance 29 (Princeton, N.J.: International Finance Section, Department of Economics, Princeton University, 1971), p. 47. See Harrod, *Life of Keynes,* pp. 691, 752−53.

15. Acheson, *Present at the Creation,* p. 83; Harrod, *Life of Keynes,* pp. 575−76.

16. Keynes, *Activities 1941−1946,* pp. 215, 227.

17. Paraphrasing of Article 1, in A. W. Hooke, *The International Monetary Fund: Its Evolution, Organization and Activities,* IMF Pamphlet Series 37, 1981; reprint ed. April 1982, p. 2.

18. Keynes, *Activities 1941−1946,* p. 215.

19. World Bank, *The World Bank, IDA, and IFC: Policies and Operations,* June 1969, p. 3.

20. U.S. Congress, House, Committee on Banking and Currency, *Participation of the United States in the International Monetary Fund and the International Bank for Reconstruction and Development,* p. 4.

21. U.S. Treasury Department, *Questions and Answers on the International Monetary Fund* (Washington, D.C., 1944), quoted in Mason and Asher, *World Bank,* p. 18. See World Bank, *Articles of Agreement of the International Bank for Reconstruction and Development (As Amended Effective December 17, 1965),* art. 1.

22. On this, see World Bank, *Articles of Agreement,* art. 3, sec. 1; Acheson, *Present at the Creation,* p. 84; Oliver, *Early Plans,* p. 42; and Gardner, *Sterling-Dollar Diplomacy,* p. 85.

23. Gardner, *Sterling-Dollar Diplomacy,* p. 291.

24. World Bank, *Articles of Agreement,* art. 3, sec. 1(a).

25. Ibid., art. 3, sec. 3(c).

26. Mason and Asher, *World Bank,* p. 430; on these early loans, see pp. 153−54.

27. See Kolko and Kolko, *Limits of Power,* pp. 85−86; Gabriel Kolko, *The Roots of American Foreign Policy* (Boston: Beacon Press, 1969), p. 70; Mason and Asher, *World Bank,* p. 504.

28. IMF, *Articles of Agreement of the International Monetary Fund* (July 22, 1944), art. 5, sec. 4. Section 3 is also of relevance. See Joseph Gold, "Use of the Fund's Resources," in *International Monetary Fund*, ed. Horsefield, vol. 2, pp. 522–23.

29. Communication from IMF managing director to Chilean government preceding September 1947 loan, quoted in Horsefield, *International Monetary Fund*, vol. 1, p. 192; see also pp. 223–24.

30. Emil G. Spitzer, "Stand-by Arrangements: Purposes and Form," in *International Monetary Fund*, ed. Horsefield, vol. 2, p. 484; Frank A. Southard, Jr., *The Evolution of the International Monetary Fund*, Essays in International Finance 135 (Princeton, N.J.: International Finance Section, Department of Economics, Princeton University, 1979), p. 19; Samuel Lichtensztejn, *The IMF and the Experience of Latin America's Southern Cone*, DEE/D/41/i (Mexico: Instituto Latinoamericano de Estudios Transnacionales, June 1980). See Per Jacobson, *International Monetary Problems, 1957–63* (Washington, D.C.: IMF, 1964), p. 20, for a summary of these different "degrees of conditionality."

31. The Executive Board's decision adopting the principle of conditionality was taken on February 13, 1952. See Gold, "Use of the Fund's Resources," in *International Monetary Fund*, ed. Horsefield, vol. 2, pp. 523–24, 526–30; and IMF, "Selected Decisions of the Executive Directors (as of December 31, 1965)," in ibid., vol. 3, pp. 228–30. According to Dell (*On Being Grandmotherly*, p. 10), "it was a desire to enlist the cooperation of the United States as the principal source of credit that prompted other Fund members to give way to American views on the question of conditionality, rather than any conviction on their part that the adoption of the U.S. concept of conditionality was indispensable for a successfully functioning IMF." See also John Williamson, *The Lending Policies of the International Monetary Fund*, Policy Analyses in International Economics 1 (Washington, D.C.: Institute for International Economics, 1982), p. 11.

32. Quoted in J. Keith Horsefield and Gertrud Lovasy, "Evolution of the Fund's Policy on Drawings," in *International Monetary Fund*, ed. Horsefield, vol. 2, p. 404. See also Dell, *On Being Grandmotherly*, pp. 10–11.

33. Margaret de Vries, "The Process of Policymaking," in *International Monetary Fund*, ed. Horsefield, vol. 2, p. 11. See also Southard, *Evolution*, pp. 19–20; and Cheryl Payer, *The Debt Trap: The International Monetary Fund and the Third World* (New York: Monthly Review Press, 1974), appendix 2, p. 219. Member countries are represented by twenty full-time executive directors. Southard was U.S. executive director to the IMF from February 1949 to November 1962, and IMF deputy managing director from then until February 1974.

34. World Bank, *Articles of Agreement*, art. 4, sec. 10. "Although there is no similar provision in the Articles of the Fund, the last sentence of Article I . . . has been understood to imply what is made express in the Bank's provision on political

activity" (Joseph Gold, *The Rule of Law in the International Monetary Fund*, IMF Pamphlet Series 32, 1980, p. 59).

35. IBRD, *Second Annual Report, 1947–1948*, 1948, p. 14. On the Polish loan, see also Gardner, *Sterling-Dollar Diplomacy*, p. 296. Poland subsequently withdrew from the Bank.

36. Interview with Dragoslav Avramović, Geneva, Switzerland, July 2, 1982. See Mason and Asher, *World Bank*, pp. 28, 105–49, 151, 158.

37. World Bank, *Third Annual Report, 1947–1948*, 1948, p. 20; and World Bank, *The International Bank for Reconstruction and Development, 1946–53* (Baltimore: Johns Hopkins University Press, 1954), p. 112.

38. Mason and Asher, *World Bank*, p. 422.

39. World Bank, *Fifth Annual Report, 1949–1950*, 1950, pp. 11–12.

40. World Bank, *Tenth Annual Report, 1954–1955*, 1955, p. 35.

41. Mason and Asher, *World Bank*, p. 701; see also p. 291.

42. Ibid., pp. 316, 437.

43. Ibid., pp. 172, 689–91. The $75 million loan to Iran in 1957 is of particular interest, as it was the Bank's first program loan to an LDC. However, unlike program loans to developed countries, this balance-of-payments support came with conditions. In particular, through the vehicle of the loan, the Bank played an important role in Iran's seven-year development plan and in building an institution to implement the plan. On this, see ibid., p. 274.

44. Ibid., pp. 297, 324–31, 438. On EDI, see also Guy de Lusignan, "The Bank's Economic Development Institute," *Finance and Development* 23 (June 1986): 28–31; "The World Bank's Economic Development Institute," *World Bank News* 3 (August 30, 1984): 3–4; James Morris, *The Road to Huddersfield: The Story of the World Bank* (n.p.: Minerva Press, 1963), pp. 53–54; and Robert Stauffer, *Transnational Corporations and the Political Economy of Development: The Continuing Philippine Debate*, Research Monograph 11 (Sydney, Australia: Faculty of Economics, University of Sydney, 1980), p. 12.

45. The ECLA document in this regard is Raul Prebisch, *The Economic Development of Latin America and Its Principal Problems*, United Nations/ECLA, E/CN.12/89/Rev. 1, Santiago, Chile, 1950. For some interesting archival research on import substitution, see Sylvia Maxfield and James H. Nolt, "Protectionism and the Internationalization of Capital: U.S. Sponsorship of Import Substitution Industrialization in the Philippines, Turkey, and Argentina," draft, Chicago: University of Chicago, May 22, 1986.

46. Mason and Asher, *World Bank*, pp. 372, 455.

47. Including IDA and IFC loans: ibid., p. 678.

48. For more on India, see ibid., pp. 99, 372–73, 422, 455, 458, 494, 514–17; and Payer, *Debt Trap*, pp. 166–83. The Indian consortium was the Bank's first effort at what evolved into the consultative group.

49. Mason and Asher, *World Bank*, p. 426.

50. On Brazil, see Payer, *Debt Trap*, pp. 143–65; Payer, *The World Bank: A Critical Analysis* (New York: Monthly Review Press, 1982), pp. 99–104; *Manchester Guardian*, June 30, 1958; Mason and Asher, *World Bank*, pp. 160, 425, 464; and Horsefield, *International Monetary Fund*, vol. 1, p. 381. The Bank, in general, found it "difficult, if not impossible, to impose conditions on a borrower unless some elements in the borrowing country consider it to be in the country's interest to meet these conditions" (Mason and Asher, *World Bank*, p. 438).

51. Philippines (Republic), *Philippine Trade Act of 1946*, Title 3, sec. 2. This act is known as the Bell Trade Act.

52. For more on the Philippines during the late 1940s and 1950s, see Miguel Cuaderno, Sr., *Problems of Economic Development (The Philippines—A Case Study)* (Manila: n.d.). This covers the fifteen-year period (1946–1960) when Cuaderno was governor of the Central Bank of the Philippines. See also Miguel Cuaderno, Sr., *Guideposts to Economic Stability and Progress: A Selection of the Speeches and Articles of Miguel Cuaderno, Sr., Governor of the Central Bank of the Philippines*, rev. ed. (Manila: Bookman Printing House, for Central Bank of the Philippines, 1960); Shirley Jenkins, *American Economic Policy Toward the Philippines* (Stanford, Calif.: Stanford University Press, for American Institute of Pacific Relations, 1954); David Wurfel, "Problems of Decolonization," in *The United States and the Philippines*, ed. Frank H. Golay (Englewood Cliffs, N.J.: Prentice-Hall, for American Assembly, Columbia University, 1966), pp. 149–73; Robert E. Baldwin, *Foreign Trade Regimes and Economic Development: The Philippines* (New York: Columbia University Press, for National Bureau of Economic Research, 1975), pp. 17–49; Frank H. Golay, *The Philippines: Public Policy and National Economic Development* (Ithaca, N.Y.: Cornell University Press, 1961), pp. 140–62; and Payer, *Debt Trap*, pp. 50–65.

53. Richard N. Cooper, *The Economics of Interdependence: Economic Policy in the American Community* (New York: McGraw-Hill, for Council on Foreign Relations, 1968), p. 40; Harry Magdoff, *The Age of Imperialism: The Economics of U.S. Foreign Policy* (New York: Monthly Review Press, 1969), pp. 103–4; and Block, *Origins*, pp. 140–63. See also Robert Triffin, *Gold and the Dollar Crisis: The Future of Convertibility*, rev. ed. (New Haven, Conn.: Yale University Press, 1961), p. 160, table 20.

54. Despite accounting for a third of Bank membership in 1967, African countries had less than 8 percent of the voting power (Mason and Asher, *World Bank*, pp. 63–64). Similar shifts were, of course, reflected in IMF membership, which is a prerequisite for Bank membership (Margaret de Vries, "Setting Par Values," in *International Monetary Fund*, ed. Horsefield, vol. 2, pp. 87–89; de Vries, *International Monetary Fund, 1966–1971*, vol. 1, p. 570; and interview with Ernest Leung, Metro-Manila, Philippines, January 30, 1981).

55. For the U.S. role in postwar coups, see Noam Chomsky and Edward S. Herman, *The Political Economy of Human Rights,* vol. 1: *The Washington Connection and Third World Fascism* (Boston: South End Press, 1979); and Richard J. Barnet, *Intervention and Revolution: America's Confrontation with Insurgent Movements Around the World,* rev. ed. (New York: New American Library, 1972).

56. The Bank largely stopped lending to developed countries by 1967 (Mason and Asher, *World Bank,* pp. 227, 458; Hooke, *International Monetary Fund: Its Evolution, Organization and Activities,* p. 4; interviews with Avramović, July 2, 1982; and Leung, January 30, 1981).

57. De Vries, *International Monetary Fund, 1966–1971,* vol. 1, chapter 28, "Growth of Responsibilities." This refers to the 1966–1971 period.

58. Margaret de Vries, "The Consultations Process," in *International Monetary Fund,* ed. Horsefield, vol. 2, p. 238.

59. De Vries, *International Monetary Fund, 1966–1971,* vol. 1, pp. 575–76.

60. On these facilities, see Horsefield and Lovasy, "Evolution of the Fund's Policy on Drawings," in *International Monetary Fund,* ed. Horsefield, vol. 2, pp. 415–27; de Vries, *International Monetary Fund, 1966–1971,* vol. 1, part 3, "General Resources: New Challenges and Responses," pp. 253–428; Calleo and Rowland, *America and the World Political Economy,* pp. 337–38, n. 2; Blake and Walters, *Politics,* pp. 46–47; Hooke, *International Monetary Fund: Evolution, Organization and Activities,* pp. 41–48.

61. Interview with Avramović, July 2, 1982.

62. William Dale at conference on IMF conditionality, sponsored by Institute for International Economics, Airlie House, Virginia, March 24–26, 1982, quoted in Williamson, *Lending Policies,* p. 12.

63. Lichtensztejn, *The IMF and the Southern Cone,* p. 11; see Payer, *Debt Trap.*

64. See Mason and Asher, *World Bank,* pp. 663–64.

65. On Brazil, see Payer, *Debt Trap,* pp. 143–65.

66. See Horsefield, *International Monetary Fund,* vol. 1, pp. 554–55, 604; de Vries, *International Monetary Fund, 1966–1971,* vol. 1, p. 588. For the expansion of other IMF technical advice, see ibid., p. 579; and *Manchester Guardian Weekly* (May 7, 1978).

67. Quoted from Mason and Asher, *World Bank,* p. 376, also pp. 332, 376–77; and de Vries, *International Monetary Fund, 1966–1971,* vol. 1, pp. 576, 590. The study on India was the Bank's *Report to the President of IBRD and IDA on India's Economic Development Effort,* 14 vols., 1965. Among the other studies were Ian Little, Tibor Scitovsky, and Maurice Scott, *Industry and Trade in Some Developing Countries: A Comparative Study* (London: Oxford University Press for the Development Centre of OECD, 1971); and Bela Balassa et al., *The Structure of Protection in Developing Countries* (Baltimore: Johns Hopkins University Press, 1971).

68. Mason and Asher, *World Bank*, p. 455. In this battle with nationalist factions, India became the Bank's largest borrower by the early 1960s and (up to mid-1967) the LDC that had most heavily borrowed from the IMF (ibid., p. 678; Payer, *Debt Trap*, p. 166).

69. Mason and Asher, *World Bank*, pp. 432–33.

70. Teresa Hayter, *Aid as Imperialism* (Harmondsworth: Penguin, 1971), pp. 57–58.

71. Quoted from David Lilienthal, *The Journals of David Lilienthal*, vol. 5: *The Harvest Years* (New York: Harper & Row, 1971), p. 538 (entry for December 19, 1963). Bruce Nissen, "Building the World Bank," in *The Trojan Horse: A Radical Look at Foreign Aid*, ed. Steve Weissman (Palo Alto, Calif.: Ramparts Press, 1975), p. 53; Mason and Asher, *World Bank*, p. 203. In 1963 the United States controlled 30 percent of the total voting power in the World Bank (Morris, *Road to Huddersfield*, pp. 44–45).

72. The 1,057 loans and credits of the Bank group as of June 30, 1971, broke down as follows: 30 were program or nonproject; 1,027 were project. "With the exception of a loan to Iran in 1957, all the Bank program loans, until the loan to Nigeria in 1971, were made to developed member countries" (Mason and Asher, *World Bank*, pp. 229, 265, 430).

73. The loan's conditions were basically provisions for consultations; there were no strict performance clauses (de Vries, *International Monetary Fund, 1966–1971*, vol. 1, pp. 338–47; Dell, *On Being Grandmotherly*, pp. 12–13).

74. Mason and Asher, *World Bank*, p. 547; on this earlier period, see also ibid., pp. 538–50; and Horsefield, *International Monetary Fund*, vol. 1, pp. 340–43.

75. Mason and Asher, *World Bank*, p. 505.

76. Ibid., p. 512, table 15-1, and p. 536. For more on consultative groups, see ibid., pp. 510–28; and de Vries, *International Monetary Fund, 1966–1971*, vol. 1, pp. 612–13; Escott Reid, *Strengthening the World Bank* (Chicago: Adlai Stevenson Institute, 1973), pp. 146–48.

77. Both men entered office in 1963 (Mason and Asher, *World Bank*, p. 550). These memoranda followed on the heels of a January 1966 paper on Bank and Fund collaboration (IMF, "Further Steps for Collaboration with the IBRD," EBD/66/9, Revision 1, January 19, 1966, revised February 17, 1966).

78. IMF, "Memorandum on Fund-Bank Collaboration," from the IMF managing director to department heads, December 13, 1966, unnumbered p. 1.

79. Ibid., unnumbered pp. 1–2.

80. IMF and World Bank, "Further Steps for Collaboration Between the IMF and the IBRD," joint memorandum by the managing director of the IMF and president of the IBRD, February 19, 1970, unnumbered p. 1.

81. De Vries, *International Monetary Fund, 1966–1971*, vol. 1, p. 613.

82. IMF and World Bank, "Collaboration Between the IMF and the IBRD," unnumbered p. 1.

83. See Diosdado Macapagal, *Five-Year Integrated Socio-Economic Program for the Philippines,* Address on the State of the Nation to the Fifth Congress of the Republic of the Philippines, January 22, 1962. This glosses over the question of exactly what sort of industrialization the Philippine economy underwent in the 1950s. On this, see especially Payer, *Debt Trap,* pp. 54–60; Edberto M. Villegas, *The Philippines and the IMF–World Bank Conglomerate,* Philippines in the Third World Papers, Series 17 (Quezon City: Third World Studies Center, University of the Philippines at Diliman, May 1979), pp. 6–7; and Guy Whitehead, "Philippine-American Economic Relations," *Pacific Research* 4 (January–February 1973): 3–6.

84. Quentin Reynolds and Geoffrey Bocca, *Macapagal: The Incorruptible* (New York: David McKay, 1965), p. 174; Diosdado Macapagal, *A Stone for the Edifice: Memoirs of a President* (Quezon City: MAC Publishing House, 1968), pp. 60–61; and interview with Macapagal, Metro-Manila, Philippines, March 27, 1981.

85. Interview with Macapagal, March 27, 1981.

86. Ibid.; see also Macapagal, *Memoirs,* p. 60.

87. The head of the IMF's Asian Division registered a complaint against this U.S. interference (interview with Leung, January 15, 1981).

88. For details, see Macapagal, *Memoirs,* annex A, p. 31; and J. Keith Horsefield, "Charges, Repurchases, Selection of Currencies," in *International Monetary Fund,* ed. Horsefield, vol. 2, table 22, p. 462. Ironically, the Philippines never made use of that $28.3 million committed by the IMF (interview with Macapagal, March 27, 1981; verified by data provided by Department of Economic Research, Central Bank of the Philippines, April 15, 1981).

The literature concerning the IMF conditions and the economic and political aftereffects of decontrol is fairly extensive: see Payer, *Debt Trap,* chap. 3, "Exchange Controls and National Capitalism: The Philippines Experience," pp. 50–74; Alejandro Lichauco, "The Lichauco Paper: Imperialism in the Philippines," *Monthly Review* 25 (July–August 1973): 1–111; Benito Legarda y Fernandez [Benito Legarda, Jr.], "Foreign Exchange Decontrol and the Redirection of Income Flows," *Philippine Economic Journal* 1 (First Semester 1962): 18–27; M. Treadgold and R. Hooley, "Decontrol and the Direction of Income Flows: A Second Look," *Philippine Economic Journal* 6 (Second Semester 1967): 117–20; John Power and Gerardo Sicat, *The Philippines: Industrialization and Trade Policies* (London: Oxford University Press, for Development Centre of the OECD, 1971), pp. 38–50; Vicente B. Valdepeñas, Jr., and Gemiliano M. Bautista, *The Emergence of the Philippine Economy* (Manila: Papyrus Press, May 1977), pp. 188–224; and Robin Broad, *International Actors and Philippine Authoritarianism* (Manila: Nationalist Resource Center, September 1981), pp. 8–9.

89. Quoted from interview with Avramović, July 2, 1982. Interview with Armand Fabella, Metro-Manila, Philippines, December 8, 1980.

90. Interview with Fabella, December 8, 1980.

91. Interview with Avramović, July 2, 1982.

92. Fabella (December 8, 1980) called it a "joint mission." Interviews with Macapagal, March 27, 1981; and with Hilarion Henares, Jr., Metro-Manila, Philippines, February 27, 1981.

93. Macapagal, *Memoirs,* p. 69; and Macapagal, *Five-Year Integrated Socio-Economic Program for the Philippines,* appendix 2, "Economic Growth in the Philippines: A Preliminary Report Prepared by the Staff of the IBRD, January 4, 1962," pp. 1–73.

94. Interview with Avramović, July 2, 1982; and C. Hsieh, *Employment Problems and Policies in the Philippines,* United Nations, International Labour Organization, Employment Research Papers (Geneva, 1969), p. 27. Already during this period, Avramović began airing the views that would lead to his departure from the Bank. "On the sly," according to Macapagal's National Economic Council chairman, Henares, "Avramović advised us not to let the IMF and the World Bank control us" (interview with Henares, February 27, 1981). The Program Implementation Agency, staffed by "young technical people," was renamed the Presidential Economic Staff during Marcos's first term. After martial law, Marcos merged his own economic staff with the by then less powerful, more nationalist-oriented National Economic Council, to form the National Economic and Development Authority, the nation's highest economic planning body (Romeo B. Ocampo, "Technocrats and Planning: Sketch and Exploration," *Philippine Journal of Public Administration* 15 [January 1971]: 31–64).

95. Interview with Benito Legarda, Jr., Metro-Manila, Philippines, February 2, 1981. Legarda was then assistant director of the Central Bank's Department of Economic Research.

96. Ibid.

97. Interview with Fabella, December 8, 1980.

98. Interview with Armado Castro, Metro-Manila, Philippines, January 20, 1981.

99. Interview with Legarda, February 2, 1981. This was up from the pre-float level of 3.90 to 1.00 (ibid.). IMF officials obviously did not totally understand the economic forces at work, either.

100. Ibid. On the specific conditions as well as the economic and political aftereffects of the 1970 IMF program, see Payer, *Debt Trap,* pp. 71–74; Lichauco, "Lichauco Paper"; Villegas, *Philippines,* p. 10; and Broad, *International Actors,* pp. 9–10. Specifically on the investment acts, see Gonzalo M. Jurado, "Industrialization and Trade," in *Philippine Economic Problems in Perspective,* ed. Jose Encarnacion, Jr. (Quezon City: Institute of Economic Development and Research,

School of Economics, University of the Philippines, 1976), p. 318; and Robyn Lim, "The Multinationals and the Philippines Since Martial Law," in *A Multinational Look at the Transnational Corporation,* ed. Michael T. Skully (Sydney: Dryden Press Australia, 1978), pp. 127–28.

101. Quoted in Robert Stauffer, "The Political Economy of Refeudalization," in *Marcos and Martial Law in the Philippines,* ed. David A. Rosenberg (Ithaca, N.Y.: Cornell University Press, 1979), p. 196.

102. This was, more officially, House Joint Resolution 2, signed into law by Marcos on August 4, 1969 (Alejandro Lichauco, "IMF–World Bank Group, the International Economic Order and the Philippine Experience," amended initial draft of paper presented at St. Scholastica's College, Manila, September 3, 1976, pp. 63–66).

103. Cited in Williamson, *Lending Policies,* p. 23.

Chapter 3

1. Michael Moffitt, *The World's Money: International Banking from Bretton Woods to the Brink of Insolvency* (New York: Simon and Schuster, 1983), p. 30.

2. For the early effects of the Vietnam War on the U.S. economy, see Gabriel Kolko, *The Roots of American Foreign Policy* (Boston: Beacon Press, 1969), pp. v–vi, 88–132.

3. In 1975, the Washington, D.C.–based Indochina Resource Center estimated the U.S. expenditure on the Indochina wars at $150 billion, compared with approximately $3 billion channeled to the North Vietnamese and National Liberation Front from China and the Soviet Union (Indochina Resource Center, *A Time to Heal: The Effects of the War on Viet Nam, Laos, Cambodia and America* [Washington, D.C.: Indochina Resource Center, 1976], p. 4).

4. David P. Calleo and Benjamin M. Rowland, *America and the World Political Economy: Atlantic Dreams and National Realities* (Bloomington: Indiana University Press, 1973), p. 120.

5. The subject of the early 1970s dollar crises and the related shifting U.S. international political position has been dealt with extensively by both political scientists and economists. Some key readings in this broad literature are David H. Blake and Robert S. Walters, *The Politics of Global Economic Relations* (Englewood Cliffs, N.J.: Prentice-Hall, 1976); Calleo and Rowland, *America and the World Political Economy;* Susan Strange, "The Politics of International Currencies," *World Politics* 23 (January 1971): 215–31; Fred Block, *The Origins of International Economic Disorder: A Study of United States International Monetary Policy from World War II to the Present* (Berkeley and Los Angeles: University of California Press, 1977), pp. 164–225; Margaret G. de Vries, *The International Monetary Fund, 1966–1971: The System Under Stress,* 2 vols. (Washington, D.C.: IMF, 1976), vol. 1,

pp. 527–30; Stephen D. Cohen, *International Monetary Reform, 1964–1969* (New York: Praeger, 1970); John Williamson, *The Failure of World Monetary Reform, 1971–1974* (New York: New York University Press, 1977), chapter 9, "Why Bretton Woods Collapsed"; and Robert Triffin's classic *Gold and the Dollar Crisis: The Future of Convertibility*, rev. ed. (New Haven, Conn.: Yale University Press, 1961), which warned of the impending breakdown of the Bretton Woods system.

6. See Neil Sheehan, Hedrick Smith, E. W. Kenworthy, and Fox Butterfield, *The Pentagon Papers* (New York: Bantam Books, 1971), pp. 589–93.

7. Kolko, *Roots,* p. 88.

8. Willy Brandt, Chairman, *Report of the Independent Commission on International Development Issues—North-South: A Program for Survival* (Cambridge, Mass.: MIT Press, 1980), p. 203 (hereafter cited as Brandt Commission Report).

9. William H. Branson, "Trends in United States International Trade and Investment Since World War II," in *The American Economy in Transition,* ed. Martin Feldstein (Chicago: University of Chicago Press, for National Bureau of Economic Research, 1980), p. 185.

10. For details of the interactions, see Branislav Gosović and John Ruggie, "On the Creation of a New International Economic Order," *International Organization* 30 (Spring 1976): 309–45. A more detailed description of what these new international economic order demands entailed can be found in the Brandt Commission Report; "The International Monetary System and the New International Economic Order," *Development Dialogue,* no. 2 (1980); and E. A. Brett, "The International Monetary Fund, the International Monetary System and the Periphery," *IFDA Dossier,* no. 5 (March 1979): 1–15. Perhaps the best overview of the scholarly debate over the significance of the North-South negotiations can be found in Michael W. Doyle, "Stalemate in the North-South Debate: Strategies and the New International Economic Order," *World Politics* 35 (April 1983): 426–64. Two perceptive analyses of what the North-South dialogue does and does not mean are Richard Nations, "The Long Hard Road from Algiers to Cancún," *Far Eastern Economic Review* (November 6, 1981): 108–10; and Elizabeth Bradshaw and Henry Holland, "Cancún: Rhetoric and Reality," *Economic and Political Weekly* (November 12, 1981): 1897–99.

11. Although more research is currently being undertaken on the new international division of labor, the questions it encompasses are, as yet, not sufficiently studied. The work by members of West Germany's Max Planck Institute, Folker Fröbel, Jürgen Heinrichs, and Otto Kreye, *The New International Division of Labour: Structural Unemployment in Industrialized Countries and Industrialization in Developing Countries,* trans. Pete Burgess (Cambridge, England: Cambridge University Press, 1980; trans. of original edition, Hamburg: Rowohlt Taschenbuch, 1977), which includes a detailed account of West Germany's textile and apparel industry, stands as a classic in the field. André Gunder Frank's review, "New Inter-

national Division of Labour?" (*Economic and Political Weekly* [December 17, 1977]: 2093–96) is also useful. Samir Amin's work should be consulted; for example, "The New International Economic Order and the Future of International Economic Relations," paper presented at the International Conference of Alternative Development Strategies and the Future of Asia, New Delhi, March 11–17, 1980. See also Dieter Ernst, ed., *The New International Division of Labor, Technology, and Underdevelopment: Consequences for the Third World* (Frankfurt: Campus, 1980); and Gary Hawes, "Southeast Asian Agribusiness: The New International Division of Labor," *Bulletin of Concerned Asian Scholars* 14 (October–December 1982): 20–29.

12. A brief but insightful historical overview of the rise of corporate power over the last hundred years can be found in UNCTAD, *Fibres and Textiles: Dimensions of Corporate Marketing Structure*, TD/B/C.1/219, Geneva, November 19, 1980, pp. 3–19.

13. Calculated from Table 3.

14. In 1980, for example, average profit rates on U.S. direct investment abroad were above 30 percent in South Africa, Indonesia, Malaysia, Singapore, Hong Kong, Nigeria, Libya, Egypt, the Bahamas, and Argentina (calculated from computer printouts on U.S. direct foreign investment abroad, supplied by the U.S. Department of Commerce, November 1981). Profit rate equals income plus fees and royalties as percentage of total investment.

15. *Survey of Current Business* (February 1981): 41, 51.

16. See Walter Kiechel III, "Playing the Global Game," *Fortune* (November 16, 1981): 111–26.

17. The U.S. government (particularly the military), for example, invested substantial funding and effort in electronics research and development. By 1980, the Pentagon financed almost a third of U.S. research and development; the Ministry of International Trade and Industry financed 16 percent of Japan's (*International Herald Tribune*, December 2, 1981).

18. Kiechel, "Playing the Global Game," p. 114.

19. Ibid., pp. 111–26.

20. Many volumes have been written on the microprocessor revolution. A good but already somewhat outdated bibliography can be found in Mary Alison Hancock, comp., *Women and Transnational Corporations: A Bibliography*, Working Papers of the East-West Center Culture Learning Institute, Impact of Transnational Interactions Project (Honolulu: East-West Center, 1980), pp. 42–44. Of particular note are A. Sivanandan, "Imperialism in the Silicon Age," *Monthly Review* 32 (July–August 1980): 24–42; Barbara Ehrenreich and Annette Fuentes, "Life on the Global Assembly Line," *Ms. Magazine* (January 1981): 53; Rachel Grossman, "Women's Place in the Integrated Circuit," *Southeast Asia Chronicle*, no. 66 (Janu-

ary–February 1979), and *Pacific Research* 9 (July–August 1978); Peter Marsh, *The Silicon Chip Book* (London: Sphere Books, 1981); J. Rada, *The Impact of Microelectronics: A Tentative Appraisal of Information Technology*, United Nations, International Labour Organization, World Employment Programme Study (Geneva, 1980). With special reference to the Philippines, see Enrico Paglaban, "Philippines: Workers in the Export Industry," *Pacific Research* 9 (March–June 1978).

21. The microprocessor work carried out in developing countries involves tedious, vision-impairing microscopic work and dangerous chemical baths. For details, see Grossman, "Women's Place"; Council for Primary Health Care (Manila), "Eye Care in the Electronics Industry: Whose Main Concern?" *Health and Workers Bulletin*, no. 2 (February 1984); and Thomas H. Gassert, *Health Hazards in Electronics: A Handbook* (Hong Kong: Asia Monitor Resource Center, 1985).

22. Grossman, "Women's Place," p. 7; Mary Alison Hancock, *Electronics: The International Industry*, Working Papers of the East-West Center Culture Learning Institute, Impact of Transnational Interactions Project (Honolulu: East-West Center, 1980), p. 29, table 7.

23. This refers to c.i.f. (cost, insurance, and freight) value at current prices for Item 729.3 of the Standard International Trade Classification (SITC), which also includes such things as thermionic valves and tubes, and transistors. In 1972 the value was $346 million; by 1976 it had surged to $1,357 million (Rada, *Impact of Micro-electronics*, p. 22, citing statistics from OECD, *Trade by Commodities*, Series C, 1972 and 1976).

24. These data refer to the total semiconductor imports to the United States under U.S. tariff code items 806.30 and 807 (United Nations Industrial Development Organization, Global and Conceptual Studies Branch, Division for Industrial Studies, *Restructuring World Industry in a Period of Crisis—The Role of Innovation: An Analysis of Recent Developments in the Semi-conductor Industry*, UNIDO/IS.285, December 17, 1981, pp. 246, table 6.8, and 247).

25. Rada, *Impact of Micro-electronics*, p. 22.

26. UNCTAD, *Fibres and Textiles*, pp. 237–44, presents a specific breakdown of the technological advances in spinning, weaving, and knitting.

27. Ibid., p. 167, table 45. Indeed, LDCs' share of the global apparel market is greater than their share of any other industrial sector.

28. See UNCTAD, *Fibres and Textiles*, p. 171, chart 18, for comparison of capital invested per employee in twenty U.S. manufacturing sectors.

29. In the world of textile exporters, the case of India, which deliberately stuck to its labor-intensive handlooms, is something of an anomaly. Figures aggregating textile exports from LDCs can be somewhat misleading; spun yarn makes up a good portion of the total amount and, in countries such as Pakistan, is not necessarily the output of modern enterprises. In 1977, developing countries

exported 19.4 percent of world textile yarn and fabric exports; developed countries, 72.7 percent (ibid., p. 167, table 45; p. 185, table 49).

30. This, of course, blurs the critical LDC world-order distinction: the industrial activity was not spread uniformly throughout the developing world but was concentrated in thirty or so LDCs.

31. IMF, *Philippines: Recent Economic Developments,* July 18, 1980, p. 32; *Philippine Development* (Manila) 6 (December 28, 1979): 29. *Manufactured exports* here refer, more precisely, to what the Philippine government calls "nontraditional" manufactured exports. Nontraditional manufactured exports accounted for 40 percent of total exports in 1980, whereas their share was less than 10 percent in 1970 (*World Business Weekly* [August 20, 1981]: 49).

32. *Economist* (December 20, 1980): 67.

33. See, e.g., W. Arthur Lewis, *Growth and Fluctuations, 1870–1913* (Cambridge, England: George Allen & Unwin, 1978), pp. 26, 29, and 280–81, table A-11; Charles Kindleberger, *Foreign Trade and the National Economy* (New Haven, Conn.: Yale University Press, 1962), pp. 23–25. Freight charges as a percentage of value of imports in overall world trade fell from 7.75 in 1970 to 6.55 in 1979, for example (UNCTAD, *Review of Maritime Transport, 1980,* TD/B/C.4/222, May 25, 1981, p. 40, table 25).

34. It is true that certain factories that are essentially assembly-line, e.g., for automobiles, were set up in a few LDCs in the 1960s, but these were largely restricted to the richer LDCs with large internal markets, such as Brazil, Mexico, and Iran.

35. TNCs could carry out these minor operations directly, or indirectly through an operation called *subcontracting* or *outward processing.*

36. Kennedy's Alliance for Progress was a precursor of this strategy. See Jerome Levinson and Juan de Onis, *The Alliance That Lost Its Way: A Critical Report on the Alliance for Progress,* Twentieth Century Fund Study (Chicago: Quadrangle Books, for Twentieth Century Fund, 1970).

37. Jonathan E. Sanford, *Multilateral Banks: Can U.S. Limit Use of Its Contributions?* U.S. Library of Congress, Congressional Research Service, Issue Brief IB79114, January 13, 1980, update of October 19, 1979, p. 5. See also Margaret G. Goodman and Jonathan E. Sanford, *The United States and the Multilateral Development Banks,* U.S. Library of Congress, Congressional Research Service, for Congress, House, Committee on Foreign Affairs (Washington, D.C.: Government Printing Office, 1974).

38. Statement of W. Michael Blumenthal, Secretary of the Treasury, in U.S. Congress, House, Committee on Appropriations, *Hearings Before the Subcommittee on Foreign Operations on Foreign Assistance and Related Appropriations for 1980,* 96th Cong., 1st sess., March 14, 1979, p. 13; and statement of C. Fred Bergsten, As-

sistant Secretary of the Treasury, in U.S. Congress, House, Committee on Appropriations, *Hearings Before the Subcommittee on Foreign Operations on Foreign Assistance and Related Appropriations for 1978*, 95th Cong., 1st sess., February 16, 1977, p. 150.

39. Results of a 1975 Harris poll cited in Walden Bello and Severina Rivera, eds., *The Logistics of Repression and Other Essays* (Washington, D.C.: Friends of the Filipino People, 1977), p. 4. See United Nations Association of the U.S.A., *United States Foreign Policy and Human Rights* (New York: United Nations Association of the U.S.A., 1979).

40. Jonathan E. Sanford, *U.S. Foreign Policy and Multilateral Development Banks* (Boulder, Colo.: Westview Press, 1982), pp. 34–37; Victoria E. Marmorstein, "World Bank Power to Consider Human Rights Factors in Loan Decisions," *Journal of International Law and Economics* 13, no. 1 (1978): 113–36; Elizabeth P. Spiro, "Front Door or Back Stairs: U.S. Human Rights Policy in the International Financial Institutions," in *Human Rights and U.S. Foreign Policy*, ed. Barry M. Rubin and Elizabeth P. Spiro (Boulder, Colo.: Westview Press, 1979), pp. 134–37.

41. See James Petras and Morris Morley, *The United States and Chile: Imperialism and the Overthrow of the Allende Government* (New York: Monthly Review Press, 1975), pp. 83–105, 162–67; Jonathan E. Sanford, "The Multilateral Development Banks and the Suspension of Lending to Allende's Chile," in U.S. Congress, House, Committee on Foreign Affairs, Subcommittee on Inter-American Affairs, *The United States and Chile During the Allende Years, 1970–1973* (Washington, D.C.: Government Printing Office, 1975), pp. 417–48; and David Gisselquist, "IMF Primer," *International Policy Report* (June 1981). The question of why the IMF continued lending to the Allende government, albeit on a small scale, has yet to be adequately analyzed.

42. Quoted in *Philippines Daily Express* (Manila), May 21, 1976. That loan was, in fact, hotly debated by the Bank's board of directors, but the Scandinavian countries, not the United States, led the debate. Reportedly, the loan required the first actual vote by the Bank's board on any of the more than two hundred loans in that fiscal year.

On the overall question of bilateral and multilateral aid and support for authoritarian regimes, see Noam Chomsky and Edward S. Herman, *The Political Economy of Human Rights,* vol. 1: *The Washington Connection and Third World Fascism* (Boston: South End Press, 1979); Walden Bello and Elaine Elinson, *Elite Democracy or Authoritarian Rule?* (Oakland, Calif.: Philippine Solidarity Network and the Coalition Against the Marcos Dictatorship, June 1981); and Sanford, *U.S. Foreign Policy.*

43. The Philippines is a case in point. See World Bank, *Philippines—Country Program Paper,* March 26, 1976, p. 2. Officials at U.S. AID in Bangkok acknowledged that this trend could also be found in assistance to Thailand (interviews with

officials [anonymity requested], U.S. AID, Bangkok, Thailand, July and August 1979).

44. Robert L. Ayres, "Breaking the Bank," *Foreign Policy* (Summer 1981): 113; *Business in Thailand* (October 1980): 5; *Asian Wall Street Journal*, June 6, 1978.

45. The Committee of the Board of Governors on the Reform of the International Monetary System and Related Issues existed from July 1972 to June 1974, when it gave its final recommendations. Its successor was the Interim Committee, so named because it was supposed to give way to an IMF Council. For an in-depth analysis of the work of the Committee of Twenty in the arena of international monetary reform, see Williamson, *Failure of World Monetary Reform*.

46. Norman Girvan, Richard Bernal, and Wesley Hughes, "The IMF and the Third World: The Case of Jamaica, 1974–80," *Development Dialogue*, no. 2 (1980): 116; John Williamson, *The Lending Policies of the International Monetary Fund*, Policy Analyses in International Economics 1 (Washington, D.C.: Institute for International Economics, 1982), p. 22; A. W. Hooke, *The International Monetary Fund: Its Evolution, Organization and Activities*, IMF Pamphlet Series 37, 1981, p. 45. Likewise, as UNCTAD negotiated its integrated program for commodities, the Big Five provided more support for the IMF's expanded compensatory finance facility. The IMF's interest-subsidy scheme is another example of a marginal concession to the South's demands. As of 1982, the IMF guidelines permitted "an annual use of its resources up to 150 percent of quota and up to 450 percent of quota over a period of three years" (Joseph Gold, *Order in International Finance, the Promotion of IMF Stand-By Arrangements, and the Drafting of Private Loan Agreements*, IMF Pamphlet Series 39, 1982, p. 41). By 1984, the IMF was reversing this trend of "enlarged access" as it moved to tighten its loan limits.

47. Williamson, *Lending Policies,* p. 20.

48. Sidney Dell, *On Being Grandmotherly: The Evolution of IMF Conditionality*, Essays in International Finance 144 (Princeton, N.J.: International Finance Section, Department of Economics, Princeton University, 1981), p. 27.

49. IMF, *Annual Report of the Executive Board for the Financial Year Ended April 30, 1980* (Washington, D.C.: IMF, 1980), p. 116; Michael Zammit Cutajar, comp., "Background Notes on the International Monetary Fund," *Development Dialogue*, no. 2 (1980): 111; and *Asian Wall Street Journal*, August 16, 1979.

50. The May 1981 loan agreement marked the fourth time the Saudis provided funds to the IMF under special borrowing arrangements. *Asian Wall Street Journal*, May 9, 1981; *Far Eastern Economic Review* (April 24, 1981): 92; "The IMF and World Economic Stability—Interview with Richard Erb, U.S. Executive Director at IMF," *Challenge* (September–October 1981): 23.

51. Formally the Intergovernmental Group of 24 on International Monetary Affairs, the Group of 24 is a subset of the Group of 77. However, the Group of 24 styles itself more as an offshoot of the IMF than of UNCTAD, and IMF publica-

tions, such as *IMF Survey,* tend to give it credibility and legitimacy by reporting on its activities as if it were an official IMF committee.

52. *Asian Wall Street Journal,* June 20, 1980. This is not to ignore the expansion in the Fund's resources, beginning with the extended fund facility in 1974. This was, however, overshadowed by the Bank's expansion in the second half of the 1970s (*Finance and Development* 15 [September 1978]: 2–3). The IMF was not a net lender in either 1977 or 1978, or even in the first half of 1979 (*Economist* [November 3–9, 1979]: 92). Moreover, there has continually been a large gap between the commitments claimed by the IMF and the net disbursements made; see UNCTAD's *Trade and Development Report 1981* (Geneva, 1981) on this subject.

53. When Robert McNamara assumed the presidency of the Bank in 1968, he brought with him the experience of seven difficult years as U.S. secretary of defense, where he stood as President Johnson's chief deputy overseeing the war effort. Although McNamara's background, as "whiz kid" turned Ford Motor Company president, endowed him with a technocratic and authoritarian style that he never relinquished during his reign at the Bank, his Pentagon days left the deepest imprint on his views of development and revolution. An extremely revealing article by a former World Bank vice-president (whose term at the Bank almost precisely overlapped McNamara's) describes McNamara's development policies as emanating from his sense of impotence over what, by 1964, had been dubbed "McNamara's War." These views matured at the Bank as American black ghettos exploded in race and class wars in the mid and late 1970s (William Clark, "Robert McNamara at the World Bank," *Foreign Affairs* [Fall 1981]: 167–84).

A number of books and articles have been written about McNamara's thirteen years as Bank president; two men obviously close to McNamara and the inner sanctums of the World Bank wrote exceptionally revealing ones. In addition to Clark, see Robert L. Ayres, *Banking on the Poor: The World Bank and World Poverty* (Cambridge, Mass.: MIT Press, in cooperation with the Overseas Development Council, 1983); and Ayres, "Breaking the Bank."

McNamara voiced his support for economic aid even earlier, during his term as secretary of defense. In 1966, addressing the American Society of Newspaper Editors, he noted "the certain connection between economic stagnation and the incidence of violence," a relationship suggesting that, if the situation were left, "the years . . . ahead for the nations in the southern half of the globe [would be] pregnant with violence" (*New York Times,* May 19, 1966).

54. Ayres, *Banking on the Poor,* p. 5.

55. Ibid., p. 226.

56. The phrase is the Bank's own (William Ascher, "Political and Administrative Bases for Economic Policy in the Philippines," World Bank, November 6, 1980, p. 4 [hereafter cited as Ascher Memorandum]).

57. What "basic needs" means and does not mean has been debated elsewhere

at length. For the World Bank's own sense of "defensive modernization," see its 1975 *Assault on Poverty,* its 1975 *Sector Policy Paper* on rural development, and McNamara's speeches. Critical assessments include Cheryl Payer, *The World Bank: A Critical Analysis* (New York: Monthly Review Press, 1982); and Walden Bello et al., *Development Debacle: The World Bank in the Philippines* (San Francisco: Institute for Food and Development Policy, 1982), pp. 67–99. See also Frances Moore Lappé, Joseph Collins, and David Kinley, *Aid as Obstacle: Twenty Questions About Our Foreign Aid and the Hungry* (San Francisco: Institute for Food and Development Policy, 1980); Betsy Hartmann and James Boyce, *Needless Hunger: Voices from a Bangladesh Village* (San Francisco: Institute for Food and Development Policy, 1979); and Aart J. M. Van de Laar, *The World Bank and the Poor* (Boston: Martinus Nijhoff, 1980).

58. Ayres's own estimate ("Breaking the Bank," p. 108) is that "considerably more than one-half and perhaps as much as two-thirds of combined bank and IDA lending remains traditional."

59. For a more detailed sense of this ministerial meeting and the Group of 77 demands, see Cutajar, "Background Notes on the International Monetary Fund," p. 105; Clark, "Robert McNamara," pp. 181–82; and Ho Kwon Ping, "A Deadlock on Development," *Far Eastern Economic Review* (October 3, 1980): 56–57.

60. See Robert McNamara, *Address to the Board of Governors, Belgrade, Yugoslavia, October 2, 1979* (Washington, D.C.: World Bank, n.d.).

61. Justinian F. Rweyemamu, "Restructuring the International Monetary System," *Development Dialogue,* no. 2 (1980), p. 86. See also Brandt Commission Report, pp. 232–34, 255, 274.

62. Andres Federman, "The Third World Bank: Making the Break," *South* (September 1981): 8.

63. Figures cited in *Asian Wall Street Journal,* October 8, 1980; *Far Eastern Economic Review* (April 24, 1981): 87. See also *Economist* (September 4, 1982): 46. These aims are explicitly stated by the World Bank Development Policy Staff's Senior Adviser, E. D. Wright, in "World Bank Lending for Structural Adjustment," *Finance and Development* 17 (September 1980): 21–23.

64. Williamson, *Lending Policies,* p. 21.

65. Ibid., p. 22.

66. Ibid., p. 21.

67. A packet of Bank and Fund memos and reports was put together for discussions the two institutions held on structural adjustment lending. Included in this packet were four memos and reports that summarized recent discussions: World Bank, "Structural Adjustment Lending—Collaboration with the IMF," memorandum from Ernest Stern, vice-president of operations, to regional vice-presidents, June 9, 1980; IMF, "Statement by the Managing Director on Fund

Collaboration with the Bank in Assisting Member Countries, Executive Board Meeting, May 28, 1980," 80/103, May 15, 1980; IMF, "The Chairman's Summing Up at the Conclusion of the Discussion on Fund Collaboration with the Bank in Assisting Member Countries, Executive Board Meeting, May 28, 1980," 80/114, June 2, 1980; and IMF, "Fund Collaboration with the Bank in Assisting Member Countries," memorandum from the managing director to department, bureau, and office heads, June 9, 1980. The quote is from IMF, "Chairman's Summing Up."

A Fund-Bank Development Committee (formally the Joint Ministerial Committee of the Boards of Governors of the Bank and Fund on the Transfer of Real Resources to Developing Countries) publicly and privately endorsed the expanded collaboration and cooperation between the two international financial institutions. Set up in 1974 after the Committee of 20 recommended that more be done to transfer resources to the South, the Development Committee was at this time headed by the Philippine finance minister, Cesar Virata (Cesar Virata, Chairman, Development Committee, *Provisional Record of Discussion of the Twelfth Meeting of the Development Committee, Belgrade, Yugoslavia, September 30, 1979,* DC/79–14 [Washington, D.C.: World Bank, 1979]; and "Development Committee's 16th Meeting Held in Gabon on May 22, 1981," *Press Communiqué* [May 22, 1981]).

68. The literature on the World Bank and the IMF and the international division of labor is sparse. Fawzy Mansour breaks new ground in "The World Bank: Present Role and Prospects—An Outsider's View (draft)" (Dakar: U.N. African Institute for Economic Development and Planning, 1979), which stands as a critique of most radical critics of the Bank and the Fund (including Payer and Hayter). One of the few works from the Philippines dealing with the new international division of labor is the seven-part series "A Scenario of Neo-Colonialism," by Merlin Magallona of the University of the Philippines Law Center, published in the January and February 1981 issues of *Makati Trade Times.*

69. Bela Balassa, "A 'Stages Approach' to Comparative Advantage," in *Economic Growth and Resources,* ed. Irma Adelman, proceedings of the Fifth Congress of the International Economic Association, Tokyo, Japan, 1977, vol. 4 (London: Macmillan, 1979), pp. 121–56. A growing literature criticizes the neoclassical notion of comparative advantage and studies the dynamics of international exchange from a Marxist perspective. These works dispute—many in theoretical terms—Ricardo's theory of comparative costs and the Hecksher-Ohlin-Samuelson trade models that built on Ricardo's work. See Anwar Shaikh, "Foreign Trade and the Law of Value: Part I," *Science and Society* 43 (Fall 1979): 281–302; Shaikh, "Foreign Trade and the Law of Value: Part II," *Science and Society* 44 (Spring 1980): 27–57; John Weeks, "A Note on the Underconsumptionist Theory and the Labor Theory of Value," *Science and Society* 46 (Spring 1982): 60–76; Samir Amin, *Unequal Development: An Essay on the Social Formation of Peripheral Capitalism,* trans.

Brian Pearce (New York: Monthly Review Press, 1976); Arghiri Emmanuel, *Unequal Exchange: A Study of the Imperialism of Trade* (New York: Monthly Review Press, 1972).

70. Bela Balassa, *The Process of Industrial Development and Alternative Development Strategies,* Essays in International Finance 141 (Princeton, N.J.: International Finance Section, Department of Economics, Princeton University, 1980), pp. 25−26. This essay contains the Graham Memorial Lecture by Balassa at Princeton University, April 17, 1980.

71. Bela Balassa, "Industrial Policies in Taiwan and Korea," in *International Economics and Development: Essays in Honor of Raul Prebisch,* ed. Luis Eugenio Di Marco (New York: Academic Press, 1972), p. 179.

72. Robert McNamara, *Address to the United Nations Conference on Trade and Development, Manila, Philippines, May 10, 1979* (Washington, D.C.: World Bank, n.d.), pp. 29, 15, 27.

73. World Bank, *Annual Report 1981* (Washington, D.C.: World Bank, 1981), pp. 70−71. Cf. World Bank, *Annual Report 1980* (Washington, D.C.: World Bank, 1980), pp. 67−68.

74. Williamson, *Lending Policies,* p. 22.

75. *International Herald Tribune,* March 18, 1981. On the growth of TNB lending to LDCs over the 1970s, see Deborah L. Riner, "Borrowers and Bankers: The Euro-Market and Political Economy in Peru and Chile," Ph.D. dissertation, Princeton University, 1982.

76. Mansour, "World Bank," p. 42, citing the preliminary work of the Brandt Commission.

77. Arthur Burns, "The Need for Order in International Finance," speech at annual dinner of Columbia University Graduate School of Business, April 12, 1977, pp. 13, 14, 21, quoted in Howard M. Wachtel, *The New Gnomes: Multinational Banks in the Third World* (Washington, D.C.: Transnational Institute, 1977), p. 36.

78. United States, Council of Economic Advisers, *Economic Report of the President* (Washington, D.C.: Government Printing Office, 1977), p. 130.

79. An overview of the influence of powerful business groups and councils is presented in Lawrence Shoup and William Minter, *Imperial Brain Trust: The Council on Foreign Relations and United States Foreign Policy* (New York: Monthly Review Press, 1977). See also Kim McQuaid, *Big Business and Presidential Power: From FDR to Reagan* (New York: William Morrow, 1982).

80. World Bank, *Annual Report 1980,* p. 70. As early as mid-1981, bankers, wary of the Philippines' already inflated debt, said that loans to the Philippines continued to carry favorable terms because of the structural adjustment program (*Far Eastern Economic Review* [September 17, 1981]: 43).

81. Articles 806.30 and 807 of the Tariff Classification Act of 1962 permit temporary export of raw materials and components for further assemblage and processing abroad. On reentry to the United States, duty on the product is assessed only on its value added; earlier laws taxed the product on its full value. Similar laws exist in Western Europe (UNCTAD, *Intra-Industry Trade and International Subcontracting*, TD/B/805/Supp. 2, August 6, 1980).

82. For more on subcontracting, see UNCTAD, *Fibres and Textiles*, pp. 202–6; and Dimitri Germidis, ed., *International Subcontracting: A New Form of Investment*, Development Centre Studies (Paris: OECD, 1980).

83. Eleven countries in Asia, nine in Latin America, and five in Africa composed the twenty-five. Frank, "New International Division of Labour?" p. 2095; Tsuchiya Takeo, "Free Trade Zones in Southeast Asia," *Monthly Review* 29 (February 1978): 31–32; *Ibon Facts and Figures*, no. 22 (July 15, 1979): 2.

84. Among the best work on EPZs has been done by Pacific Asia Resources Center (PARC), a Japanese research group. See PARC, "Free Trade Zones and Industrialization of Asia," *Ampo: Japan-Asia Quarterly Review* (1977), which shows how the World Bank worked with UNIDO in its promotion of EPZs.

Chapter 4

1. That the IMF's and the World Bank's contacts would evolve historically to those suggested in Figure 2 was not predictable from the charter of either institution. Indeed, both institutions' Articles of Agreement (World Bank, *Articles of Agreement of the International Bank for Reconstruction and Development [As Amended Effective December 17, 1965]*, art. 3, sec. 2; IMF, *Articles of Agreement of the International Monetary Fund* [July 22, 1944], art. 5, sec. 1) state that each member shall deal with the Bank and Fund (and vice versa) "only through its Treasury, central bank, stabilization fund or similar fiscal agency."

2. World Bank, *Philippines—Country Program Paper*, August 29, 1980, p. 13.

3. The Philippines was the second country to enter into an EFF arrangement with the IMF; the first, Kenya, dropped its EFF (which had begun some nine months prior to that of the Philippines) in midstream (IMF, *Annual Report 1980* [Washington, D.C.: World Bank, 1980], p. 116; *Asian Wall Street Journal*, August 14, 1979).

4. Interview with Gregorio S. Licaros, Metro-Manila, Philippines, April 1, 1981.

5. IMF, *Annual Report 1980*, p. 116, table 1.7.

6. Paragraph based on interviews with Escolastica B. Bince, Metro-Manila, Philippines, December 2, 1980; Carmelita Areñas, Metro-Manila, Philippines, January 15, 1981; Mercy Suleik, Metro-Manila, Philippines, December 15, 1980;

Leung, January 15 and 30, 1981; and Licaros, April 1, 1981. While these targets were, for the most part, confidential, there are a few written sources on the subject: *Asian Wall Street Journal*, August 14, 1979; *Times Journal* (Manila), August 18, 1977; World Bank, *World Development Report 1982* (New York: Oxford University Press for the World Bank, 1982), pp. 76–77.

7. Quoted from interview with IMF official (anonymity requested), Metro-Manila, Philippines, November 25, 1980. Over the EFF period, the peso-dollar rate remained a fairly stable 7.4 (IMF, *Philippines—Recent Economic Developments,* July 18, 1980, p. 41).

8. Quote is from interview with IMF official (anonymity requested), Metro-Manila, Philippines, November 25, 1980. Paragraph based on interviews with Bince, December 2, 1980; Areñas, January 15, 1981; Suleik, December 15, 1980; Licaros, April 1, 1981; and Leung, January 15 and 30, 1981. Written sources were *Asian Wall Street Journal*, June 19, 1978, July 24, 1979, August 14, 1979; Philippines (Republic), Central Bank, *Economic and Financial Development During the First Nine Months of 1977,* preliminary report from Amado R. Briñas, senior deputy governor, to Ferdinand Marcos, October 4, 1977; and World Bank, *Philippines— Country Program Paper,* 1980, p. 13.

9. Interviews with IMF official (anonymity requested), November 25, 1980; Leung, January 30, 1981; Bince, December 2, 1980; and Licaros, April 1, 1981, among others.

10. By 1978, nontraditional manufactured exports exceeded one billion dollars, representing almost a third of total export earnings (Barend de Vries, *Transition Toward More Rapid and Labor-Intensive Industrial Development: The Case of the Philippines,* World Bank Staff Working Paper 424, October 1980, p. 5). As officially defined by the Philippines' 1981 Omnibus Investments Code, nontraditional exports are to be distinguished from traditional exports, which are products whose total Philippine export value exceeded five million dollars in 1968.

11. Interviews with Suleik, December 15, 1980; Ofelia Soliven, Metro-Manila, Philippines, November 17, 1980. Philippines (Republic), Central Bank of the Philippines, Interagency Committee on IMF-EFF, "Preliminary Outline: Manual of Demand Policies," Manila, 1978 (mimeographed).

12. Interview with Bince, December 2, 1980. Bince was the Central Bank's chief negotiator with the IMF.

13. Interview with Licaros, April 1, 1981.

14. Interviews with Ministry of Finance staff members (anonymity requested), Metro-Manila, Philippines, December 3, 1980, and March 26, 1981; Central Bank staff member (anonymity requested), Metro-Manila, Philippines, April 15, 1981.

15. Interview with Licaros, April 1, 1981. The associate director and assistant head of the Central Bank's Public Relations Service, Office of the Governor, Oscar

A. de los Santos—who was Licaros's righthand man—used the same description (interview with de los Santos, Metro-Manila, Philippines, March 30, 1981).

16. Interview with Licaros, April 1, 1981. Cf. Licaros's quotes in *Asian Wall Street Journal*, June 21, 1980.

17. Figures from Business International, *Roundtable with the Government of the Philippines, Manila, May 11–14, 1980: Briefing Paper* (n.p.: Business International, n.d.) (hereafter cited as Business International, *Briefing Paper*), p. 30; *Wall Street Journal*, February 10, 1981; World Bank, *World Debt Tables* (Washington, D.C.: World Bank, April 1986), pp. 226–29.

18. Interview with Wilhelm G. Ortaliz, Metro-Manila, Philippines, January 19, 1981.

19. Interview with Ministry of Finance staff member (anonymity requested), Metro-Manila, Philippines, December 17, 1980.

20. Interview with Leung, January 15, 1981.

21. Interview with former Central Bank deputy governor (anonymity requested), Metro-Manila, Philippines, February 9, 1981. For more on Cheryl Payer's *The Debt Trap: The International Monetary Fund and the Third World* (New York: Monthly Review Press, 1974), see Chapter 1, above.

22. Interview with Edgardo P. Zialcita, Metro-Manila, Philippines, January 21, 1981. In this informal interview, Zialcita was speaking broadly about secrecy in both IMF projections and models, although he clearly realized the distinction between the two.

23. Interviews with Bienvenido M. Noriega, Jr., Metro-Manila, Philippines, January 30 and April 20, 1981; NEDA official (anonymity requested), Metro-Manila, Philippines, December 5, 1980; Ortaliz, January 19, 1981; Benito Legarda, Jr., February 2, 1981.

24. Interview with Ortaliz, January 19, 1981.

25. Interview with Leung, January 30, 1981.

26. World Bank, *Report and Recommendation of the President of the International Bank for Reconstruction and Development to the Executive Directors on a Proposed Structural Adjustment Loan to the Republic of the Philippines,* Report P–2872–PH, August 21, 1980, p. 1 (hereafter cited as World Bank, *Report and Recommendation,* August 21, 1980).

27. World Bank, *Philippines—Country Program Paper,* 1980, p. 3.

28. World Bank, *Philippines—Country Program Paper,* March 26, 1976, p. 19.

29. Ibid., p. 2. The Philippines' 1972–1976 experience with World Bank project loans and IMF yearly standby loans has been analyzed elsewhere. See Walden Bello and Severina Rivera, eds., *The Logistics of Repression and Other Essays* (Washington, D.C.: Friends of the Filipino People, 1977); Walden Bello et al., *Development Debacle: The World Bank and the Philippines* (San Francisco: Institute for Food

and Development Policy, 1982); Robin Broad, *International Actors and Philippine Authoritarianism* (Manila: Nationalist Resource Center, 1981); Edberto M. Villegas, *The Philippines and the IMF–World Bank Conglomerate*, Philippines in the Third World Papers, Series 17 (Quezon City: Third World Studies Center, University of the Philippines at Diliman, 1979).

30. World Bank, *Philippines—Country Program Paper*, 1976, p. 17.

31. "Guinea pig" and "testing ground" were terms used by a wide-ranging group of Philippine government officials during the course of interviews. Among them: Areñas, January 15, 1981; Bince, December 2, 1980; Noriega, April 20, 1981; and NEDA official (anonymity requested), December 5, 1980.

32. Interview with Licaros, April 1, 1981.

33. Interview with Castro, January 20, 1981. Basic economic reports, restricted documents within the Bank, are working documents covering macroeconomic issues. Some of these basic economic reports have been published—after some censoring, like most Bank documents that reach the public document stage—by the Bank as a series of World Bank Country Economic Reports. Cheetham's report became *The Philippines: Priorities and Prospects for Development*, 1976.

34. Other references were United Nations, International Labour Organization, *Sharing in Development: A Program of Employment, Equity and Growth for the Philippines* (Geneva: ILO, 1974); IMF, *Philippines—Use of Fund Resources*, Report EBS/76/133, March 16, 1976. See, among others, World Bank, *Philippines: Domestic and External Resources for Development*, economic memorandum for 1979 Consultative Group Meeting, Report 2674–PH, November 12, 1979, pp. i, iii; and World Bank, *Report and Recommendation of the President of the International Bank for Reconstruction and Development to the Executive Directors on a Proposed Loan to the Republic of the Philippines for a Third Urban Development Project*, February 1980, pp. 2, 3. Cf. U.S. Agency for International Development, *FY1982 Country Development Strategy Statement—Philippines* (Manila: AID, 1980), p. 28 and annex D, p. 1.

35. Interview with Flordeliza Dizon, Metro-Manila, Philippines, December 8, 1980. Dizon worked on the five-year plan as a member of the Subcommittee on Credit Resources and the Subcommittee on External Financing.

36. World Bank, *Philippines—Country Program Paper*, 1976, p. 17.

37. See Cheetham, *Priorities and Prospects;* Philippines (Republic), *Five-Year Development Plan 1978–1982*, September 1977. The term *take off,* repeated frequently by top Philippine policymakers and Bank and Fund officials during interviews, is taken from the work of W. W. Rostow; see esp. *The Stages of Economic Growth: A Non-Communist Manifesto* (London: Cambridge University Press, 1960).

38. Cesar Virata, minister of finance, to Robert McNamara, president of World Bank, letter, "Re: Philippine Industrial Development Policy," August 12, 1980. With the letter were attachment 1, "Statement on Industrial Policy for the 1980s," and attachment 2, "Industrial Development Policy."

39. Philippines (Republic), Ministry of Industry, *Measures/Steps Taken by the Government in Connection with the Industrial Policy Recommendations Contained in the World Bank's Industrial Sector Report,* Working Paper of the Government of the Philippines (Manila: Ministry of Industry, 1979).

40. World Bank, *Economic Perspectives on Southeast Asia and Asia,* April 19, 1978, p. 74.

41. World Bank, *Philippines—Country Program Paper,* 1976, p. 11.

42. Ibid., pp. 21, 22.

43. As a foreign consultant paid through World Bank loan 1374–PH, Power spent eighteen months (1977–1979) working with the School of Economics research project. That project was headed by Romeo Bautista, who, in turn, went from the project to the World Bank, where he spent the thirteen months from July 1979 to August 1980 working on the question of exchange-rate flexibility and trade flows. From there, Bautista returned to the Philippines as a deputy director-general of NEDA (interviews with Romeo Bautista, Metro-Manila, Philippines, December 15, 1980, and with John Power, Honolulu, Hawaii, October 29, 1980; Romeo Bautista, John H. Power et al., *Industrial Promotion Policies in the Philippines* [Manila: Philippine Institute for Development Studies (at NEDA), 1979]; and World Bank, *Report and Recommendation,* August 21, 1980, pp. 17–18).

44. The World Bank and the Philippine government subsequently began to rotate the preparation of these economic memos for the Consultative Group (interview with NEDA official [anonymity requested], December 5, 1980).

45. Interview with Wilfredo Nuqui, Metro-Manila, Philippines, March 10, 1981. It seemed to be the Bank's job to prepare the special report on that topic.

46. *Nominal tariff rate* refers to the rate of protection on output, whereas *effective tariff rate* is the rate of protection on value added, taking into account tariffs on imported inputs. See W. M. Corden, "The Structure of a Tariff System and the Effective Protective Rate," *Journal of Political Economy* 74 (June 1966): 221–37. The effective rate of protection is the more meaningful measure, but the Bank at this point in its conceptualization of how best to embark the Philippines on export-oriented industrialization referred solely to the nominal rates. World Bank, *The Philippines: Country Economic Memorandum,* Report 1765–PH, October 26, 1977, p. 11 and annex A, pp. 11–13.

47. World Bank, "Consultative Group for the Philippines," *Bank News Release,* December 2, 1977. It was at this Consultative Group meeting that the government's 1978–1982 Five-Year Development Plan was formally presented (*New Philippines Daily Express* [Manila], December 7, 1977).

48. World Bank, *Philippines—Country Program Paper,* 1978, cited by World Bank, *Report and Recommendation of the President of the International Bank for Reconstruction and Development to the Executive Directors on a Proposed Loan to the Central Bank of the Philippines with the Guarantee of the Republic of the Philippines for an*

Industrial Finance Project, Report P–3028–PH, April 13, 1981, p. 17 (hereafter cited as World Bank, *Report and Recommendation,* April 13, 1981); and *Philippines—Country Program Paper,* 1980, p. 15.

49. World Bank, *Report and Recommendation,* April 13, 1981, p. 17. The sectoral content of the World Bank lending program is taken from *Philippines— Country Program Paper,* 1980, table on p. 20.

50. World Bank, *Philippines: Industrial Development Strategy and Policies,* World Bank Country Study, May 1980, p. vi (hereafter cited as World Bank, *Industrial Development Strategy,* May 1980).

51. The Bank has a well-documented history of covering up the fact that it, and not its client LDCs, typically initiated plans for projects to be funded by the Bank. This has been discussed extensively elsewhere. See Edward Mason and Robert Asher, *The World Bank Since Bretton Woods* (Washington, D.C.: Brookings Institution, 1973), p. 308; Susan George, *How the Other Half Dies: The Real Reasons for World Hunger* (Montclair, N.J.: Allanheld, Osmun, 1977), p. 226; Michael Scott, *Aid to Bangladesh: For Better or Worse?* (San Francisco: Institute for Food and Development Policy, 1979), p. 9; and Judith Tendler, *Inside Foreign Aid* (Baltimore: Johns Hopkins University Press, 1975), pp. 86–87, 93–95.

52. *Philippines Daily Express* (Manila), February 16, 1979.

53. *Business Day* (Manila), February 26, 1979; *Philippines Daily Express* (Manila), February 27, 1979.

54. World Bank, *Industrial Development Strategy,* May 1980. The three volumes, at this stage, were published together in one document.

55. World Bank, *Industrial Development Strategy and Policies in the Philippines,* Report 2513–PH, 3 vols., October 29, 1979: vol. 1: *Summary Report;* vol. 2: *Main Report;* vol. 3: *Statistical Appendix and Annexes.* There were at least two even earlier versions of this, one in May 1979, the other in July 1979.

56. World Bank, *Industrial Development Strategy,* May 1980, p. 22.

57. World Bank, *Report and Recommendation,* August 21, 1980, p. 32.

58. Quoted in *New York Times,* May 26, 1980. The mission relayed the hope of making the Philippine SAL the Bank's first such loan to top Philippine officials (interview with Noriega, January 30, 1981). The Philippines did not quite make it to number one, but its SAL was the first in Asia and followed on the heels of its three forerunners, in Turkey, Kenya, and Bolivia. All four loans were approved within six months.

59. *Business Day* (Manila), August 22, 1979.

60. Quoted from interview with Ortaliz, January 19, 1981.

61. From the start the Bank made it clear that this $200 million loan would be the first of many. Interviews with Ortaliz, January 19 and April 13, 1981; Noriega, January 30 and April 20, 1981; and NEDA official (anonymity requested), December 5, 1980.

62. World Bank, *Economic Perspectives on Southeast Asia and Asia,* April 19, 1978, p. 74.

63. World Bank, "World Bank Approves $200 Million Loan for Structural Adjustment in the Philippines," *Bank News Release,* 81/5, September 18, 1980; and World Bank, "Loan Agreement for Loan [No. 1903–PH]" (draft), July 14, 1980. The final version of the loan agreement for the SAL was the same as this draft (interview with Philippine government official [anonymity requested], Metro-Manila, Philippines, April 21, 1981).

64. Guillermo Soliven, special assistant to the governor, Central Bank of the Philippines, and Lawrence Hinkle, World Bank, to Jose Leviste, Jr., deputy minister of industry, Republic of the Philippines, cable, July 9, 1980.

65. Ibid. As is discussed below, government documents indicate that the SAL's first installment (of $100 million peso-equivalent) would help finance the cement industry's coal conversion program (in keeping with the Bank's industrial restructuring and modernization program); help finance the Cavite, Davao, and Legaspi EPZs; and help create a financing fund to assist exporters (Roberto Ongpin, "Re: Utilization of Peso Proceeds of SAL," memorandum from minister of industry to Cesar Virata, minister of finance, November 27, 1980; and Rafael Sison, "Re: $50 Million Peso Equivalent of SAL," memorandum from DBP chairman to Cesar Virata, minister of finance, October 13, 1980).

66. World Bank, "Aide-Mémoire," outcome of discussions between World Bank and Philippine government, Manila, Philippines, August 20–31, 1979 (mimeographed).

67. Ibid., unnumbered pp. 2–3. As the Bank noted in retrospect in *Report and Recommendation,* August 21, 1980, p. 32, a substantial part of the reason it was decided to push for a structural adjustment loan was that "the specific solutions to the major problems . . . were readily available, and the Bank was . . . then in a position to help formulate these."

68. World Bank, "Aide-Mémoire," cover memo, unnumbered p. i.

69. Ibid., unnumbered p. 10.

70. Interview with Noriega, January 30, 1981. Noriega's sentiments were corroborated by others.

71. Interview with NEDA official (anonymity requested), December 5, 1980.

72. World Bank, *Report and Recommendation,* August 21, 1980, p. 29.

73. Statement of Roberto Ongpin, cited in World Bank, *Meeting of the Consultative Group for the Philippines, Washington, D.C., December 13 & 14, 1979—Report of Proceedings by the Chairman plus Annexes,* PHL–80–1, March 20, 1980, annex 6, p. 1.

74. Statement of Michael Gould, Philippines programs division chief, World Bank, cited in *Meeting of Consultative Group, December 13 & 14, 1979,* annex 12, p. 18. See also World Bank, *Philippines: Domestic and External Resources for Devel-*

opment, p. 26. Also released at this time was the Bank's financial-sector report (No. 2546).

75. Interview with NEDA official (anonymity requested), December 5, 1980.

76. Interview with Noriega, January 30, 1981.

77. Interview with Nuqui, March 10, 1981.

78. See, e.g., John Power and Gerardo Sicat, *The Philippines: Industrialization and Trade Policies* (London: Oxford University Press, for Development Centre of the OECD, 1971); and Gerardo Sicat, *Economic Policy and Philippine Development* ([Metro-Manila]: University of the Philippines Press, 1972).

79. World Bank, *Philippines—Country Program Paper,* 1980, p. 7. It was opportune to have a new industry minister at just this point. "Ongpin could be a strong factor in pushing the changes along because criticism of the industrial structure was not criticism of the Ministry of Industry under *him*" (interview with Power, October 29, 1980).

80. Quoted from Ascher Memorandum, p. 6.

81. Interview with Ortaliz, January 19, 1981.

82. Interview with NEDA official (anonymity requested), December 5, 1980.

83. Interview with Noriega, January 30, 1981.

84. Interview with Corpus, February 11, 1981. Corpus added that he did the same with other aid institutions, both bilateral and multilateral, but that the "World Bank has been the most influential."

85. Interview with Bince, December 2, 1980.

86. Gerardo Sicat, "Economic Development Programs and Tariff Policies," speech presented at Policy Conference on Tariff Reforms, Metro-Manila, Philippines, April 22, 1981.

87. World Bank, *Philippines—Country Program Paper,* 1976, p. 2.

88. B. de Vries, *Transition Toward Industrial Development,* p. 3.

89. World Bank, *Philippines—Country Program Paper,* 1980, p. 15.

90. Ascher Memorandum, p. 6.

91. Interview with Ortaliz, January 19, 1981.

92. Interview with deputy minister of industry (anonymity requested), Metro-Manila, Philippines, November 17, 1980. The word is derived from the Spanish *compadre.*

93. World Bank, *Philippines—Country Program Paper,* 1980, p. 21.

94. William D. Clark, World Bank vice-president for external affairs, quoted in *Asian Wall Street Journal,* June 6, 1978.

95. Interview with Ortaliz, January 19, 1981. For list of the committee's membership, see World Bank, *Industrial Development Strategy,* May 1980, pp. 100–102.

96. World Bank, *Report and Recommendation,* August 21, 1980, p. 32. The IMF mission that was simultaneously in-country for its annual November review

likewise lent a hand. See Chapter 5 for more on the IMF role in SAL reforms.

97. World Bank, *Report and Recommendation,* August 21, 1980, p. 33; interview with Ortaliz, January 19, 1981. The amount—$50,000—showed up in the loan agreement as a "project preparation advance" (World Bank, "Loan Agreement for Loan [No. 1903–PH]").

The Bank's veto over contractors and consultants is covered by a standard clause in most loan agreements. What happens when an LDC government tries to elude Bank approval of consultants was shown in the case of the Bank's withdrawal of a $250 million loan for an Indian fertilizer-plant complex in January 1981. The loan was terminated after the Indian government switched consultants, from the American firm with which it had originally contracted, to an Italian firm. For more on this, see Mohan Ram and Richard Nations, "Questions About a Lapsed Loan," *Far Eastern Economic Review* (January 16, 1981): 46–48; and Jane Merriman, "India Strays from World Bank," *South* (February 1981): 73–79.

98. See, for instance, World Bank, *Report on Government-IBRD Project Implementation Review,* 1980, p. 4; and statement of Michael Gould cited in World Bank, *Meeting of Consultative Group, December 13 & 14, 1979,* annex 12, p. 18.

99. Interview with Nuqui, March 10, 1981.

100. Interviews with Nuqui, March 10, 1981; Noriega, April 20, 1981; and Michael Bamberger, Metro-Manila, Philippines, March 19, 1981.

101. Interview with NEDA official (anonymity requested), December 5, 1980.

102. Interview with Ortaliz, January 19, 1981.

103. Interview with Noriega, January 30, 1981.

104. Interview with Noriega, April 20, 1981.

105. Interview with Ortaliz, January 19, 1981. This was echoed by Noriega in an interview on April 20, 1981. The Bank wanted indirect tax realignment included as a condition for the first SAL; it maintained that the move went along with tariff revisions. Philippine technocrats did not disagree, but felt that it was too much to include at that time (interviews with Ortaliz, April 13, 1981; and Noriega, January 30, 1981).

106. Interview with Ortaliz, January 19, 1981.

107. Interview with Noriega, April 20, 1981.

108. Interview with Ministry of Finance staff member (anonymity requested), December 17, 1981.

109. Fund preconditions, covering such policies as exchange rates and food prices (as opposed to performance clauses) are almost "never put in documents as they are all to be done beforehand" (interview with Leung, January 15, 1981; cf. Teresa Hayter, *Aid as Imperialism* [Harmondsworth: Penguin, 1971], pp. 57–58).

110. Interview with Bince, December 2, 1980. Areñas's response was strikingly similar: "We don't have that in writing" (interview with Areñas, January 15, 1981).

111. Interview with Ortaliz, January 19, 1981; *Far Eastern Economic Review* (August 8, 1980): 46; *Business Day* (Manila), July 22, 1980.

112. At board meetings of the Bank, as at those of the Fund, there is relatively little formal voting and even fewer surprises: it is quite unusual for loan proposals to make it that far and then be vetoed. On this, see Escott Reid, *Strengthening the World Bank* (Chicago: Adlai Stevenson Institute, 1973), p. 195; and Margaret de Vries, "The Process of Policymaking," in *The International Monetary Fund, 1945– 1965: Twenty Years of International Monetary Cooperation*, ed. J. Keith Horsefield, 3 vols. (Washington, D.C.: IMF, 1969), vol. 2, p. 9.

113. Soliven and Hinkle to Leviste, cable, July 9, 1980.

114. The aim was to establish a tariff system with nominal rates between 10 and 50 percent, which meant that "most effective rates of protection will be brought within a range of 10–80 percent" (World Bank, *Report and Recommendation*, August 21, 1980, p. 22).

115. Virata to McNamara, August 12, 1980, p. 3. The ten were cement, iron and steel, automotive, wood and wood products, motorcycles and bicycles, glass and ceramics, furniture, domestic appliances, machinery and other capital equipment, and electrical and electronic goods.

116. Interview with Noriega, January 30, 1981; Razon T. Haresco, speech presented at Policy Conference on Tariff Reforms, Metro-Manila, Philippines, April 22, 1981.

117. World Bank, *Report and Recommendation*, August 21, 1980, p. 22. On Philippine effective rates of protection in the 1950s and 1960s, see Robert E. Baldwin, *Foreign Trade Regimes and Economic Development: The Philippines* (New York: Columbia University Press, for National Bureau of Economic Research, 1975).

118. *Business Day* (Manila), October 6, 1980; IMF, *Philippines: Recent Economic Developments*, July 18, 1980, p. 46.

119. World Bank, *Report and Recommendation*, August 21, 1980, pp. 21, 29.

120. Strengthening the linkages meant that domestically oriented industries would produce more for export.

121. World Bank, *Report and Recommendation*, August 21, 1980, pp. 22, 23, 29.

122. Interview with Nuqui, December 8, 1980. Reiterated in interview with Power, October 29, 1980.

123. Vice-President and Secretary, World Bank, *Summaries of Discussions at the Meeting of the Executive Directors of the Bank and IDA, September 16, 1980*, SD80–52, November 20, 1980, p. 9.

Chapter 5

1. World Bank, "World Bank Approves $200 Million Loan for Structural Adjustment in the Philippines," *Bank News Release*, 81/5 (September 18, 1980).

2. Interviews with, for instance, a NEDA official (anonymity requested), December 5, 1980; Noriega, January 30, 1981; and Ortaliz, March 31, 1981.

3. See Philippines (Republic), *Executive Order 609: Modifying the Rates of Import Duty on Certain Imported Articles as Provided Under Presidential Decree No. 1464, Otherwise Known as the Tariff and Customs Code of 1978, as Amended,* August 1, 1980; and Philippines (Republic), *Executive Order 632A: Modifying the Rates of Import Duty on Certain Imported Articles as Provided Under Presidential Decree No. 1464, Otherwise Known as the Tariff and Customs Code of 1978, as Amended,* November 28, 1980.

4. The rehabilitation and modernization of the textile sector under a Bank project loan was to be the first of these. See Chapter 6.

5. *Executive Order 609; Executive Order 632A;* and "Special Report: Tariff Reforms," *Business Day* (Manila), April 22, 1981. The average effective rate of protection for consumer goods fell from 77 percent to 41 percent (World Bank, *Report and Recommendation,* August 21, 1980, pp. 22–23).

6. For more on this subject of intra-industry trade, see Paul Krugman, "Economies of Scale, Imperfect Competition and Trade: An Exposition," July 1981 (mimeographed); and Bela Balassa, *Intra-Industry Trade and the Integration of Developing Countries in the World Economy,* World Bank Staff Working Paper 312, January 1979, pp. 24–32.

7. Ascher Memorandum, p. 2. Official Bank statements, attempting to counteract the damaging effects of the leaking of the Ascher Memorandum, argued that William Ascher was simply a Johns Hopkins University political risk analyst and that the memo thus represented onetime Bank consultant Ascher's outside views and work. But this was a cover-up. Ascher's name appeared in the April 1981 World Bank phone book as a member of the Central Projects Staff's Projects Advisory Staff (with a Bank office and phone extension); moreover, he was aided in his work by members of the Bank's East Asia Division.

8. World Bank, "Background Notes for Press," December 7, 1981, reprinted in *IMF Survey* (December 14, 1981): 395–96.

9. See U.S. Treasury Department, *Assessment of U.S. Participation in the Multilateral Development Banks in the 1980s—Consultation Draft,* September 21, 1981, annex 5, pp. 44–45.

10. *Central Bank* (of the Philippines) *Review* (August 1981): 7.

11. Guillermo Soliven, special assistant to the governor, Central Bank of the Philippines, and Lawrence Hinkle, World Bank, to Jose Leviste, Jr., deputy minister of industry, Republic of the Philippines, cable, July 9, 1980. The other $5 million of the total $200 million loan is a technical-assistant component, primarily funding World Bank–approved foreign consultants.

12. Interview with Ortaliz, January 19, 1981.

13. Ibid.

14. Interview with Ortaliz, March 31, 1981.

15. Interview with Noriega, January 30, 1981.

16. Chulia Azarcon, Tariff Commission commissioner, statement during open forum of Policy Conference on Tariff Reforms, Metro-Manila, Philippines, April 23, 1981; *Executive Order 609; Executive Order 632A.*

17. Returned to Marcos's fold (in public statements, at least), the influential Philippine Chamber of Food Manufacturers "hailed" the government's "speedy action on the request" for a more gradual reduction of tariff duties on sausages, preserved meat, chocolate, macaroni and spaghetti, roasted cereals and cereal products, and tapioca and sago (*Bulletin Today* [Manila], February 3, 1981; *Executive Order 609; Executive Order 632A*).

18. Soliven and Hinkle to Leviste, cable, July 9, 1980. These caveats are repeated in World Bank, *Report and Recommendation,* August 21, 1980, pp. ii, 33, and annex 3, p. 63, under the heading "Special Bank Implementation Actions."

19. Interviews with Noriega, January 30, 1981, and April 20, 1981.

20. Interview with Noriega, April 20, 1981. Cf. Pierre M. Landell-Mills, "Structural Adjustment Lending: Early Experience," *Finance and Development* 18 (December 1981): 17–21.

21. The so-called paper lifting of martial law left Marcos's powers intact. The election, boycotted by all major opposition parties, likewise brought only cosmetic changes. See Civil Liberties Union of the Philippines, *Tuloy Ang Ligaya* (*On with the Circus*), New Year's Statement of the Civil Liberties Union of the Philippines (Quezon City: Civil Liberties Union of the Philippines, January 1, 1981); and Civil Liberties Union of the Philippines, *The Plebiscite and the Foreign Connection* (Quezon City: Civil Liberties Union of the Philippines, March 26, 1981). Excellent in this regard are the *Far Eastern Economic Review* articles by Sheila Ocampo over the relevant period; see, for instance, "Landslide Win for Marcos," *Far Eastern Economic Review* (June 19, 1981): 13.

22. Interview with Ortaliz, March 31, 1981. Diokno, Ortaliz added, was "taking advantage of the situation."

23. "Marcos' circle" refers to the so-called cronies within the transnationalist business faction, who, as the Ascher Memorandum explained elsewhere (p. 8), have "particularly good connections with the Marcos administration [and] are consolidating their advantages." On the cronies, see Chapter 8. Note that the Bank acknowledged the existence of Peter Evans's "triple alliance" in the Philippines.

24. Ascher Memorandum, pp. 8–9; see also p. 1.

25. Interview with Ortaliz, April 13, 1981.

26. World Bank, *Report and Recommendation,* April 13, 1981, p. 47 (under the heading "Projects in Execution").

27. The Tariff Commission assumed administrative responsibility for changes in tariff rates. Its recommendations went to a transnationalist-dominated minis-

terial-level Board on Tariff Policy. The board's decisions then went to President Marcos for approval.

28. Azarcon at Policy Conference on Tariff Reforms, April 23, 1981.

29. Ramon J. Farolan, Customs commissioner, "Bureau of Customs: Programs for the Eighties," speech presented at Policy Conference on Tariff Reforms, April 23, 1981.

30. Norma A. Tan, "Tariff Reforms and the Structure of Protection," speech presented at Policy Conference on Tariff Reforms, April 23, 1981. Tan, then a consultant to the Tariff Commission, wrote the chapter entitled "The Structure of Protection and Resource Flows in the Philippines" in Romeo Bautista, John H. Power et al., *Industrial Promotion Policies in the Philippines* (Manila: Philippine Institute for Development Studies [at NEDA], 1979), pp. 129–71, which was an edited version of her Ph.D. dissertation (University of the Philippines, School of Economics, April 1979).

31. Sicat at Policy Conference on Tariff Reforms, April 22, 1981.

32. Edgardo Tordesillias, deputy minister of industry, "Industrial Development Programs and Tariff Structure," speech presented for Roberto Ongpin, Policy Conference on Tariff Reforms, April 22, 1981 (emphasis added).

33. The author was an invited guest of *Business Day* at the conference. These impressions came from conversations with audience members as well as from overheard conversations in which the author was not directly involved.

34. The full second tranche was made available to the Philippine government by the end of 1981 but was not budgeted for disbursement as part of the Philippine budget until 1982 (IMF, *Philippines—Staff Report for 1982 Article IV Consultations*, SM/82/55, March 24, 1982, p. 2, n. 1, and p. 6).

35. Conversation with Ortaliz at Policy Conference on Tariff Reforms, April 23, 1981. Having "the hearings and meetings made it easier to sell phase IV to the President" (interview with Noriega, April 20, 1981).

36. *Business Day* (Manila), October 6, 1980; Cesar Virata, minister of finance to Robert McNamara, president of the World Bank, letter, "Re: Philippine Industrial Development Policy," August 12, 1980, attachment 1, p. 10.

37. World Bank, *Report and Recommendation*, August 21, 1980, pp. 22, 24.

38. World Bank, *Industrial Development Strategy and Policies in the Philippines*, Report 2513–PH, October 29, 1979, vol. 1: *Summary Report*, p. 7.

39. *Bulletin Today* (Manila), October 23, 1980.

40. Quoted in Julie A. Amargo, "Licaros, Ver and Imelda," *Philippine Signs* (February 18–24, 1984): 8.

41. Interview with Licaros, April 1, 1981.

42. Interview with former Central Bank deputy governor (anonymity requested), February 9, 1981.

43. Interview with Noriega, April 20, 1981, repeating statements originally

made on January 30, 1981. Reiterated by Ortaliz (April 13, 1981), and by Licaros himself (April 1, 1981).

44. Interviews with Ortaliz, January 19, 1981; and Noriega, April 20, 1981.

45. Interview with Noriega, April 20, 1981.

46. Ibid.

47. Interview with Ortaliz, January 19, 1981.

48. World Bank, *Report and Recommendation*, August 21, 1980, p. 24.

49. She received the title of special assistant to the governor (interviews with Noriega, April 20, 1981; Licaros, April 1, 1981).

50. *Times Journal,* January 8, 1981.

Thus, in mid-1981, Ongpin became minister of trade and industry. Although people in the Central Bank's Department of Economic Research interviewed by the author were firm in their insistence that no such transfer of power would occur (especially Areñas, April 15, 1981), Central Bank's Robert Garcia, assistant to the governor, admitted publicly during the open forum of the Policy Conference on Tariff Reforms, April 23, 1981, that "the move of import licensing from out of the Central Bank has taken effect. It was found by the IMF and GATT that such import licensing [duties] had to be transferred."

51. This was the so-called Dewey Dee caper of early January 1981. On this, see Chapter 6, below; and Robin Broad and Walden Bello, "Structural and Other Adjustments," in Walden Bello et al., *Development Debacle: The World Bank in the Philippines* (San Francisco: Institute for Food and Development Policy, 1982), p. 180.

52. Interview with Ortaliz, April 13, 1981. Laya subsequently became enmeshed in a scandal of his own when the IMF discovered in late 1983 that the Central Bank had been overstating its foreign exchange reserves by $600 million. For this mistake in counting, Laya was "promoted" to the post of minister of education.

53. In looking at the experience of twenty-four devaluations in nineteen countries during the year following each devaluation, economist Richard Cooper has noted that "devaluation seems to increase substantially the possibility that the finance minister of the devaluing country will lose his job" (Richard N. Cooper, "Currency Devaluation in Developing Countries," in *Government and Economic Development,* ed. Gustav Ranis [New Haven, Conn.: Yale University Press, 1971], pp. 472–513).

54. Statement of Daniel A. O'Donohue, acting deputy assistant secretary, Bureau of East Asian and Pacific Affairs, Department of State, in U.S. Congress, House, Committee on Foreign Affairs, *U.S. Policy Towards the Philippines, Joint Hearings Before the Subcommittee on Asia and Pacific Affairs and the Subcommittee on Human Rights and International Organizations,* 97th Cong., 1st sess., November 18, 1981, p. 78.

55. Interview with Licaros, April 1, 1981. The purchasing-power parity theory or doctrine was developed by Sweden's Gustav Cassel around 1917 to predict the equilibrium level of a flexible exchange rate. In general terms, the theory states that the exchange rate between one currency and another is in equilibrium when, at that rate of exchange, their domestic purchasing powers are equivalent. See Bela Balassa, "The Purchasing-Power Parity Doctrine: A Reappraisal," *Journal of Political Economy* 72 (December 1964): 584–96.

56. Interview with Bince, December 2, 1980. Even Virata was quoted in the Philippine press as decrying the IMF's "questionable application of dubious economic theories such as the purchasing-power parity theory" (*Bulletin Today* [Manila], November 16, 1980).

57. Interview with Legarda, February 2, 1981. The Exchange and Trade Relations Department is the former Exchange Restrictions Department (Margaret G. de Vries, *The International Monetary Fund, 1966–1971: The System Under Stress*, 2 vols. (Washington, D.C.: IMF, 1976), vol. 1, p. 636.

58. See, e.g., IMF, *Staff Report for the 1980 Article IV Consultation and Review of Standby Arrangement*, EBS/80/159, July 16, 1980, pp. 12–14.

59. Interview with Legarda, February 2, 1981. The term has carried over from the Fund's original articles to the second amendment. The U.S. Treasury representative to the Bretton Woods Conference, Harry Dexter White, noted in 1946 that "in the drafting of the Articles of Agreement, no attempt was made to define fundamental disequilibrium." And, as Joseph Gold commented decades later, Fund officials "have not yet ventured a formal definition of it" (Joseph Gold, "The Techniques of Response," in *The International Monetary Fund, 1945–1965: Twenty Years of International Monetary Cooperation*, ed. J. Keith Horsefield, 3 vols. [Washington, D.C.: IMF, 1969], vol. 2, p. 581).

60. Interview with Legarda, February 2, 1981.

61. Ibid.

62. Ibid.; and interview with Leung, January 15, 1981.

63. Interviews with IMF official (anonymity requested), November 25, 1980; and Leung, January 15, 1981. World Bank, *Report and Recommendation*, August 21, 1980, p. 25.

64. Interview with Licaros, April 1, 1981.

65. Interview with Bince, December 2, 1980.

66. This assessment was reiterated in Business International, *Briefing Paper*, pp. 36–37.

67. Interview with Ministry of Finance staff member (anonymity requested), December 17, 1980. View repeated by Areñas, January 15, 1981, and in Business International, *Briefing Paper*, pp. 36–37. Percentages calculated from statistics supplied by Department of Economic Research, Central Bank of the Philippines, January 1981.

68. World Bank, *The Philippines: Poverty, Basic Needs, and Employment: A Review and Assessment,* draft of Report 2984–PH, n.d., pp. 124–27. The pagination refers to the 154-page, single-spaced edition of the report, not the 392-page edition. See also World Bank, *Philippines—Country Program Paper,* August 29, 1980, p. 4.

69. World Bank, *Report and Recommendation,* August 21, 1980, p. 23. See also p. 25 of that report. Cf. John Maynard Keynes, *The Collected Writings of John Maynard Keynes,* ed. Donald Moggridge, vol. 26: *Activities 1941–1946, Shaping the Post-War World: Bretton Woods and Reparations* (Cambridge, England: Macmillan, 1979), chapter 2, "Commercial Policy, December 1941–December 1945."

70. Interview with Noriega, April 20, 1981.

71. Interview with Ortaliz, April 13, 1981.

72. World Bank, *Industrial Development Strategy,* May 1980, p. ix.

73. See, e.g., *Bulletin Today* (Manila), June 6, 1980.

74. Interview with Legarda, February 2, 1981. Cf. Business International, *Briefing Paper,* p. 39.

75. Virata to McNamara, August 12, 1980, p. 4.

76. The U.S. dollar is the intervention currency.

77. A similar vow had initially been taken by Virata and Licaros in a December 1979 letter to the IMF; Cesar Virata and Gregorio Licaros to Jacques de Larosière, letter requesting a new standby arrangement from the Fund, December 14, 1979. However, the Bank acknowledged that six months later the Fund was "disappointed by the government's failure to vigorously use exchange rate policies . . . to achieve program objectives" (World Bank, *Philippines—Country Program Paper,* 1980, p. 13).

78. IMF, *Staff Report,* July 16, 1980, p. 19.

79. *IMF Survey* (October 26, 1981): 337.

80. IMF, *Philippines—Staff Report for 1982 Article IV Consultation,* March 24, 1982, p. 13. Better reflecting the peso's international purchasing power, the nominal effective exchange rate represents a trade-weighted basket of currencies. Major currencies are the U.S. dollar, the yen, the Deutsche mark, pounds sterling, and the Swiss franc. The nominal effective exchange rate divided by price differences yields the peso's real effective exchange rate.

81. Ibid.

82. In mid-1981, the Ministry of Trade also became part of the Ministry of Industry under Ongpin.

83. See, among others, World Bank, *Industrial Development Strategy,* October 29, 1979, vol. 1, pp. 3–9; and World Bank, *Report and Recommendation,* August 21, 1980, pp. 16–17, 19.

84. *Asian Business* (May 1981): 57; *Business Day* (Manila), March 17, 1981.

85. Roberto Ongpin, "Re: Utilization of Peso Proceeds of SAL," memoran-

dum from minister of industry to Cesar Virata, minister of finance, November 27, 1980.

86. World Bank, *Industrial Development Strategy,* October 29, 1979, vol. 1, p. 9.

87. Interview with Victor Ordoñez, Metro-Manila, Philippines, December 9, 1980.

88. World Bank, *The Philippines: Country Economic Memorandum,* Report 1765–PH, October 26, 1977, annex A, p. 2; and World Bank, *Industrial Development Strategy,* October 29, 1979, vol. 1, pp. 8–9.

89. *Ibon Facts and Figures,* no. 29 (October 31, 1979): 1; and *Asiaweek* (June 6, 1981).

90. IMF, *Philippines: Recent Economic Developments,* July 18, 1980, p. 34; and World Bank, *Staff Appraisal Report on the Industrial Finance Project,* Report 3331–PH, April 7, 1981, p. 7.

91. Interview with Merlin M. Magallona, Metro-Manila, Philippines, December 16, 1980.

92. IMF, *Philippines: Request for Standby Arrangement with Supplementary Financing,* EBS/80/25, February 5, 1980, p. 7; statement of Roberto Ongpin in World Bank, *Meeting of the Consultative Group for the Philippines, Washington, D.C., December 13 & 14, 1979—Report of Proceedings by the Chairman plus Annexes,* PHL–80–1, March 20, 1980, annex 6, p. 3.

93. Philippines (Republic), Board of Investments, *Rules and Regulations to Implement Presidential Decree No. 1789, Otherwise Known as the Omnibus Investments Code,* reprinted in *Business Day* (Manila), April 1, 1981.

94. *Business Day* (Manila), February 25, 1981.

95. Business International, *Briefing Paper,* pp. 26, 28; *Business Day* (Manila), February 26, 1981.

96. *Business Day* (Manila), February 25 and 26, 1981; *Far Eastern Economic Review* (February 27, 1981): 6.

97. *Asiaweek* (June 6, 1980): 24; interview with Ordoñez, December 9, 1980. Villafuerte was minister of trade until mid-1981, when the Ministry of Trade and the Ministry of Industry were merged and Villafuerte became presidential representative for trade negotiations (a post with cabinet rank).

98. World Bank, *The Philippines: Country Economic Memorandum,* Report 1765–PH, October 26, 1977, annex A, p. 12. See also World Bank, *Philippines: A Development Strategy and Investment Priorities for the Central Visayas (Region VII),* vol. 1: *The Main Report,* Report 2264–PH, January 4, 1979, p. 49.

99. World Bank, *Report and Recommendation,* August 21, 1980, p. 21. This was through Presidential Decree 1646 of October 1979 providing greater incentives for traders involved in nontraditional exports (*Far Eastern Economic Review* [August 1, 1980]: 97).

100. Statement of Roberto Ongpin, in World Bank, *Meeting of Consultative Group, December 13 & 14, 1979*, annex 6, p. 4.

101. *Far Eastern Economic Review* (August 1, 1980): 99.

102. *Asiaweek* (June 6, 1980): 28.

103. *Bulletin Today* (Manila), May 18, 1981. For more on the Philippine trading houses, see Ngo Huy Liem, *Promotion of General Trading Companies in an Export Oriented Economy: The Philippine Experience* (Freiburg, Federal Republic of Germany: Institute for Development Policy, University of Freiburg, 1982).

104. Interview with Ortaliz, April 13, 1981.

105. *Asian Wall Street Journal*, February 14, 1980; *Far Eastern Economic Review* (February 15, 1980): 49.

106. Virata to McNamara, August 12, 1980, attachment 1, p. 5. See also statement of Roberto Ongpin, in World Bank, *Meeting of Consultative Group, December 13 & 14, 1979*, annex 6, p. 4.

107. Barend de Vries, *Transition Toward More Rapid and Labor-Intensive Industrial Development: The Case of the Philippines*, World Bank Staff Working Paper 424, October 1980, p. 3.

108. Interviews with Soliven, November 17, 1980; Magallona, December 16, 1980.

109. Interview with Ortaliz, January 19, 1981. Sentiments corroborated by others.

110. Conversation with Philippine government official on interagency committee for SAL reforms (anonymity requested), April 22, 1981.

111. Interview with NEDA official (anonymity requested), December 5, 1980.

112. Ibid. View corroborated by others.

113. IMF, "The Chairman's Summing Up at the Conclusion of the Discussion on Fund Collaboration with the Bank in Assisting Member Countries, Executive Board Meeting, May 28, 1980," 80/114, June 2, 1980, p. 1.

114. Interview with IMF official (anonymity requested), November 25, 1980.

115. See, for example, World Bank, *Report and Recommendation*, August 21, 1980, p. 25; World Bank, *Country Economic Memorandum*, October 26, 1977, p. iii; World Bank, *Philippines—Country Program Paper*, 1980, attachment 4, p. 1.

116. Quoted from IMF, "Fund Collaboration with Bank in Assisting Member Countries," memorandum from the managing director to department, bureau, and office heads, June 9, 1980, p. 1.

117. This paragraph is based on an interview with an IMF official (anonymity requested), November 25, 1980, and was corroborated in an interview with one of his colleagues (anonymity requested), Washington, D.C., September 28, 1982.

118. World Bank and IMF, *The Philippines: Aspects of the Financial Sector*, World Bank Country Study, May 1980.

119. Vice-President and Secretary, World Bank, *Summaries of Discussions at the Meeting of the Executive Directors, September 16, 1980,* SD80–52, November 20, 1980, p. 7; and IMF, "Chairman's Summing Up," p. 1. See also p. 2 of the latter document.

120. IMF, "Statement by the Managing Director on Fund Collaboration with the Bank in Assisting Member Countries, Executive Board Meeting, May 28, 1980," 80/103, May 15, 1980, p. 1.

121. One such example was India, a country in which the World Bank exerted some of its strongest attempts at policy-making influence during the 1950s and 1960s. But in 1981, it was the IMF that took over that role with an EFF. On this, see Robin Broad, "Sous le Pouce du F.M.I.," *Afrique-Asie* (February 1, 1982): 45–46.

122. IMF, "Statement by Managing Director," p. 3; and World Bank, "Structural Adjustment Lending—Collaboration with IMF," memorandum from Ernest Stern, June 9, 1980, p. 1.

123. Interview with IMF official (anonymity requested), November 25, 1980.

124. IMF, *Staff Report,* July 16, 1980, p. 5.

125. On EDI and the IMF Institute, see Chapter 2, above. See also "The Fund's Technical Assistance," *Finance and Development* 19 (December 1982): 10–15; and "The World Bank's Technical Assistance," *Finance and Development* 19 (December 1982): 16–21.

126. Interview with Soliven, November 17, 1980.

127. Ascher Memorandum, p. 7.

Chapter 6

1. Pierre M. Landell-Mills, "Structural Adjustment Lending: Early Experience," *Finance and Development* 18 (December 1981): 21.

2. Barend de Vries, "Public Policy and the Private Sector," in World Bank, *Economic Development and the Private Sector,* September 1981, p. 5.

3. Ascher Memorandum, p. 1.

4. World Bank, "Aide-Mémoire," outcome of discussions between World Bank and Philippine government, Manila, Philippines, August 20–31, 1979, unnumbered p. 1.

5. Bela Balassa, *Structural Adjustment Policies in Developing Economies,* World Bank Staff Working Paper 464, July 1981, pp. 1–2.

6. World Bank, *Focus on Poverty,* 1983, quoted in Robert E. Wood, "The Aid Regime and International Debt: Crisis and Structural Adjustment," *Development and Change* 16 (April 1985): 207.

7. Remarks delivered by Jaime V. Ongpin, minister of finance of the Philip-

pines, Carnegie Endowment for International Peace, Washington, D.C., April 7, 1986.

8. Interview with political prisoner (anonymity requested), National Penitentiary, Muntinglupa, Philippines, March 29, 1981.

9. *Pilipino Muna: Bulletin of the National Economic Protectionism Association* (Manila), no. 17 (May 1986): 3.

10. Yoshihara Kunio, *Philippine Industrialization: Foreign and Domestic Capital* (Quezon City: Ateneo de Manila University Press, 1985), p. 108.

11. *Ibon Facts and Figures,* no. 140 (June 15, 1984): 7.

12. Ibid. After a 1984 interview with Concepcion, *Ibon* wrote: "Foreign brands sell better, says Jose Concepcion, noting that Swift meats is the number one selling brand in meat products."

13. Ascher Memorandum, cover memo.

14. Ibid., pp. 8, 2.

15. Peter Evans, *Dependent Development: The Alliance of Multinational, State, and Local Capital in Brazil* (Princeton, N.J.: Princeton University Press, 1979), p. 283.

16. Ascher Memorandum, p. 14 (emphasis added).

17. For a complete listing of the eleven, see Philippines (Republic), National Economic and Development Authority, *Five-Year Philippine Development Plan, 1978–1982—Draft Revisions for 1981 and 1982* (Manila: NEDA, 1980), annex 4.1.

18. *Far Eastern Economic Review* (October 31, 1980): 62.

19. Interview with Lichauco, January 13, 1981.

20. See Alejandro Lichauco, "The Lichauco Paper: Imperialism in the Philippines," *Monthly Review* 25 (July–August 1973). Lichauco became a political figure of sorts in the pre–martial law Philippines. He was elected representative from the first district of Rizal to the Constitutional Convention in progress when martial law was declared. He was imprisoned at the start of martial law.

21. Alejandro Lichauco, "The Philippine Economic Situation: Growth and Nondevelopment," in *The Ligouri Lectures,* by Jose Diokno, Alejandro Lichauco, and Francisco Claver, S.J., papers prepared for the Ligouri Lectures, Cebu City, July 30–August 1, 1979 (Cebu: Redemptorist Press, 1979), pp. 21–23.

22. "Interview: Industry Minister Ongpin on the 11 Major Industrial Projects," *Business Day* (Manila), January 19, 1981.

23. World Bank, *Philippines—Country Program Paper,* August 29, 1980, p. 7. "The World Bank and IMF are not happy" with the major industrial projects (interview with Ortaliz, January 19, 1981).

24. Barend de Vries, *Transition Toward More Rapid and Labor-Intensive Industrial Development: The Case of the Philippines,* World Bank Staff Working Paper 424, October 1980, p. 2.

25. World Bank, *Philippines—Country Program Paper,* 1980, p. 7.

26. Statement of Roberto Ongpin, in World Bank, *Meeting of the Consultative Group for the Philippines, Washington, D.C., December 13 & 14, 1979—Report of Proceedings by the Chairman plus Annexes*, PHL–80–1, March 20, 1980, annex 6, pp. 2–3.

27. Interview with Lichauco, January 13, 1981.

28. Interview with NEDA official (anonymity requested), December 5, 1980.

29. See, for instance, World Bank, *Philippines: Domestic and External Resources for Development*, economic memorandum for 1979 Consultative Group Meeting, Report 2674–PH, November 12, 1979, p. 34; World Bank, *Industrial Development Strategy*, May 1980, p. 16; and "Setbacks for Ambition," *Far Eastern Economic Review* (December 12, 1980): 55.

30. Interview with Ortaliz, January 19, 1981. The pledge was more formally made by the Philippine government in NEDA's *Economic Report on the Philippines, 1978–80* (Manila: NEDA, December 1980), which was prepared for the January 1981 Consultative Group meeting; see esp. pp. 2–7. The pledge is also mentioned in World Bank, *Philippines—Country Program Paper*, 1980, p. 7, and was stressed by an IMF official (anonymity requested) in a November 25, 1980, interview.

31. See, e.g., Cesar Virata, minister of finance, to Robert McNamara, president of the World Bank, letter, "Re: Philippine Industrial Development Policy," August 12, 1980, attachment 1, p. 12; and *Business Week* (February 28, 1981): 60.

32. Cesar Virata's remarks to the seventh annual Philippine Business Conference, Manila, Philippines, November 3, 1981, quoted in "Realism Replaces Ambition," *Far Eastern Economic Review* (November 20, 1981): 54. See also Ongpin's letter to *Far Eastern Economic Review* (December 11, 1981): 4; and *Business Day* (Manila), January 19, 1981. Cf. *Business International* (February 19, 1982): 64.

33. Ferdinand Marcos's address to the seventh annual Philippine Business Conference, Manila, Philippines, November 5, 1981, quoted in *Far Eastern Economic Review* (November 20, 1981): 54.

34. Ferdinand Marcos's speech to the University of the Philippines Law School, quoted in *Asian Wall Street Journal*, October 2, 1979. Cf. "FM Won't Relent on '11 Giants,'" *Business Day* (Manila), December 16, 1980; "Govt Won't Deter Sked [*sic*] Industrial Projects," *Bulletin Today* (Manila), November 12, 1980; and *Bulletin Today* (Manila), December 11 and 12, 1980.

35. Quoted in *Business Day* (Manila), May 7, 1982.

36. Interview with Ministry of Finance staff member (anonymity requested), May 19, 1981. By 1986, only the copper smelter, the diesel engine factory, and the fertilizer plant were operating.

37. Tordesillias at Policy Conference on Tariff Reforms, April 22, 1981. See also World Bank, *Report and Recommendation*, August 21, 1980, p. 27; and World Bank, *Philippines—Country Program Paper*, 1980, p. 21.

38. See table describing key components of structural adjustment loans in

Landell-Mills, "Structural Adjustment Lending," p. 19. "Regular Bank project loans are often needed to complement structural adjustment lending" ("Background Notes for Press," *IMF Survey* [December 14, 1981]: 396).

39. Interview with Ortaliz, March 31, 1981.

40. Interview with Ortaliz, April 13, 1981.

41. Interview with Noriega, April 20, 1981.

42. Quoted in *Business Day* (Manila), April 16, 1980.

43. The loan was given final approval in April 1982 (World Bank, "World Bank to Support Philippines $600 Million Textile Restructuring Program," *Bank News Release*, 82/77 [April 22, 1982]).

44. The cost soared from the original estimate of $250 million. *Philippines Daily Express* (Manila), March 26, 1981, cited a figure of $500 million. By the time of the general procurement notice for the loan, the figure given was $600 million (*Development Forum Business Edition* [November 30, 1981]: 11).

45. Including corporate debts of about $75 million and personal debts of approximately $12.5 million (*Economist* [January 31, 1981]: 72). For more on Dewey Dee, see Chapter 7, below.

46. Conversation with Philippine government official (anonymity requested), Metro-Manila, Philippines, April 23, 1981. Cf. *Asian Wall Street Journal,* February 3, 1981.

47. World Bank, *Philippines: Staff Appraisal Report on Textile Sector Restructuring Project,* Report 3700–PH, March 26, 1982, p. 40; *Bulletin Today* (Manila), October 28, 1980, December 16, 1980, May 23, 1981; *Business Day* (Manila), May 20, 1981. For more on requirements, see *Textile Asia* (August 1981): 88.

48. Interview with executive from Philippine textile firm (anonymity requested), Metro-Manila, Philippines, May 21, 1981.

49. *Asian Wall Street Journal,* February 3, 1981.

50. *Business Day* (Manila), February 2, 1981.

51. *Textile Asia* (July 1981): 103.

52. *Bulletin Today* (Manila), May 23, 1981.

53. UNIDO, Global and Conceptual Studies Branch, Division for Industrial Studies, *Restructuring World Industry in a Period of Crisis—The Role of Innovation: An Analysis of Recent Developments in the Semiconductor Industry,* UNIDO/IS.285, December 17, 1981, pp. 211–12.

54. *Textile Asia* (July 1981): 103.

55. *Business Day* (Manila), February 3, 1981. By 1986, about 75 percent of Unisol's yarn and knitted fabric was exported directly; the rest was sold to garment exporters (data supplied by Central Bank of the Philippines, July 1986).

56. All information on Filsyn is from Leo Gonzaga, "Buying Up the Market," *Far Eastern Economic Review* (November 27, 1981): 51–52; Mamora Tsuda, *A Pre-*

liminary Study of Japanese-Filipino Joint Ventures (Quezon City: Foundation for Nationalist Studies, 1978), pp. 160–64; and John F. Doherty, *A Preliminary Study of Interlocking Directorates Among Financial, Commercial, Manufacturing and Service Enterprises in the Philippines* (Manila, 1979), pp. 84–86. See also *Textile Asia* (February 1982): 97. By the mid-1980s, Filsyn was the sole domestic producer of polyester fiber (*Manila Bulletin* [formerly *Bulletin Today*], March 13, 1986; *Malaya* [Manila], March 31, 1986).

57. Securities and Exchange Commissioner Roserio Lopez, quoted in Leo Gonzaga, "Buying Up the Market," p. 52.

58. Interview with Fabella, December 8, 1980.

59. For more on the business groups that dominated local affiliations with TNCs, see Mamora Tsuda, *A Preliminary Study of Japanese-Filipino Joint Ventures,* and Yoshihara Kunio, *Philippine Industrialization: Foreign and Domestic Capital.*

60. Quoted from World Bank, *Staff Appraisal Report on the Industrial Finance Project,* Report 3331–PH, April 7, 1981, p. 5.

61. *Business Day* (Manila), May 20, 1981; see also *Business Day,* April 14, 1980.

62. *Business Day* (Manila), March 9, 1986.

63. According to data provided by the Central Bank of the Philippines, July 1986.

64. Interviews with NEPA official (anonymity requested), Metro-Manila, Philippines, January 27, 1981; and Magallona, January 12, 20, and 27, 1981.

65. Interviews with Magallona, January 16, 1981; and Ortaliz, April 13, 1981.

66. World Bank, *Report and Recommendation,* August 21, 1980, p. 30.

67. Interviews with national entrepreneurs (anonymity requested), Metro-Manila, Philippines, January 29, April 23, and May 13, 1981.

68. Interview with Henares, February 27, 1981.

69. Ascher Memorandum, pp. 7, 9.

70. Interviews with Nuqui, March 10, 1981; and with officer of East Asia Division, World Bank (anonymity requested), December 15, 1980, cited in Walden Bello, David Kinley, and Elaine Elinson, "The Making of McNamara's Second Vietnam," in Walden Bello et al., *Development Debacle: The World Bank in the Philippines* (San Francisco: Institute for Food and Development Policy, 1982), p. 62.

71. Statement of Daniel A. O'Donohue, acting deputy assistant secretary, Bureau of East Asian and Pacific Affairs, Department of State, in U.S. Congress, House, Committee on Foreign Affairs, *U.S. Policy Toward the Philippines, Joint Hearings Before the Subcommittee on Asia and Pacific Affairs and the Subcommittee on Human Rights and International Organizations,* 97th Cong., 1st sess., November 18, 1981, p. 78.

72. Ascher Memorandum, p. 8.

73. Interview with Henares, February 27, 1981.

74. "Background Notes for Press," *IMF Survey* (December 14, 1981): 395.

75. B. de Vries, *Transition Toward Labor-Intensive Industrial Development*, p. 20.

76. IMF, *Philippines: Recent Economic Developments,* January 24, 1975, p. 18.

77. World Bank, *Philippines: Poverty, Basic Needs, and Employment,* Report 2984–PH, draft (hereafter cited as Poverty Report 2984–PH, draft), p. 130.

78. Interview with Bince, December 2, 1980.

79. *Business Week* (June 16, 1980): 118–B–1.

80. World Bank's July 1979 draft of the industrial-sector report, cited in World Bank, *Philippines: Third Urban Development Project—Staff Appraisal Report,* Report 2703a–PH, February 26, 1980, p. 20. See also World Bank, *Industrial Development Strategy and Policies in the Philippines,* Report 2513–PH, vol. 1: *Summary Report,* October 29, 1979, p. 10. The Philippine government defines *scale* according to total assets: (1) cottage industries have total capitalization less than or equal to P100,000; (2) small-scale industries, P100,000 to P1 million; (3) medium-scale, P1 million to P4 million; and (4) large-scale industries, greater than P4 million (interview with Ortaliz, April 13, 1981; *Bulletin Today* [Manila], May 20, 1981; U.S. AID, *FY1982 Country Development Strategy Statement—Philippines* [Manila: AID, 1980], p. 48).

81. Statement of Roberto Ongpin, cited in World Bank, *Meeting of Consultative Group for the Philippines, Washington, D.C., December 13 & 14, 1979—Report of Proceedings by the Chairman plus Annexes,* PHL–80–1, March 20, 1980, annex 6, p. 6.

82. David O'Connor, "Chapter on Export-Oriented Industrialization and the World Bank in the Philippines," draft (1981), p. 15 (mimeographed).

83. World Bank, *The Philippines: Country Economic Memorandum,* Report 1765–PH, October 26, 1977, annex A, p. 7. See also United Nations, Centre on Transnational Corporations, *Transnational Corporations in the International Semiconductor Industry,* 83–45443, 1983, pp. 380–93.

84. *Bulletin Today* (Manila), April 21, 1981.

85. Statement of Roberto Ongpin, in World Bank, *Meeting of Consultative Group, December 13 & 14, 1979,* annex 6, p. 6. "Productivity in many export firms compares favorably with that in these countries" (World Bank, *Industrial Development Strategy,* October 29, 1979, vol. 1, p. 2). A study by the Asian Pacific Compensation Survey likewise showed that the average monthly wages paid by foreign corporations in the Philippines were much lower than elsewhere in the region (*Le Monde,* August 27, 1980).

86. World Bank, Poverty Report 2984–PH, draft, pp. 112–13, and 113A, table 4.3; Guy Standing and Richard Szal, *Poverty and Basic Needs: Evidence from Guyana and the Philippines*, ILO World Employment Programme Study, 1979, pp. 87–90. See also IMF, *Recent Economic Developments*, January 24, 1975, p. 17.

87. Data provided by World Bank, July 1986.

88. World Bank, Poverty Report 2984–PH, draft, pp. 112–13.

89. World Bank, *Industrial Development Strategy*, October 29, 1979, vol. 1, p. 2.

90. The two versions of the Poverty Report are: World Bank, Poverty Report 2984–PH, draft; and World Bank, *Aspects of Poverty in the Philippines: A Review and Assessment*, vol. 1: *Overview*; vol. 2: *Main Report with Annexes and Statistical Appendix*, Report 2984–PH, 2 vols., December 1, 1980 (hereafter cited as Poverty Report 2984–PH).

91. World Bank, Poverty Report 2984–PH, p. 53. The Stolper-Samuelson theorem, in brief, states that free trade between countries with different factor endowments will raise the relative price of the factor of production used intensively in the export industry and, therefore, that the owners of that factor of production stand to gain from opening the economy. The predictions of the factor-price equalization theorem follow from the Stolper-Samuelson theorem. See Wolfgang F. Stolper and Paul A. Samuelson, "Protection and Real Wages," *Review of Economic Studies* 9 (November 1941): 58–73; Paul Samuelson, "International Factor-Price Equalisation Once Again," *Economic Journal* 59 (June 1949): 181–97.

92. World Bank, Poverty Report 2984–PH, draft, pp. 125–26.

93. Ibid., p. 127. The Bank failed to mention that the 1969 devaluation was part of an IMF stabilization loan package. Cf. Romeo Bautista, John H. Power et al., *Industrial Promotion Policies in the Philippines* (Manila: Philippine Institute for Development Studies [at NEDA], 1979), p. 76, for the problems of translating the Stolper-Samuelson results into income distribution effects.

94. Ferdinand Marcos, Speech on the Occasion of the Silver Anniversary of the Central Bank of the Philippines, January 4, 1974, quoted in Felix Casalmo, *The Vision of a New Society* (Manila, 1980), p. 86.

95. IMF, *Philippines: Recent Economic Developments*, July 18, 1980, p. 12. Such differentials added to the national entrepreneurs' relative disadvantage vis-à-vis exporters.

96. Business International, *Briefing Paper*, p. 67.

97. Quoted from IMF, *Philippines: Recent Economic Developments*, January 24, 1975, p. 18. See also, for example, Omotunde Johnson and Joanne Salop, "Stabilization Programs and Income Distribution," *Finance and Development* 17 (December 1980): 3.

98. See, for instance, World Bank, *Industrial Development Strategy*, May 1980, pp. 12, 26; World Bank, *Report and Recommendation*, August 21, 1980, pp. 9, 10, 31.

99. Conversation with government official (anonymity requested), April 23, 1981.

100. Quoted in Barbara Ehrenreich and Annette Fuentes, "Life on the Global Assembly Line," *Ms. Magazine* (January 1981): 58.

101. Interview with IMF official (anonymity requested), November 25, 1980.

102. IMF, *Philippines—Request for Standby Arrangement with Supplementary Financing*, EBS/80/25, February 5, 1980, p. 16. See also IMF, *Staff Report for the 1980 Article IV Consultation and Review of Standby Arrangement*, EBS/80/159, July 16, 1980, p. 16.

103. Interview with Ortaliz, April 13, 1981.

104. Records of Wage Commission, Ministry of Labor, Manila, cited in Edberto M. Villegas, *Studies in Political Economy* (Manila: Silangan Publishers, 1983), p. 97. The basic pay plus various additional monthly cost-of-living allowances make up the effective minimum wage.

105. The average daily wage rate in rural areas followed a similar trend, falling from about 125 percent of the monthly poverty line in 1979 to just over 100 percent in 1982 (World Bank, *The Philippines—Recent Trends in Poverty, Employment and Wages*, Report 5456–PH, June 20, 1985, p. 32, table 12).

106. See, for example, Leo Gonzaga, "The Workers Are Restive," *Far Eastern Economic Review* (March 20, 1981): 51.

107. Jaime T. Infante, *The Political, Economic, and Labor Climate in the Philippines*, Multinational Industrial Relations Series 8a (Philadelphia: Industrial Research Unit, Wharton School, University of Pennsylvania, 1980), p. 52.

108. Ibid., p. 95; *Bulletin Today* (Manila), March 1981, cited in the Oakland, California, newspaper *Ang Katipunan*, September 22, 1981.

109. Sheila Ocampo, "Striking Out Alone," *Far Eastern Economic Review* (June 5, 1981): 65.

110. Interview with Filipino social worker (anonymity requested), Metro-Manila, Philippines, March 13, 1981.

111. World Bank, Poverty Report 2984–PH, draft, p. 118.

112. Interviews with Ortaliz, April 13, 1981; and Rene Ofreneo, Metro-Manila, Philippines, May 17, 1981. *Asia Monitor* 5 (Third Quarter 1981): P–5–301.

113. Conversation with government official (anonymity requested), April 23, 1981.

114. The list of so-called vital industries was long, but in 1981 it included, among others, manufacture and processing of textiles and garments, and produc-

tion of export products, particularly by firms with Central Bank or Board of Investments certificates of export orientation, including hotels and restaurants in three-, four-, or five-star categories (*Business Day* [Manila], March 27, 1981).

115. Sheila Ocampo, "Striking Out Alone," pp. 64–65.

116. *Bulletin Today* (Manila), May 16 and 19, 1981; *Guardian* (New York), June 10, 1981.

117. "Foreign Firms Confident as Labor Law Lifts Philippine Strike Ban," *Business Asia* (August 14, 1981): 259–60; Leo Gonzaga, "Jobs, Not Wages," *Far Eastern Economic Review* (January 15, 1982): 46. *Asian Wall Street Journal,* June 2, 1981, estimated that this strike ban covered 95 percent of all businesses in the Philippines.

118. World Bank, Poverty Report 2984–PH, draft, p. 112; see also p. 127.

119. From papers presented at the January 1981 Consultative Group Meeting in Paris, cited in interviews with Central Bank staff member (anonymity requested), Metro-Manila, Philippines, March 19, 1981; and Nuqui, March 10, 1981.

120. World Bank, Poverty Report 2984–PH, pp. 18–19.

121. See, e.g., IMF, *Staff Report,* July 16, 1980, p. 16.

122. World Bank, *Philippines—Country Program Paper,* March 26, 1976, p. 10.

123. Data provided by Export Processing Zone Authority, 1986.

124. B. de Vries, *Transition Toward Labor-Intensive Industrial Development,* p. 17.

125. See, for instance, Barend de Vries's statement at press conference, cited in *Philippines Daily Express* (Manila), February 27, 1979.

126. World Bank, *Report and Recommendation,* August 21, 1980, p. 31; Louis Kraar, "The Philippines Veers Toward Crisis," *Fortune* (July 27, 1981): 35; *Far Eastern Economic Review* (October 2, 1981): 36; and *Financial Times* (London), February 8, 1982.

127. World Bank, Poverty Report 2984–PH, draft, pp. 153–54.

128. Ibid., pp. 148–49.

129. Ibid., p. 143A, table 5.14.

130. Employment in clothing/footwear subsectors plunged from 514,060 (1970) to 405,430 (1975) (ibid., pp. 141–43 and p. 143A, table 5.14).

131. This was not the only problem with the Bank's employment estimates. There was also the fact that EPZs created jobs for a *new* labor force: young, single women. See Rachel Grossman, "Women's Place in the Integrated Circuit," *Southeast Asia Chronicle,* no. 66 (January–February 1979), and *Pacific Research* 9 (July–August 1978); "Filipino Women Workers Praised by MEPZ Firm," *Business Day* (Manila), May 20, 1981. For more on the employment effects of TNCs in the developing world in general, see United Nations, International Labour Organization, *Employment Effects of Multinational Enterprises in Developing Countries,* 1981.

132. World Bank, "Philippines—Random Thoughts on Rural Development," memorandum from David J. Steel to M. A. Gould and L. E. Hinkle, September 1, 1977, p. 6.

133. Cited in *Bulletin Today* (Manila), October 27, 1980.

134. *Business Asia* (May 15, 1981): 160.

135. Statement of Benigno S. Aquino, Jr., in U.S. Congress, House, Committee on Foreign Affairs, *U.S. Policy Toward the Philippines, Joint Hearings Before the Subcommittee on Asia and Pacific Affairs and the Subcommittee on Human Rights and International Organizations,* 97th Cong., 1st sess., November 18, 1981, p. 20.

136. Statistics supplied by Philippine Ministry of Trade and Industry, 1986.

137. In early 1986, the Philippine government measured unemployment at 20 percent and underemployment at 40 percent. Underemployment here refers to those who work less than half time. Remarks delivered by Jaime Ongpin, minister of finance of the Philippines, Carnegie Endowment for International Peace, Washington, D.C., April 7, 1986.

138. *Report: News and Views from the World Bank* (September–October 1978): p. 3.

139. Interview with Ministry of Finance staff member (anonymity requested), December 17, 1980. Presumably he is referring to Simon Kuznets's U-shaped curve between inequality and level of development. On this, see M. S. Ahluwalia, "Inequality, Poverty and Development," *Journal of Development Economics* 3 (December 1976): 307–42.

140. Fernando Henrique Cardoso and Enzo Faletto, *Dependency and Development in Latin America,* trans. Marjory Marringly Urquidi (Berkeley and Los Angeles: University of California Press, 1979), p. 169.

141. Interview with World Bank official (anonymity requested), Metro-Manila, Philippines, March 4, 1981.

Chapter 7

1. World Bank, *Staff Appraisal Report on the Industrial Finance Project,* Report 3331–PH, April 7, 1981, p. 27.

2. World Bank and IMF, *The Philippines: Aspects of the Financial Sector,* World Bank Country Study, May 1980 (hereafter cited as World Bank and IMF, *Philippines—Financial Sector,* May 1980), preface. Here again, a number of internal reports preceded this May 1980 "red-cover" public version: one in June 1979, another in September, and still another in October. See also World Bank, *Philippines—Country Program Paper,* August 29, 1980, p. 15; World Bank, *Report and Recommendation,* April 13, 1981, p. 17.

3. See, e.g., World Bank, *Staff Appraisal Report on Industrial Finance Project,* pp. 18–21.

4. Cesar Virata, minister of finance, to Robert McNamara, president of World Bank, letter, "Re: Philippine Government's Statement of Policy on the Future Evolution of the Financial Sector," March 13, 1981.

5. For instance, interviews with Areñas, January 15, 1981; Corpus, February 11, 1981; NEDA official (anonymity requested), December 5, 1980; and Licaros, April 1, 1981.

6. While the SAL is listed under the heading of "Nonproject: Structural Adjustment" in the Bank's 1981 *Annual Report* (Washington, D.C.: World Bank, 1981), the apex loan is listed under "Development Finance Companies: Industrial Finance—Central Bank of the Philippines," pp. 193–94.

7. World Bank, "Aide-Mémoire," outcome of discussions between World Bank and Philippine government, August 20–31, 1979, unnumbered p. 1.

8. Ibid., unnumbered p. 2.

9. *IMF Survey* (December 14, 1981): 395–96.

10. Pierre M. Landell-Mills, "Structural Adjustment Lending: Early Experience," *Finance and Development* 18 (December 1981): 18. Later it became Bank policy to use sector loans for *single-sector* restructuring and SALs for more comprehensive, multisector policy dialogues.

11. Paragraph based on Edward Mason and Robert Asher, *The World Bank Since Bretton Woods* (Washington, D.C.: Brookings Institution, 1973), pp. 166–67, 190.

12. World Bank, *Development Finance Companies,* Sector Policy Paper, April 1976, p. 3. See also World Bank, *DFC Policy Paper,* Report 823, July 28, 1975.

13. In 1968, a Department of Development Finance Companies was set up in the Bank to complement assistance provided by the IFC's Development Finance Company Division. Until that year, only private development finance companies were eligible for World Bank funds (Mason and Asher, *World Bank,* pp. 358–65, 375–78; Escott Reid, *Strengthening the World Bank* [Chicago: Adlai Stevenson Institute, 1973], p. 54; and U.S. Treasury Department, *United States Participation in the Multilateral Development Banks in the 1980s,* February 1982, pp. 27–29).

14. World Bank, *Economic Perspectives on Southeast Asia and Asia,* April 19, 1978, p. 61. DBP is the former Rehabilitation Finance Corporation.

15. Ibid.; World Bank, *Staff Appraisal Report on Industrial Finance Project,* p. 69; *Euromoney* (April 1979): 36. Although officially licensed as an investment house, PDCP performed the duties of a development bank (World Bank and IMF, *Philippines: Financial Sector,* May 1980, p. 29). PDCP was 30 percent owned by foreign stockholders, including Union Bank of Switzerland, Deutsche Bank, and the local subsidiary of the J. Walter Thompson advertising agency. In 1978, the Bank added a third conduit to the list of Philippine financial institutions servicing its medium- and long-term industrial and infrastructural financing. This was the then four-year-old, privately owned Philippine Investments Systems Organization, which also boasted foreign stockholders.

16. Quoted from World Bank, *Report and Recommendation,* August 21, 1980, p. 32. See also World Bank, *Staff Appraisal Report on Industrial Finance Project,* p. 26.

17. World Bank, *Report and Recommendation,* August 21, 1980, p. 36.

18. World Bank, *Staff Appraisal Report on Industrial Finance Project,* p. 50.

19. IMF-CB Banking Survey Commission, *The Recommendations of the Joint IMF-CB Banking Survey Commission on the Philippine Financial Sector,* September 1972, p. ii; World Bank and IMF, *Philippines: Financial Sector,* May 1980, p. 51; and Miguel Cuaderno, Sr., *Problems of Economic Development (The Philippines—A Case Study)* (Manila, n.d.), pp. 86–95.

20. This paralleled the overall rise, starting in the early 1960s, of the IMF relative to the United States in influencing LDC policy-making.

21. For a more detailed historical overview, see Margaret G. de Vries, ed., *The International Monetary Fund, 1966–1971: The System Under Stress,* 2 vols. (Washington, D.C.: IMF, 1976), vol. 1, pp. 579–82; and J. Keith Horsefield, ed., *The International Monetary Fund, 1945–1965: Twenty Years of International Monetary Cooperation,* 3 vols. (Washington, D.C.: IMF, 1969), vol. 1, pp. 552–53, on which this paragraph is based.

22. IMF-CB Banking Survey Commission, *Recommendations,* 1972, p. ii; R. S. Ofreneo et al., "A Critique of the 1972 and 1980 Financial Reforms," University of the Philippines at Diliman, 1981, p. 2 (mimeographed).

23. Interview with Fabella, December 8, 1980.

24. Ibid.

25. "It took the state of emergency to allow the amendments to the Central Bank's charter and the Banking Acts to be enacted" ("Philippines: The Economy That Came Up Smiling," *Euromoney* [April 1979]: 30).

26. IMF-CB Banking Survey Commission, *Recommendations,* 1972, cover letter.

27. Cesar Virata, "The Philippine Financial System Faces Challenge of the '80s," in *Fookien Times Philippines Yearbook, 1981–82* (Manila, 1981), p. 108; *Ibon Facts and Figures,* no. 51 (September 30, 1980); *Asian Wall Street Journal,* October 27, 1978; *Business Day* (Manila), January 19, 1981; *Philippines Daily Express* (Manila), November 4, 1975; Ofreneo et al., "Critique," p. 4. Minimum capital base levels for investment houses became P20 million (*Asian Finance* [September 15–October 14, 1976]: 87).

28. This new policy was contained in Presidential Decree 71. Maria Socorro L. Africa, "Participation of Offshore Banking Units (OBUs) in the Peso Market: Implications for Domestic Credit and the Money Supply," Master's thesis, School of Economics, University of the Philippines, 1980, pp. 1–2; Ofreneo et al., "Critique," p. 6; and interview with Diokno, May 14, 1982.

29. The term *underwriting* refers to managing the issuance of stocks.

30. World Bank and IMF, *Philippines: Financial Sector*, May 1980, pp. 51–52; "Philippines: The Economy That Came Up Smiling," *Euromoney* (April 1979): 36; Virata, "Philippine Financial System," p. 108. See Philippines (Republic), *Republic Act 37: General Banking Act Approved on July 24, 1948;* IMF-CB Banking Survey Commission, *Recommendations,* 1972, Recommendation 48, pp. 76–79, and Recommendation 68, pp. 97–100.

31. World Bank, *Staff Appraisal Report on Industrial Finance Project,* p. 12; *Business Day* (Manila), January 19, 1981.

32. Philippines (Republic), Central Bank of the Philippines, *Circular No. 739: Rules and Regulations Governing Commercial Banks and Banks with Expanded Commercial Banking Authority to Implement the Provisions of Batas Pambansa Blg. 61 Further Amending Republic Act No. 337, as Amended, and Other Relevant Provisions of Banking Laws* (July 10, 1980), p. 2.

33. The major example was the series of so-called Central Bank–IBRD loans for agricultural machinery. On these, see Eduardo Evangelista, "Agricultural Credit Programs: A Critique," Master's thesis, Asian Institute of Management, Metro-Manila, 1978, pp. 33–52, and exhibits 11–14. See also World Bank, *Staff Appraisal Report on Industrial Finance Project,* p. 26.

34. Interviews with IMF official (anonymity requested), November 25, 1980; NEDA official (anonymity requested), December 5, 1980; World Bank, *Report and Recommendation,* August 21, 1980, p. 17. The usefulness of overlapping (or parallel) missions had been stressed in the 1966 and 1970 memoranda of collaboration between the Bank and Fund. However, joint missions were another thing. As of 1972, according to the semiofficial World Bank history, "jointly sponsored missions are unknown" (Mason and Asher, *World Bank,* p. 545).

35. See, for instance, Licaros's quote in *Philippines Daily Express* (Manila), December 23, 1979.

36. Interview with Areñas, January 15, 1981.

37. Interview with NEDA official (anonymity requested), December 5, 1980.

38. Interview with IMF official (anonymity requested), November 25, 1980.

39. Interview with Noriega, April 20, 1981.

40. Interview with Licaros, April 1, 1981.

41. Central Bank of the Philippines, *Circular No. 739,* pp. 12–13, 35.

42. Interview with Licaros, April 1, 1981.

43. Philippines (Republic), *Presidential Decree No. 71: Amending Republic Act No. 337, entitled "The General Banking Act"* (November 29, 1972); Central Bank of the Philippines, *Circular No. 739,* sections 35–52; Philippines (Republic), Batasang Pambansa, *Batas Pambansa Blg. 61: An Act Amending Further Republic Act Numbered Three Hundred Thirty-Seven, as Amended, Regulating Banks and Banking Institutions and For Other Purposes, Otherwise Known as the "General Banking Act"*

(April 1, 1980), section 21; Philippines (Republic), Central Bank of the Philippines, *Circular No. 756: Amending Section 9 of Circular No. 739* (August 22, 1980).

44. See World Bank and IMF, *The Philippines: Report on Aspects of the Financial Sector*, vol. 1: *The Summary*, Report 2546–PH, June 6, 1979 (hereafter cited as World Bank and IMF, *Philippines: Financial Sector*, June 6, 1979), p. 3; and IMF, *Staff Report for the 1980 Article IV Consultation and Review of Standby Arrangement*, EBS/80/159, July 16, 1980, p. 10. In the Philippine context, short-term debts mature in less than one year; medium-term extend to five years.

45. Central Bank of the Philippines, *Circular No. 739*; Philippines (Republic), Central Bank of the Philippines, *Circular No. 740: Rules and Regulations Governing Thrift Banks to Implement the Provisions of Batas Pambansa Blg. 61, 62, and 63 Further Amending Republic Acts No. 337, as Amended, 3779, as Amended, and 4093, as Amended Respectively, and Other Relevant Provisions of Banking Laws* (July 10, 1980); Philippines (Republic), Central Bank of the Philippines, *Circular No. 741: Rules and Regulations Governing Rural Banks To Implement the Provisions of Batas Pambansa Blg. 65 Further Amending Republic Act No. 720, as Amended, and Other Relevant Provisions of Banking Laws* (July 10, 1980); Philippines (Republic), Central Bank of the Philippines, *Circular No. 742: Rules and Regulations Governing Non-Bank Financial Intermediaries Authorized to Perform Quasi-Banking Functions to Implement the Provisions of Batas Pambansa Blg. 61 Further Amending Republic Act No. 337, as Amended, Batas Pambansa Blg. 66, Amending Presidential Decree No. 129, and Other Relevant Provisions of Applicable Laws* (July 10, 1980); Philippines (Republic), Batasang Pambansa, *Batas Pambansa Blg. 61*; Philippines (Republic), Batasang Pambansa, *Batas Pambansa Blg. 62: An Act Amending Further Republic Act Numbered Three Thousand Seven Hundred Seventy-Nine, as Amended, Otherwise Known as the "Savings and Loan Association Act"* (April 1, 1980); Philippines (Republic), Batasang Pambansa, *Batas Pambansa Blg. 63: An Act Amending Further Republic Act Numbered Forty Hundred and Ninety-Three, as Amended, Otherwise Known as the "Private Development Banks Act"* (April 1, 1980); Philippines (Republic), Batasang Pambansa, *Batas Pambansa Blg. 64: An Act Amending Further Republic Act Numbered Eighty-Five, as Amended, Otherwise Known as the "Charter of the Development Bank of the Philippines"* (April 1, 1980); Philippines (Republic), Batasang Pambansa, *Batas Pambansa Blg. 65: An Act Amending Further Republic Act Numbered Seven Hundred Twenty, as Amended, Otherwise Known as the "Rural Banks Act"* (April 1, 1980); Philippines (Republic), Batasang Pambansa, *Batas Pambansa Blg. 66: An Act Amending Presidential Decree No. 129, as Amended, Otherwise Known as the "Investment Houses Law"* (April 1, 1980); Philippines (Republic), Batasang Pambansa, *Batas Pambansa Blg. 67: An Act Amending Republic Act Numbered Two Hundred and Sixty-Five, as Amended, Otherwise Known as the "Central Bank Act"* (April 1, 1980).

For a summary of these laws, see Cesar Virata, minister of finance, to Robert McNamara, president of the World Bank, letter, "Re: Philippine Industrial Development Policy," August 12, 1980, pp. 16–18.

46. *Asian Finance* (April 15, 1979): 64; *Philippines Daily Express* (Manila), November 23, 1979.

47. Fabella (December 8, 1980) used these terms.

48. World Bank, *Staff Appraisal Report on Industrial Finance Project,* pp. 2, 29; and see World Bank, *Report and Recommendation,* August 21, 1980, pp. 5, 9.

49. World Bank, *The Philippines: Country Economic Memorandum,* Report 1765–PH, October 26, 1977, annex A, p. 12. This requirement was repeated by de Vries in 1980 and at the 1980 Consultative Group meeting (Barend de Vries, *Transition Toward More Rapid and Labor-Intensive Industrial Development: The Case of the Philippines,* World Bank Staff Working Paper 424, October 1980, p. 14; *Bulletin Today* [Manila], January 1, 1981).

50. Virata to McNamara, August 12, 1980, p. 6; see also p. 16.

51. World Bank, *Staff Appraisal Report on Industrial Finance Project,* p. 23.

52. See, for example, IMF, *Staff Report,* July 16, 1980, p. 10; World Bank and IMF, *Philippines: Financial Sector,* May 1980, p. 81; Virata to McNamara, March 13, 1981, p. 1; and Virata, "Philippine Financial System," p. 110.

53. World Bank and IMF, *Philippines: Financial Sector,* June 6, 1979, p. 6. This was also cited in *Philippines Daily Express* (Manila), October 3, 1979, and by an IMF official during an interview (November 25, 1980).

54. Interview with Fabella, December 9, 1980. See World Bank, *Report and Recommendation,* April 13, 1981, p. 15; *Far Eastern Economic Review* (November 14, 1980): 8. The Joint IMF–Central Bank Banking Survey Commission of 1971–1972 was reconstituted and enlarged in 1979. The Philippine side of this group was informally known as the Financial Reforms Committee.

55. Interviews with Noriega, April 20, 1981; and Leung, January 15, 1981.

56. Interview with former Central Bank deputy governor (anonymity requested), February 9, 1981.

57. Interview with Fabella, December 8, 1980.

58. Interview with IMF official (anonymity requested), November 25, 1980.

59. World Bank and IMF, *Philippines: Financial Sector,* May 1980, p. 72, n. 1; see also pp. 3 and 6 of the June 6, 1979, version of this report. For a later admission of this lack of data, see Millard Long, *Review of Financial Sector Work,* World Bank Industry Department, October 1983, pp. 39–41.

60. Central Bank of the Philippines, *Circular No. 739,* p. 8 (emphasis added); see also pp. 2, 7.

61. Interview with Licaros, April 1, 1981.

62. Interview with Areñas, January 15, 1981.

63. Interview with Bince, December 2, 1980.

64. Interview with Legarda, February 2, 1981.

65. Philippines (Republic), Central Bank of the Philippines, memorandum for CB Panel, Joint IMF-CBP Banking Survey Commission, "Subject: Report of the Joint IMF-WB Mission on Aspects of the Financial Sector of the Philippines," by Arnulfo B. Aurellano, special assistant to the governor, October 8, 1979, pp. 5–9 (hereafter cited as Aurellano Memorandum).

66. Ibid., pp. 1, 5, 9.

67. Quoted in *Bulletin Today* (Manila), September 4, 1979.

68. See Investment House Association of the Philippines, "IHAP Position on Universal Banking," Manila [1979]; and *Business Day* (Manila), June 8, 1979.

69. David SyCip, chairman, Committee to Study Multi-Purpose Financial Institutions Proposal, "Statement of Views re: Proposal to Permit/Encourage the Development of Multi-Purpose Financial Institutions," Bankers' Association of the Philippines, Manila, November 20, 1979; interviews with Magallona, December 16, 1980, and January 16, 1981; *Business Day* (Manila), June 8, 1979; *Ibon Facts and Figures,* no. 51 (September 30, 1980): 8; and *Philippines Daily Express* (Manila), September 30, 1979, August 18, 1980.

70. Interviews with Gabriel Singson, Metro-Manila, Philippines, February 23, 1981; Central Bank staff member (anonymity requested), December 3, 1980; and Areñas, January 15, 1981.

71. Interview with Noriega, April 20, 1981.

72. Ibid.

73. Interview with Fabella, December 8, 1980.

74. See Central Bank of the Philippines, *Circular No. 739,* p. 11. By comparison, the minimum capital base of a commercial bank was P20 million, raised to P100 million as of 1973.

75. Interview with Fabella, December 8, 1980.

76. Even Minister Virata admitted that the Philippine banking reforms were in line with the German universal-banking model (*Makati* [Manila] *Trade Times,* March 6–12, 1981).

77. Interview with Fabella, December 8, 1980.

78. Variations of this phrase were used by Licaros (April 1, 1981); Singson (February 23, 1981); national entrepreneurs (anonymity requested, May 13, 1981); Zialcita (January 21, 1981); and Ministry of Finance staff member (anonymity requested, December 17, 1980).

79. Interview with Legarda, February 2, 1981.

80. Interview with Licaros, April 1, 1981.

81. Interview with former Central Bank deputy governor (anonymity requested), February 9, 1981.

82. See, for example, *Far Eastern Economic Review* (January 23, 1981): 38–39; *Business Day* (Manila), September 26, 1979; *Asian Wall Street Journal,* February 26, 1980; *Asian Wall Street Journal Weekly* (October 25, 1982): 25. Reiterated in interview with Corpus, February 11, 1981.

83. Philippine press reports cited by Magallona, December 16, 1980; Fabella, December 8, 1980; and Gonzalo Jurado, Metro-Manila, Philippines, January 27, 1981.

84. Interview with Central Bank staff member (anonymity requested), April 19, 1981, citing phrase used by others.

85. Philippines (Republic), Central Bank, "Apex Development Finance Unit," annex A, unnumbered p. 1 (mimeographed).

86. *Asian Finance* (June 15, 1980): 24. Cf. World Bank and IMF, *Philippines: Financial Sector,* June 6, 1979, p. 8.

87. Interview with Eduardo Villanueva, Metro-Manila, Philippines, February 23, 1981.

88. This handout was Central Bank, "Apex Development Finance Unit," annex A.

89. Interview with Central Bank staff member (anonymity requested), December 3, 1980. Statements to this effect were repeated during a number of other interviews with Central Bank staff and officials.

90. Interview with Villanueva, February 23, 1981.

91. Ibid.

92. Interviews with Singson, February 23, 1981; Legarda, February 2, 1981; former Central Bank deputy governor (anonymity requested), February 9, 1981; Areñas, January 15, 1981; and de los Santos, March 30, 1981.

93. See, for example, World Bank, *Staff Appraisal Report on Industrial Finance Project,* pp. 52–53; World Bank, *Philippines—Country Program Paper,* 1980, p. 9.

94. World Bank, *Report and Recommendation,* April 13, 1981, p. 18.

95. World Bank, *Staff Appraisal Report on Industrial Finance Project,* pp. 49–50 (emphasis added).

96. *Manila Journal,* November 3–9, 1980.

97. Interview with Licaros, April 1, 1981.

98. Ibid., and interview with Singson, February 23, 1981.

99. World Bank, *Staff Appraisal Report on Industrial Finance Project,* p. 31.

100. Ibid., p. 31 and p. 5, annex 2; and interview with Villanueva, February 23, 1981. The Monetary Board directs the Central Bank's management, operations, and administration by preparing the necessary rules and regulations for these purposes. Under Marcos, the Monetary Board was composed of the Central Bank governor (Licaros at the time of the ADFU's birth, then Laya, then Jose Fernandez), minister of finance (Virata), minister of industry (Ongpin), minister of planning

and economic policy (Sicat until July 1981, then Placido Mapa), and a representative of the private sector.

101. Interview with Villanueva, February 23, 1981.

102. World Bank, *Staff Appraisal Report on Industrial Finance Project*, pp. 30–32, 53.

103. Interview with Licaros, April 1, 1981.

104. Interview with Imelda Macaraig, Metro-Manila, Philippines, February 23, 1981. Up to eight more professional positions were, at that point, allotted in the ADFU (World Bank, *Staff Appraisal Report on Industrial Finance Project*, p. 31).

105. Interview with Diokno, April 11, 1981.

106. Interviews with Villanueva, February 23, 1981, and Macaraig, February 23, 1981; *Bulletin Today* (Manila), April 27, 1981. See also World Bank, *Staff Appraisal Report on Industrial Finance Project*, p. 31.

107. Interview with Diokno, January 17, 1981; *Christian Science Monitor*, September 18, 1980.

108. Interview with Philippine government official (anonymity requested), April 21, 1981.

109. Interview with World Bank official (anonymity requested), March 4, 1981.

110. Interview with Philippine government official (anonymity requested), April 21, 1981.

111. Interview with Villanueva, February 23, 1981.

112. *Bulletin Today* (Manila), April 27, 1981. On EDI, see Chapter 2, above.

113. World Bank, *Staff Appraisal Report on Industrial Finance Project*, pp. 32, 53.

114. Following a common pattern of World Bank and UNDP collaboration, the Bank was the executing agency for these UNDP funds. Interview with Macaraig, February 23, 1981; World Bank, *Report and Recommendation*, April 13, 1981, p. 19; World Bank, *Staff Appraisal Report on Industrial Finance Project*, p. 32.

115. Interview with Macaraig, February 23, 1981.

116. World Bank, *Staff Appraisal Report on Industrial Finance Project*, p. 32.

117. Interview with Villanueva, February 23, 1981.

118. Interview with Macaraig, February 23, 1981.

119. Ibid.

120. World Bank, *Staff Appraisal Report on Industrial Finance Project*, p. 14.

121. Paragraph based on World Bank, *Staff Appraisal Report on Industrial Finance Project*, pp. 33, 48–49; World Bank, *Report and Recommendation*, April 13, 1981, p. 20. See also *Business Day* (Manila), April 24, 1981. The Bank relied on an SGV study for the figures cited in this paragraph, as the citation for p. 159, table 7, of the *Staff Appraisal Report* disclosed.

122. List of participatory financial institutions, as of April 1986, was provided by the Central Bank of the Philippines, July 1986.

123. World Bank, *Staff Appraisal Report on Industrial Finance Project*, pp. 49–50.

124. Interview with Villanueva, February 23, 1981. See, for instance, World Bank, *Report and Recommendation*, April 13, 1981, p. 23; *Staff Appraisal Report on Industrial Finance Project*, p. 33.

125. Interview with Macaraig, February 23, 1981; World Bank, *Staff Appraisal Report on Industrial Finance Project*, p. 30; World Bank, "World Bank to Assist Industrial Sector in the Philippines," *Bank News Release*, 81/84 (May 11, 1981); and *Business Day* (Manila), April 24, 1981. Cf. World Bank, *Development Finance Companies*, pp. 36–37, 47; Mason and Asher, *World Bank*, p. 317, n. 37.

126. Interview with Villanueva, February 23, 1981.

127. Interview (by telephone) with Macaraig, March 5, 1981; *Manila Journal*, December 10, 1979; World Bank, "World Bank to Assist Industrial Sector in the Philippines," *Bank News Release*, 81/84 (May 11, 1981); World Bank, *Report and Recommendation*, April 13, 1981, pp. 18–19; World Bank, *Staff Appraisal Report on Industrial Finance Project*, p. 50.

128. World Bank, "World Bank to Assist Industrial Sector in the Philippines," *Bank News Release*, 81/84 (May 11, 1981); and "Top 1,000 Corporations in the Philippines," *Fookien Times Philippines Yearbook, 1981–82*, pp. 126–40. This list of the 1980 top corporations is taken from the Philippine Securities and Exchange Commission records. Although approximately 550 firms fall within this asset range, not all fulfill the "export-oriented" and "labor-intensive" criteria.

129. This included the $100 million co-finance component of the apex loan (World Bank, "World Bank to Assist Industrial Sector in the Philippines," *Bank News Release*, 81/84 [May 11, 1981]).

130. Interview with Macaraig, February 23, 1981.

131. World Bank, *Staff Appraisal Report on Industrial Finance Project*, pp. 52–53; interview with Macaraig, February 23, 1981.

132. World Bank, *Report and Recommendation*, April 13, 1981, pp. 18–19. The ADFU and, in turn, the World Bank were given specific power to review these subloans. On this, see World Bank, *Staff Appraisal Report on Industrial Finance Project*, pp. 34, 62–65.

133. *Bulletin Today* (Manila), April 27, 1981.

134. *Wall Street Journal*, June 24, 1981; World Bank, *Report and Recommendation*, April 13, 1981, p. ii.

135. Years here refer to World Bank fiscal years (July–June); World Bank, *Co-Financing* (Washington, D.C.: World Bank, September 1983), pp. 20–21, table 2; and "Co-Financing: World Bank Tries Harder," *The Banker* (January 1983): 66. At the end of 1980, twenty-six LDCs were in arrears over repayment to private banks (*International Herald Tribune*, October 29, 1981). At roughly that same time, the World Bank publicized the fact that there had never been a default on its

loans, never a payment missed (Eugene H. Rotberg, *The World Bank: A Financial Appraisal* [Washington, D.C.: World Bank, March 1978], p. 12; World Bank, *Co-Financing: Review of World Bank Activities,* December 1976; World Bank, *Annual Report 1980* [Washington, D.C.: World Bank, 1980], pp. 68–70; *Asian Finance* [September 15, 1977]: 5; Brandt Commission Report, p. 275). Even in the early 1980s, however, the Bank's boast warranted somewhat deeper investigation. At that point, there were at least two cases in which late payments occurred: Chile (under Allende) and Tanzania (1982). See Cheryl Payer, *The World Bank: A Critical Analysis* (New York: Monthly Review Press, 1982), pp. 46–50; and *International Herald Tribune,* October 23–24, 1982. On the question of the Bank's debt-renegotiation role historically, see Mason and Asher, *World Bank,* pp. 224–26.

136. World Bank, *Co-Financing,* 1976, pp. 15, 17.

137. World Bank, *Philippines—Country Program Paper,* 1980, p. 25; World Bank, *Annual Report 1980,* p. 70.

138. *Times Journal* (Manila), November 1, 1980.

139. *Times Journal* (Manila), December 21, 1980.

140. Interview with Licaros, April 1, 1981.

141. World Bank, *Report and Recommendation,* April 13, 1981, pp. 49–50.

142. *World Business Weekly* (August 31, 1981): 49.

143. World Bank, *Co-Financing,* 1983, p. 9. See also *Asian Finance* (September 17, 1977): 5.

144. World Bank, *Co-Financing,* 1976, pp. 12, 15.

145. Interview with Macaraig, February 23, 1981.

146. See, e.g., World Bank, *Staff Appraisal Report on Industrial Finance Project,* p. 62.

147. Interview with Licaros, April 1, 1981.

148. Ibid.

149. World Bank, *Staff Appraisal Report on Industrial Finance Project,* p. 30.

150. *Business Day* (Manila), April 24, 1981.

151. World Bank, "Operating Policy Guidelines of the Apex Development Finance Unit, Central Bank of the Philippines," April 1, 1981, p. 1. These guidelines also appeared as annex 2 of the project's *Staff Appraisal Report on Industrial Finance Project.*

152. World Bank, *Staff Appraisal Report on Industrial Finance Project,* p. 27.

153. In a survey of New York bankers, "practically every major New York lender interviewed warned of hazards" for the Philippines (*Asian Wall Street Journal,* January 20, 1981).

154. Interview with IMF official (anonymity requested), November 25, 1980.

155. World Bank, *Co-Financing,* 1976, p. 14.

156. Interview with Villanueva, February 23, 1981.

157. *Asiaweek* (May 1, 1981): 36–37; James Bartholomew, "The Shockwave Spreads," *Far Eastern Economic Review* (February 6, 1981): 87; Louis Kraar, "The Philippines Veers Toward Crisis," *Fortune* (July 27, 1981): 37–39.

158. World Bank, "Aide-Mémoire," unnumbered page 5.

159. Reportedly, the limit on banks' net domestic-assets increase stood at approximately 16 percent—as opposed to a 1980 inflation rate of about 25 percent (*Far Eastern Economic Review* [June 12, 1981]: 81). On this, see also Chemical Bank, Economic Research Department, *Asian Economic Trends* (New York: Chemical Bank, January 1982), p. 26; and *Far Eastern Economic Review* (May 1, 1981): 53.

160. Philippines (Republic), Central Bank, Office of the Governor, ADFU, "Industrial Finance Fund: Proposed Statement of Policy and Operating Procedures," April 1981, p. 1.

161. Ibid., pp. 1, 2.

162. Philippines (Republic), Central Bank, Office of the Governor, ADFU, "Industrial Finance Fund," April 1981, p. 1. This document and the paper cited in the two immediately preceding notes are separate papers.

163. Conversation with Philippine government official (anonymity requested), Policy Conference on Tariff Reforms, April 23, 1981.

164. Central Bank, "Industrial Finance Fund," pp. 1–3; and Central Bank, "Industrial Finance Fund: Proposed Statement of Policy and Operating Procedures," p. 4. The four "lead banks" were PNB, United Coconut Planters Bank, DBP, and Land Bank of the Philippines.

165. Marc Frons, "A Little Help for Some Friends?" *Newsweek* (August 10, 1981): 40; "Helping Hand in Manila," *Far Eastern Economic Review* (April 3, 1981): 43; James Bartholomew, "Sweetheart Firm May Get Special Deal," *New Statesman* (June 19, 1981): 4. See also "With a Little Help from Their Friend," *Economist* (June 27, 1981): 79.

166. This is discussed further in Chapter 8, below. Quote is from Central Bank, "Industrial Finance Fund," p. 1. For more on the history of these businessmen, see Kraar, "Philippines Veers Toward Crisis," pp. 34–39; Walden Bello, David O'Connor, and Robin Broad, "Technocrats Versus Cronies," in Walden Bello et al., *Development Debacle: The World Bank in the Philippines* (San Francisco: Institute for Food and Development Policy, 1982), pp. 183–95; and *Ibon Facts and Figures*, no. 73 (August 30, 1981): 5–7.

Chapter 8

1. Aurellano Memorandum, p. 9.

2. Diwa Guinigundo, "What Is Unibanking?" *Diliman Review* 28 (May–June 1980): 3–6.

3. Interviews with priest (anonymity requested), Metro-Manila, Philippines, May 19, 1981; priest (anonymity requested), Bukidnon, Mindanao, Philippines, December 23, 1980; priest (anonymity requested), Metro-Manila, Philippines, March 12, 1981; priest (anonymity requested), Metro-Manila, Philippines, March 6, 1981. Cf. John Doherty, S.J., "The Government's New Export Offensive," *Diliman Review* 28 (September–October 1980): 25–28.

4. Interviews with commercial bank executive (anonymity requested), Metro-Manila, Philippines, March 9, 1981; investment house executive (anonymity requested), Metro-Manila, Philippines, May 24, 1981; investment house executive (anonymity requested), Metro-Manila, Philippines, December 14, 1980, and March 11, 1981; and administrative assistant to commercial bank president (anonymity requested), Metro-Manila, Philippines, April 10, 1981.

5. Central Bank, *Circular No. 739,* p. 22.

6. World Bank and IMF, *Philippines: Financial Sector,* June 6, 1979, p. 6.

7. Cesar Virata, minister of finance, to Robert McNamara, president of World Bank, letter, "Re: Philippine Government's Statement of Policy on the Future Evolution of the Financial Sector," March 13, 1981, p. 2; World Bank and IMF, *Philippines: Aspects of the Financial Sector,* World Bank Country Study, May 1980, p. 79. See also *Philippines Daily Express* (Manila), September 26, 1979. Virata's description was repeated by Leung (January 15, 1981).

8. Central Bank, *Circular No. 739,* p. 7.

9. World Bank and IMF, *Philippines: Financial Sector,* June 6, 1979, pp. 6–7.

10. IMF, *Staff Report for the 1980 Article IV Consultation and Review of Standby Arrangement,* EBS/80/159, July 16, 1980, p. 10.

11. Central Bank, *Circular No. 739,* p. 19.

12. Ibid., pp. 19, 26. See *Manila Journal,* March 17–23, 1980.

13. On this, see Sixto K. Roxas, "Unibanking: The Philippines Third Wave," *Fookien Times Philippines Yearbook 1981–82* (1981), p. 164.

14. Interviews with IMF official (anonymity requested), November 25, 1980; and World Bank official (anonymity requested), March 4, 1981. See any of the versions of the World Bank and IMF joint report on the Philippine financial sector.

15. Interview with Fabella, December 8, 1980. Cf. Fabella's quotes in *Times Journal* (Manila), February 8, 1980; and Leo Gonzaga, "Buying Up the Market," *Far Eastern Economic Review* (November 27, 1981): 51.

16. Interview with Fabella, December 8, 1980.

17. The 1,034 rural banks controlled only 2.3 percent of the financial system's assets. See Ibon Databank, *The Philippine Financial System—A Primer* (Manila: Ibon Databank, 1983), p. 9. This excellent primer by the Manila-based Ibon research institute is the best reference source on the Philippine financial sector.

18. The five were PNB, United Coconut Planters Bank, Metropolitan Bank

and Trust Co., Philippine Commercial and Industrial Bank, and Allied Banking Corp. (Guy Sacerdoti, "Postscripts to a Trauma," *Far Eastern Economic Review* [March 26, 1982]: 89).

19. This former savings bank was Family Bank, which became a commercial bank in 1981 and an ECB in September of 1982. Of the top fifteen banks (ranked by assets as of 1978)—PNB, Citibank, Bank of the Philippine Islands, Metropolitan Bank and Trust Company, Allied Banking Corporation, United Coconut Planters Bank, Far East Bank and Trust Company, China Banking Corporation, Rizal Commercial Banking Corporation, Philippine Commercial and Industrial Bank, Consolidated Bank and Trust Company, Equitable Banking Corporation, Pacific Banking Corporation, Manila Banking Corporation, and Insular Bank of Asia and America—only six (China Bank, Rizal Commercial, Consolidated, Equitable, Pacific, and Insular) had not become ECBs as of August 1982 (Philippines: The Economy That Came Up Smiling," *Euromoney* [April 1979]: 33; "Financial Fiasco," *Ibon Facts and Figures,* no. 143 [July 31, 1984]: 7; and Ibon Databank, *The Philippine Financial System—A Primer,* pp. 103–6).

20. *Ibon Facts and Figures,* no. 143 (July 31, 1984): 7.

21. *Far Eastern Economic Review* (January 15, 1982): 6. See also Leo Gonzaga, "More and More of the Brightest Bankers Are Going Commercial," *Far Eastern Economic Review* (September 24, 1982): 95–96.

22. *Business Day* (Manila), April 22, 1981; *Euromoney* (April 1979): 36–37.

23. *Times Journal* (Manila), July 27, 1978; *Philippines Daily Express* (Manila), July 22, 1980; *Financial Times* (London), November 11, 1980; *Business Day* (Manila), March 9, 1981; R. S. Ofreneo et al., "A Critique of the 1972 and 1980 Financial Reforms," University of the Philippines at Diliman, 1981, appendix A–1 (mimeographed).

24. *Asia Monitor* 5 (Third Quarter 1981): P–5–303; *Euromoney* (April 1979): 37; *Business Day* (Manila), April 20, 1981; *Bulletin Today* (Manila), October 27, 1980.

25. Quoted from *Euromoney* (April 1979): 36. John F. Doherty, *A Preliminary Study of Interlocking Directorates Among Financial, Commercial, Manufacturing and Service Enterprises in the Philippines* (Manila, 1979), p. 13. Among other links, J. B. Fernandez, Jr. (later Marcos's and then Aquino's Central Bank governor) was Bancom's vice-chairman and (as of early 1981) Far East Bank and Trust's president and chairman of the board (Ofreneo et al., "Critique," appendices B–1, B–2; *Bulletin Today* [Manila], January 7 and March 26, 1981).

26. Defense Minister Enrile was chairman of the board of United Coconut Planters Bank and a director of PDCP (Ofreneo et al., "Critique," appendix B–1; and "Some Are Smarter Than Others" [Manila, n.d.], p. 14 [the latter citation refers to an opposition article that was privately circulated in Manila in 1979]).

Panfilo Domingo was PNB's president and chairman of the board and also PDCP's chairman of the board (Ofreneo et al., "Critique," appendix B–2).

27. Quoted in *Business Day* (Manila), April 14, 1981. Cf. *Business Day* (Manila), April 15, 1981.

28. Leo Gonzaga, "The Wizards Are Disappearing," *Far Eastern Economic Review* (November 15, 1984): 85.

29. Interviews with Licaros, April 1, 1981; former Central Bank deputy governor (anonymity requested), February 9, 1981; Central Bank staff member (anonymity requested), March 19, 1981; and Ministry of Finance staff member (anonymity requested), December 3, 1980.

30. Remarks of the United Democratic Opposition (UNIDO), quoted in *Business Day* (Manila), January 16, 1981.

31. Interview with Philippine government official (anonymity requested), March 6, 1981.

32. Central Bank deputy governor, quoted in *Euromoney* (April 1979): 30; and Ibon Databank, *Primer on Philippine Commercial Banking* (Manila: Ibon Databank, 1979), p. 13. Prior to 1972, TNBs had been barred from taking equity in the Philippine financial sector, but the four wholly foreign-owned banks (Bank of America, Citibank, Hong Kong and Shanghai, and Standard and Chartered Group) that were active in the country before the 1947 ban were allowed to retain their operations (Maria Socorro L. Africa, "Participation of Offshore Banking Units [OBUs] in the Peso Market: Implications for Domestic Credit and the Money Supply," Master's thesis, School of Economics, University of the Philippines, 1980, pp. 1–2; Robert Stauffer, "Philippine Martial Law: The Political Economy of Refeudalization," in *Marcos and Martial Law in the Philippines,* ed. David A. Rosenberg [Ithaca, N.Y.: Cornell University Press, 1979], p. 214).

33. "How Successful Was the Bank Build-Up Drive?" *Asian Finance* (January 1976): 29.

34. Interview with IMF official (anonymity requested), November 25, 1980. The Philippine government added other incentives to spur this TNB involvement in 1981. See *Far Eastern Economic Review* (September 11, 1981): 81.

35. World Bank and IMF, *Philippines: Financial Sector,* June 6, 1979, p. 3.

36. Ibon Databank, *Philippine Financial System—A Primer,* pp. 194–96. See also Robyn Lim, "The Multinationals and the Philippines Since Martial Law," in *A Multinational Look at the Transnational Corporation,* ed. Michael T. Skully (Sydney: Dryden Press Australia, 1978), p. 131; and Renato Constantino, *The Nationalist Alternative* (Quezon City: Foundation for Nationalist Studies, 1979), p. 35.

37. Frederick R. Dahl, "International Operation of U.S. Banks," *Law and Contemporary Problems* 32 (Winter 1967): 111.

38. Aurellano Memorandum, p. 9.

39. Interviews with Licaros, April 1, 1981; former Central Bank deputy governor (anonymity requested), February 9, 1981; Central Bank staff member (anonymity requested), March 19, 1981; and Finance Ministry staff member (anonymity requested), December 3, 1980.

40. "OBUs Join Credit Debate," *Asian Finance* (June 15–July 14, 1977): 85. Cf. World Bank, Poverty Report 2984–PH, draft, p. 129.

41. Interview with national entrepreneur (anonymity requested), March 13, 1981. Similar statements made by Henares, February 27, 1981.

42. On this global phenomenon, see Richard J. Barnet and Ronald E. Müller, *Global Reach: The Power of Multinational Corporations* (New York: Simon and Schuster, 1974), p. 152; and UNCTAD, *Marketing and Distribution of Tobacco*, TD/B/C.1/205, 1978, p. 21.

43. *Asian Finance* (June 15–July 14, 1977): 86. For more statistical information on TNCs' penetration among the top 1,000 Philippine corporations, see United Nations, Economic and Social Commission for Asia and the Pacific, Joint CTC/ESCAP Unit on Transnational Corporations, *Monitoring and Regulating Transnational Corporations in the Philippines*, Working Paper 11, August 1980.

44. IMF, *Philippines: Recent Economic Developments*, July 18, 1980, p. 46.

45. Walden Bello, David O'Connor, and Robin Broad, "Export-Oriented Industrialization: The Short-Lived Illusion," in Walden Bello et al., *Development Debacle: The World Bank in the Philippines* (San Francisco: Institute for Food and Development Policy, 1982), p. 155.

46. Interview with Central Bank staff member (anonymity requested), April 14, 1981.

47. Calculated from computer printouts on U.S. direct foreign investment abroad, supplied by U.S. Commerce Department, 1981. Profit rate equals income plus fees and royalties as percent of total investment.

48. Nationalist Resource Center, *U.S. Imperialism in the Philippines (An Anti-Imperialist's Sourcebook)* (Manila: Nationalist Resource Center, 1980), p. 38.

49. "Philippines: The Economy That Came Up Smiling," *Euromoney* (April 1979): 30.

50. Quoted in E. P. Patanne, "Slow Development in Manila," *Asian Business* (July 1981): 44.

51. Louis Kraar, "The Philippines Veers Toward Crisis," *Fortune* (July 27, 1981): 36. It should be emphasized that illegalities are not completely alien to TNCs themselves. A 1980 *Fortune* study examining the activities of 1,043 major TNCs concluded that 11 percent had committed at least one of the following five crimes between 1971 and 1978: bribery (including kickbacks and illegal rebates), criminal fraud, illegal political contributions, tax evasion, or price fixing. The 11 percent figure is actually a minimum, as *Fortune* included only cases of actual

conviction on federal criminal charges or cases resulting in consent decrees ("How Lawless Are Big Companies?" *Fortune* [December 15, 1980]: 57).

52. Peter Evans, *Dependent Development: The Alliance of Multinational, State, and Local Capital in Brazil* (Princeton, N.J.: Princeton University Press, 1979), p. 162.

53. For more on what *Fortune* (July 27, 1981, p. 37) calls the "crony problem," see Walden Bello, David O'Connor, and Robin Broad, "Technocrats Versus Cronies," in Bello et al., *Development Debacle*, pp. 183–95.

54. Philippines (Republic), Central Bank, Office of the Governor, "Industrial Finance Fund: Proposed Statement of Policy and Operating Procedures," April 1981, p. 4.

55. *Asiaweek* (May 1, 1981): 36.

56. World Bank, "Operating Policy Guidelines of ADFU," April 1, 1981, p. 2. See "IMF Stand-by Arrangement with RP," *Central Bank* (of the Philippines) *Review* (August 1981): 8.

57. *Asian Wall Street Journal,* February 10, 1981.

58. Interview with Manila-based TNC executive (anonymity requested), February 13, 1981.

59. As was explained in Chapter 1, the use here of the term *triple alliance* focuses only on Filipino institutions, whereas Evans's *triple alliance* includes both international and national institutions.

60. For more on how this industry-finance-government hookup works in Japan, see Andreas R. Prindl, *Japanese Finance: A Guide to Banking in Japan* (Chichester: John Wiley and Sons, 1981); Alexander K. Young, *The Sogo Shosha: Japan's Multinational Trading Companies* (Boulder, Colo.: Westview Press, 1979); Hugh Patrick, ed., with Larry Meissner, *Japanese Industrialization and Its Social Consequences* (Berkeley and Los Angeles: University of California Press, 1976); Hugh Patrick and Henry Rosovsky, *Asia's New Giants: How the Japanese Economy Works* (Washington, D.C.: Brookings Institution, 1976); Chalmers Johnson, *MITI and the Japanese Miracle: The Growth of Industrial Policy, 1925–75* (Stanford, Calif.: Stanford University Press, 1982).

61. Interview with IMF official (anonymity requested), November 25, 1980. See Gonzaga, "More and More of the Brightest Bankers Are Going Commercial," pp. 95–96.

62. See Aurellano Memorandum, p. 6; Ibon Databank, *Philippine Financial System—A Primer,* pp. 42–49.

63. Doherty, *Preliminary Study of Interlocking Directorates,* p. 100; John Doherty, S.J., "Who Controls the Philippine Economy?" in *Cronies and Enemies: The Current Philippine Scene,* ed. Belinda A. Aquino (Honolulu: Philippine Studies Program, Center for Asian and Pacific Studies, University of Hawaii, 1982), pp. 7–35.

64. Vyvyan Tenorio, "A Blueprint Bogged Down," *Far Eastern Economic Review* (August 1, 1980): 99. See also John Doherty, "The Government's New Export Offensive," *Diliman Review* (September–October 1980): 25; and Ngo Huy Liem, *Promotion of General Trading Companies in an Export-Oriented Economy: The Philippine Experience* (Freiburg: Institute for Development Policy, 1982).

65. For specific names and holdings, see Doherty, *Preliminary Study of Interlocking Directorates,* and "Who Controls the Philippine Economy?"; Ofreneo et al., "Critique," p. 64 and appendix B–1; *Asian Finance* (May 15, 1980): 76; *Manila Journal,* March 17–23, 1980.

66. Aurellano Memorandum, p. 6.

67. Ibid.

68. Interview with Fabella, December 8, 1980. Cf. Central Bank, *Circular No. 739,* p. 22.

69. Philippines (Republic), Batasang Pambansa, *Batas Pambansa Blg. 61,* sec. 21–B; Central Bank, *Circular No. 739,* pp. 54–55. These limits were generous when compared to other countries where such financial-industrial equity hookups are allowed. In Japan, the limit for a single investment has fluctuated between 5 and 10 percent of a financial institution's capital (Young, *Sogo Shosha,* p. 36; Prindl, *Japanese Finance,* p. 25). In Singapore, the limit on total equity investment stands at approximately 40 percent of net worth; in Mexico, at about 25 percent of total resources (David SyCip, "Statement of Views re: Proposal to Permit/Encourage the Development of Multi-Purpose Financial Institutions," Bankers' Association of the Philippines, Manila, November 20, 1979, p. 3).

70. Central Bank, *Circular No. 739,* p. 54.

71. SyCip, "Statement of Views," p. 3.

72. NEDA, *Economic Report on the Philippines, 1978–1980* (Manila: NEDA, December 1980), p. 3. Cf. World Bank and IMF, *Philippines: Financial Sector,* May 1980, p. v.

73. World Bank and IMF, *Philippines: Financial Sector,* May 1980, p. 76.

74. Ibid., pp. 76–77. Cf. Millard Long, *Review of Financial Sector Work,* World Bank Industry Department, October 1983, p. 39.

75. Cesar Virata, minister of finance, to Robert McNamara, president of World Bank, letter, "Re: Philippine Industrial Development Policy," August 12, 1980, attachment 1, p. 4.

76. Interview with Macaraig, February 23, 1981. See *Far Eastern Economic Review* (April 16, 1982): 5.

77. IMF, *Philippines—Staff Report for the 1982 Article IV Consultation,* SM/82/55, March 24, 1982, p. 9; *Far Eastern Economic Review* (April 30, 1982): 41. The original 1981 net domestic asset ceiling (an IMF performance criterion) was raised during the IMF's mid-1981 review "to accommodate the financial rescue operation" (IMF, *Staff Report,* March 24, 1982, pp. 6, 9).

78. IMF, *Staff Report,* March 24, 1982, p. 9.

79. Evans, *Dependent Development,* p. 278.

80. "On the Takeover Trail," *Far Eastern Economic Review* (September 11, 1981): 61.

81. Ibid.; Leo Gonzaga, "High Noon in Manila," *Far Eastern Economic Review* (March 19, 1982): 74; *Business Day* (Manila), April 20, 1981.

82. Leo Gonzaga, "The High Cost of Help," *Far Eastern Economic Review* (October 4, 1981): 104.

83. Marc Frons, "A Little Help for Some Friends?" *Newsweek* (August 10, 1981): 40.

84. Leo Gonzaga and Guy Sacerdoti, "Operation Cold Comfort," *Far Eastern Economic Review* (May 14, 1982): 87.

85. Ibid.; see also Guy Sacerdoti, "Delta's Dire Straits," *Far Eastern Economic Review* (April 16, 1982): 63.

86. Gonzaga, "High Noon in Manila," p. 74.

87. Quoted in Kraar, "The Philippines Veers Toward Crisis," p. 37. See Ascher Memorandum, pp. 2, 12, 14.

88. Conversation with Philippine government official (anonymity requested), Policy Conference on Tariff Reforms, April 23, 1981. Sentiments repeated by other government officials.

89. For more on these appointees, see *Central Bank* (of the Philippines) *Review* (August 1981): 13; Bello, O'Connor, and Broad, "Technocrats Versus Cronies," pp. 183–85; *World Business Weekly* (August 24, 1981): 11–12; Renato Constantino, "The World Bank's Trojan Horses," *Far Eastern Economic Review* (August 14, 1981): 39.

Chapter 9

1. GATT, *International Trade 1980/81* (Geneva: GATT, 1981), p. 2, table 1.

2. Ibid. From 1948 to 1971, world trade (volume) grew at an average annual rate of 7.3 percent, while from 1958 to 1978, the average annual growth rate for manufactured exports was between 9.5 and 10 percent (UNCTAD, Secretariat, *Trade and Development Report 1981* [Geneva: UNCTAD, 1981], p. 2, table 4; GATT, *Networks of World Trade,* 1978, cited in Vijay L. Kelkar, "Post-War Growth in World Trade in Manufactures," *Economic and Political Weekly* [April 7, 1984]: 596, table 1).

3. GATT, "International Trade in 1981 and Present Prospects," *GATT Press Release,* GATT/1313, March 23, 1982, p. 2, table 1.

4. The figures compared are year-over-year declines (GATT, "International Trade in 1981," pp. 1 and 2, table 2).

5. World Bank, *World Development Report 1979* (New York: Oxford University Press, 1979), p. 17.

6. Calculated from IMF, *Annual Report of the Executive Board for the Financial Year Ended April 30, 1981* (Washington, D.C.: IMF, 1981), p. 8, table 1. In the decade before 1975, the rate was 5 percent (World Bank, *World Development Report 1978* [New York: Oxford University Press, 1978], p. 9).

7. IMF, *World Economic Outlook: A Survey by the Staff of the IMF,* Occasional Paper 9 (Washington, D.C.: IMF, 1982), p. 31.

8. OECD report, cited in *International Herald Tribune,* May 4, 1982.

9. Ibid.

10. Jan Tumlir, director, GATT economic department, quoted in *International Herald Tribune,* January 25, 1982.

11. United States, Council of Economic Advisers, *Economic Report of the President* (1982), quoted in *International Herald Tribune,* February 26, 1982.

12. On the "new protectionism," see Robert McNamara, *Address to the United Nations Conference on Trade and Development, Manila, Philippines, May 10, 1979* (Washington, D.C.: World Bank, n.d.), pp. 6–9; Douglas R. Nelson, *The Political Structure of the New Protectionism,* World Bank Staff Working Paper 471, July 1981; Bela Balassa, *The Newly Industrializing Countries in the World Economy* (New York: Pergamon Press, 1981), p. 113. See also Robert E. Baldwin, *The Inefficiency of Trade Policy,* Essays in International Finance 150 (Princeton, N.J.: International Finance Section, Department of Economics, Princeton University, 1982), p. 20. This essay was presented as the Frank D. Graham Memorial Lecture, Princeton University, October 7, 1982.

13. OECD official, quoted in *International Herald Tribune,* January 25, 1982.

14. Hollis B. Chenery and Donald B. Keesing, *The Changing Composition of Developing Country Exports,* World Bank Staff Working Paper 314, January 1979, p. 42. Cf. World Bank, *Philippines: Domestic and External Resources for Development,* Economic Memorandum for 1979 Consultative Group Meeting, Report 2674–PH, November 12, 1979, p. 26; McNamara, *Address to UNCTAD, 1979,* p. 6.

15. In early 1982, the Multi-Fiber Arrangement controlled four-fifths of textile and apparel world trade (*International Herald Tribune,* April 16, 1982). For more on the MFA, see John Cavanagh, "Northern Transnationals Can Use New MFA to Sew Up Markets," *South* (May 1982): 70–71; Diana Tussie, "GATT and the MFA: Counter to 'Free Trade,'" *South* (January 1982): 21; and Malcolm Subhan, "Alive But Struggling," *Far Eastern Economic Review* (January 1, 1982): 34–35; "Coming Apart at the Seams," *Far Eastern Economic Review* (March 19, 1982): 52–54; Malcolm Subhan, "Not Quite Sewn Up," *Far Eastern Economic Review* (April 30, 1982): 44–46. With special reference to Asia, see almost any early-1980s issue of *Textile Asia.*

16. Jonathan Power, "A Rich-Poor Alliance Against Protectionism," *International Herald Tribune*, February 26, 1982.

17. Tussie, "GATT and the MFA," p. 21.

18. As a result, these products were taxed at a 16 percent rate (*Asia Monitor* 5 [Third Quarter 1981]: P-5-305).

19. See IMF, *Philippines: Recent Economic Developments*, July 18, 1980, appendix, p. 51, table 9.

20. Robert McNamara, *Address to the Board of Governors, Washington, D.C., September 30, 1974* (Washington, D.C.: World Bank, 1974), p. 12.

21. World Bank, *Philippines—Country Program Paper*, March 26, 1976, p. 6. In 1980, Philippine exports and imports accounted for 43 percent of GNP (*Business Day* [Manila], May 6, 1981).

22. McNamara, *Address to UNCTAD, 1979*, p. 6. See also World Bank, *The Philippines: Country Economic Memorandum*, Report 1765-PH, October 26, 1977, annex A, p. 12.

23. Barend de Vries, *Transition Toward More Rapid and Labor-Intensive Industrial Development: The Case of the Philippines*, World Bank Staff Working Paper 424, October 1980, p. 19.

24. Statement of Andreas Abadjis, senior adviser, Asian Department, IMF, and head of IMF delegation to 1979 Consultative Group meeting, in World Bank, *Meeting of the Consultative Group for the Philippines, Washington, D.C., December 13 & 14, 1979—Report of Proceedings by the Chairman plus Annexes*, PHL-80-1, March 20, 1980, annex 5, p. 2. See also World Bank, *Philippines: Domestic and External Resources for Development*, p. 26; World Bank, *Industrial Development Strategy*, October 29, 1979, vol. 1, p. 32; IMF, *Philippines: Recent Economic Developments*, p. 34; IMF, *Philippines—Request for Standby with Supplementary Financing*, EBS/80/25, February 5, 1980, p. 19.

25. See, for example, World Bank, *Report and Recommendation*, August 21, 1980, p. 31; World Bank, *World Development Report 1978* (New York: Oxford University Press, 1978), p. 32.

26. B. de Vries, *Transition Toward Labor-Intensive Industrial Development*, p. 17; World Bank, *Philippines—Country Program Paper*, 1976, p. 14; and World Bank, *Industrial Development Strategy*, October 29, 1979, p. 2. See also, for example, World Bank, *Report and Recommendation*, August 21, 1980, p. 30; and World Bank, *Staff Appraisal Report on the Industrial Finance Project*, Report 3331-PH, April 7, 1981, p. 11.

27. Interview with Power, October 29, 1980; and Romeo Bautista, John H. Power et al., *Industrial Promotion Policies in the Philippines* (Manila: Philippine Institute for Development Studies, 1979), pp. 74-75. For more on Power and Bautista's book and involvements, see Chapter 4, above. Cf. IMF, *Philippines—Staff Report for 1982 Article IV Consultation*, March 24, 1982, p. 19.

28. Chenery and Keesing, *Developing Country Exports,* p. 43.

29. B. de Vries, *Transition Toward Labor-Intensive Industrial Development,* p. 17. Similarly, Balassa, in his April 1980 Frank D. Graham Memorial Lecture at Princeton University, shared optimistic projections concerning the growth of LDC-manufactured exports to industrial countries even with the "maintenance of the Multi-Fiber Arrangement." The catch is that the MFA was not simply being maintained, as Balassa suggested; it was being tightened (Bela Balassa, *The Process of Industrial Development and Alternative Development Strategies,* Essays in International Finance 141 [Princeton, N.J.: International Finance Section, Department of Economics, Princeton University, 1980], p. 25).

30. World Bank, *Report and Recommendation,* August 21, 1980, p. 31.

31. Vice-President and Secretary, World Bank, *Summaries of the Discussions at the Meeting of the Executive Directors of the Bank and IDA, September 16, 1980,* SD80–52, November 20, 1980, p. 8.

32. Ibid. See also World Bank, *Philippines—Country Program Paper,* 1976, p. 9.

33. This paragraph and the preceding one are based on the World Bank's *World Development Report 1981* (New York: Oxford University Press, 1981), pp. 10–11; and *World Development Report 1978* (New York: Oxford University Press, 1978), pp. 26–29, quotation from p. 32. Earlier projections also appeared in Chenery and Keesing, *Developing Country Exports,* p. 36.

34. See, for example, World Bank, *China: Socialist Economic Development,* vol. 1: *The Main Report,* Report 3391-CHA, June 1, 1981, p. 169. In this instance, the *World Development Report 1981* high-assumption scenario was used with only the caveat that this assumed that protectionist barriers would not increase "significantly."

35. Interview with Ortaliz, January 19, 1981. Similar sentiments were expressed by Sicat in a speech presented at Policy Conference on Tariff Reforms, April 22, 1981; by Minister of Labor Blas Ople speaking on a 1980 Philippine television program (quoted in *Business Day* [Manila], December 5, 1980); by Bince, December 2, 1980; and by a Ministry of Finance staff member (anonymity requested), May 19, 1982.

36. Sicat, speech presented at Policy Conference on Tariff Reforms, April 22, 1981.

37. See World Bank, *Progress Report on Structural Adjustment Lending,* SecM84–461, May 23, 1984, p. 7, table 3; and Pierre M. Landell-Mills, "Structural Adjustment Lending: Early Experience," *Finance and Development* 18 (December 1981): 19, table 1.

38. Interview with Bank of Thailand official (anonymity requested), Bangkok, Thailand, July 1979.

39. World Bank, *Thailand: Toward a Development Strategy of Full Participation,*

Basic Economic Report 2059–TH, September 1, 1978; World Bank, *Industrial Development Strategy in Thailand,* June 5, 1980; World Bank, *Thailand: Coping with Structural Change in a Dynamic Economy,* August 1980; Santi Mingmongkol, "The World Bank and Thailand: New Wine in an Old Bottle," *Southeast Asia Chronicle,* no. 81 (December 1981): 20–24; *Bangkok Bank Monthly Review* (November 1980): 401–6 and (November 1981): 434–49; and *Far Eastern Economic Review* (May 23, 1980): 40–46; (February 13, 1981): 40–44; and (June 4, 1982): 56–61.

40. See, for example, World Bank, *Indonesia: Selected Issues of Industrial Development and Trade Strategy,* Report 3182–IND, October 29, 1980, annex 1: *The Structure of the Manufacturing Sector;* and World Bank, *Chile: An Economy in Transition,* Report 2390–CH, 3 vols., June 21, 1979, vol. 1: *The Main Report;* vol. 2: *The Annexes.*

41. The similarities are detailed further in Robin Broad, "Behind Philippine Policy Making: The Role of the World Bank and International Monetary Fund," Ph.D. dissertation, Princeton University, 1983, pp. 469–97.

42. Quoted in *Christian Science Monitor,* September 18, 1980.

43. Advertisement by Investment Promotion Division of the Greater Colombo Economic Commission, Colombo, Sri Lanka, in *Far Eastern Economic Review* (October 16, 1981): 71.

44. Interview with government official on Interagency Committee for SAL reforms (anonymity requested), April 22, 1981. Similar phrase used by Bautista, December 15, 1980.

45. Interview with Bince, December 2, 1980.

46. Interview with Manila-based TNC executive (anonymity requested), February 13, 1981.

47. Chenery and Keesing, *Developing Country Exports,* p. 47.

48. World Bank, *Report and Recommendation,* August 21, 1980, p. 31.

49. World Bank, *Industrial Development Strategy,* October 29, 1979, vol. 1, p. 2.

50. Quoted in John Kelly and Joel Rocamora, "Indonesia: A Show of Resistance," *Southeast Asia Chronicle,* no. 81 (December 1981): 16.

51. Barbara Ehrenreich and Annette Fuentes, "Life on the Global Assembly Line," *Ms. Magazine* (January 1981): 58.

52. World Bank, *China: Socialist Economic Development,* vol. 1, p. 168. China, a fledgling member of the Bank and the Fund, is a good example of a country trying to move into light-manufactured exports in its free trade zones, although it is not yet a would-be NIC.

53. See, for instance, UNIDO, Global and Conceptual Studies Branch, Division for Industrial Studies, *Restructuring World Industry in a Period of Crisis—The Role of Innovation: An Analysis of Recent Developments in the Semiconductor Industry,* UNIDO/15.285, December 17, 1981, p. 225.

54. John Cavanagh, "Textile Multinationals: Profiting from Protectionism," Geneva, 1981, p. 4 (mimeographed). See *Textile Asia* (August 1981): 87.

55. On South Korea, for example, see IMF, *Korea—Recent Economic Developments,* SM/82/70, April 15, 1982, pp. 54, 56, and appendix, p. 93, table 20, and p. 94, table 21; Hyan-Chin Lim, "Dependent Development in the World-System: The Case of South Korea, 1963–1979," Ph.D. dissertation, Harvard University, 1982; and *Far Eastern Economic Review* (February 19, 1982): 40–41.

56. "The 'Four Dragons' Lose Fire," *Business Week* (March 28, 1983): 64.

57. W. Arthur Lewis, *Development Economics: An Outline,* University Programs Modular Studies (Morristown, N.J.: General Learning Press, 1974), p. 10.

58. George L. Hicks and Geoffrey McNicoll, *Trade and Growth in the Philippines: An Open Dual Economy* (Ithaca, N.Y.: Cornell University Press, 1971); Douglas S. Paauw, "The Philippines: Estimates of Flows in the Open, Dualistic Economy Framework, 1949–1965," draft, Washington, D.C.: National Planning Association, Center for Development Planning, 1968; Douglas S. Paauw and Joseph L. Tyron, "Agriculture-Industry Interrelationships in an Open Dualistic Economy: The Philippines, 1949–1964," in *Growth of Output in the Philippines,* ed. Richard W. Hooley and Randolph Barker (Manila: School of Economics, University of the Philippines, and International Rice Research Institute, 1967).

59. See, for instance, World Bank, Poverty Report 2984–PH, vol. 1, p. 20; World Bank, *Staff Appraisal Report on Industrial Finance Project,* p. 10; and World Bank, *Philippines—Country Program Paper,* August 29, 1980, p. 7.

60. World Bank, *Philippines—Country Program Paper,* 1976, p. 13.

61. Statement of Shahid Husain, cited in World Bank, *Meeting of the Consultative Group for the Philippines, Washington, D.C., November 30 & December 1, 1978—Report of Proceedings by the Chairman,* 1979, p. 66.

62. Roberto V. Ongpin, "A New and Revitalized Ministry of Trade and Industry," *Fookien Times Philippines Yearbook 1981–1982* (1981), p. 118.

63. "Export Processing Zone Authority—An Agent for Development," Export Processing Zone Authority advertisement for Bataan Export Processing Zone, 1979.

64. Ibid.

65. Interviews with Ortaliz, April 13, 1981; Noriega, April 20, 1981; Licaros, April 1, 1981; and Bince, December 2, 1980, among others.

66. World Bank, *Philippines: Domestic and External Resources for Development,* p. 29; World Bank, *Staff Appraisal Report on Industrial Finance Project,* p. 4. See also World Bank, *Industrial Development Strategy,* October 29, 1979, p. 13.

67. *CACP* [Citizens' Alliance for Consumer Protection] *Journal* (Manila) 1 (Second Quarter 1981): 29.

68. Mary Soledad Perpiñan, R. G. S., "Women and TNCs: The Philippine Experience," Manila, March 1981, p. 6 (mimeographed).

69. World Bank, *Industrial Development Strategy*, October 29, 1979, p. 32. According to the Textile Mills Association of the Philippines, the value added under Republic Act 3137 (the so-called Embroidery Law, which allows garment manufacturers to import, on consignment, duty-free raw materials for local processing and subsequent re-export) was only 30 percent (Ibon Databank, *Primer on Garment Industry* [Manila: Ibon Databank, 1981], p. 19).

70. Calculated from World Bank, *Philippines: Domestic and External Resources for Development*, p. 61, table 3.5, and p. 64, table 3.8.

71. Calculated from United Nations, Statistical Office, *1977 Supplement to the World Trade Annual Report: Trade of the Industrialized Nations with Eastern Europe and the Developing Nations*, vol. 5: *The Far East* (New York: Walker, 1979), pp. v–554, v–579.

72. UNIDO, *Restructuring World Industry*, p. 250. The figure would, however, have to be closer to the lower estimate if the World Bank's aggregate average value-added figure of 25 percent is to hold. Clearly, none of these three estimates is a precise calculation, but they provide useful approximations.

73. See Ibon Databank, *Primer on Garment Industry*, p. 18.

74. World Bank, *Philippines: Domestic and External Resources for Development*, p. 4.

75. "Coming Apart at the Seams," *Far Eastern Economic Review* (March 19, 1982): 52; "Tough Year Ahead for Textile Talks," *South* (June 1982): 72; John Cavanagh, "Northern Transnationals Can Use New MFA." On subcontracting, see Chapter 3, above.

76. World Bank, *Country Economic Memorandum*, annex A, p. 11. The Bank's 1979 projections for Philippine import payments of intermediate goods destined for export-processing industries likewise indicated that overall import dependence was expected to remain high (World Bank, *Philippines: Domestic and External Resources*, p. 29).

77. This refers to total tariff item 806.30/807 imports to the United States.

78. Paragraph based on UNIDO, *Restructuring World Industry*, pp. 237, 244–51; quote is from p. 249. See also United Nations, Centre on Transnational Corporations, *Transnational Corporations in the International Semiconductor Industry*, 83–45443, 1983.

79. See J. Rada, *The Impact of Micro-electronics: A Tentative Appraisal of Information Technology*, United Nations, International Labour Organization, World Employment Programme Study, 1980.

80. James A. Norling, international manager for Motorola's semiconductor group, quoted in *Business Week* (March 15, 1982): 38.

81. UNIDO, *Restructuring World Industry*, p. 237. On this question of employment, see Chapter 6, above; and United Nations, International Labour Orga-

nization, *Employment Effects of Multinational Enterprises in Developing Countries*, 1981, p. 82.

82. Walden Bello, David O'Connor, and Robin Broad, "Export-Oriented Industrialization: The Short-Lived Illusion," in Walden Bello et al., *Development Debacle: The World Bank in the Philippines* (San Francisco: Institute for Food and Development Policy, 1982), p. 153.

83. Peter Evans, *Dependent Development: The Alliance of Multinational, State, and Local Capital in Brazil* (Princeton, N.J.: Princeton University Press, 1979), pp. 314–15.

84. "Manila Export Zones Lure Business," *Christian Science Monitor,* September 18, 1980; *Peacemaker* (Manila) 1 (September 1981): 7. The Bataan Zone cost $192 million to build in 1973, earned only $82 million in ten years of operation, generated only half of the predicted direct employment, and had a *negative* net present value (Peter G. Warr, *Export Processing Zones in the Philippines* [Kuala Lumpur and Canberra: ASEAN-Australian Joint Research Project, 1985]). See also Judy S. Castro, *The Bataan Export Processing Zone,* United Nations, International Labour Office, Asian Employment Programme Working Paper, September 1982. The $2.1 billion was nearly $1 billion higher than had been projected in the plant's 1976 agreement. In the immediate aftermath of the April 1986 accident at the Chernobyl nuclear power plant, the Aquino government decided to "mothball" the Bataan plant.

85. Philippine government estimates. For a discussion of the impact of such infrastructure investments, see *Ibon Facts and Figures,* no. 60 (February 15, 1981).

86. Business International, *Briefing Paper,* p. 33.

87. Ibid.

88. World Bank, *Philippines—Country Program Paper,* 1980, p. 5; World Bank, *Staff Appraisal Report on Industrial Finance Project,* p. 4. NEDA's *Five-Year Philippine Development Plan, 1978–82—Draft Revisions for 1981 and 1982* (December 1980, pp. 8–9) targeted $3.082 billion for 1982. See also *Bulletin Today* (Manila), February 19, 1981. The World Bank, however, slated the $3 billion current-account deficit mark for the following year, 1983 (World Bank, *Philippines—Country Program Paper,* 1980, attachment 3C).

The current account measures how much a country earns versus how much it spends internationally exclusive of borrowing and foreign investment; the balance-of-payments figure includes capital flows from abroad.

89. World Bank, *World Debt Tables* (Washington, D.C.: World Bank, 1986), pp. 226–29; and Philippines (Republic), Central Bank, "External and Financial Development in the Philippines in 1981: Year-End Report of the Central Bank of the Philippines to President of the Philippines on the State of the Economy and the Financial System," Manila, 1982.

90. This was from $1.2 billion (1980) to $2.05 billion (1981) (IMF, *Staff Report,* March 24, 1982, p. 4).

91. By World Bank estimates, the debt service ratio for 1979 was already at 21 percent (World Bank, *Philippines: Domestic and External Resources for Development,* p. 4).

92. World Bank, *Philippines—Country Program Paper,* 1976, p. 17. In the past, the Philippine government got around this limit by changing its definition of debt service ratio. See note 93, below.

93. IMF, *Staff Report,* March 24, 1982, pp. 13, 17, and appendix 1, p. 23. Debt service ratio, as calculated by the IMF, refers to the ratio of debt service net of IMF obligations and prepayments to the current year's current-account earnings. In other words, the IMF defines the debt service as payments on medium-term and long-term loans divided by the export of goods and services. The denominator of the World Bank's debt service ratio calculation excludes transfers and investment income (which the IMF includes). The real discrepancy in calculations is not between these two, but between these and the Philippine government's calculation. The Philippine government uses total debt service as the numerator and the previous year's receipts on current *and capital accounts* as the denominator. By counting the proceeds from foreign loans as receipts, the Philippine government's calculation diminishes the ratio.

Passing from debt service ratios to the actual dollar terms behind them puts the Philippines' dilemma in starker focus. According to Business International, 1979 Philippine debt service payments totaled $1.56 billion (*Briefing Paper,* p. 33). As the IMF calculated in 1980, debt service payments on loans with maturities over one year would hit $2 billion in 1982 (as against the previous year's gross export earnings of somewhat more than double that amount) and top $3 billion by 1985 (IMF, *Staff Report,* July 16, 1980, p. 14; Central Bank, "Economic and Financial Development in the Philippines in 1981").

94. Cited in *Economist* (November 27, 1982): 88. This figure includes interest and amortization of medium- and long-term debt plus short-term debt outstanding at start of year.

95. Interviews with Purita Neri, Central Bank of the Philippines, November 17, 1980; and with Central Bank staff member (anonymity requested), January 22, 1981; and E. S. Browning, "East Asia in Search of a Second Economic Miracle," *Foreign Affairs* (Fall 1981): 145.

96. Interview with officer of World Bank's East Asia Division (anonymity requested), December 15, 1980, by Walden Bello. The situation was exacerbated because the rapidly rising interest rates in the West bloated that portion of the debt borrowed on a variable-interest-rate basis, which embraced more than one-third of Philippine debt in 1981 (*Far Eastern Economic Review* [December 12, 1981]: 50).

97. World Bank, *Philippines—Country Program Paper,* 1976, p. 8.

98. World Bank, *Economic Perspectives on Southeast Asia and Asia*, April 19, 1978, p. 5.

99. World Bank, *Philippines—Country Program Paper*, 1980, p. 7.

100. These figures are from the Bank's "high borrowing, high growth of GDP and manufactured exports scenario" for China (World Bank, *China: Socialist Economic Development*, vol. 1, pp. 175, 180–81).

101. Interview with IMF official (anonymity requested), November 25, 1980.

102. Interview with Ministry of Finance staff member (anonymity requested), December 17, 1980.

103. Interview with Zialcita, January 21, 1981. Cf. Guillermo Soliven, quoted in "Bringing the Banks Up to Date," *Euromoney* (April 1979): 26.

104. Interviews with (among others) Zialcita, January 21, 1981; Corpus, February 11, 1981; and NEDA official (anonymity requested), December 5, 1980.

105. "Chairman's Opening Statement," in World Bank, *Meeting of Consultative Group, December 13 & 14, 1979*, p. 17.

106. World Bank, *Philippines—Country Program Paper*, 1980, p. 5.

107. Philippines (Republic), NEDA, *Five-Year Philippine Development Plan, 1978–1982* (Manila: NEDA, 1977), p. 26, table 2.5; Philippines (Republic), *Philippines Development Report 1980* (Manila: Central Bank, 1981); interview with Ferdinand Marcos in *Asian Wall Street Journal*, February 21, 1981; *Business Day* (Manila), January 23, 1981.

108. Quoted in *Business Day* (Manila), January 23, 1981.

109. Interviews with staff economist (anonymity requested), Center for Research and Communications, Metro-Manila, Philippines, May 20, 1981; and with official (anonymity requested), Asian Development Bank, Metro-Manila, Philippines, March 20, 1981. "Certain foreign estimates put it [the 1980 growth rate] at only 3%" (*Far Eastern Economic Review* [January 16, 1981]: 50).

110. *World Business Weekly* (August 24, 1981): 12.

111. *Textile Asia* (July 1981): 102, and (November 1981): 100. The total value "rose moderately" (*Textile Asia* [August 1981]: 87).

112. NEDA, *Five-Year Plan—Revision for 1981 and 1982*, preface. See also *Bulletin Today* (Manila), February 19, 1981. Once again, government figures did not always mesh. *Business Day* (Manila), March 3, 1981, claimed President Marcos's "revised" target for 1981 was 5.9 percent and that realized growth for 1980 was 5.7 percent.

113. IMF, *Staff Report*, March 24, 1982, p. 6.

114. Ibid. The 1980 population growth rate was 2.7 percent (*Euromoney* [April 1982]: 27). On the population growth rate, see also World Bank, *World Development Report 1981* (Washington, D.C.: World Bank, 1981), p. 166, table 17; and *Far Eastern Economic Review* (July 16, 1982): 42.

115. *Asia Monitor* 6 (Second Quarter 1982), P–6–206; and *Far Eastern Eco-*

nomic Review (April 30, 1982): 40. The average real growth for non-oil Asian LDCs was 5 percent in 1981 (*Far Eastern Economic Review* [June 11, 1982]: 91).

116. Guy Sacerdoti, "Recession's Net Spreads," *Far Eastern Economic Review* (April 23, 1982): 88.

117. Central Bank of the Philippines, *Annual Report 1981,* draft, cited in Sacerdoti, "Recession's Net Spreads," p. 90; Chemical Bank (January 1982): 27. The Central Bank figure cited is for sales including a component of receivables.

118. "Nontraditional exports increased by 14.2 percent in 1981, compared with 29.0 percent in 1980" (IMF, *Staff Report,* March 24, 1982, p. 11, n. 1).

119. *Economist* (November 27, 1982): 88; *Institutional Investor* (October 1982): 245–46; *Philippines Daily Express* (Manila), December 5, 1982; and *Far Eastern Economic Review* (November 5, 1982): 59.

120. The same, the Bank reported, was true for Thailand and Malaysia (World Bank, *Economic Perspectives on Southeast Asia and Asia,* pp. 21–22).

121. Interview with Ordóñez, December 9, 1980. Sentiments reiterated by other government officials during interviews.

122. World Bank, "Philippines—Random Thoughts on Rural Development," memorandum from David J. Steel to M. A. Gould and L. E. Hinkle, September 1, 1977, p. 5.

123. Statement of Barend de Vries in World Bank, *Meeting of Consultative Group, December 13 & 14, 1979,* annex 7, p. 1.

124. See, for instance, World Bank, *Philippines—Country Program Paper,* 1976, p. 13; World Bank, *Staff Appraisal Report on Industrial Finance Project,* p. 10; World Bank, *Meeting on Consultative Group, November 30 and December 1, 1978,* p. 66.

125. World Bank, *Third Urban Development Project—Staff Appraisal Report,* Report 2703a–PH, February 26, 1980, p. 3. See also U.S. AID, *FY1982 Country Development Strategy Statement—Philippines* (Manila: AID, 1980), annex D. For more on World Bank loans to the Philippine urban sector, see Walden Bello and Vincent Bielski, "Counterinsurgency in the City," in Bello et al., *Development Debacle,* pp. 101–25.

126. See *Business Day* (Manila), March 17, 1981, and May 10, 1982.

127. See Vivencio R. Jose, "Re-Orienting Philippine Education," in *Mortgaging the Future: The World Bank and IMF in the Philippines,* ed. Vivencio R. Jose (Quezon City: Foundation for Nationalist Studies, 1982), pp. 128–58; World Bank, "Philippines to Improve Elementary Education with $100 Million Loan," *Bank News Release,* 81/129 (July 2, 1981); and Nationalist Resource Center, *What's Behind the Education Act of 1982?* ([Manila]: Nationalist Resource Center, 1982).

128. World Bank, Poverty Report 2984–PH, draft, p. 65; interview with World Bank official (anonymity requested), March 4, 1981; interview with pro-

fessor (anonymity requested), Asian Institute of Management, Metro-Manila, Philippines, March 18, 1981; interview with Grace Goodell, International Rice Research Institute, Los Baños, Philippines, March 15, 1981; interview with Glenn Denning, International Rice Research Institute, Los Baños, Philippines, March 16, 1981; *Far Eastern Economic Review* (March 12, 1982): 39; and Rene E. Ofreneo, "Modernizing the Agricultural Sector," in *Mortgaging the Future,* ed. Jose, pp. 98–127. These World Bank cash crop projects were alongside other Bank projects that furthered the counterinsurgency (or legitimacy) goal. See Walden Bello, David Kinley, and Vincent Bielski, "Containment in the Countryside," in Bello et al., *Development Debacle,* pp. 67–99.

129. See Walden Bello, "The World Bank in the Philippines: A Decade of Failures," *Southeast Asia Resource Chronicle,* no. 81 (December 1981): 3.

130. First post-martial law debate between Marcos's Kilusang Bagong Lipunan (KBL or New Society Movement), represented by Assemblymen Arturo M. Tolentino and Emmanuel Palaez, and opposition representatives Assemblymen Salvador Laurel and Francisco "Soc" Rodriguez, February 15, 1981. On this, see *Bulletin Today* (Manila), February 17, 1981. Cf. *Asian Wall Street Journal,* December 21, 1981; *Bulletin Today* (Manila), January 19, 1981.

131. Interview with Ministry of Finance staff member (anonymity requested), Metro-Manila, Philippines, January 15, 1981. Similar statement made by another Ministry of Finance staff member (anonymity requested), Metro-Manila, Philippines, December 17, 1980.

132. André Gunder Frank, *Crisis in the World Economy* (New York: Holmes and Meier, 1980); Raul Prebisch, "The Crisis of Capitalism in the Periphery," speech presented at first annual Raul Prebisch Lectures, UNCTAD, Geneva, Switzerland, July 6, 1982; UNIDO, *Restructuring World Industry.*

133. John Hein, *Major Forces in the World Economy: Concerns for International Business,* Conference Board Report 807 (New York: Conference Board, 1981), p. 8; and *Business Asia* (May 15, 1981): 106.

134. Jacques de Larosière, "The Need for International Economic Adjustment: The Role of the IMF," address to the Annual Meeting of the French-American Chamber of Commerce, Minneapolis, Minnesota, March 4, 1982, pp. 1–2.

Chapter 10

1. World Bank projections for developing-country GDP growth for 1980–1985 were substantially higher every year than the actual growth rates. Bank projections, published in annual *World Development Reports* (New York: Oxford University Press, various years), were 5.1 percent (high case) and 4.4 percent (low case) for GNP in 1980; 5.3 percent (high) and 4.1 percent (low) in 1981; 5.7 percent

(high) and 4.5 percent (low) for 1980–1990 in 1982; 4.5 percent (average) for 1982–1985 in 1983; 2.8 percent (average) in 1984; 3.0 percent (average) in 1985; and 3.3 percent (average) in 1986. In 1986 the United Nations calculated GDP growth for developing countries from 1980 to 1984 at 0.8 percent and for 1985 at 2.0 percent. See World Bank, *World Development Reports* for 1980 (pp. 11, 99); 1981 (p. 15); 1982 (p. 37); 1983 (p. 27); 1984 (p. 35); 1985 (p. 138); and 1986 (p. 44). See also UNCTAD, *Trade and Development Report, 1986,* 1986, p. 150.

2. United Nations, Department of International Economic and Social Affairs, *World Economic Survey 1986: Current Trends and Policies in the World Economy,* 1986, p. 12. Output in China grew annually at an average rate of 9.8 percent (1981 to 1985).

3. Ibid., p. 45.

4. Louis Kraar, "Reheating Asia's 'Little Dragons,'" *Fortune* (May 26, 1986): 134.

5. See articles by James Clad in *Far Eastern Economic Review:* "Trade-Zone Benefits Built on Shifting Sand" (February 14, 1985): 89; "Call for New Carrots" (February 28, 1985): 86–87; and "Penang Road to Growth on Shifting Foundations" (September 19, 1985): 79–85.

6. United Nations, *World Economic Survey 1986,* p. 85.

7. Ibid., p. 49.

8. World Bank, *World Development Report 1986* (New York: Oxford University Press, 1986), p. 44. The high projection was 7.1 percent annual growth for exports, 7.7 percent for imports; the low projection was 3.2 percent for exports, 3.4 percent for imports.

9. United Nations, *World Economic Survey 1986,* p. 4. Moreover, a substantial debt write-off would be necessary to stimulate real growth in the largest debtors.

10. *Wall Street Journal,* August 21, 1985, p. 28.

11. Both quotes are from *Wall Street Journal,* August 7, 1986, p. 22.

12. *IMF Survey* (June 30, 1986): 205. See also *Financial Times* (London), October 28, 1985, p. 8A; *Wall Street Journal,* January 23, 1986; Carol T. Loomis, "Why Baker's Debt Plan Won't Work," *Fortune* (December 23, 1985): 98–102.

13. World Bank, *World Development Report 1986,* pp. 125–36. The only major LDC recipients of foreign investment that are not among the top debtors are Hong Kong and Singapore.

14. See Table 12; and IMF, *World Economic Outlook: A Survey by the Staff of the International Monetary Fund* (Washington, D.C.: IMF, 1986), p. 229.

15. Inter-American Development Bank, *Economic and Social Progress in Latin America, 1985 Report—External Debt: Crisis and Adjustment* (Washington, D.C.:

Inter-American Development Bank, 1985), p. 22. The seven are Argentina, Brazil, Chile, Colombia, Mexico, Peru, and Venezuela.

16. For more detailed treatment of the origins of the debt crisis, see Cheryl Payer, *The Debt Trap: The International Monetary Fund and the Third World* (New York: Monthly Review Press, 1974); and John Cavanagh, Fantu Cheru, Carole Collins, Cameron Duncan, and Dominic Ntube, *From Debt to Development: Alternatives to the International Debt Crisis* (Washington, D.C.: Institute for Policy Studies, 1985).

17. IMF, *Annual Report of the Executive Board for the Financial Year Ended April 30, 1985* (Washington, D.C.: IMF, 1985), p. 64.

18. Extended fund facilities are repaid five to ten years after drawing.

19. Net flows were $5.7 billion in 1981 and in 1982, and $4.2 billion in 1984 (IMF, *International Financial Statistics*, various issues).

20. These were Vietnam, Cambodia, Liberia, Sudan, Guyana, and Peru.

21. See Willy Brandt, *Arms and Hunger* (New York: Pantheon Books, 1986).

22. The facility was financed by reflows to the IMF from a trust fund set up for low-income LDCs in 1976. That trust fund was financed through the sale of some of the IMF's gold holdings. See "The IMF's Structural Adjustment Facility," *Finance and Development* 23 (June 1986): 39.

23. Ibid.

24. *Wall Street Journal*, July 25, 1985, p. 24.

25. "World Bank Tries Harder," *The Banker* (January 1983): 66; "World Bank Announced New Co-Financing Instruments," *Bank News Release* (January 13, 1983); World Bank, *Co-Financing*, 1983, pp. 11–13 and 20–21, table 2.

26. See "Brief Notes: International Finance," *IMF Survey*, July 15, 1985; *Wall Street Journal*, July 1, 1985; Katherine Roberts and Peter Kornbluh, "U.S. Bolsters Chile Despite Repression," *San Jose Mercury News*, July 21, 1985.

27. During fiscal years 1984 and 1985, the World Bank used the program to disburse an additional sum of $4.5 billion to 44 recipient countries. See A. W. Clausen, *Address to Board of Governors, Seoul, Korea, October 8, 1985* (Washington, D.C.: World Bank, 1985), p. 10.

28. Quoted in Robert E. Wood, "The Aid Regime and International Debt: Crisis and Structural Adjustment," *Development and Change* 16 (April 1985): 194.

29. For details of MIGA's operations, see "The Multilateral Investment Guarantee Agency: An Update," *Finance and Development* 22 (December 1985): 54.

30. As early as July 1985, Federal Reserve Board Chairman Paul Volcker testified to the House Banking Committee that the World Bank's role in debtor countries "is likely to be more critical" as the IMF role diminishes. Volcker cited Colombia as an example, where the Bank was the major multilateral lender (with a SAL),

but where the IMF did not have a standby arrangement (*Washington Post,* July 31, 1985).

31. Data provided by World Bank official, July 1986.

32. "Washington's Gambit to Head Off a Debtor Revolt," *Business Week* (September 23, 1985): 35.

33. See Stanley Please, *The Hobbled Giant: Essays on the World Bank* (Boulder, Colo.: Westview Press, 1984), p. 41.

34. Elliot Berg and Alan Batchelder, "Structural Adjustment Lending: A Critical View," paper prepared by Elliot Berg Associates of Alexandria, Virginia, for World Bank, Country Policy Department, January 1985, p. 15.

35. World Bank, *Sector Adjustment Lending,* World Bank News Special Report, April 1986, p. 2.

36. Paragraph based on ibid., pp. 1–13; quoted matter on p. 9.

37. *Washington Post,* April 14, 1986; *Time* (July 14, 1986): 45.

38. Quoted in *Wall Street Journal,* July 3, 1986, p. 21. Conable was hand-picked by Treasury Secretary James Baker.

39. Jaime Ongpin, minister of finance of the Philippines, "Briefing Notes on the Philippine Economy (After 30 Days in Office)," March 1986, p. 3. This dismal list ends with an ironic final item: "business confidence returning."

40. Remarks delivered by Jaime Ongpin, minister of finance of the Philippines, Carnegie Endowment for International Peace, Washington, D.C., April 7, 1986, p. 2. Two American academics put it similarly in *Foreign Affairs:* "The root causes [of economic decline] lay in the mismanagement of macroeconomic policy and the resultant decline in industrial efficiency. . . . The heart of the problem was the complete politicization of entrepreneurship" (Carl Landé and Richard Hooley, "Aquino Takes Charge," *Foreign Affairs* [Summer 1986]: 1089–90). See also Paul Gigot, "Crony Capitalism Slaps Philippines," *Asian Wall Street Journal,* November 8, 1983.

41. It should be noted that in 1982 the Philippines had already suffered a trade deficit of $2.6 billion. For an excellent analysis of this period, see Joel Rocamora, "The Marcos Dictatorship, the IMF and the Philippine Economic Crisis," in *Sourcebook on the Philippine Crisis,* ed. Joel Rocamora (Berkeley, Calif.: Philippine Resource Center, n.d.), p. 3.

42. For Ongpin's views in 1984, see T. K. Seshadri, "Manila Awaits Its Moment of Truth," *Asian Finance* (May 15, 1984).

43. Roy Rowan, "Business Talks Tough to Marcos," *Fortune* (November 28, 1983): 146.

44. Norman Peagam, "The Spectre That Haunts Marcos," *Euromoney* (April 1984): 51. A superb three-part series broke the capital-flight story: Peter Carey, Katherine Ellison, and Lewis M. Simons, "Hidden Billions: The Draining of the

Philippines," *San Jose Mercury News,* June 23, 24, 25, 1985. See also follow-up articles of June 28 and October 27, 1985.

45. Phil Bronstein, "U.S. Seeks to Hold Marcos at Arm's Length," *San Francisco Examiner,* September 15, 1985.

46. Senator Paul Laxalt, "My Conversations with Ferdinand Marcos: A Lesson in Personal Diplomacy," *Policy Review* (Summer 1986): 205.

47. To fill in this brief summary of events in the Philippines from Benigno Aquino's assassination to Cory Aquino's victory, see Walden Bello, "Benigno Aquino: Between Dictatorship and Revolution in the Philippines," *Third World Quarterly* 6 (April 1984): 283–309; Walden Bello, "Philippines in Turmoil," *Intervention* 1 (1985): 26–33; Walden Bello, "Edging Toward the Quagmire: The United States and the Philippine Crisis," *World Policy Journal* 3 (Winter 1985): 29–58; A. James McGregor, *Crisis in the Philippines—A Threat to U.S. Interests* (Washington: Ethics and Public Policy Center, 1984); U.S. Congress, Senate, Select Committee on Intelligence, *The Philippines: A Situation Report,* Staff Report, 99th Cong., 1st sess., October 31, 1985; Marjorie Niehaus, *Philippine Internal Conditions: Consequences of the Aquino Assassination,* U.S. Library of Congress, Congressional Research Service, Issue Brief IB84114–update, November 19, 1985; Daniel B. Schirmer and Stephen Rosskamm Shalom, eds., *The Philippines Reader: A History of Colonialism, Neocolonialism, Dictatorship, and Resistance* (Boston: South End Press, 1987); Robert Shaplen, "A Reporter at Large: From Marcos to Aquino," *New Yorker* (August 25, 1986): 33–73 and (September 1, 1986): 36–64; Raymond Bonner, *Waltzing with a Dictator: The Marcoses and the Making of American Policy* (New York: Times Books, 1987).

48. "Under Attack—And Caught in a Dilemma," *Far Eastern Economic Review* (October 10, 1985): 77. The analysis of the Philippines as guinea pig was widespread in the country after a Philippine edition of *Development Debacle* appeared in late 1982 (Walden Bello et al., *Development Debacle: The World Bank in the Philippines* [San Francisco: Institute for Food and Development Policy, 1982]).

49. See *Washington Post,* October 14, 1984. It took another five months for the Philippines to reach agreement on the rest of the rescue package—a $10 billion rescheduling package with 483 creditor banks, finally signed in May 1985.

50. World Bank, *Economic Adjustment Policies in the Philippines,* Background Paper Prepared for the Meeting of the Consultative Group of the Philippines to be Held in Paris in July 1983, May 25, 1983, p. 9.

51. Ibid., p. 11.

52. United States, Agency for International Development, "An Overview of the Philippine Structural Adjustment Program" (Manila: U.S. AID, February 1984), p. 6.

53. Ibid., p. 10.

54. See Nayan Chanda, "Vote of No Confidence," *Far Eastern Economic Review* (September 13, 1984): 16.

55. A good review of SAL programs as of July 1983 is provided in World Bank, *Economic Adjustment Policies in the Philippines.*

56. IMF, *Philippines—Staff Report for the Article IV Consultation,* EBS/84/117, May 29, 1984, p. 45.

57. Interview with World Bank official (anonymity requested), Washington, D.C., July 10, 1986.

58. "EPZA Goes to Cavite," *Metro-Manila Times,* January 27, 1986.

59. See *Business Day* (Manila), March 27, 1986, p. 3.

60. Percentages measured in value terms (*Ibon Facts and Figures,* no. 145 [August 31, 1984]: 2).

61. These figures refer to value of exports (IMF, *Philippines: Recent Economic Developments,* SM/84/132, June 8, 1984, p. 113).

62. In value terms using 1972 constant prices. Statistics provided by Philippine Ministry of Trade and Industry, June 1986.

63. *Ibon Facts and Figures,* no. 182 (March 15, 1986): 1, based on statistics from the Central Bank of the Philippines and the National Census and Statistics Office.

64. Bernardo Villegas, "The Philippines in 1985: Rolling with the Political Punches," *Asian Survey* 26 (February 1986): 135–36.

65. Statistics provided by the Philippine Ministry of Trade and Industry, June 1986.

66. Estimates vary. See Jose Gonzaga, "The Turn of the Screw," *Far Eastern Economic Review* (February 9, 1984): 54–55; *Journal of Commerce,* March 27, 1985, p. 11A; and *Los Angeles Times,* August 23, 1985.

67. Jose Gonzaga, "Inflation Turns Downward," *Far Eastern Economic Review* (May 9, 1985): 86.

68. Reported in *Business Day* (Manila), January 13, 1984.

69. Data provided by World Bank official, July 1985.

70. Statistics from the Philippine Export Processing Zone Authority, various years.

71. For a complete listing, see *Manila Times,* January 27, 1986.

72. *Manila Bulletin,* June 9, 1986, p. 17.

73. See "Why Marcos Can't Last Much Longer," *Business Week* (February 24, 1986): 47.

74. Among those to exercise this option in 1985 were Del Monte, Procter and Gamble, Coca-Cola, Bayer, Avon, and McDonald's. See *Ibon Facts and Figures,* no. 169 (August 31, 1985): 6.

75. World Bank, "Aide-Mémoire," minutes of meetings between World Bank and Philippine Government ministers, March 17–24, 1986, p. 2.

76. Interview with World Bank official (anonymity requested), Washington, D.C., August 1986.

77. World Bank, *The Role of Industry in Economic Recovery in the Philippines*, June 1986, p. 27. The Bank targeted five areas for its new industrial restructuring: trade liberalization, industrial investment incentives, industry financing, export policies, and technology policy.

78. Ibid., p. 43.

79. Data provided by Central Bank, June 1986; "Under Attack—And Caught in a Dilemma," *Far Eastern Economic Review* (October 10, 1986): 78; Ibon Data-bank, *The Philippine Financial System—A Primer* (Manila: Ibon Databank, 1983), p. 134.

80. *Ibon Facts and Figures,* no. 170 (September 15, 1985): 4.

81. Jose Galang, "After All That Drama, Look for Useful Reform," *Far Eastern Economic Review* (May 8, 1986): 84.

82. *Ibon Facts and Figures,* no. 170 (September 15, 1985): 2–3.

83. *Asian Wall Street Journal,* January 8, 1984, p. 3. By mid-1985, a Manila banker would predict, "Over time, I'd expect the number of banks here to shrink from 35 to 20" (Robert Winder, "The Philippine Way to Reschedule," *Euromoney* [July 1985]:84).

84. Guy Sacerdoti, "Bank Takeover Launches Crusade," *Far Eastern Economic Review* (September 6, 1984): 10; and Winder, "The Philippine Way to Reschedule," p. 84.

85. *Ibon Facts and Figures,* no. 170 (September 15, 1985): 3.

86. World Bank, "Aide-Mémoire," March 17–24, 1986, p. 2. See also Galang, "After All That Drama, Look for Useful Reform," pp. 84–86.

87. Interview with World Bank official (anonymity requested), Washington, D.C., August 1986. See also World Bank, "Aide-Mémoire," March 17–24, 1986, for conversation with Fernandez.

88. John E. Lind, *Philippine Debt to Foreign Banks* (San Francisco: Northern California Interfaith Committee on Corporate Responsibility, 1984), pp. 12–13.

89. Ibid., p. 13.

90. Ibid., p. 12.

91. *Washington Post,* August 6, 1984, p. 30. Ongpin claimed that $6 to $7 billion of the country's foreign debt was wasted on the cronies. Ironically, in April 1986, evidence emerged that Ongpin's Benguet Corporation had been owned by Imelda Marcos's brother, crony Benjamin "Kokoy" Romualdez. See *Wall Street Journal,* April 4, 1986.

92. Peter Evans, "State, Local and Multinational Capital in Brazil: Prospects for Stability of the 'Triple Alliance' in the Eighties," in *Latin America in the World Economy: New Perspectives,* ed. Diana Tussie (New York: St. Martin's Press, 1983), p. 140.

93. He was referring to crony bailouts as well as to the falsification of Central Bank data (*Wall Street Journal*, January 23, 1984, p. 25).

94. *Asian Wall Street Journal*, December 7, 1983, p. 1.

95. *Financial Times* (London), July 4, 1984.

96. Remarks of Jose Concepcion, minister of trade and industry of the Philippines, Carnegie Endowment for International Peace, Washington, D.C., June 20, 1986.

97. American Express converted $26 million of its loans for the Bataan nuclear power plant into Interbank equity (Leo Gonzaga, "Ex-Herdis Banks Well," *Far Eastern Economic Review* [December 13, 1984]: 87; Guy Sacerdoti, "Long-Term Deposits," *Far Eastern Economic Review* [May 8, 1986]: 141).

98. A 1984 International Labour Organization study on Asian countries found a strong correlation between a country's reliance on exports and the amount of damage that a deep recession in the world economy will inflict on it. See United Nations, International Labour Office, "Developing Asia Hit Where It Really Hurts," special press kit, December 1984.

99. Hollis Chenery et al., *Redistribution with Growth* (London: Oxford University Press, 1974), p. 17.

100. Thorough analyses of this "poverty crusade" are found in Robert L. Ayres, *Banking on the Poor: The World Bank and World Poverty* (Cambridge, Mass.: MIT Press in cooperation with the Overseas Development Council, 1983); and Sheldon Annis, "The Shifting Grounds of Poverty Lending at the World Bank," in *Between Two Worlds: The World Bank's Next Decade*, ed. Richard E. Feinberg (Washington: Overseas Development Council, 1986), pp. 87–109. Ayres singles out two problems: insufficient attention by the Bank to the factors that generate poverty, and lack of a sophisticated political theory for implementing the proposed distributional redirections (pp. 74–80). Both an excellent overview of participatory development and an extensive bibliography of development literature are found in Guy Gran, *Development by People* (New York: Praeger, 1983).

101. World Bank, *Sector Adjustment Lending*, p. 3.

102. Even the nationalist Philippine National Economic Protectionism Association is quite critical of the 1950s import-substitution industrialization in the Philippines: "The import substitution period of the 1950s was characterized by massive inflow of foreign investment. . . . Filipino savings were being spent more on consumer goods and services rather than being reinvested. . . . Filipino businessmen were looking into the foreign markets rather than developing the local market" (Jorge V. Sibal, "The History of NEPA Is the History of Economic Nationalism," *Pilipino Muna: Bulletin of the National Economic Protectionism Association* [Manila], no. 17 [May 1986]: 4). For more on import-substitution strategies, see Raul Prebisch, *The Economic Development of Latin America and Its Principal Prob-*

lems, United Nations, Economic Commission on Latin America, E/CN.12/89/ Rev. 1, 1950; Albert O. Hirschman, *The Strategy of Economic Development* (New Haven, Conn.: Yale University Press, 1958).

103. Albert O. Hirschman, "The Rise and Decline of Development Economics," in *The Theory and Experience of Economic Development,* ed. Mark Gersovitz, Carlos F. Díaz-Alejandro, Gustav Ranis, and Mark R. Rosenweig (London: George Allen & Unwin, 1982), p. 372.

104. Paul Streeten, *Development Perspectives* (London: Macmillan, 1981), p. 91.

105. Marc Nerfin, ed., *Another Development: Approaches and Strategies* (Uppsala: Dag Hammarskjöld Foundation, 1977); William H. Matthews, ed., *Outer Limits and Human Needs: Resource and Environmental Issues of Development Strategies* (Uppsala: Dag Hammarskjöld Foundation, 1976); "What Now? Another Development," 1975 Dag Hammarskjöld Report, *Development Dialogue,* no. 1−2 (1975).

106. "Another Development with Women," *Development Dialogue,* no. 1−2 (1982).

107. Carlos Díaz-Alejandro, "Delinking North and South: Unshackled or Unhinged?" in *Rich and Poor Nations in the World Economy,* ed. Albert Fishlow, Council on Foreign Relations 1980s Project (New York: McGraw-Hill, 1978), pp. 87−162.

108. Organization of African Unity, *Lagos Plan of Action for the Economic Development of Africa, 1980−2000* (Geneva: International Institute for Labour Studies, 1981). See also Timothy M. Shaw, "Debates About Africa's Future: The Brandt, World Bank and Lagos Plan Blueprints," *Third World Quarterly* 5 (April 1983): 330−44.

109. Giovanni Andrea Cornia, Richard Jolly, and Frances Stewart, eds., *Adjustment with a Human Face: Protecting the Vulnerable and Prompting Growth,* A Study by UNICEF (New York: Oxford University Press, 1987). Also see Bernadette Orr, "Adjustment with a Human Face," *International Health News* (National Council of International Health) 7 (June 1986): 3, 9, and (August 1986): 5, 11; and Khadija Haq and Uner Kirdar, eds., *Human Development: The Neglected Dimension,* Papers Prepared for the Istanbul Roundtable on Development: The Human Dimension, September 2−4, 1985 (Islamabad: North South Roundtable, 1986); North South Roundtable and UNDP Development Study Programme, *Salzburg Statement on Adjustment and Growth with Human Development, 7−9 September 1986* (Islamabad: North South Roundtable; New York: UNDP, 1986).

110. Albert Fishlow, "The State of Latin American Economics," chapter 5 in Inter-American Development Bank, *Economic and Social Progress in Latin America, 1985 Report—External Debt: Crisis and Adjustment,* 1985, pp. 123−48.

111. Bolivia also initiated its own program along these lines. See Inter-American Development Bank, *Economic and Social Progress in Latin America, 1985 Report—*

External Debt: Crisis and Adjustment, 1985; and United Nations, *World Economic Survey 1986,* p. 23.

112. Alvin Levie, *Nicaragua: The People Speak* (South Hadley, Mass.: Bergin and Garvey, 1985); George Black, *Triumph of the People: The Sandinista Revolution in Nicaragua* (London: Zed Press, 1982).

113. Florian A. Alburo et al., *Economic Recovery and Long-Run Growth: Agenda for Reforms* (Manila: Philippine Institute for Development Studies, May 1, 1986); and Philippines (Republic), National Economic and Development Authority, "Policy Agenda for People-Powered Development," draft [1986].

114. "Prescriptions for 'People-Powered' Development," *Ibon Facts and Figures,* no. 191 (July 31, 1986).

115. One of the better World Bank studies, *Poverty and Hunger: Issues and Options for Food Security in Developing Countries* (Washington, D.C.: World Bank, 1986), admits what many of its critics have long argued and Bank hierarchy has long disclaimed: hunger is partially rooted in distribution and poverty problems. The study fails, however, to make the connection between the World Bank's emphasis on cash crops for exports and the incidence of hunger.

LIST OF PERSONS INTERVIEWED

(Biographic details as of last date interviewed)

Anderson, James. Cultural anthropologist, Stanford University; consultant to World Bank, on mission, Metro-Manila, Philippines. Interview (by telephone), March 4, 1981.

Areñas, Carmelita. Assistant director, Department of Economic Research, Central Bank, Metro-Manila, Philippines. Interviews, November 17, 1980; January 15, 1981; April 15, 1981.

Asian Development Bank official (anonymity requested). Metro-Manila, Philippines. Interview, March 20, 1981.

Asian Institute of Management professor (anonymity requested). Metro-Manila, Philippines. Interview, March 18, 1981.

Avramović, Dragoslav. World Bank staff member (1953–1977); director of Secretariat and *ex officio* member of the Independent Commission on International Development Issues (Brandt Commission, 1978–1979); senior adviser on economic cooperation, UNDP–UNCTAD, Geneva, Switzerland. Interview, July 2, 1982.

Bamberger, Michael. Urban and Regional Economics Division, Development Economics Department, World Bank; on mission, Metro-Manila, Philippines. Interview, March 19, 1981.

Bautista, Romeo. Former professor, University of the Philippines School of Economics; World Bank (1979–1980); deputy director-general, NEDA, Metro-Manila, Philippines. Interview, December 15, 1980.

Bince, Escolastica B. Deputy governor, Research Sector, and chief negotiator with the IMF, Central Bank, Metro-Manila, Philippines. Interview, December 2, 1980.

Butalid, Ted, S. J. Share and Care Apostolate for Poor Settlers, Metro-Manila, Philippines. Interview, May 19, 1981.

Castro, Armado. Professor, University of the Philippines School of Economics, Metro-Manila, Philippines. Interview, January 20, 1981.

Center for Research and Communications staff economist (anonymity requested). Metro-Manila, Philippines. Interview, May 20, 1981.

Central Bank deputy governor (former, anonymity requested). Metro-Manila, Philippines. Interview, February 9, 1981.

Central Bank staff member (anonymity requested). Metro-Manila, Philippines. Interviews, December 3, 1980; January 22, 1981; January 28, 1981; March 19, 1981.

Central Bank staff member (anonymity requested). Metro-Manila, Philippines. Interviews, February 23, 1981; May 19, 1981.

Central Bank staff member (anonymity requested). Metro-Manila, Philippines. Interviews, April 13, 1981; April 15, 1981; May 13, 1981; May 23, 1981.

Central Bank staff member (anonymity requested). Metro-Manila, Philippines. Interview, April 15, 1981.

Central Bank staff member (anonymity requested). Metro-Manila, Philippines. Interview, April 19, 1981.

Commercial bank, administrative assistant to president (anonymity requested). Metro-Manila, Philippines. Interview, April 10, 1981.

Commercial bank executive (anonymity requested). Metro-Manila, Philippines. Interview, March 9, 1981.

Community organizers (anonymity requested). Metro-Manila, Philippines. Interviews, March 2–3, 1981.

Cool, John. Ford Foundation, Metro-Manila, Philippines. Interview, December 11, 1980.

Corpus, Eduardo. Assistant director-general, Programs and Projects Office, NEDA, Metro-Manila, Philippines. Interview, February 11, 1981.

Cunanan, Reverend Jose. Nationalist Resource Center, Metro-Manila, Philippines. Interviews, March 12, 1981; May 18, 1981.

David, Randolph. Coordinator, Third World Studies, University of the Philippines, Metro-Manila, Philippines. Interviews, November 27, 1980; January 27, 1981.

Del Mar, Thomas F. Director, Slum Improvement Project, Cebu, Philippines. Interview, January 7, 1981.

De los Santos, Oscar A. Associate director and assistant head, Public Relations Service, Office of the Governor, Central Bank, Metro-Manila, Philippines. Interviews, March 20, 1981; March 30, 1981; April 1, 1981.

Denning, Glenn. International Rice Research Institute, Los Baños, Philippines. Interview, March 16, 1981.

Deputy minister of industry (anonymity requested). Ministry of Industry, Metro-Manila, Philippines. Interview, November 17, 1980.

Dimaranan, Marianni, C.F.I.C. Task Force for Detainees, Metro-Manila, Philippines. Interview, November 5, 1980.

Diokno, Jose W. Attorney; former minister of justice (under Macapagal administration); former senator and chairman of Senate Committee on Economic Affairs; former political detainee (1972); chairman, Civil Liberties Union of the Philippines, Metro-Manila, Philippines. Interviews, January 17, 1981; January 31, 1981; April 11, 1981; May 14, 1982.

Dizon, Flordeliza. Staff economist, Economic Planning and Research Staff, Planning and Policy Office, NEDA, Metro-Manila, Philippines. Interview, December 8, 1980.

Export Processing Zone Authority official (anonymity requested). Metro-Manila, Philippines. Interview, December 4, 1980.

Fabella, Armand. Former director-general, Program Implementation Agency (1962); co-chairman, Central Bank Panel, Joint IMF-CBP Banking Survey Commission (1971–1972, reconstituted 1979); member, Commission of Presidential Reorganization; consultant to Central Bank on the financial and banking system; Metro-Manila, Philippines. Interview, December 8, 1980.

Ganapin, Delfin, Jr. Professor of forestry, University of the Philippines, Los Baños, Philippines. Interview, February 24, 1981.

Goodell, Grace. Rockefeller Foundation fellow, International Rice Research Institute, Los Baños, Philippines. Interviews, December 5, 1980; March 15, 1981.

Government official (anonymity requested). Metro-Manila, Philippines. Interview, March 6, 1981.

Government official (anonymity requested). Metro-Manila, Philippines. Interview, March 11, 1981.

Government official (anonymity requested). Metro-Manila, Philippines. Interview, April 21, 1981.

Gultiano, Edgardo. Officer-in-charge, Slum Improvement Project, Cagayan de Oro, Philippines. Interview, January 5, 1981.

Henares, Hilarion, Jr. Former president, Philippine Chamber of Industries; former chairman, National Economic Council (under Macapagal administration); president, Philippine Pigment and Resin Corporation, Metro-Manila, Philippines. Interviews, February 20, 1981; February 27, 1981; March 27, 1981.

IMF official (anonymity requested). On mission, Metro-Manila, Philippines. Interview, late 1980 (exact date withheld upon request).

IMF official (anonymity requested). On mission, Metro-Manila, Philippines. Interview, November 25, 1980.

IMF official (anonymity requested). Washington, D.C. Interview, September 28, 1982.

Investment house executive (anonymity requested). Metro-Manila, Philippines. Interview, May 24, 1981.

Investment house executive (anonymity requested). Metro-Manila, Philippines. Interviews, December 14, 1980; March 11, 1981.

Jose, Vivencio. Professor, University of the Philippines, Metro-Manila, Philippines. Interview, April 21, 1981.

Jurado, Gonzalo. Professor, University of the Philippines School of Economics, Metro-Manila, Philippines. Interviews, November 27, 1980; January 27, 1981.

Kerkvliet, Benedict. Professor of political science, University of Hawaii, Honolulu, Hawaii. Interviews, October 21, 1980; October 29, 1980.

Labor leader (anonymity requested). Kilusang Mayo Uno (May 1st Movement), Metro-Manila, Philippines. Interview, July 29, 1982.

Lappé, Francis Moore. Institute for Food and Development Policy, San Francisco, California. Interview, October 15, 1980.

Legarda, Benito, Jr. Central Bank staff member (1951–1980); deputy governor, Central Bank (until June 1980); special assistant to the minister, Ministry of Finance, Metro-Manila, Philippines. Interview, February 2, 1981.

Leung, Ernest. Alternate executive director to the IMF (1976–1978); Ministry of Finance, Metro-Manila, Philippines. Interviews, January 15, 1981; January 30, 1981.

Licaros, Gregorio S. Governor of Central Bank (January 1970–January 1981), Metro-Manila, Philippines. Interview, April 1, 1981.

Lichauco, Alejandro. Attorney; former president, Philippine Petroleum Association; representative to 1972 Constitutional Convention; former political detainee (1972), Metro-Manila, Philippines. Interviews, January 13, 1981; January 29, 1981; May 13, 1981.

Lindsey, Charles W. Fulbright research grantee and visiting professor, University of the Philippines School of Economics, Metro-Manila, Philippines. Interview, February 21, 1981.

Macapagal, Diosdado. Fifth president of the Philippines (1962–1965), Metro-Manila, Philippines. Interview, March 27, 1981.

Macaraig, Imelda. Assistant to head, ADFU, Central Bank, Metro-Manila, Philippines. Interviews, February 23, 1981; (by telephone) March 5, 1981.

Magallona, Merlin M. Associate professor of law, University of the Philippines; research associate, University of the Philippines Law Center, Metro-Manila, Philippines. Interviews, December 16, 1980; January 12, 1981; January 16, 1981; January 20, 1981; January 27, 1981; February 21, 1981; February 27, 1981.

Mangahas, Mahar. Professor, University of the Philippines School of Economics, Metro-Manila, Philippines. Interview, November 12, 1980.

Ministry of Budget official (anonymity requested). Metro-Manila, Philippines. Interview, February 18, 1981.

Ministry of Finance staff member (anonymity requested). Metro-Manila, Philippines. Interviews, December 3, 1980; May 19, 1981.

Ministry of Finance staff member (anonymity requested). Metro-Manila, Philippines. Interviews, December 10, 1980; January 20, 1981.

Ministry of Finance staff member (anonymity requested). Metro-Manila, Philippines. Interview, December 17, 1980.

Ministry of Finance staff member (anonymity requested). Metro-Manila, Philippines. Interview, January 15, 1981.

Ministry of Finance staff member (anonymity requested). Metro-Manila, Philippines. Interviews, March 26, 1981; May 23, 1981.

Ministry of Human Settlements staff member (anonymity requested). Metro-Manila, Philippines. Interviews, November 11, 1980; December 5, 1980; February 19, 1981.

Ministry of Industry staff member (anonymity requested). Metro-Manila, Philippines. Interviews, November 26, 1980; January 16, 1981.

Ministry of Industry staff member (anonymity requested). Metro-Manila, Philippines. Interview, January 12, 1981.

Ministry of Industry staff member (anonymity requested). Metro-Manila, Philippines. Interviews, February 11, 1981; February 12, 1981.

Ministry of Labor staff member (anonymity requested). Metro-Manila, Philippines. Interview, February 13, 1981.

Ministry of Local Government official (anonymity requested). Metro-Manila, Philippines. Interview, January 14, 1981.

National Economic and Development Authority official (anonymity requested). Metro-Manila, Philippines. Interview, December 5, 1980.

National Economic Protectionism Association official (anonymity requested). Metro-Manila, Philippines. Interview, January 27, 1981.

National entrepreneurs (anonymity requested). Metro-Manila, Philippines. Interviews, January 29, 1981; March 13, 1981; April 23, 1981; May 13, 1981.

Neri, Purita. Director, Department of Economic Research, Central Bank, Metro-Manila, Philippines. Interview, November 17, 1980.

Noriega, Bienvenido M., Jr. Director, Policy Coordination Staff, NEDA, Metro-Manila, Philippines. Interviews, January 30, 1981; April 20, 1981.

Nuqui, Wilfredo. Director, Economic Planning and Research Staff, Planning and Policy Office, NEDA, Metro-Manila, Philippines. Interviews, December 8, 1980; March 10, 1981.

Ofreneo, Rene. Training specialist, Asian Labor Education Center, Metro-Manila, Philippines. Interviews, January 16, 1981; February 21, 1981; May 17, 1981.

Ordoñez, Victor. Consultant to the minister of trade, Ministry of Trade, Metro-Manila, Philippines. Interview, December 9, 1980.

Ortaliz, Wilhelm G. Director, Bureau of Industrial Coordination, Ministry of Industry, Metro-Manila, Philippines. Interviews, January 19, 1981; January 28, 1981; March 31, 1981; April 13, 1981.

Pantabangan residents (anonymity requested). Pantabangan, Philippines. Interviews, February 25, 1981.

Perpinan, Mary Soledad, R.G.S. Ibon Databank, Metro-Manila, Philippines. Interviews, December 13, 1980; January 17, 1981; January 31, 1981; May 14, 1981.

Pimentel, Aquilino. Mayor, Cagayan de Oro, Philippines. Interviews, January 2, 1981; August 10, 1982.

Political prisoner (anonymity requested). National Penitentiary, Muntinglupa, Philippines. Interview, March 29, 1981.

Power, John. World Bank consultant; professor of economics, University of Hawaii, Honolulu, Hawaii. Interview, October 29, 1980.

Priest (anonymity requested). Bukidnon, Mindanao, Philippines. Interview, December 23, 1980.

Priest (anonymity requested). Metro-Manila, Philippines. Interview, March 6, 1981.

Priest (anonymity requested). Metro-Manila, Philippines. Interview, March 12, 1981.

Priest (anonymity requested). Metro-Manila, Philippines. Interview, May 19, 1981.

Reforma, Mila. Director, Research Department, College of Public Administration, University of the Philippines; consultant to World Bank on Tondo project through Research and Analysis Division, National Housing Authority, Metro-Manila, Philippines. Interview, April 24, 1981.

Rocamora, Joel. Southeast Asia Resource Center, Berkeley, California. Interviews, October 2–19, 1980.

Roumasset, James. Professor of economics, University of Hawaii; resource associate, Resource Systems Institute, East-West Center, Honolulu, Hawaii. Interview, October 29, 1980.

Singson, Gabriel. Senior deputy governor, Central Bank, Metro-Manila, Philippines. Interview, February 23, 1981.

Social worker (anonymity requested). Metro-Manila, Philippines. Interview, March 13, 1981.

Soliven, Ofelia. Coordinating director, Balance of Payments Section, Department of Economic Research, Central Bank, Metro-Manila, Philippines. Interview, November 17, 1980.

Stauffer, Robert B. Professor of political science, University of Hawaii, Honolulu, Hawaii. Interviews, October 20–29, 1980.

Subido, Chita. Technical Board on Agricultural Credit, Metro-Manila, Philippines. Interview, December 1, 1980.

Suleik, Mercy. Assistant director, Department of Economic Research, Central Bank, Metro-Manila, Philippines. Interviews, December 15, 1980; January 28, 1981.

Taguba, Cesar. Ecumenical Center for Development, Metro-Manila, Philippines. Interviews, December 16, 1980; March 6, 1981.

Textile firm executive (anonymity requested). Philippine-owned firm, Metro-Manila, Philippines. Interview, May 21, 1981.

TNC executive (anonymity requested). Manila-based, Metro-Manila, Philippines. Interview, February 13, 1981.

Tsuda, Mamoru. Visiting research associate, University of the Philippines, College of Public Administration, Metro-Manila, Philippines. Interviews, December 1, 1980; May 22, 1981.

Villanueva, Eduardo. Head, ADFU, Central Bank, Metro-Manila, Philippines. Interview, February 23, 1981.

Villegas, Edberto M. Professor of political science and history, De La Salle University, Metro-Manila, Philippines. Interviews, November 7, 1980; February 20, 1981; May 13, 1981.

Wada, Richard. Senior economist, Asian Development Bank, Metro-Manila, Philippines. Interview, January 29, 1981.

World Bank consultant (anonymity requested). Metro-Manila, Philippines. Interviews, February 26, 1981; March 14, 1981.

World Bank official (anonymity requested). On mission, Metro-Manila, Philippines. Interview, March 4, 1981.

World Bank official (anonymity requested). On mission, Metro-Manila, Philippines. Interview, March 31, 1981.

World Bank official (anonymity requested). Washington, D.C. Interview, July 10, 1986.

World Bank official (anonymity requested). Washington, D.C. Interview, August 1986 (exact date withheld on request).

Zialcita, Edgardo P. Special assistant to the governor, Research Sector, and coordinator with IMF of technical aspects of loans, Central Bank, Metro-Manila, Philippines. Interview, January 21, 1981.

INDEX

"Adjustment with growth," xx. *See also* Baker Plan

Africa, 28, 135, 211–12, 235. *See also* Less developed countries; Would-be NICs; *and names of individual countries*

Agency for International Development (AID) (U.S.), 221

Agricultural sector: loans for, in Philippines, 32, 66, 68, 199–200, 219, 221, 222; in Philippines, 57, 94, 178, 213, 227, 231; and World Bank loans, 53, 231. *See also names of individual agricultural subsectors*

Allende, Salvador, 47

Alliance for Progress, 258n.36

Alliances among institutions, 17, 18. *See also* Transnationalist factions; Triple alliance

American Express International Banking Corporation, 167, 230

Amin, Samir, 243n.30

Apex Development Finance Unit (ADFU), 170, 171, 175; and co-financing, 155–58, 159; creation of, 12, 148–49; and extension of control by World Bank and IMF, 159–61; strategy of World Bank and IMF in, 150–55, 225, 227. *See also* Apex loan; Central Bank of the Philippines; Industrial finance fund

Apex loan (World Bank), 10, 12–13, 129, 140, 148, 162, 226; criteria for applicants for, 152–53; defined, 132–34. *See also* Apex Development Finance Unit; Financial sector in Philippines; Industrial finance fund; World Bank

Apparel industry, 5, 44, 45, 87, 96, 125; effects of SAL on, in Philippines, 198, 223; protectionism in, 180, 181; value

added in, 192, 193. *See also* Export processing zones; Exports, nontraditional; Textile sector in Philippines

Aquino, Benigno, assassination of, xix, xxi, 105, 126, 175, 218

Aquino, Corazon, xxi, 218, 225, 227, 230

Areñas, Carmelita, 139, 144

Argentina, 31, 54, 231, 235

Arruda, Marcos, 244n.44

Ascher, William, 107, 275n.7. *See also* Ascher Memorandum

Ascher Memorandum (World Bank), 82, 85, 102, 104, 116

ASEAN (Association of Southeast Asian Nations), 118

Asia. *See* Less developed countries; Newly industrializing countries; Would-be NICs; *and names of individual countries*

Asia Pacific Capital, 176

Asiaweek, 97

Assembly line, global, 42–43, 45, 155, 208–9. *See also* Electronics industry; Export processing zones; Exports, nontraditional; International division of labor; Transnational corporations

Atrium Capital, 176

Aurellano, Arnulfo, 144, 145, 163, 169, 173–74

Avramović, Dragoslav, 30, 33, 34, 253n.94

Ayala, 106, 167; Ayala-Zobel family, 173

Ayres, Robert, 50

Bagong Alyansang Makabayan (BAYAN), 236

Bailouts. *See* Government sector; Industrial finance fund

Baker, James, xxi. *See also* Baker Plan; Treasury Department (U.S.)

ing, 155–57; and financial reforms, 129, 153, 157–59, 167, 168–69, 170–71; before 1979, 34, 135, 137, 145, 306 n.32; after 1982, 226–27, 230, 325 n.49, 328 n.97; and transnationalists, 7, 13, 106–7, 172
—See also Apex loan; Debt, Philippine; Debt crisis, international; Financial sector in Philippines; *and names of individual institutions*
Transnational corporations (TNCs), 6–7, 30, 38, 41–42, 212, 307 n.51; and borrowing in host country, 169; influence of, on LDCs, 17–18, 54, 229; and international division of labor, 42–46, 53, 55, 185, 186, 195, 206–9
—and Philippines, 115, 116, 154, 178; and bonded villages, 95–96; and borrowing from domestic banks, 169–70; and electronics sector, 117–18, 192–94; and EPZs, 3, 11, 224; and financial reforms, 170, 171–72; and industrial reforms, 4, 64–65, 85, 96–98, 111, 186–87; and major industrial projects, 109–10; before 1979, 33, 35, 108; after 1982, 224–25, 229, 326 n.74; and Omnibus Investments Code, 96–97; and textile sector, 112, 113–14, 118; and transnationalists, 7, 13, 73, 106–7, 172
—See also Assembly line, global; Joint ventures; Mergers, corporate; Subcontracting; *and names of individual sectors and institutions*
Transnationalist factions, 7, 18, 41, 231–32; and alliances with World Bank and IMF, 35, 48–49, 50–52, 57, 59, 184–85, 233; strengthened by World Bank and IMF, xviii, 13, 19, 26, 27, 31–32; and technocratization, 35
—in Philippines: ADFU and, 128, 150–52, 160, 171; alliances of, with World Bank and IMF, 3, 72–77, 90, 94, 97, 102, 126, 162, 184; and apex reforms, 164, 165; in conflict with Philippine nationalists, 10, 11, 61–62, 88; cronies as, 171, 219, 228–29; historical position of, in government, 33; power of, in private sector, 13, 97–98, 104, 113–15, 151, 154, 176; power of, as technocrats in government, xix, 7, 12, 63, 64, 65, 67, 87, 89, 90, 103, 106, 107, 143, 176, 177, 230; in private sector, described, 106–7; as technocrats in Aquino government, xxi, 217, 230

—See also Apex Development Finance Unit; Government sector; Nationalist factions; Triple alliance; *and names of individuals and ministries*
Treasury Department (U.S.), xxii, 25, 47, 221. See also Baker, James; Baker Plan
Trickle-down theory of growth, 50, 117, 129. See also Development theories
Triple alliance, 13, 17, 85, 172–77, 276 n.23; post-1982, 228–31. See also Government sector; Private sector; Transnationalist factions
Turkey, 47, 53, 185, 213

Ul-Haq, Mahbub, 185
Ulloa, Manuel, 185
Underwriting, 141
Unemployment. See Employment levels
UNICEF, 235
Unisol Industries and Manufacturing Corporation, 113–14, 115
United Kingdom, 21, 30, 32, 42, 169, 223
United Nations agencies, 6. See also UNICEF; *and names of other agencies*
United Nations Conference on Trade and Development (UNCTAD), 53
United Nations Development Program (UNDP), 152
United Nations Economic Commission for Latin America (ECLA), 27
United Nations General Assembly, 41
United Nations' Group of 77, 51
United States, 24, 25, 30, 42, 92, 223; economic hegemony of, 21–22, 23, 37–39; influence of, in LDCs, 44, 46, 47; and Philippines, 32, 33, 67, 84, 92, 218, 221, 222; post–World War II economy of, 28; power of, in World Bank and IMF, 46–47, 80; role of, in current global market, 38, 169, 186. See also *names of specific agencies, departments, and administrations*
United Technologies, 208
Universal banks. See Expanded commercial banks
University of the Philippines School of Economics, 66–67
Uruguay, 31

Value added, 179, 190, 191–94
Vietnam War, 37, 38, 40
Villafuerte, Luis, 97
Villanueva, Eduardo, 148, 150, 151, 153, 154, 160

Compositor: G & S Typesetters
Printer: Edwards Bros., Inc.
Binder: Edwards Bros., Inc.
Text: 10/13 Galliard
Display: Friz Quadrata